PAN-ARABISM before NASSER

Egyptian Power Politics and the Palestine Question

MICHAEL DORAN

OXFORD
UNIVERSITY PRESS

OXFORD
UNIVERSITY PRESS

Oxford   New York
Auckland   Bangkok   Buenos Aires   Cape Town   Chennai
Dar es Salaam   Delhi   Hong Kong   Istanbul   Karachi   Kolkata
Kuala Lumpur   Madrid   Melbourne   Mexico City   Mumbai   Nairobi
São Paulo   Shanghai   Singapore   Taipei   Tokyo   Toronto

and an associated company in Berlin

Published by Oxford University Press, Inc.
198 Madison Avenue, New York, New York 10016

www.oup.com

First issued as an Oxford University Press paperback, 2002

Oxford is a registered trademark of Oxford University Press

Library of Congress Cataloging-in-Publication Data
Doran, Michael Scott, 1962–
Pan-Arabism before Nasser : Egyptian power politics and the
Palestine question / Michael Doran.
    p.   cm.—(Studies in Middle Eastern history)
Includes bibliographical references.
ISBN 0-19-512361-1; 0-19-516008-8 (pbk.)
1. Egypt—Politics and government—1919–1952.   2. Pan-Arabism.
3. Egypt—Foreign relations—Arab countries.   4. Arab-Israeli
conflict.   I. Title.   II. Series: Studies in Middle Eastern history
DT107.82.D67   1999
962.05—dc21   98-23001

9 8 7 6 5 4 3 2 1

Printed in the United States of America
on acid-free paper

For
Mark Mancall

Pan-Arabism before Nasser

Studies in Middle Eastern History

BERNARD LEWIS, ITAMAR RABINOVICH, AND ROGER SAVORY
General Editors

Other volumes are in preparation.

Acknowledgments

I WELCOME this opportunity to thank Professor L. Carl Brown, who supported me in this project from the beginning, and who made many useful comments on the manuscript. His professionalism will always be a model for me. I owe an immense debt of gratitude to Professor Michael Cook, who helped me refine my ideas, read every draft chapter, and made invaluable suggestions. Many thanks are due to Professor Robert Tignor, who also read the entire draft and offered many helpful comments. Professor Bernard Lewis directed me to a number of valuable sources, read several draft chapters, and bolstered my confidence. Professor Abraham Udovitch also read parts of the manuscript; when workspace and moral support were in short supply, he provided both. Professor Norman Itzkowitz read two chapters and made helpful comments.

My views on the postwar Middle East developed in tandem with those of Joshua Landis, from whom I have learned much about Syria. Joe Maiolo read and commented on two chapters; more important, he actually enjoyed talking at length about the balance of power. Professor Yohanan Friedmann, Professor Andras Hamori, Shahab Ahmed, and Abdelmajid Hannoum helped me with translations. Avraham Sela's unpublished Ph.D. thesis aided me in more ways than my footnotes indicate, not least of all because it demonstrated the immense value of the second volume of the memoirs of Taha al-Hashimi. Muhammad al-Masri introduced me to Jordan; he opened his library, providing me with rare sources that do not bear directly on this book but nonetheless inform its perspective. I benefited more than once from the critical eye of Stephen Larsen, who deserves many thanks.

The writing of this book would not have been possible were it not for the backing that I received from the Department of Near Eastern Studies at Princeton, and, in particular, from its Chairman, Professor Andras Hamori. In addition, I am very grateful for the generous financial support that I received from the Fulbright-Hays Research Committee and from Princeton University. Mary Craparotta, Kathleen Knight-O'Neill, David Redman, and Nancy Carnes offered many kindnesses beyond their obligations. At the Oxford University Press, Thomas LeBien was particularly helpful and patient; Barry Katzen's copyediting improved my text.

My parents cannot be adequately acknowledged in this space; nor can Melanie, who waited.

Contents

Note on Transliteration and Terminology

W HEN transliterating Arabic and Hebrew, I have adopted simplified versions (no diacritical marks) of the standard systems.

It is impossible to avoid confusion over the name of the state now called Jordan. In 1946, the authorities in Amman officially changed the name, but many people—including British diplomats—continued to refer to it as Transjordan. Historians often assume erroneously that the name changed in 1950, when the Hashimite Kingdom annexed parts of Arab Palestine. For the period starting in 1946, I consistently use the name Jordan, but I quote from documents that do not.

Anyone familiar with the sources on which this book is based knows that American diplomats tended to write much longer telegrams than their British colleagues, even though the State Department, unlike the Foreign Office, instructed its representatives to omit as many words as possible from their cables. These rather unsuccessful efforts of the Americans to be concise have produced texts of an inferior literary quality. Some historians tackle this problem by inserting the missing words in brackets. I have taken the liberty of replacing the missing words without placing them in brackets, which are annoying to the eye.

Pan-Arabism before Nasser

Introduction

The Problem

Egyptian foreign policy has traced a pattern that poses a riddle for historians. Consider, for instance, the first Arab–Israeli war. During the period 1947–1948, leaders in Cairo recoiled time and again when other Arab statesmen asked them to participate in military operations against the emerging state of Israel. In fact, Cairo did not decide to send troops into Palestine until 11 May 1948, just four days before the end of the British Mandate. Although Egyptian leaders initially displayed great uncertainty about joining the war, once they had mobilized their army, they proceeded to dominate the Arab coalition against the Jewish state; in addition, they appeared to exhibit a staunch commitment to the Palestinian cause. However, when their war fortunes had soured in early 1949, Egyptian statesmen abandoned the fight and, leaving their allies in the lurch, became the first Arab leaders to sign an armistice agreement with the Israelis. Egypt jumped in last, took charge, then jumped out first.

This pattern—ambivalence, leadership, abdication—is characteristic of more than just the actions of Cairo during eight or nine months in 1948. It also describes the trajectory of Egyptian policy toward the Arab–Israeli conflict in general. In the period before the 1948 War, leaders in Egypt displayed ambivalence toward the Arab struggle against Zionism. But by 1955 all signs of doubt had disappeared. For the next eighteen years, Cairo guided the Arab states in such a resolute manner that many observers came to believe that Egyptian leadership of the Arab side was a natural and permanent component of the Middle Eastern scene. Then, in 1977 President Anwar Sadat challenged this belief by making a dramatic appeal for peace with Israel. Suddenly, without consulting its Arab allies, Egypt had again jumped out first.

What is puzzling about this pattern? There is certainly nothing odd about the first stage, the period of ambivalence. On the contrary, it would have been strange if leaders in Cairo had been eager to fight, both because Egypt was already locked in a conflict with Britain, and because sober statesmen are often fearful of war. Similarly, whether we are analyzing policy during the 1948 War itself or during the entire span of the Arab–Israeli conflict, there is nothing odd about the last stage, the period of abdication. In 1948, Cairo signed an armistice agreement because its losses on the battlefield had rendered the Egyptian army ineffective; in 1977, Anwar Sadat went to Jerusalem because the cost of continuing the war against Israel was simply too much for Egypt to bear. In both cases the Egyptian state pursued a practical policy motivated by concern for its military and economic well-being.

By themselves, the stages of ambivalence and abdication require little explanation. Greater difficulties arise, however, when one attempts to explain the relationship between these and the middle stage, the period of leadership. On the face of it, states that reluctantly join coalitions and then quit without warning would hardly seem to possess the stuff of which international leadership is made. Yet, with seemingly little effort, Egypt assumed—in the 1948 War and in the period after 1955—the dominant position among the Arab states.

The problems of analysis raised by Egyptian leadership of the Arab world in its conflict with Israel are, of course, part of a much larger matter: The Egyptian attitude toward other Arab countries, and, more precisely, toward the movement for Arab unity. Thus, the ambivalence–leadership–abdication pattern emerges not just in the policy of Cairo toward the Arab–Israeli conflict but, in addition, in its policy toward the Middle East in general. We may therefore ask how it was possible for the Egyptian state to become the architect of pan-Arabism in the 1950s and 1960s, only to abandon the role in the 1970s.

State versus Society

The goal of this book is to explore this puzzling pattern in Egyptian foreign policy. The few studies that grapple with this matter directly (together with the works that address it indirectly) rest on the presupposition—rarely if indeed ever explicitly stated—that Egyptian public opinion forced the twin policies of pan-Arabism and anti-Zionism on the Egyptian state. This literature assumes that the 1952 Revolution swept away a corrupt elite and swept in Gamal Abd al-Nasser and his fellow Free Officers, who, being from a humbler class, were in closer touch with an authentic Egypt. According to this view, the Free Officers, in contrast to their predecessors, adopted policies that tapped into the mainstream of Egyptian culture and society. Through these men, it is implied, the popular goals of establishing strong bonds with the Arab world and of liberating the Middle East from foreign control began for the first time to animate high policy. Hence, profound cultural and social forces threw Egypt into the thicket of inter-Arab relations and the Arab–Israeli conflict. In short, these studies unconsciously accept the view of Egyptian history—favored by the Nasser regime itself—that pan-Arabism rose from the street.

Out of a desire to deepen our understanding of Egyptian pan-Arabism, this study suggests a new perspective on its origins. My approach proceeds from the top down; it restores the state to the central role that it deserves in the analysis of Egyptian politics and foreign policy. The adoption by Cairo of a pan-Arab strategy, I argue, cannot be understood without examining the pressure placed on the Egyptian elite by the demands of the Middle Eastern international system.

An approach that focuses on state interest does not deny the importance of social and cultural movements in the history of pan-Arabism; rather, it views them as but two of many forces that imposed themselves on the leadership in Cairo. After all, pan-Arabism was not simply a popular idea, it was also a policy. This idea had a profound historical impact, because leaders in Cairo threw the weight of the most powerful Arab state behind it. Historians, therefore, must direct their attention beyond the realm of social and cultural developments; they must address the argument that state interest made pan-Arabism attractive to leaders in Cairo.

The view of history that emphasizes social and cultural roots cannot make sense of the puzzling pattern of Egyptian foreign policy. For instance, it cannot explain the jettisoning of pan-Arabism following the 1973 Arab–Israeli war. If it was simply the case that profound social and cultural forces made pan-Arabism attractive to Gamal Abd al-Nasser, then those forces must have been operating with equal force on his fellow Free Officer, Anwar Sadat. Moreover, to acknowl- edge that reasons of state led President Sadat to abandon Egyptian leadership of the Arab world is to recognize the state itself as an independent actor in history— to understand it as an agent mediating, if not directing, social and cultural cur- rents. Therefore, a state-centered approach to the study of pan-Arabism can provide us with a framework for understanding the ambivalence–leadership– abdication pattern of Egyptian foreign policy.

The Argument

What new international order should arise in the Middle East? This question cast a long shadow over the region for more than a decade after World War II; this book seeks to reconstruct the answer that the Egyptian elite gave to it. I focus on the years 1945–1948, but the book is haunted by the specter of Gamal Abd al- Nasser. This is because the pan-Arabism of the 1950s and 1960s grew out of the vision of regional order that Egyptian leaders developed in the late Faruq era. In the immediate aftermath of World War II, the old regime contended simulta- neously with war in Palestine, the Anglo-Egyptian conflict, and struggles with Arab rivals. These issues forced the Egyptian government to formulate a coherent vision of the postwar Middle East. After the Revolution in 1952, the new leaders in Cairo inherited the grand strategy of the old regime.

Chapter 1 examines the legitimacy crisis that developed in Egypt during 1946, when the government of Prime Minister Ismail Sidqi found itself caught between the dictates of the international system and the angry demands of Egyptian na- tionalists. On the one hand, the British government, temporarily unchallenged by any other great power in the region, demanded that Egypt remain within the imperial sphere of influence. On the other hand, nationalist opinion claimed the right to withdraw from the British security zone and called for the unity of Egypt and the Sudan under the crown of King Faruq. Thus the international and do- mestic political systems pulled the Egyptian government in opposite directions. In October 1946, Ismail Sidqi and British Foreign Minister Ernest Bevin com- promised, arriving at a draft for a new treaty. The agreement, fundamentally illegitimate in almost all Egyptian political circles, aroused intense opposition to the Sidqi government, which fell as a result. Subsequent governments concluded that it was impossible to renew the treaty with Great Britain and still remain legitimate at home.

Chapter 2 follows Ismail Sidqi's successor, Mahmud Fahmi al-Nuqrashi, as he attempted to enlist the support of the United States in an effort to break the British grip on Egypt. The al-Nuqrashi government, hoping to capitalize on the tensions created by the Cold War, placed the question of Anglo-Egyptian relations before the United Nations, demanding the abrogation of the existing treaty of alliance. The Egyptian appeal to the Security Council was in essence a call for help from the United States government. Considerable support for the Egyptian position did exist in Washington, where many officials feared that the Anglo-Egyptian conflict would redound to the detriment of the West in its struggle against the Soviet Union. Nonetheless, the Americans regarded the continuation of the Anglo-Egyptian military alliance as necessary for the defense of the Middle East. Consequently, they took a line in the Security Council that in effect killed the Egyptian appeal.

Chapter 3 examines inter-Arab relations within the context of the Anglo-Egyptian dispute. It demonstrates that the attempt by Cairo to use the Arab League—which it dominated—as an anti-British instrument led to the formation of two blocs in the Middle East, which I shall call the Turco-Hashimite Entente (Iraq, Jordan, Turkey) and the Triangle Alliance (Egypt, Syria, Saudi Arabia). The alliance led by Egypt sought to oust the British from their role as the predominant military power in the Middle East, and it sought to contain, if not weaken, Jordan and Iraq, both of which harbored plans to expand at the expense of Syria and Palestine.

This book argues that protecting the Triangle Alliance and ousting the British from Egypt gradually led the elite in Cairo to develop a plan for international revolution in the Middle East. The government of Ismail Sidqi pursued a vision of regional order that would have diminished, but not eliminated, British participation in regional defense. The Empire, according to the Bevin–Sidqi Agreement, would have retained military bases in Egypt, but direct British control of those bases would have been sharply restricted. By contrast, the al-Nuqrashi government pursued a vision of a new Middle Eastern order, one devoid of a significant British presence. Between March 1947 and February 1948 it became clear that al-Nuqrashi sought to replace the British security system with a bloc of Arab states led by Egypt and organized under the aegis of the Arab League. By eliminating Britain as the predominant power in the region, Cairo would have dealt a severe blow to Iraq and Jordan, the clients of Britain. Thus the new Arab order would have been dominated by Egypt and her close allies, Syria and Saudi Arabia.

It was in the midst of this struggle over regional order, and partly as a result of it, that the British withdrew from Palestine. Chapters 4 through 6 analyze Egyptian policy toward the Palestine question against the background of the conflict between the Turco-Hashimite Entente and the Triangle Alliance. These three chapters develop the view that, despite the strength of popular anti-Zionism, the elite in Cairo never formulated policy purely according to the dictates of ideology. The question "What new order should arise in the Middle East?" always remained the central concern of Egyptian strategists.

Thus Cairo fought against Israel primarily in order to preserve the position of Egypt as the dominant power in the Arab world. The Egyptian elite directed operations on the battlefield with the aim not of destroying Israel but rather of preserving the special status of Egypt among the Arab states.

This book concludes with the events of 1948. All the same, the policy problem that it analyzes informs the specific strategies and tactics of Egyptian foreign policy from the push for complete independence after World War II until the debacle of 1967.

ONE

The Taproot of Egyptian Foreign Policy

The Bevin–Sidqi Agreement: A False Path

On 20 December 1945 the Egyptian prime minister, Mahmud Fahmi al-Nuqrashi, delivered a Note to the British Government stating that "the manifest interests of Anglo-Egyptian friendship and alliance" required the revision of the 1936 treaty between the two countries. One month later, on 26 January 1946, the British government responded grudgingly: The Foreign Office Note of reply expressed a willingness to undertake "a review" of the treaty arrangements, but it also took leave to observe that the events of World War II proved "the essential soundness of the fundamental principles" of the treaty.[1] Since these principles included, among other things, extraterritorial privileges for the British military in Egypt, the reluctance of the British to revise the treaty enraged Egyptian nationalists. The publication of the two Notes in Egypt sparked off student riots organized by the opposition Wafd party. On the one hand, the protesters attacked the government for opening talks over "revision" of a treaty that, in their eyes, should have been summarily abolished; on the other hand, the students attacked the British for their expressed desire to preserve the status quo. The riots precipitated a cabinet crisis that ended when King Faruq dismissed al-Nuqrashi Pasha and called on Ismail Sidqi to form a new government.

Under the circumstances of conflict between the Wafd and the government, the king's choice for the premiership had powerful symbolic significance. A political independent, Sidqi Pasha had served as prime minister once before, during the period 1930–1933, when he displayed a willingness to engage in open combat with the Wafd.[2] In support of his policies during that first stint in office, Sidqi had not hesitated to jail party leaders and to shut down Wafdist newspapers. By selecting him now to follow through with the process of negotiation initiated by al-Nuqrashi Pasha, King Faruq signaled to the Wafd that he would aggressively resist its attempts to dictate policies to the government. Thus Sidqi Pasha set about the task of negotiating with the British while in open conflict with the most powerful political organization in Egypt. Constant pressure from the opposition left the prime minister little room for maneuver.

Mustafa al-Nahhas, the veteran leader of the Wafd, had one major goal in the conflict with the government: To bring it down. The Wafd had boycotted the elections of January 1945 and, consequently, it had no representation in the Chamber of Deputies (although it did retain seats in the Senate). Since Nahhas Pasha could reasonably expect that the new elections would result in a landslide victory for his party, he searched for every means possible to discredit the policies of Ismail Sidqi. To achieve that end, the Wafd, together with all opposition parties, attempted to present the attitude of the Sidqi government toward the Anglo-Egyptian negotiations as a betrayal of fundamental nationalist values. Since nationalist attacks had already succeeded in bringing down the al-Nuqrashi cabinet, the Wafd and other opposition groups reasoned that they could also topple Sidqi's government.

The new prime minister, then, walked a tightrope between the nationalists at home and the British abroad. In order to remain legitimate in Egypt, Sidqi Pasha required a new agreement with the British that could be plausibly presented to the Egyptian public as the fulfillment, or near fulfillment, of its fundamental nationalist aspirations. These had remained largely the same since the time of Sa'd Zaghlul: Complete independence from Britain, as well as Egyptian sovereignty over the Sudan. Since the Notes exchanged between the Egyptian and British governments had defined the goal of negotiations as revision, not abrogation, of the 1936 treaty, the very act of negotiating with the British appeared to a nationalist public as, at best, appeasement of the imperialists. The Wafd, of course, lost no opportunity to highlight this appearance; consequently the government was on the defensive at home from the moment it sat down at the negotiating table.

Despite his advanced age, Sidqi Pasha displayed a dogged determination to get the best bargain possible from the British. The tortuous negotiations, punctuated by cabinet crises and constant attacks from the opposition, lasted from March until October 1946, when they culminated in the Bevin–Sidqi Agreement, a draft treaty which the British foreign minister and the Egyptian prime minister intended to lay before their parliaments for ratification. The Agreement dealt with three basic issues: the evacuation of British troops from Egypt, the new terms of the Anglo-Egyptian military alliance, and the status of the Sudan.

Before the ink had dried on the agreement, however, Bevin and Sidqi immediately quarreled over their differing interpretations of the Sudan Protocol, a single paragraph that laid out a new Anglo-Egyptian understanding in the Sudan. The first sentence of the passage stated:

> [T]he policy which the High Contracting Parties undertake to follow in the Sudan within the framework of the unity between the Sudan and Egypt under the common Crown of Egypt will have for its essential objectives to assure the well-being of the Sudanese, the development of their interests, and their active preparation for self-government and consequently the exercise of their right to choose the future status of the Sudan.

Composition by committee rarely produces elegant prose: the tortured syntax reflected a deep gulf between the two delegations. This sentence conveys two contradictory principles: self-determination for the Sudanese, championed by Bevin, and Egyptian sovereignty over the Sudan, championed by Sidqi.

Relations between Egypt and Britain became troubled as soon as the Egyptian prime minister stepped off the plane that brought him back to Cairo. While still at the airport, he announced that he had brought the Sudan home to Egypt. The statement provoked a storm of outrage among Sudanese supporters of independence, and among their British patrons in the Sudanese Government. Partly as a result of pressure emanating from those quarters, London felt compelled to disavow immediately Sidqi Pasha's interpretation of the Protocol. Since Bevin was en route to New York, it fell to Prime Minister Attlee to state in Parliament that the Bevin–Sidqi Agreement did not in fact deliver up the Sudan to the Egypt. Following this statement, Bevin demanded from Cairo that an exchange of letters be appended to the Bevin–Sidqi Agreement stating that the Protocol would not lead to a change in the status quo of the Sudan, where in practice the British wielded power.

Given the nationalist pressure on the Egyptian government, the prime minister could not afford to go back on his original interpretation of the Protocol. In mid-December, therefore, after further discussions with the British government had failed to produce an agreement, Sidqi—who was suffering from poor health, exhausted from the negotiations, and beleaguered by the opposition attacks at home—resigned from office. The Bevin–Sidqi Agreement had died.

Since the British foreign minister and the Egyptian prime minister did, after surmounting many obstacles, actually agree on a draft treaty, and since the two men subsequently fell out over the Sudan Protocol, the sequence of events has left the lasting impression that the Sudan question killed the chances for an Anglo-Egyptian rapprochement.[3] Although this interpretation draws strength from the actual course of events, it fails to take into account the powerful opposition *in Egypt* to the other clauses of the Bevin–Sidqi Agreement. It ignores, in particular, the revulsion that the most powerful Egyptian political parties felt at the very notion of an Anglo-Egyptian alliance, which constituted the basic framework of the agreement. Certainly the controversy over the Sudan did wreck an understanding between two men, Sidqi and Bevin; it is not the case, however, that the chances for cooperation between two states, Egypt and Britain, were dashed on the rocks of the Sudan. The profound strength of anti-British feeling in Egypt in the postwar period, not to mention the fundamental weakness of the Sidqi government, raises serious doubts regarding the possibility of the proposed alliance ever functioning in a manner that would have been acceptable to the two governments.

To argue that the Bevin–Sidqi Agreement would not have provided a sound basis for an alliance is not to quibble over what might have been in history, but rather to highlight the dominant forces that actually determined the course of Anglo-Egyptian relations throughout the entire postwar period. A perspective that views the Sudan question as the spoiler of Anglo-Egyptian friendship presupposes a completely different kind of interaction between Britain and Egypt than what actually existed. More particularly, it blinds us to the dominant trends in Egyptian political thinking.

Perhaps one reason that historians continue to emphasize the Sudan as the issue that scuttled a rapprochement between the two powers is that even after the event Great Britain and the United States continued to see the Bevin–Sidqi Agreement as a glass half full. Both powers had an abiding interest in roping Egypt into an alliance with the West: In an effort to solve their Cold War dilemmas in the Middle East, they kept alive for years the basic assumption of the agreement—the notion that an Anglo-Egyptian alliance could be made politically acceptable to the Egyptians. Yet an understanding of the course that events actually followed requires looking beyond the attitudes of the Western powers; it requires examining the interaction between Western and Egyptian thinking. And in Cairo no prime minister after Sidqi Pasha ever displayed a desire to negotiate within the framework of the Bevin–Sidqi agreement.

The attraction that diplomats in the West felt for the Bevin–Sidqi formula, and the revulsion it generated among Egyptians, are the basic factors that governed the course of Egyptian relations with the United States and Great Britain until 1954. In that year, Western diplomatic pressure and temporary Egyptian weakness resurrected the Bevin–Sidqi framework in the form of the Anglo-Egyptian Agreement of October 1954. To grasp the causes for the unraveling of that later agreement, and for the consequent crisis and war in 1956, we must first examine the divergent attitudes that developed in Egypt and the West during the Bevin–Sidqi negotiations.

The Wafd, the Government, and Anglo-Egyptian Relations

On 13 June 1945 the Egyptian government voted to rescind some of the more onerous martial-law restrictions that it had enacted in September 1939 when the British declared war against Nazi Germany.[4] While the Egyptian state still retained certain extraordinary powers allowing it to monitor and regulate the political activities of its citizens, in June it began gradually to lift press censorship. After nearly six years of control, the political parties once again engaged in something like open debate. As the curtain of censorship rose above the political stage, the Egyptian public discovered that the developments of World War II had created deeper and more bitter divisions among the major political actors than had ever existed before.

Although many of the basic divisions among the Egyptian ruling elite dated back to World War I and its aftermath, the constellation of forces that emerged from the press blackout had moved into alignment as a result of the events of 4 February 1942. On that day Miles Lampson, the British ambassador in Cairo, surrounded Abdin Palace with armored cars and delivered an ultimatum to King Faruq: If the British did not receive word immediately that a new government under Wafd leader al-Nahhas had been appointed, then they would take drastic action to ensure their interests. Lampson installed the Wafd in power at gunpoint in order to purge the Egyptian government of Axis collaborators, potential and real, at a moment when Rommel's Afrika Korps had nearly penetrated as far east as the Nile Delta. Only the Wafd, the largest and most prestigious political party in the country, wielded the power and the authority necessary to impose a pro-British discipline on the entire Egyptian political system.[5]

The government of Mustafa al-Nahhas remained in power until October 1944, when the war had moved far from the borders of Egypt and King Faruq felt that circumstances would now permit him to again wield a free hand in Egyptian politics. He dismissed the prime minister and called on Ahmad Mahir, a Sa'dist, to form a new government. The three-year ascendancy of the Wafd had not gone smoothly for the rivals of the party: Al-Nahhas allegedly used the cover provided by British patronage and martial law to punish enemies and to feather his nest.[6] But, if the opponents of the Wafd suffered a setback, al-Nahhas did not gain as much as he might have expected from his tenure in office. Against the background of his attempts to promote favorites and siphon profits from the public trough, al-Nahhas fell out with the finance minister (and secretary-general of the party), Makram Ubayd Pasha, who had aggressively opposed some of the prime minister's more dubious ventures. Unwilling to brook opposition from within the party, al-Nahhas engineered the ouster of Ubayd from the government. Ubayd retaliated in 1944 by publishing *The Black Book*, which detailed corruption and abuse of power that, he claimed, characterized the government of al-Nahhas.[7] In addition, he established his own splinter party, the Independent Wafdist Bloc, which quickly became the bête noire of the Wafd.

In January 1945, three months after Mustafa al-Nahhas fell from power, the new prime minister, Ahmad Mahir, called a general election; as mentioned previously, the Wafd refused to participate, claiming, no doubt with some justification, that the government would use the powers accorded it under the martial law legislation to rig the outcome. As a result of the boycott, the largest party in Egypt ceased to have any representatives in the Chamber of Deputies.[8]

To make matters worse for al-Nahhas, Makram Ubayd and several of his colleagues from the Independent Wafdist Bloc figured prominently in the new government, also headed by Ahmad Mahir. Ubayd used his position of power to organize and lead a special ministerial committee of inquiry that would, investigate the malfeasance of the Wafd government, with an eye to bringing criminal charges.[9] Throughout 1945 Ubayd obstinately provoked a number of crises in the cabinet in an effort to force the government to put al-Nahhas on trial; Ubayd may have hoped that if al-Nahhas were jailed the way would be clear for Ubayd to assume leadership of the party.[10]

While many in the government certainly shared the interest of Ubayd in blackening the reputation of al-Nahhas, powerful forces lobbied against actually bringing criminal charges against him. A trial would have complicated relations with the British, who, having installed al-Nahhas by force, felt compelled to protect his—and their own—reputation.[11] In addition, the present government had, according to the American Ambassador, its share of skeletons in the closet: Initiating a precedent whereby members of new governments prosecute their immediate predecessors in office could be dangerous. Although King Faruq seems to have supported the efforts of Ubayd, other ministers contented themselves with publicizing the findings of the special committee, thereby destroying the reputation of al-Nahhas without actually dragging the matter into the courts. Nevertheless, Ubayd persisted. His efforts to stand al-Nahhas before a judge ultimately failed; however, he did succeed—by repeatedly threatening to resign—in severely weakening the cabinet. The pursuit of this vendetta exacerbated deep divisions within the government that, in order to stay in power, forced it to rely heavily on the coercive power that it enjoyed thanks to the regime of martial law.

Thus, as free debate returned to the Egyptian political arena, a shaky government, propped up by the palace, was locked in bitter conflict with the Wafd. Given the circumstances, therefore, Mustafa al-Nahhas sought to bring down the government and to arrange for new elections, which (the charges of corruption notwithstanding) would undoubtedly fill the Chamber of Deputies with a Wafdist majority.[12] Since neither the King (who had not forgotten the humiliation of 4 February 1942) nor the government had any wish to see the Wafd return to power, the scene was set for a long and costly struggle. Not surprisingly, the Wafd countered the charges of corruption by playing the nationalist card. Under any circumstances, al-Nahhas Pasha might have been expected to agitate for a revision of the Anglo-Egyptian Treaty of 1936, but the need to erase the stigma of wartime collaboration with the British gave him a special incentive to prove his patriotism by accusing the government of neglecting the duties of Egyptian nationalism.

From June to September 1945 the Wafd orchestrated a propaganda campaign in the press: The government, it claimed, was illegitimate; new elections must be held. The newspapers of the party, which included several of the most popular in Egypt, charged that the end of the war had created a new world that rendered the terms of the 1936 Anglo-Egyptian Treaty obsolete. In order to seize the opportunities presented by this historic moment, the Wafd cried, a government broadly representative of the Egyptian people must take power and aggressively seek complete independence for Egypt. Unfortunately, so the argument went, the ruling clique did not have the power, the authority, or the wherewithal to exploit the possibilities of this critical moment. The Wafd, by contrast, had always championed the national aspirations of the Egyptian people and, therefore, it functioned as the only vehicle appropriate for leading the Egyptians to freedom and to unify them with the Sudanese. Since an unfair election carried out under abnormal circumstances had produced a nonrepresentative Chamber of Deputies, the government had no choice but to resign. A neutral cabinet—that is, one not hostile to the Wafd—should be appointed to preside over fair and open elections.[13]

The drumbeat of Wafdist propaganda struck a deep resounding chord in Egyptian political sensibilities. Establishment politicians felt pressure from all sides to extricate Egypt from the terms of the 1936 treaty, which in its day had been touted as a legal bulwark against British domination. However, the flood of foreign soldiers that had poured over Egyptian shores during the war had shown this bulwark up as a pillar of sand. The first serious sign of a dangerous mood in the country had come when the al-Nuqrashi Pasha's predecessor, Ahmad Mahir, lost his life to an assassin's bullet in February 1945. The prime minister had died for declaring war against the Axis—a step interpreted by nationalists as an act of subservience to Britain.[14] Supporters of the declaration of war justified it as an action designed to secure for Egypt a seat at the peace conference, where it would be better placed to lobby for complete independence. The declaration of war by Mahir raised expectations that the new world order would benefit Egypt; his assassination, however, served as a warning to others regarding the dangers of cooperating with Britain.

The belief that the new international order, founded on the principles of the Atlantic Charter, would strengthen the hand of Cairo against British imperialism grew in strength during the San Francisco Conference, which established the United Nations. The Egyptian delegate to the conference worked assiduously, yet in vain, to advance the cause of nations subservient to the great powers and to weaken the status of the British Empire in international affairs. In addition, the delegate sought to promote the particular interests of Egypt. The view gained ground in Cairo that the Egyptians, as founding members of the Arab League and the leaders of the Arab world, deserved a permanent seat on the Security Council.[15] Thus considerable disappointment resulted when the political elite in Cairo realized that the Great Powers, Britain among them, would dominate the Security Council and would function as the policemen of the world.

Despite the disappointment, official Egyptian opinion held to the view that the Charter of the United Nations rendered null and void the special rights in Egypt accorded to Britain by the 1936 Anglo-Egyptian Treaty. It is impossible to say whether the elite in Cairo truly believed that the Charter abrogated the alliance with Britain. But, given its need to find a legal basis on which to oppose the British position in Egypt, Cairo had a manifest interest in promoting this interpretation of the new international order.[16] The currency of such views, however, ultimately worked in favor of the Wafdist propaganda campaign. As many countries, including Syria and Lebanon, received independence, Egyptian nationalist opinion grew angry and impatient. The Wafd, playing on these feelings, accused the government of shameful inaction.

In September 1945, al-Nahhas began to direct his attacks against the prime minister personally, claiming that al-Nuqrashi Pasha was willfully neglecting Egyptian national aspirations. Each day the press requested to know when the prime minister would place before the British the demands for complete independence and for sovereignty over the Sudan. After all, the government itself had embraced these as the basis of its own policy. The Wafd argued that al-Nuqrashi, concerned only with staying in power, had in fact no intention of approaching the British. London, it argued, would inevitably reject Egyptian nationalist demands. In that case the government would be forced to admit failure: It would have no choice but to resign and call for an election.[17]

The prime minister had no effective retort: The strength of nationalist feeling in Egypt had reached such a fevered pitch—and the belief that the new world order would work to the advantage of Egypt had such plausibility—as to deprive the prime minister of ideological resources. Moreover, the Wafdist critique had a strong basis in reality. Officials in London did not, in fact, desire to enter into complex negotiations with the Egyptians, both because they had more pressing matters on their agenda and because they, too, considered the cabinet of al-Nuqrashi weak and nonrepresentative.

The British calculated their moves toward the al-Nuqrashi cabinet by using as a model the negotiations for the 1936 treaty, which had been carried out between the British government and a delegation of Egyptians composed of all major political parties, the Wafd included.[18] The requirements of Britain in the Middle East necessitated an agreement that would stand on a solid political base in Egyptian domestic politics: A treaty negotiated with a weak, minority government would be subjected to constant attack in Egypt and, therefore, would not stand the test of time. As Miles Lampson stated to the American Ambassador in Egypt, the king and the anti-Wafdist politicians had conspired against Britain and the Wafd by throwing al-Nahhas out of office in October 1944; now they would have to settle their own internal differences.[19] If al-Nuqrashi had little means of countering the attacks of the Wafd, the British Ambassador reasoned, he was caught in a dilemma of his own making. London would adopt a posture of aloofness from the Egyptian political fray.

In the light of this unresponsiveness, the Egyptian government had little choice but to play for time, as long as it refused to call for elections. Thus al-Nuqrashi limply answered the attacks of the Wafd by stating that Anglo-Egyptian relations were complex and delicate, that it would be dangerous to jump precipitously into negotiations; first, he said, the groundwork had to be prepared. He counseled patience.[20] Meanwhile, the government, using the material from Makram Ubayd's special committee, continued to attack the credibility of the Wafd. In addition, al-Nuqrashi and his supporters tried to turn nationalist sentiment against the Wafd by, for the first time, publicizing the details of the ultimatum presented to King Faruq by Lampson on 4 February 1942.[21] In effect, the progovernment press now accused the Wafd not just of corruption but also of collaboration with the British.

While these attacks may in fact have diminished the personal stature of al-Nahhas, they did little if anything to relieve the cabinet from the pressure generated by the accusation that it did not have the gumption to stand up to the British. At issue for the prime minister and his colleagues was not the legitimacy of the Wafd but the persuasiveness of the claim that historic opportunities were being squandered. By September 1945 a sense had developed among the Egyptian political elite that the al-Nuqrashi cabinet stood on its last legs. Rumors spread regarding the composition of the successor government; politicians jockeyed for position. For instance, Husayn Haykal Pasha, the president of the Senate, began to associate himself with the moderate wing of the Wafd, with whom he allegedly intended to form a new coalition.[22] In addition, Makram Ubayd led a faction of "dissident elements" within the cabinet who put heavy pressure on al-Nuqrashi to confront London.[23]

Even the most conservative supporters of the government encouraged it to take direct action in Anglo-Egyptian relations. The effort to save the cabinet focused on the "Committee of Elder Statesmen," an informal body of experienced politicians on whom al-Nuqrashi had come to rely, especially in the realm of foreign affairs. The committee placed the government under the wide umbrella of elite support, thus shielding it from the Wafdist criticism of being nonrepresentational. Despite its nonconstitutional status, the committee wielded considerable moral authority.[24] On 23 September, it issued the following statement:

> The . . . Committee unanimously considers that the National Rights, as affirmed by the entire nation and proclaimed by the Government, are the withdrawal of the British forces and the realization of the unity of Egypt and the Sudan according to the will of the inhabitants of the Nile Valley. Further, the Committee esteem the present moment most opportune to work for the realization of national aspirations and . . . to begin negotiations with our ally with the object of arriving at an accord on this basis. . . . [25]

The elder statesmen tacitly acknowledged that Wafdist propaganda had cut deeply into al-Nuqrashi's base of support. The government subsequently voted to approve the statement and, therefore, committed itself to bringing the British to the negotiating table.

Yet, despite the mounting pressure coming even from conservative supporters of the government, al-Nuqrashi continued to temporize: He assured supporters that, in fact, he had taken action on Anglo-Egyptian relations but refused to offer details of his actions, arguing that the matter required silence. Against the background of these assurances, a storm broke out in Egypt in late October when Ernest Bevin, the British foreign minister, inadvertently proved al-Nuqrashi to be a liar. In answer to a question in Parliament, Bevin remarked that he had not received from the Egyptian government any official demands regarding the status of the Sudan.[26] The statement prompted at least two prominent members of the Committee of Elder Statesmen, including Ismail Sidqi, to tender their resignations. .

The departure of Sidqi threatened to precipitate the complete dissolution of the committee—a development that would have severely weakened the authority of the government. King Faruq, therefore, took the extraordinary step of mediating between the committee and the government. In a hurried round of meetings, the monarch brokered a deal between the committee and the prime minister: In return for a commitment by the government to confront Britain, the committee would remain intact. Faruq issued a public call for support of the cabinet, thereby staking the royal reputation on the good faith of the government.[27]

Social Unrest Feeds the Nationalist Impulse

The cabinet crisis cannot be understood against the background of the rivalry among the establishment parties alone. By September 1945 a wide array of extraparliamentary forces had openly sided with the Wafd in its demand that the prime minister should take immediate action in pursuit of Egyptian national aspirations. In addition to a number of prominent Independents in the Chamber of Deputies, the following groups all endorsed the Wafdist position: the Muslim Brothers, the Young Egypt Party, student organizations, workers syndicates, and the lawyers guild.[28] The support of the nonparliamentary organizations had a particularly explosive potential: At the center of the Egyptian political stage stood radical groups that espoused revolutionary ideologies and that displayed a willingness to take violent actions against the government and the British alike. To be an opposition group in Egyptian politics in the 1940s and 1950s meant by definition to be anti-British, and the Muslim Brothers, the Young Egypt Party, and the Communists all took a maximalist line on the question of independence.[29] Regardless of the nature of their formal relations with Wafd, therefore, they all sang its tune.

These radical groups had a powerful hold over the imagination of the generation of 1936—that is, those who came to political maturity under the shadow of the Anglo-Egyptian Treaty of that year. To them, the very real gains in independence that Egypt had achieved under the treaty seemed, at best, hollow. The British ultimatum to Faruq in 1942 had belied all the verbiage of alliance between sovereign states; the treaty, in their eyes, was a sham; the traditional political actors, squabbling among themselves, had no ability or inclination to treat the root causes of the Egyptian national dilemma. These radical groups had divergent diagnoses of what ailed Egypt, but all agreed that the traditional political and social system suffered from a pernicious disease. Despite their different perspectives, all regarded the imperialist presence as a cancerous tumor in the Egyptian body politic: They viewed the inability of the traditional politicians to treat the disease as proof of its severity and of the need for a radical cure. The massive influence of the British held the Egyptians in thrall not just to Western military power but to insidious Western ideas as well. For the Muslim Brothers, the British presence encouraged people to stray from the fundamental tenets of Islam; for the followers of Young Egypt, it corrupted the national character; and for the Communists, it entangled Egypt in the capitalist web.

The nature and scope of these ideas created a body of thought that inextricably tied the question of relations with Britain to social, economic, and cultural problems. These doctrines encouraged their advocates to organize social groups (such as students or workers) and to imbue them with the sense that their parochial concerns had an intimate connection to the larger, national dilemma. Radical propaganda wove diverse issues—ranging from the causes of unemployment to the role of movie theaters in cultural life—into a coherent pattern at the center of which always stood the foreign presence in Egypt.

For the government, the role of the Muslim Brothers in fomenting anti-British sentiment posed the greatest threat. After the Wafd, they controlled the largest political following in the country—and certainly the most devoted. By 1947 they could plausibly claim to speak for one million Egyptians. Although the Brotherhood was not technically a political party, its size and organization gave it a central place in national life. The Brothers wielded considerable financial power; they ran businesses, social welfare agencies, and youth clubs, and they printed their own newspaper. Alarmingly, they controlled a large clandestine paramilitary organization. The Muslim Brothers had fielded candidates for office in the elections of January 1945. After losing seats in districts where they commanded a clear majority, however, they declared the political system corrupt, withdrawing from electoral politics. They did not, therefore, function as a traditional political party, yet no government could ignore their presence.

Ismail Sidqi Rises with the Crowd

The government limped along until early December 1945. One minister resigned due to illness and another minister died. Hafiz Ramadan Pasha resigned from the cabinet under pressure from the right wing of his Nationalist Party, the slogan of which was "Egypt for the Egyptians" and "No Negotiations until Evacuation."[30] This resignation brought into sharp relief the inability of the government to present itself successfully to the Egyptian people as its representative before the British.[31] As the cabinet tottered in this weakened state, Makram Ubayd exposed its deep divisions by criticizing in his party organ the unwillingness of the government to take action in the Anglo-Egyptian arena. Meanwhile, it emerged that the Egyptian foreign minister had returned empty-handed from London, where he had conducted talks regarding the opening of negotiations. Makram Ubayd then delivered a public ultimatum to the Egyptian prime minister. If al-Nuqrashi failed to demand publicly from the British that they respond to the Egyptian call for negotiations within a fixed period of time, then he would resign from the government along with at least two of his colleagues from the Independent Wafdist Bloc.[32]

Once again the cabinet was saved from dissolution by King Faruq, who now mediated between the prime minister and his rebellious finance minister. The outcome of this second round of royal mediation shifted the balance of power within the cabinet to the advantage of Makram Ubayd, who succeeded in forcing al-Nuqrashi to issue the Note of 20 December requesting that the British "fix an early date for an Egyptian delegation to proceed to London to negotiate with them the revision of the treaty of 1936."

This concession, however, did not bridge the open rift between the two rivals within the government. Although Ubayd held a personal grudge against al-Nahhas, the ideology of the Independent Wafdist Bloc did not differ significantly from the ideology of the Wafd. From December 1945 until the signing of the Bevin–Sidqi Agreement, Ubayd played to the nationalist grandstand, consistently proving, at the expense of the government, the purity of his nationalist credentials by advocating an aggressive position on Anglo-Egyptian relations. The weak tone of the Note to the British embarrassed Ubayd and functioned as a magnet for renewed criticism of the government.

Nationalist attacks grew even more hostile when the Egyptian foreign minister was quoted in the local press as having stated in London that it would be pointless to raise the matter of Anglo-Egyptian relations before the Security Council, where, coincidentally, the Soviet Union had launched a campaign against British policy toward Indonesia and Greece. The report created a storm in Egypt, where every politician continued to espouse the view that the creation of the United Nations nullified the Anglo-Egyptian Agreement.[33] At a moment when the Security Council functioned as an anti-imperial instrument, the Egyptian government appeared to have denied the need for United Nations intervention and, moreover, had implicitly delivered a message praising the alliance with Britain. The public in Cairo gained the impression that its government had conspired with the British against Egyptian national aspirations. One prominent newspaper went so far as to allege that the Egyptian foreign minister had issued the statement in consultation with the British in order to prevent the Soviet Union from raising in the Security Council the status of Egypt together with the status of Greece and Indonesia.[34]

The British responded, on 25 January, to the Egyptian Note in a manner that confirmed the worst suspicions of Egyptian nationalists. By affirming the "essential soundness" of the terms of the 1936 treaty, London revealed that, despite its expressed willingness "to undertake a review" of the treaty, its would in no way agree to relax the imperial grip on Egypt. Given the basic ideological currents in Egyptian politics, the two Notes provided the Wafd and the Muslim Brothers with highly combustible material. Both groups took a stand in favor of complete independence from Britain and portrayed the government's policy of attempting to revise the treaty as treachery. Mustafa al-Nahhas issued a manifesto in the name of his party in which he characterized the Egyptian Note and the British reply as "a shameful conspiracy" and "a disaster unparalleled in modern history."[35] The long manifesto concluded with a veiled call to arms:

> Egyptians, now is the time to raise your voice against the weakness of Egypt's policy and against the greed and ambition of the British. . . . No Egyptian proud of his country and jealous of his rights will hesitate to go forth in battle. The Wafd, chosen by you to achieve your independence, announces in the name of the Egyptian nation that it cannot be bound by the result of negotiations conducted by weak and inexperienced men. Forward, to strive and struggle for you country's cause. . . . Let us, one and all, raise our voice to tell all that there are people in Egypt who will not be subjugated.[36]

The Muslim Brothers, who also published a manifesto, responded in a similar vein. Attacking the notion of alliance with Britain, Hasan al-Banna announced that the term "partnership" was simply a new word for imperialism. "The Sons of the Nile," his manifesto declared, "will yield to no oppressor and will band together to demand their rights, ready to give their lives in the cause of justice."[37]

The two mass parties did not restrict their activities to the publication of manifestos: With the aid of their university organizers, they took their struggle to the streets. The student protesters addressed a letter with demands to King Faruq and then began a march on Abdin palace. As several thousand demonstrators reached the Abbas bridge they clashed with the police, who opened fire and wounded 150 people. Further protests continued on the following days in both Cairo and Alexandria, resulting in a total of twelve dead over a period of four days. Since the police in Cairo were still controlled by British commanders, the violence greatly strengthened anti-British feeling and created a general atmosphere hostile to the government's policy.[38]

As a result of the deaths and the anger they provoked, the position of al-Nuqrashi proved embarrassing to Makram Ubayd, who remained concerned with preserving the nationalist credentials he had won for himself in December, when he had forced the government to take action on treaty negotiations. Accordingly, he attacked the prime minister openly in the Senate and in his newspaper. He then tendered his resignation to the king on 13 February, protesting that the government reaction to the demonstrations had been excessive and that he had not been consulted.[39] Faced with the impossibility of bringing Mahmud Fahmi al-Nuqrashi and Makram Ubayd together yet again, King Faruq, who himself was no doubt embarrassed by the deaths, asked the government to resign. He called on Ismail Sidqi to form a new cabinet, which took office on 17 February.[40] With the exception of the prime minister, political nonentities populated the new government: Competent technocrats, few with formal party affiliations, held all the major portfolios.[41] Such a government, unlike its fractious predecessor, would clearly be subservient to the will of the prime minister, but its composition raised doubt about whether it would be capable of managing the opposition forces in the streets.

By choosing Sidqi, who during the period 1930–1933 had displayed his ability to police the Wafd, King Faruq signaled his continued refusal to countenance a government led by Mustafa al-Nahhas. Yet no Egyptian prime minister in 1946 could hope to swim directly against the powerful nationalist currents flowing through the country. The lukewarm vote of confidence the new government received from the Chamber of Deputies, which had no Wafdist members, spoke for itself: 105 deputies supported the cabinet, 3 opposed it, 78 abstained from voting, and 79 were absent. Makram Ubayd, who did not receive a portfolio, voted in favor, but announced that the support of the Independent Wafdist Bloc, which commanded twenty-nine deputies, had been given on a conditional basis. Thus although he would not hold a ministry he would continue to hold the government hostage.[42]

In effect, Sidqi had the choice of ruling the country by quasidictatorship or of attempting to co-opt as much of the nationalist program as possible. The first steps of the government demonstrated that it would attempt to present itself as the representative of nationalist opinion, and that it would attempt to steal a march on the Wafd and the Muslim Brothers. Thus the foreign minister announced that he, too, would seek total independence from the British and unity between Egypt and the Sudan. He also stated that the existence of the Security Council did make the Anglo-Egyptian Treaty an anachronism, but that since the Egyptian government had in 1936 signed an alliance that would last twenty years, it was preferable to attempt to extricate Egypt from it by direct negotiations with the British.

In an attempt to flow with the nationalist tide, and, perhaps, to increase his bargaining power over the British, Ismail Sidqi permitted protesters throughout the country to stage large anti-British demonstrations on 21 February. Demonstrators, led primarily by Wafdist and Muslim Brother student organizers, called for the immediate evacuation of British troops from the major population centers.[43] In Alexandria and Port Said the protest remained peaceful. In Cairo, however, events quickly turned violent, leading to one of the worst incidents of unrest in the postwar period. Thousands of angry youths, armed with clubs and baskets of rocks, rallied in Khedive Ismail square, the location of a number of British military institutions, including a large barracks and the headquarters of the British Air Force in Egypt. The demonstrators stoned the buildings; the men inside responded with gunfire. When four British army trucks strayed into the square, protesters leaped onto them; soldiers knocked them back onto the road, wounding eight people and killing one. The angry mob burned the trucks and "manhandled" their drivers.[44] Elsewhere in Cairo the police turned back a crowd en route to the British embassy; the protesters vented their anger instead on the Anglican cathedral. The quick arrival of troops stymied the attempt to torch the church, but the crowd managed to sack the bishop's residence. Hours after the main action had dissipated, small bands still roamed the city, destroying and looting European establishments.[45]

The next day calm returned to Cairo as the British army lurked about in tanks and trucks mounted with machine guns; the Egyptian police manned strategic intersections.[46] The day of violence left many wounded: The total number of dead stood, according to the Egyptian prime minister, at around fifteen.[47] The student leadership, held under police guard at the university, sent representatives to the government to inform it of their decision to call a three-day student strike and to initiate a boycott of British goods.[48]

The events of 21 February prompted London to issue a strong protest to Sidqi and to Faruq, claiming that the policy of the government had created a climate that encouraged violent anti-British activities. British officials in Cairo had bristled at the decision by Sidqi to allow the demonstration, and they deeply resented the attitude of King Faruq. For three days prior to the demonstration, the monarch had warmly received numerous delegations of student protesters who marched to his palace chanting anti-British slogans. The British military commanders blamed the king in particular: They contemplated calling on him themselves but abandoned the idea because they feared it would be received in Egypt as a repetition of Lampson's ultimatum to Faruq on 4 February 1942.[49]

Nonetheless, on 22 February, the British ambassador delivered a letter to the Egyptian government demanding punishment for those responsible for the violence, compensation for damage to British property, and assurance of arrangements designed to prevent violence in the future. Ismail Sidqi rejected the British demands, arguing that the demonstrators simply expressed the Egyptian national will and that improper behavior by the British had caused the disturbances.[50] On 22 February, in an act that no doubt enraged the British, the prime minister toured Cairo, receiving a thunderous applause from a crowd that numbered between 12,000 and 15,000 people.[51] The conservative statesman and the crowd were enjoying their honeymoon, which was destined to be short.

A Delegation Is Formed

The incident did not bode well for the success of the impending Anglo-Egyptian talks: nonetheless, when the dust from the demonstration had settled, the prime minister set about organizing (on the model of the 1936 treaty negotiations) a delegation composed of representatives from all the major parties. Mustafa al-Nahhas agreed to join only on the conditions that he would lead the delegation and that the group would begin its work only after a caretaker government took power with the intention of conducting a general election. In effect, therefore, he called for negotiations only after a government by the Wafd had been formed. Sidqi rejected the conditions and put together a delegation devoid of Wafdist representatives—a delegation, that is, that would suffer from the persistent opposition of al-Nahhas and his ideological allies. In contrast to the Wafd, however, Makram Ubayd agreed to join the delegation, where he would persist in performing the role of in-house nationalist agitator.

Thus, although Sidqi had succeeded in composing a cabinet that would not suffer from the divisiveness of the previous government, his relations with Makram Ubayd within the delegation would develop along the same lines as the al-Nuqrashi–Ubayd relationship. A powerful personality, Sidqi Pasha would prove more adept at handling Ubayd, yet his problem remained essentially the same: Under the prevailing political conditions there existed no possibility of composing a delegation capable of standing united in the face of the militant anti-British call of the Wafd, the Muslim Brotherhood, and numerous other nationalist organizations. However noble his intentions, in order to survive in power Ismail Sidqi stood before two simple tests: He had to achieve total independence for Egypt and he had to bring the Sudan under the sovereignty of the Egyptian crown. Failure to achieve these demands would not ruin the reputation of the prime minister—as long as he remained faithful to their spirit. If, however, he tried to sell something less to the Egyptian public, he could expect serious trouble. These had been the demands of Egyptian nationalists since the time of Sa'd Zaghlul, and they constituted the official policy of the Sidqi government.

Egypt in the British Strategic Vision

Because of the strategic importance of Egypt to the British Empire, and because the Egyptian demands for Treaty revision coincided with complex British-American-Soviet negotiations over the nature of the postwar world order, diplomatists in London formulated their policy toward Egypt with an eye on global considerations. The British attitude toward the nationalist wave sweeping Cairo, therefore, cannot be understood without surveying the place of the Middle East in the negotiations between the great powers over the postwar settlement.

Prior to the Suez Crisis, the British regarded their Empire as a third force in world affairs—a power squeezed uncomfortably between the capitalist United States, with which it shared many interests, and the Communist Soviet Union, which it feared greatly.[52] While Whitehall planners still saw themselves as players on the global stage, they also recognized that the ability of Britain to behave as the equal of its wartime allies had come under grave threat. The war had exhausted Britain, while, at the same time, it had fostered the spectacular expansion of Soviet and American might; moreover, it had eliminated Germany and Japan as great powers. Consequently, on the Eurasian land mass, the Soviet Union had no rival; in the Western hemisphere and in the Pacific, the Americans towered over all. Sandwiched between the emerging superpowers, strategists in London feared that their counterparts in Moscow and Washington would squeeze Britain out of the top ranks of diplomacy and relegate her to the status of a second-rate power.

Complete pessimism, however, did not overtake British diplomatists, who still nursed some hope concerning the strength of Britain in the future.[53] Yet they perceived clearly the dangers of their current exhaustion. The weakness of Britain vis-à-vis the superpowers compelled statesmen in London to gird themselves for a struggle with their wartime allies, who, purely on the basis of the arrogance of power, might not be inclined to respect British interests in the postwar era. Contemplating the present differential in capabilities and gambling that the economic recovery of Britain would diminish that differential, British diplomatists resolved that they must refuse to relinquish control over traditional spheres of interest. They believed that if their government, as a result of temporary weakness, allowed its international position to erode, then even after an economic recovery it would be impossible for Britain to regain the status of a great power. Retreat, they reckoned, would be permanent; hunkering down offered the only basis for hope.[54]

As Whitehall planners catalogued the international assets that they deemed worthy of stubborn preservation, they placed primary importance on the traditional British position in the Middle East and the Mediterranean, the only area of global geostrategic importance in which Britain still played the predominating role. The region, of course, had great intrinsic value for Britain: It sat athwart crucial routes of imperial communications—land, air, and sea—that London deemed vital both economically and strategically. In addition, the Middle East contained massive reserves of cheap crude oil that played an ever-increasing role in European industrial life. Under any circumstances, therefore, the British could have been expected to guard their privileged position with extreme jealousy. However, as the Egyptians delivered their demands for treaty revision, statesmen in London were calculating the value of their position in the Middle East at a rate even higher than its intrinsic worth to Britain. Whitehall planners believed that the very existence of Britain as a global player depended upon maintaining its role as the preponderating power in the region.[55] Moreover, the dissipation of their influence in the Middle East would have disastrous ramifications far beyond the borders of the British Isles: Nothing less than the future of Europe, they believed, was at stake in the Middle East.

In the course of 1945–1946, the British position in the region had come under severe threat from the north. In the final year of the war, the massive expansion of Soviet military power, the general opacity of Soviet intentions, and the demonstrated appetite of Stalin for territory and control in Eastern Europe, the Balkans, and the Middle East forced diplomatists in London to regard the Soviet Union as a rival in the Mediterranean and the Middle East. The dominant view among imperial strategists held that if the Soviets succeeded in breaking the British grip on the greater Mediterranean region, not only would Britain become a second-class power but all of continental Europe would likely fall under the shadow of Communism. In such circumstances, Great Britain would become a client of either the United States or the Soviet Union.[56]

The greatest threat to the established British position in the Middle East came as a result of Soviet pressure on Turkey and Iran. The interest of Moscow in these countries had predated the German invasion of Russia: Nazi diplomatic correspondence, captured during the war, documented an early Soviet desire to play a major role there. In November 1940, when Soviet and German representatives attempted to thrash out an agreement over spheres of influence, Vyacheslav Molotov, the Soviet foreign minister, demanded from the Germans "the establishment of a base for land and naval forces of the USSR within range of the Bosporus and the Dardanelles by means of a long term lease." In addition, Molotov affirmed that "the area south of Batum and Baku in the general direction of the Persian Gulf is recognized as the center of the aspirations of the Soviet Union."[57] The German invasion of Russia had deflected Moscow from these aspirations, which gradually revived—together with Soviet power—following the defeat of the Nazi armies at Stalingrad.

Soviet expansion into the Middle East first became a British obsession during the period 1944–1945. After the Red Army flooded across Eastern Europe and the Balkans, Moscow aggressively pursued five major policies, all clearly animated by the same desires to which Molotov had earlier given expression: (1) the scrapping of the Montreux Convention of 1936, which regulated the control of shipping through the Black Sea Straits; (2) the right, to be established by treaty with Ankara, to construct a military base on Turkish soil along the straits; (3) the ceding of territory in Eastern Turkey—around Kars and Ardahan—to the Soviet Union; (4) the maintenance, under Soviet bayonets, of puppet regimes in northern Iran; and (5) the attempt to wrest an exclusive oil concession from the government in Tehran.[58]

The Montreux Convention of 1936 gave the Turkish government sole responsibility for the defense of the Dardanelles and the Bosporus, both of which Turkey had closed to the warships of all nations during times of war. Stalin, in an expansive mood following the successes of the Red Army over the Nazis, now sought new terms that would open the straits to the Soviet navy and that would make the Soviet Union directly responsible for the defense of the waterways, whose security would be guaranteed by the construction of a Soviet base. Such a development, of course, would radically shift the regional balance of power by eliminating the traditional influence of the British in Ankara. Moreover, allowing the Soviets to build a base and giving them the territory they claimed in the East would lay the groundwork for Moscow to create a pliant political system in Turkey. Experience suggested that Moscow would follow its insistence on territory and a base with efforts to subvert the Turkish political system.

To British eyes, the pressure on Ankara appeared even more sinister when viewed against the background of Soviet actions in northern Iran, which the Red Army had occupied as a result of the Anglo-Russian-Persian Agreement of 1942. Although the agreement called for noninterference in the internal affairs of the country, the Soviets had nonetheless deprived Tehran of any say in the governance of Azerbaijan and Kurdistan, where Moscow established puppet Azerbaijani and Kurdish governments. These policies demonstrated that the Soviets were laying the foundation for a permanent position in the northern Iran, notwith-standing their acceptance of the clauses in the 1942 agreement that required both the British and the Soviets to evacuate completely all troops within six months of the cessation of hostilities. Faced with irrefutable evidence that Moscow had no intention of honoring its commitments, the Iranian, American, and British governments began pressuring the Soviets to demonstrate good faith. Not sur-prisingly, Moscow met these pleas with a stone wall.

If successful, Soviet policies toward Iran and Turkey would give Moscow a springboard with which to extend its influence not just over the states immedi-ately adjacent to the Soviet Union but farther south as well, down to the oil-producing regions of the Persian Gulf, "the center of the aspirations of the Soviet Union," as Molotov had described it to the Nazis. The importance of oil in the calculations of Moscow expressed itself directly when the Soviets demanded from the Iranian government an exclusive oil concession in the north—a demand that Tehran successfully foiled. Moscow, however, may have been casting its gaze beyond the oil of Iran. The creation of the Kurdish Republic of Mahabad, cen-tered directly opposite the Iraqi border and running north along the Turkish frontier, suggested that the Soviets coveted Iraqi oil as well.

Support for a Kurdish state in Iran certainly dovetailed with the other policies toward Turkey, where a large Kurdish minority also harbored bitter grievances against Ankara. The cessation of Kars and Ardahan, together with the establish-ment of autonomous Kurdish and Azerbaijani states in northern Iran, would inevitably spread Soviet influence throughout the Kurdish population of eastern Turkey, thereby significantly increasing the leverage of Moscow over Ankara. In addition, of course, Kurdish nationalism could also function as a powerful means of pressuring the Iraqi government, whose army had, between 1942 and 1945, forcefully subdued a Kurdish insurrection led by Mustafa al-Barzani. The links between Soviet policy toward Iran and Turkey, on the one hand, and to-ward Iraq, on the other, were not simply hypothetical: Following the failure of his rebellion in northern Iraq, al-Barzani fled, along with some 3,000 of his men, to the Republic of Mahabad, where he solidified ties with the Soviets that con-tinued for years after. If Moscow were allowed, therefore, a free hand in eastern Turkey and northern Iran, its goodwill toward the British position in Iraq would stand as the only impediment to Soviet pressure being brought to bear directly on Iraqi Kurdistan, which guarded the valuable oil fields around Kirkuk. What-ever the conscious intentions of Moscow toward Iraq and its oil, playing the ethnic card in Iran could not but awaken powerful fears in Baghdad, Ankara, and London.

Direct Soviet pressure on Turkey and Iran also caused British officials to regard gravely the indirect influence of Moscow over events in Greece, where local Com-munists played a leading role in an incipient civil war. In late 1945, the British attempted to install in Athens a government loyal to London and hostile to Moscow; much to British dismay, however, a significant portion of the Greek public regarded that government as illegitimate. Since the Communist party led the revolt against the British-sponsored regime, diplomatists in London had good reason for believing that a successful Soviet bid for influence over Turkey would greatly strengthen the rebels in Greece, whose other neighbors had already fallen under Communist control.

In contrast to the cases of Turkey and Iran, however, Moscow, out of deference to the British, did not attempt to bludgeon the Greek government into submission. In October 1944, Stalin and Churchill had arrived at their famous agreement that portioned out, by percentage, Soviet and British influence in the Balkan states: The Soviets, in return for a relatively free hand in the countries under their occupation, acquiesced in the British demand for the lion's share (90 percent) of control over Greece.[59] Having relegated the country to the British sphere of interest, Stalin refrained from making any direct demands on Athens.

At the same time, however, the Russians did nothing to help the British quell the domestic upheaval in Greece.[60] Allowing the Greek sore to fester, within the confines of the Anglo-Soviet understanding, served Soviet interests in the postwar bargaining over spheres of influence. Whenever the British or the Americans protested against the heavy-handed policy of the Russians in countries and territories under Soviet occupation, Moscow found it convenient to counter the accusations by pointing to the British use of force in Greece. Thus, for instance, at the London Conference of Foreign Ministers, in September 1945, the Russians raised the Greek question when the Americans pressured them over Romania. Also, on 19 January 1946, when the Iranian government appealed to the United Nations Security Council in protest over the Soviet occupation of northern Iran, Moscow responded two days later by placing before the Council the British occupation of Greece (and, for good measure, Indonesia as well).[61] Since Iran had been subject to the percentages agreement, Soviet actions toward Greece demonstrated that Moscow regarded that agreement as a loose understanding: It might inform policy as long as the Soviets found British goodwill useful, but it would certainly not remove the Greek issue from the international agenda. The frontiers remained porous between the British and Soviet spheres of influence.

Although Turkey, Iran, and Greece obviously constituted the kernel of dispute between Moscow and London, the attitude of the Russians toward the Mediterranean in general also fueled the fears of British diplomatists. As part of the postwar settlement, the great powers faced the task of determining the future of a number of territories along the Mediterranean littoral, most of them former Italian possessions.[62] In the discussions of the Big Three (Britain, the United States, and the Soviet Union), related to these issues, Moscow displayed a tendency to dilute the dominant influence of Britain in the region. For instance, on various occasions Stalin and his lieutenants pushed for a Soviet role in the trusteeship of Libya and Tangier; they resisted the British effort to give the Dodecanese Islands to Greece; they sought to extend the sovereignty of Communist Yugoslavia over Trieste; and they pressured the British and the French to evacuate Syria and Lebanon.[63] To be sure, the Soviets did not pursue these Mediterranean demands with the aggressiveness that characterized their policies toward Turkey and Iran.[64] Nonetheless, given the fluid nature of international affairs in early 1946, officials in London were in no mood to gamble on the future goodwill of the Soviet Union.

Tension between London and Moscow did not simply play itself out behind the closed doors of diplomatic chambers. In fact, it became a major public spectacle when it formed the theme of the first meeting of the United Nations Security Council, which convened in London in early 1946. The Council considered four issues: the British occupations of Indonesia, Greece, and the Levant states, and the Soviet occupation of northern Iran. Predictably, Moscow pushed for an early withdrawal of troops from the territories under British control, while London pressed the Soviets to evacuate Azerbaijan and Kurdistan.[65]

The discussions in the Security Council, which were characterized by tedious debates over matters of procedure, no doubt did little to resolve the problems in a manner that fulfilled the pious hopes of United Nations architects; nonetheless, the very existence of such an arena had a significant influence on the relations between Great Britain and its clients in the Middle East. The structure of the Security Council conspired with the rivalry between the great powers to create an international environment that tended to benefit small states nursing grievances against the British Empire. On the face of it, the power of veto enjoyed by Britain as a permanent member might have been expected to shield the Empire from such claims. In actual fact, however, the Security Council functioned as a mechanism for capturing diffuse anti-imperial forces and channeling them against the British (and, for that matter, the French), especially on matters over which London and Washington were not in accord.

Being the weakest of the Big Three, Britain would sooner modify its policies in most areas than step out of line with the United States; Britain needed U.S. support on the Security Council in order to counter the power and expansiveness of the Soviet Union. While the Americans did tend to support the interests of Britain over those of the Soviets, they also deemed necessary British concessions to local nationalism. Thus, in cases where the Americans and British were not in total agreement, a lesser power could capitalize on great-power discord simply by placing its claims before the Security Council, where the public nature of the debate encouraged the participants to force their policies to conform in appearance to their avowed principles.

The case of the British and French forces in the Levant illustrates well the manner in which the new world order gave small states a court of appeal against Britain. Before turning to the Security Council, the Syrians had attempted to introduce the Soviets into the equation. On the eve of the Potsdam conference of July 1945, Damascus appealed directly to Moscow in a bid for Soviet aid in ousting the British and French troops from Syria and Lebanon.[66] This direct appeal, however, had little effect. Although Stalin raised the question at the conference, he—no doubt having more important matters on his agenda—did not attempt to pressure the British and the French. Following this failure, the Syrians, in concert with the Lebanese, placed the matter before the Security Council, defining the issue as a dispute with the occupying powers. The terms of the appeal—which suggested that Britain had been collaborating with French imperialism—surprised London, which had initially encouraged the Syrians to play their hand at the United Nations. On the basis of their rather anti-French policies in the Levant, the British believed erroneously that they had created reservoirs of goodwill among the Syrian and Lebanese elites.[67] By contrast, leaders in Damascus and Beirut knew well that the Soviets would not side publicly with Britain and France on such an issue; in addition, they knew that the Americans also wished to avoid being painted as the supporters of European imperialism. Thus by taking the issue out of the back channels of diplomacy, the small states of the Levant capitalized on the international ideological positions of Moscow and Washington.[68] In the event, the Security Council deadlocked when the Soviets vetoed an American-authored resolution. Nonetheless, international exposure forced the British and French governments to propitiate Washington by pledging to honor the terms of the defeated resolution, which in effect called for the swift withdrawal of their troops from Lebanon and Syria. Therefore, the appeal to the United Nations, though by no means a resounding affirmation of the sovereignty of small nations, still bore some fruit.

The nature of this new world order influenced Anglo-Egyptian relations in an indirect, yet significant, manner. Leaders in Cairo, unlike their counterparts in the Levant, did not, in fact, appeal directly either to Moscow or to the United Nations; nonetheless Anglo-Soviet discord cast a long shadow over all that transpired in the Anglo-Egyptian arena.

The threat of the Soviet Union and Egypt cooperating against Britain certainly informed the attitude of London toward the Egyptian question from as early as July 1945, when, at the Potsdam Conference, Stalin suddenly raised the question of the British position in Egypt. In the course of a discussion between the Big Three regarding the Soviet demands for a base on the Black Sea Straits, Truman and Churchill attempted to deflect Stalin from pressing his demands. Stalin, however, would have nothing of it; crossing swords with Churchill, he won a tactical victory in the debate:

STALIN: I am afraid we won't reach an agreement on the straits. Our ideas differ widely. Perhaps we can pass over this point now.

CHURCHILL: I think that the freedom of the straits in war and in peace, for war and merchant vessel[s], should be guaranteed by the three great powers. That is a proposal worthy of discussion.

STALIN: We are also for the freedom of all traffic.

CHURCHILL: We should think that an international guaranty would be more than the equivalent of a base.

STALIN: What will be done about the Suez Canal?

CHURCHILL: It will be open.

STALIN: What about international control?

CHURCHILL: That question has not been raised.

STALIN: I am raising it.

CHURCHILL: We have an agreement, with which we are satisfied. There have been no complaints.

STALIN: Egypt should be consulted.

CHURCHILL: We have a treaty.

STALIN: You suggest that international control is preferable. We want a treaty with Turkey.

Faced with the clear parallel between the Turkish and the Egyptian cases, and with the threat of the Soviets becoming directly involved in Anglo-Egyptian relations, Churchill retreated, quickly agreeing with Stalin's initial assertion that they should pass over the point: "I quite agree," he said, "that this must be put off."[69]

By raising the Egyptian issue in the context of a discussion over Turkey, Stalin demonstrated that Turkey, not Egypt, was the matter of vital interest for the Soviet Union. Just as the issue of Greece had provided a means for Stalin to combat Western pressure over Soviet policy in Romania and Iran, threatening to attack the legitimacy of the Suez Canal Zone bases functioned as an effective means of pressuring Churchill for concessions over the straits. Moreover, given all of the important issues—in Europe and elsewhere around the globe—that still remained unsettled between the Soviet Union, Britain, and the United States, it seems unlikely that Stalin would wish to needlessly antagonize the British by attacking one of their most vital imperial strongholds.[70] Such an attack would certainly not succeed and might well drive the British and the Americans even closer together.

Nevertheless, while the Soviets no doubt saw little interest in launching a direct attack on the British position in Egypt, they certainly had, as in the case of Greece, a great interest in indirectly fostering discord between the British and the Egyptians—if only to keep the Egyptian question in an unsettled state, to allow the Soviets to pressure the British whenever they saw fit. In addition, if Egyptian nationalism could independently weaken the British position in the Middle East, so much the better for the Soviet Union, which had no long-term interest in keeping the British ensconced in the region. Thus, while Soviet diplomatists refrained from intervening in Anglo-Egyptian relations, Soviet publicists pumped a continual stream of anti-British and pronationalist propaganda into the Middle East.[71] Moreover, Moscow may well have conducted clandestine relations with the Egyptian opposition—the Wafd and the Communists in particular—encouraging attacks on the British in Egypt and funneling information to the opposition which would provide the basis for a well-informed critique of Anglo-Egyptian relations.[72]

The logic of this bifurcated Soviet policy suggested that, in the event of the Anglo-Egyptian dispute becoming public and international—for instance, by being placed before the Security Council—the Soviets would not hesitate to take an anti-British position, just as they had done in the cases of Indonesia, Greece, and the Levant. The British, therefore, had a powerful interest in restricting the Egyptian question, in keeping it strictly within the confines of bilateral relations between London and Cairo.[73]

Of course, the possibility of the Soviet Union and Egypt tacitly cooperating at the United Nations against Britain depended not just on the policies of Moscow but on those of Cairo as well. Here, too, the British had good cause for worry. During the first meeting of the Security Council, the Egyptian delegation, which held one of the temporary seats, displayed an alarming tendency to support the anti-British initiatives of the Soviet Union. In the case of Indonesia, for instance, the Egyptians were the only members of the council who voted together with the Poles and the Soviets for the immediate withdrawal of British troops; in the case of the Levant, the Egyptians also pursued an anti-British line. Though less aggressive on the matter of Greece, Cairo nonetheless did not fall in directly behind London. Since the occupation of northern Iran had, in Egyptian eyes, much in common with the British control of the Canal Zone, Cairo refrained from supporting the position of the Soviets. The absence, however, of a consistently pro-Soviet bias did not preclude the likelihood of Soviet–Egyptian cooperation in the event of an appeal to the council to annul the 1936 Anglo-Egyptian Treaty. Cairo could be expected to follow its own sense of self-interest, to pursue an anti-imperial line in every instance.

The attitude of the Egyptian government placed the British on the horns of a dilemma. Given the strength of the view in Egypt, fostered by the political opposition, that the new world order rendered the 1936 Anglo-Egyptian Treaty obsolete, London came under strong pressure to negotiate with the Egyptians, lest Cairo follow the example of Syria and Lebanon. From a strictly legal point of view, nothing compelled the British to honor the Egyptian request for talks: The 1936 treaty would remain valid for twenty years; a special clause of the treaty also stipulated that revisions would be made only when both parties deemed them necessary. From a political point of view, however, a rejection of the request would almost inevitably force the Egyptian government to bow to the will of the opposition and appeal to the United Nations, thereby directly involving the Soviet Union (and the United States) in the Anglo-Egyptian dispute. But, if the British feared that the Egyptian issue might yet become another subject for great-power bargaining, they also loathed the idea of sitting down directly opposite Egyptian negotiators, who, given the nature of Egyptian domestic politics, would undoubtedly call for a withdrawal of British forces from the Canal Zone. In British eyes, the evacuation of imperial forces from Egypt would constitute as great a blow to British dominance of the Middle East as would the success of Soviet policy toward Turkey and Iran. London, therefore, was trapped. Failure to respond to the Egyptian demand would vastly complicate the issue; responding, however, would provide Egyptian nationalists with an opportunity to challenge the foundation of British power in the Middle East.

When speaking of Britain as "dominant" in the region, we refer to a status that certainly entailed political and economic dimensions; fundamentally, however, "dominance" boiled down to the question of military power, to the preponderant position of Britain in the regional security system. Practically speaking, the British hoped that great powers and regional powers alike would recognize— without London being forced to resort to a public declaration—a kind of British Monroe Doctrine over the Middle East.[74] In order for London to remain dominant in the area, no potentially hostile state could be permitted bases in the region. Moreover, no local state could be allowed to conduct a foreign policy indifferent to British security interests. Creating conditions in which all countries would regard the Middle East as an exclusively British security zone required

Britain to project the image of a power capable of defending the region against all comers. Influential groups in London believed that without control of the bases in the Canal Zone, the projection of such an image would be impossible. Only the facilities in Egypt could provide a military infrastructure adequate for creating the impression of Britain as a Middle Eastern colossus.

Diplomatists in London, therefore, sought to safeguard the essential features of the 1936 treaty: the right to maintain British bases on Egyptian soil; the right to expand their forces in time of war; and commitment on the part of Egypt to undertake no international responsibilities and no domestic policies that endangered the interests of Britain. The rhetoric of the document implied a mutual relationship between equals: It affirmed that each state would come to the aid of the other in time of war. In essence, however, the 1936 treaty was a unilateral agreement; it gave Britain near complete control over matters pertaining to the defense of Egypt. The "aid"—laid out in tedious details filling numerous clauses—that Cairo provided Britain amounted to transforming the country in time of war into a British air base, barracks, supply center, and machine shop all rolled into one. Egypt, as defined by the 1936 treaty, was simply the world's largest aircraft carrier and transport vessel, permanently docked in the Middle East.

In relation to the other facilities that Britain controlled in the region, the Canal Zone resembled the dense center of a spider's web. If Egyptian nationalism were to rip it away from the greater network, then the British facilities in Jordan, Iraq, Palestine, Malta, and Cyprus would be left dangling like so many strands of a tattered web. Without the sobering effect of a massive imperial force stationed on the ground in the Middle East, British diplomatists would find it difficult in the extreme to convince, for instance, the Iraqis that Britain actually possessed the ability to defend their country against the Soviets—especially since the Soviets, thanks to geography, enjoyed the advantage of naturally dominating the Eurasian land mass. Under circumstances of attenuated imperial power, therefore, the Iraqis (and other Arab states) could be expected to find new friends to help defend their oil wealth.

The desire, then, to keep Egypt firmly bound to the British regional security system arose not only from the strict logic of military thinking but also from calculations regarding the political and economic implications of strategy. Although the region was divided into numerous autonomous states, London regarded these as components of an integrated unit. The Arab world—which shared strong social, religious, linguistic, and cultural ties—functioned like a vast echo chamber: Political ideas expressed in one country could be heard reverberating immediately throughout the region.[75] The size, independence, cultural power, and relative stability of Egypt coalesced to form a regional bullhorn, projecting the ideas current in Cairo into the political debates of Damascus, Jerusalem, Baghdad, and Amman. If the Egyptian state, as the Wafd and the Muslim Brotherhood desired, broke completely out of the British orbit, the Egyptians would set the pace for relations between Britain and her other clients. Nationalists in Baghdad, for instance, would then see complete independence as a realistic option. They would, after the example of the Egyptian opposition in the fall and winter of 1945, attack their pro-British government for failure to exercise that option; the government, officially pledged to the nationalist cause, would stand stripped of ideological resources with which to justify a special relationship with Britain.

Even prior to the Egyptian Note of December 1945, the nationalist tide seemed to be flowing against Britain. Independence movements threatened the British overtly in Palestine and in Egypt; Syria was gaining complete independence from European power; and, in Iraq, the force of anti-British feeling had already been demonstrated during the war by the Rashid Ali coup. If the British were to remain the preponderant power in the region, this tide of nationalism had to be stemmed: The Canal Zone base was the final bulwark against the flood.

When the Egyptians, then, presented their demand for negotiations, there emerged two major (and as yet uncoordinated) threats to the British position in the Middle East: The Soviet danger in the north and the Egyptian danger in the center. The success of British strategy required, in the best of all worlds, keeping Iran, Turkey, and Egypt sympathetic to the British security system (Syria, Palestine, Transjordan, and Iraq could be expected to follow the lead of these, the major regional players). The Soviet Union, therefore, must not be permitted significant influence over the non-Arab countries of the north, and the Egyptians must not be allowed to tear the Canal Zone from the fabric of the imperial security system. Moreover, under no circumstances could the British allow the Egyptian question to become enmeshed in the tangle of great-power negotiations over the postwar order, lest the two uncoordinated dangers to Britain form themselves into twin prongs of a single fork.

The restrained attitude of the Soviets toward Egypt offered some hope for keeping Anglo-Soviet and Anglo-Egyptian relations on separate tracks. It remained to be seen if the Egyptians would continue to accept their status as the custodians of an imperial aircraft carrier. London had no choice but to attempt to convince by means of negotiation. As stated at the start of this chapter, Britains's reluctance was manifest in its response of 26 January 1946 to the Egyptian demand for negotiations: On the one hand, the British Note stated that "his Majesty's government declare themselves willing to undertake with the Government of Egypt a review of the treaty arrangements between them"; on the other hand, it also affirmed "the essential soundness of the principles on which the Anglo-Egyptian treaty of 1936 was based."[76] The British would negotiate but they were unwilling to alter the status quo. This attitude, inevitably, would not hold up for long.

British Concessions

Sidqi Pasha, had he so wished, could have placed the Egyptian question before the Security Council; he refrained, however, from internationalizing the dispute. That he considered the option is indisputable: The call to submit the Egyptian case to the United Nations had risen daily from a number of quarters since late 1945. The prime minister probably calculated that the position of Egypt in the international system made an appeal to the Security Council pointless. For when

he took the reins of power he faced an international environment that, on balance, tended to work in favor of the perpetuation of a special relationship with
Britain.

Cairo did not command the power and resources adequate for the task of
dislodging Egypt from the imperial grip. The events of 4 February 1942 provided
a model of the British response to any attempt by the Egyptian authorities to
organize a violent movement against the British. If Egypt could not be liberated
by force, neither could it be freed by diplomacy. The Soviet Union—regardless
of what Moscow might have been telling the Wafd—did not have the means to
pry the country away from the British. The deadlock in the Security Council over
the Levant resolution proved that unless the United States worked to oust the
British forces from Egypt, they would remain stationed in the Canal Zone.

Whether Sidqi Pasha actually reasoned along these lines, he clearly chose not
to challenge the dominant British role in the Middle East. He sought, instead, a
kind of partnership with Britain—a relationship between equals that would continue to accord London the predominant role in the regional security system.
Though it would certainly serve British goals, this relationship would also pay
greater respect to Egyptian sovereignty. Cairo pursued a policy designed to stake
out a middle ground between the call for complete independence rising from the
street and the demand for the maintenance of the status quo coming from London. While this strategy no doubt reflected a sober analysis of the realities of the
international system, it was hardly the stuff from which nationalist heroes are
made. Sidqi Pasha would be hard pressed to sell his policy of the golden mean
to a public fixated on the slogan "*al-Istiqlal al-tamm!*"—complete independence.
In the hothouse of Egyptian politics, the very act of negotiating with the British
on the basis of perpetuating the alliance, in whatever form, could easily be painted
as treachery.

The attitude of the Wafd greatly increased the difficulty of legitimating the
policy of compromise. When Sidqi Pasha decided, in the face of a Wafdist refusal
to participate in the talks with London, to press ahead with the composition of
a multiparty delegation responsible for conducting the negotiations, he implicitly
reconciled himself to the fact that any agreement with Britain would be wrapped
in controversy. Al-Nahhas Pasha had made it perfectly clear that he would only
accept a treaty negotiated by a delegation that the Wafd dominated. By rejecting
the demands of al-Nahhas, Sidqi Pasha ensured that the most powerful political
party in the country would violently reject the work of the Egyptian negotiators.

The delegation, then, took on great importance as the primary instrument for
legitimating a new Anglo-Egyptian treaty. In the wake of al-Nahhas's obstruc-
tionism, the success of the policy of the government required the unwavering
support of every other major political party and of most leading independent
politicians. Without a strong political foundation for the new treaty, the Wafd
could effectively characterize any agreement as the work of a minority government—a band of toadies kowtowing to the British. Under these circumstances,
a new treaty would not usher in a new stage of cooperation in Anglo-Egyptian
relations; it would simply inaugurate another phase in the struggle for complete
independence.

The negotiations themselves were long (lasting from April to October), tumultuous (appearing repeatedly to be on the verge of collapse), and controversial (sparking a virulent debate between the Tory and Labor parties in Britain and provoking nearly continuous demonstrations and acts of violence on the streets of Cairo). They fell clearly into three separate stages:

1. From April, when the British delegation headed by Lord Stansgate arrived in Cairo, to 9 May, when Ernest Bevin announced in the House of Commons the intention to evacuate British troops from Egypt.
2. From May through September, when the delegations conducted countless rounds of talks in Cairo that ended in deadlock and the return home of the Stansgate mission.
3. The weeklong conference in London in late October between Bevin and Sidqi, who emerged from their negotiations with a draft proposal for a treaty to be placed before the Egyptian and British parliaments for approval.

The reserves of legitimacy with which Sidqi Pasha fueled his policy decreased considerably as the negotiations advanced to each successive stage. By the time he returned from London, his pursuit of the golden mean between British security interests and Egyptian nationalism had floundered.

The first stage of the negotiations went well for the Egyptian government, because London made some rather bold concessions in an attempt to create a favorable atmosphere. Sidqi Pasha had informed the British delegation, immediately upon its arrival in Cairo, that official talks would not be opened until London agreed in principle to evacuate completely its forces from Egypt. In order to save the negotiations from stillbirth, Foreign Minister Bevin bowed to the will of the Egyptian government and dramatically announced in the House of Commons the readiness of his government, under the proper conditions, to evacuate the troops.[77]

The statement, which raised the ire of the Tory Party—and of Churchill in particular—sparked off an angry debate in Parliament. Bevin had cut British policy loose from the 1936 treaty, with all of the guarantees it gave to the British in terms of physical control over Egyptian bases. To the Tories this step threatened to undermine the Empire. In response to their criticisms Bevin assured them that he "would not leave a vacuum in the Middle East," although he did not explain how this would be accomplished in the absence of forces on the ground.

As part of his new policy, the foreign minister also announced the immediate and unconditional withdrawal of soldiers from Cairo and Alexandria. This evacuation from urban centers—which was completed within a period of ten months—began immediately: by 4 July the British had returned to the Egyptian government the Citadel of Muhammad Ali, which had served as the British military headquarters for more than sixty years. In London, Bevin's concessions appeared, depending on one's politics, as either a noble recognition of Egyptian sovereignty or as a shameful retreat from an imperial stronghold. In keeping with the terms of this debate, Bevin attempted to sell the Egyptians the line that the British decision to withdraw from the urban areas constituted a magnanimous gesture of goodwill.

To be sure, Bevin certainly displayed great political courage when he scrapped the conception of Anglo-Egyptian relations that informed the 1936 treaty. But even these bold concessions could not possibly mollify Egyptian nationalists—as represented, say, by the Wafd and the Muslim Brothers—who viewed both the evacuation from the cities and the statement of willingness to withdraw troops from the Canal Zone as meaningless gestures.[78]

No doubt Sidqi Pasha and other members of the Egyptian elite understood the full extent of the forces arrayed against the policy of Ernest Bevin; no doubt they sincerely appreciated the manner in which the British foreign minister faced his enemies at home. In 1946, however, Egyptian politicians, whatever their private thoughts, were not in the business of publicly praising British policy. Especially in the view of the Egyptian opposition, London made concessions to Egypt not out of some inherent magnanimity, but rather out of fear of the Soviet threat. Moreover, for Egyptian nationalists there was nothing noble about returning stolen property to its rightful owners. It scarcely escaped notice in Cairo that the purportedly generous removal of troops from the streets of the cities actually served British self-interest by rendering the soldiers less vulnerable to attack, and by reducing the points of friction between British personnel and the local population. Given the currency of such feelings, Sidqi Pasha had no legitimate basis on which to extol publicly the courage of Ernest Bevin.

Thus, while the British concessions did no harm to the position of Sidqi Pasha, they in no way altered his fundamental dilemma. For Egyptian nationalists, the bottom line was this: Bevin himself had insisted that a vacuum would not be left in Egypt; clearly, then, the British did not intend to leave, but rather to substitute one form of control for another. Sidqi Pasha, therefore, faced the challenge of persuading his public that, in fact, his agreement with Britain would ensure that Egypt no longer constituted the plaything of the Empire. During the remaining stages of the negotiations, when London would demand concessions from Cairo, the impossibility of this task would become clear to everyone. As a result, the balance of power, would shift—away from the government and in favor of the opposition.

Makram Ubayd Aligns with the Wafd

In early June tension developed between the prime minister and his colleagues as a result of Sidqi Pasha's tendency to arrogate to himself responsibility for making policy toward Britain. By the end of the month a rupture developed between the prime minister and Makram Ubayd, who returned to the role of in-house nationalist agitator—the role that he had played to the detriment of al-Nuqrashi Pasha's government. Although not part of the cabinet, Ubayd was a member of the negotiating delegation, where he was almost as great a thorn in the side of Ismail Sidqi as he had been in the side of the previous prime minister. As a result, the Egyptian negotiating team, just like al-Nuqrashi's cabinet, divided into two camps—one forming around the prime minister, the other loosely around Ubayd.

The future of the Anglo-Egyptian alliance was the main source of contention between the prime minister, who was willing to continue the alliance, and Makram Ubayd, who was not. Bevin had agreed in principle to a complete withdrawal of forces from Egyptian bases, but he still insisted that the Canal Zone continue to play a major role in the global British strategic network. Therefore, he aggressively sought assurance from Sidqi that Britain would be permitted to reoccupy the Egyptian bases in the event of war. The British desire for the right of return posed serious political problems for Sidqi Pasha. A provision in the new treaty according the British bases on Egyptian territory would appear to nationalists as yet another mechanism of imperial control over the country. Ultimately, the roots of the hostility toward the British demand for the right to reoccupy the bases lay in the collective Egyptian experience in both world wars. Hordes of foreign soldiers swarmed over the cities, and statesmen in London dictated the policies of Cairo. Granting the British the ability to return yet again seemed, in the eyes of many, like inviting a repetition of the indignities that Egypt had already suffered twice in the past. In order to make the British alliance palatable to the Egyptian people, therefore, Sidqi needed a formula that would allow him, at the very least, to guarantee that Egyptian sovereignty would not be compromised for yet a third time.

By June the two negotiating teams had hit upon the concept of a "Joint Defense Board," a consultative committee that would be composed of both British and Egyptian representatives. In the eyes of its architects, this committee would continuously examine the international situation in order to maintain the bases at a level of readiness appropriate for countering the existing threats to Egyptian security. In the event of an international crisis, the defense board would determine whether British forces should be permitted to use the bases. In theory, the mechanism would have given the Egyptian government the ability to veto any unwanted attempt by the British to occupy the Canal Zone. It would have put an end to the extraterritoriality that Britain enjoyed under the 1936 treaty. In order to take advantage of Egyptian military facilities, statesmen in London would be required to persuade their counterparts in Cairo that it was obviously in the interest of Egypt to open its doors to British troops.

Since the concept of the defense board did, in fact, reduce the level of British direct control over Egypt, Sidqi Pasha could characterize it in good faith as a real achievement for Egypt. He could not, however, plausibly present it as the realization of the desire for complete independence. The concept was simply too legalistic and too bureaucratic to satisfy the symbolic needs of an aggrieved nationalism.

Continuous press leaks kept the Egyptian public informed about the progress of the negotiations.[79] The defense board scheme came under severe public scrutiny already in late June. The Wafd, of course, violently criticized the scheme; in addition, Makram Ubayd, despite his position on the delegation, also lent his voice to the rising public chorus of denunciation. His newspaper described the defense board as a means of extending a British protectorate over Egypt; the paper warned against believing that the mechanism would ever be merely consultative.[80] One interviewer, responding to Ubayd's rejection in principle of any alliance with Great Britain, asked why he remained on the negotiating delegation. Ubayd replied: "I am fulfilling my duty to the end. At the moment of signature I shall leave my place blank."[81]

For six months, from June until the death of the Bevin–Sidqi Agreement in December, Makram Ubayd maintained a ceaseless attack on the proposed Anglo-Egyptian military alliance, calling on the government to publicize the content of the negotiations with the British, to break off negotiations, and to refer the Egyptian question to the United Nations. This position, of course, did not differ in substance from the stance of the Wafd, which also turned up the heat on Sidqi following the disclosures to the press regarding the Joint Defense Board. Although the ideological differences between the Wafd and the Independent Wafdist Bloc had always been negligible, the animosity between the leaders had previously prevented cooperation between them. In a surprising development, however, in early August 1946 Mustafa al-Nahhas (the jailer of Ubayd in 1943) and Makram Ubayd (the would-be jailer of al-Nahhas in 1945) proclaimed common cause and pronounced a truce between their parties.[82] Sidqi Pasha found himself facing an opposition more united than ever before. That the concept of the defense boards could engender even a modicum of cooperation between two sworn enemies was a significant measure of its illegitimacy in Egypt.

The startling decision by Makram Ubayd to cozy up to the Wafd arose not from a flight of personal whimsy, but rather from a sober analysis of the prospects for success of the Anglo-Egyptian negotiations, which during the months of July and August teetered on the verge of complete breakdown. In their attempt to reach agreement, the negotiators confronted significant difficulties over three main issues: the precise authority of the defense board; the length of time to be allotted for the troop withdrawal; and the relationship between Egypt and the Sudan. The distance between the British and Egyptian positions on each of these issues gave rise to the feeling in Cairo that the negotiations would fail and that, as a result, the Sidqi government would fall.

Speculation among the political elite regarding the probable constitution of the successor government caused the star of the Wafd to rise.[83] To many informed observers it appeared that, one way or another, the Wafd would inevitably wind its way in from the political wilderness. Given the shaky position of the government, it would appear that Makram Ubayd, by adopting an uncompromising position toward the negotiations, intended to position himself in the vanguard of the nationalist movement when a new government would be formed.[84] He sought a truce with the Wafd because al-Nahhas would likely hold the balance of power.

The Muslim Brothers Align with the Wafd

The instability of the government, which bore a striking resemblance to the trouble faced by al-Nuqrashi some ten months earlier, undoubtedly served as a warning to Sidqi Pasha. Nevertheless, he showed no signs of caving into the opposition, nor did he follow the example of his predecessor and simply allow matters to drift. On the contrary, he launched a counterattack. In early July the government drove through parliament an anti-Communist law that restricted some forms of public demonstration and forbade the newspapers to publicize information regarding protests and strikes. The legislation also gave the state wide powers to detain individuals and confiscate publications.

Although ostensibly directed against Communists, the law also proved itself as an effective weapon for harassing the Independent Wafdist Bloc and the Wafd, the left wing of which the government claimed was cooperating with Communist elements. For instance, when Wafdist-led student groups attempted to organize a nationwide strike on 11 July to commemorate the anniversary of the British conquest of Egypt in 1882, the prime minister responded by confiscating the organ of Makram Ubayd's party and two papers published by the Wafd; all three publications had printed statements in favor of the strike. In addition, the police detained numerous organizers. Meanwhile, under the pretext of conducting a broad sweep for Communists—which entailed house searches, the arrest of scores of activists, and the confiscation of publications—the government indefinitely suspended several newspapers, including *al-Wafd al-Misri*, the mouthpiece of the left-wing of the party.[85]

In his effort to weaken al-Nahhas, Sidqi enjoyed not just the coercive power of the state but, in addition, the veiled support of the Muslim Brotherhood, which between July and September engaged in an extremely acrimonious struggle with the Wafd. The bad blood between the two mass political organizations ran thick, as a result (among other things) of their competition for the loyalty of the same social groups. In addition, the policies of Sidqi Pasha exacerbated the rivalry, because in an effort to weaken the Wafd he entered into an informal alliance with the Muslim Brothers.

The exact terms of this alliance remain unclear. Without doubt, however, the Muslim Brothers received government subsidies for a number of their activities.[86] The authorities also turned a blind eye to the violent acts of the secret paramilitary organization of the Brotherhood, whose activities, though illegal, tended to benefit the government. Paramilitary activists channeled their energies into harassing the British, thereby increasing the pressure on London to compromise with Sidqi. Violent attacks against British soldiers—many, if not most, conducted by members of the Muslim Brothers—were commonplace throughout 1946. The Wafd also suffered the blows of resurgent Islam. In July and August a number of pitched battles between supporters of the Muslim Brothers and the Wafd broke out on the streets of Cairo, Port Said, and Ismailiyya.[87] The failure of the government to prosecute paramilitary activists cannot be attributed to ignorance of their existence, because all participants in Egyptian politics knew of the Muslim Brothers' secret organization.[88]

In return, apparently, for adopting an indifferent attitude toward the secret paramilitary organization, the government probably received a greater reward than simply the harassment of its enemies. The Muslim Brothers may also have agreed to avoid calling for mass action designed to counter Ismail Sidqi's policies.

It is certainly striking that, whereas the Muslim Brothers rejected in principle the attempt by the government to seek an accommodation with the British, before September they never took action designed directly to discredit the government.[89] In short, Sidqi Pasha bought some breathing space from Hasan al-Banna, leader of the Brotherhood.

The limits of this purchase became apparent during the first week in September, when al-Banna's antinegotiation policy sharpened, and he became overtly critical of the government. This new direction found expression at a national congress of the Muslim Brothers which drafted a manifesto demanding that the government break off the negotiations, renounce the 1936 treaty, force the British to withdraw their troops within one year, and refuse to sign any new treaty with the British until after they completed their evacuation and after the consideration of the Egyptian question by the Security Council.[90] As a result of this shift in policy, on the major issue of the day no difference existed between the position of the Wafd, the Independent Wafdist Bloc, and the Muslim Brothers, not to mention many other smaller groups, including the Communists. All had turned sharply against the perpetuation of the Anglo-Egyptian alliance in any form.

The threat that this alignment presented to the government became clear a few weeks after the national congress of the Muslim Brothers, when Hasan al-Banna and Mustafa al-Nahhas sent out feelers, exploring the possibility of an understanding between their organizations.[91] In a development as striking as the rapprochement concluded one month earlier between al-Nahhas and Ubayd, these contacts also proved successful. The Muslim Brothers, like the Independent Wafdist Bloc before them, proclaimed a truce with their erstwhile rivals. Although scant potential existed for long-term cooperation between the Wafd and the Muslim Brothers, even an alliance of convenience between the two giants of Egyptian politics boded ill for the government. It testified dramatically to the inherent difficulty of refurbishing the Anglo-Egyptian alliance.

The new policy the Muslim Brothers adopted in September 1946 was yet another reflection of the progressive deterioration of Sidqi Pasha's strategy of seeking an accommodation with London. After the August meetings between British and Egyptian representatives, the differences between them on the three main issues—length of time allotted for the evacuation, the wartime responsibilities of Egypt to Britain under the new terms of alliance, and the Sudan—remained significant. Consequently, many members of the Egyptian delegation actively opposed the continuation of the negotiations, and they kept the public well informed regarding the specific nature of the disagreements between London and Cairo.[92] By leaking this information to the press, these rebellious delegates, led by Makram Ubayd, assured that any compromises made by Sidqi Pasha would appear as proof that the prime minister had caved in under British pressure.

In late August speculation redoubled regarding the inevitable fall of the government; prominent members of the delegation now favored the participation of the Wafd in both the government and the delegation itself. To make matter worse for the prime minister, public signs of a reconciliation between the Wafd and King Faruq added substance to the speculation.[93]

The Last Gasp of a Dying Policy

Sidqi Pasha, ever tenacious, pressed on. In an attempt to shore up his position, he reshuffled the cabinet during the first two weeks of September, bringing into the government the Sa'dists, who, together with the Liberal Party, were the only supporters of his policy.[94] On the face of it, the cabinet reconstruction might appear to have given the prime minister a new lease of life. In actual fact, however, the maneuver underscored the growing isolation of Sidqi Pasha. Since the cabinet changes occurred against the background of the rebellion in the delegation, they appeared as preparation for the granting of concessions to the imperialists.

Following the reconstitution of the cabinet, another set of meetings between the negotiators provoked a new crisis for the government. When the Egyptian delegation convened to discuss the British proposals—characterized by London as its final offer—the split between the factions led by Sidqi and Ubayd came to a head, prompting the prime minister to conclude that any further attempt to press forward was fruitless. He tendered his resignation to the king, who immediately took steps to install a government in which the Wafd would participate.[95] These efforts failed, however, when Mustafa al-Nahhas made familiar demands for a monopoly over the levers of power. As a consequence, King Faruq rejected Sidqi Pasha's resignation. This crisis at least allowed the prime minister to wring from the king a public statement of support for his policy. However, there could be no denying that, as a British diplomat wrote, "it seems likely Sidki Pasha's leading influence has been further weakened by this controversy."[96]

In the light of the rebellion within the delegation, the prime minister, in order to pursue his policy to its logical conclusion, had no choice but to continue the negotiations with the British on his own. Since the British delegation had returned to London after presenting its final offer, Sidqi Pasha proposed (despite the public protests of the rebels in the Egyptian delegation) to travel to Britain himself in order to present the Egyptian position to Ernest Bevin in person.[97] Even the Sa'dist and Liberal Party leaders, who publicly endorsed the proposed trip, distanced themselves from Sidqi's venture by declining to join him. In response to the proposed meetings in London, the Wafd issued a new manifesto that attacked the British and the government alike in the harshest terms yet, accusing Sidqi Pasha of treason and calling in veiled terms for the violent overthrow of the government.[98] An air of unrest hung over Cairo.

The meetings, therefore, between Bevin and Sidqi, which took place on 18–25 October 1946, enjoyed little legitimacy in Egyptian politics; they are best understood as the last gasp of a strong-willed but isolated prime minister. By the time Sidqi Pasha traveled to London, his policy suffered from the hostility of the two mass political organizations—the Wafd and the Muslim Brotherhood—as well as of the Egyptian delegation to the negotiations, the very committee designed to confer legitimacy on a new understanding with the British. In addition, the strength of this opposition led many erstwhile supporters of Sidqi Pasha to distance themselves from his decision to pursue his policy to the bitter end.

The crux of the dispute between the prime minister and his opponents was not simply the question of the Sudan but the legitimacy of committing Egypt to continued participation in a military alliance with Great Britain. Such an alliance was almost universally recognized in Egypt as an antiquated legacy of colonial domination and as a mechanism for dominating the politics and economy of the country. In this view, the strategic importance of Egyptian territory to the Empire had made the Egyptians the puppets of the British during two world wars; perpetuation of the alliance in any form would, in the event of a third war, assure the reappearance of the puppet master.

Behind the ideological conflict between Sidqi Pasha and the opposition, of course, stood the naked power struggle between the Wafd and its enemies. Clearly, playing the nationalist card was the most effective means for the Wafd to regain power and credibility following the political developments of World War II. By October 1946, however, after more than a year of agitation against an accommodation with Britain, the Wafd had staked out a position that it could abandon only at the cost of losing credibility in nationalist circles. Mustafa al-Nahhas had committed his organization, irrevocably, to placing the Egyptian question before the United Nations.

As discussed earlier in this chapter, when Sidqi returned from London, he immediately emphasized Bevin's affirmation of Egyptian sovereignty over the Sudan. He advanced an understanding of the Sudan Protocol that flatly contradicted the interpretation of the British foreign minister, thereby provoking a storm of outrage in London.[99] Sidqi Pasha portrayed the Sudan Protocol as a victory for Egypt because he had manifestly failed to secure complete independence. The British recognition of Egyptian sovereignty over the Sudan constituted, in the final round of negotiations, the greatest concession to the Egyptian point of view. Thus for Sidqi, who returned to a public that was well informed on the differences between the British and Egyptian positions, the Sudan Protocol provided the best material from which to fashion a claim that he had forced the British to retreat. In other words, the opposition attacks directed at the government for its willingness to renew the military alliance forced Sidqi to hail the Sudan Protocol as a great victory for Egyptian national claims.

While the call for the "Unity of the Nile Valley" certainly occupied a place of importance in the pantheon of Egyptian national claims, it did not enjoy greater importance than the call for total independence. Even Sidqi Pasha's tendentious reading of the Sudan Protocol could not, therefore, render the Bevin–Sidqi Agreement attractive enough to rally the wavering members of the delegation. In the weeks following his return to Cairo, the prime minister, with the aid of King Faruq, attempted in vain to persuade the independents on the delegation to endorse the Bevin–Sidqi Agreement.[100] As a result of their implacable opposition, Sidqi Pasha decided to bypass them altogether by calling for a vote of confidence in the lower house of parliament—a maneuver that prompted the dissidents in the delegation to make their position known to the public.[101]

The Liberal Party, together with the Sa'dists, offered the only organized support for Sidqi's policy. But even they did not wholeheartedly endorse the draft treaty; they agreed to vote for it only on the condition that the British agree to amendments that would unambiguously affirm Sidqi's interpretation of the Sudan Protocol. Thus, with the hesitant backing from the Liberal Party and the full support of the Sa'dists, Sidqi did manage to secure a vote of confidence in the Chamber of Deputies for his policy. The British authorities, however, now demanded that, before signing the treaty into law, an exchange of letters interpreting the Sudan Protocol in a manner favorable to London must be attached. The two governments remained deadlocked, and the Bevin–Sidqi Agreement never passed into law. Exhausted by his efforts, Ismail Sidqi resigned. Meanwhile, in the streets the opposition to Sidqi's policy took an aggressive turn; the month of November witnessed some of the worst violence of 1946, a violent year in any case.

On the face of it, the Sudan question ultimately constituted the greatest obstacle to an Anglo-Egyptian rapprochement. But given the massive opposition to the draft treaty, the significance of the vote in parliament must not be overstated. Sidqi Pasha secured that endorsement only by offering a tendentious presentation of his agreement with Ernest Bevin, and only after circumventing the Egyptian delegation to the negotiations. Moreover, the claims of the Wafd regarding the nonrepresentative nature of the lower chamber of parliament could not easily be ignored.

Therefore, the government's ability to muster a majority in the lower house of parliament in favor of the Bevin–Sidqi Agreement did not prove that its policy of granting the British base rights on Egyptian soil enjoyed a solid base of support. The proposed Anglo-Egyptian alliance would never have functioned in a manner acceptable to either Cairo or London. The Joint Defense Board, a consultative body, would have required the wholehearted support of the Egyptian authorities in order to conduct its affairs. With the Wafd, the Muslim Brothers, Makram Ubayd's party, the student organizations, and a host of prominent politicians all implacably hostile to the draft treaty, such support had no hope of emerging. The Joint Defense Board, had it ever appeared, would inevitably have been subjected to violent attacks. Far from resolving the differences between London and Cairo, the treaty would simply have ushered in a new era in the Anglo-Egyptian conflict.

The experience of Sidqi Pasha in 1946 proved that the Anglo-Egyptian military alliance was illegitimate in Egyptian politics. It would not be long before this truism clearly guided the policy of Cairo.

TWO

In the American Era

A New Policy

In the beginning of 1947, voices from across the Egyptian political spectrum demanded that the government, now led once again by Mahmud Fahmi al-Nuqrashi, work to terminate the alliance with Britain by appealing to the United Nations. According to advocates of this position, the international community would surely help Egypt realize its national aspirations. Because the fall of Sidqi Pasha had indeed demonstrated the illegitimacy of the Anglo-Egyptian alliance, the new prime minister enjoyed almost no room for maneuver. Having himself already fallen once from power for failing to pursue the national aims aggressively, he could not afford to appear dilatory again. Within a few months of taking office, therefore, al-Nuqrashi Pasha stole a plank from the platform of the radical nationalists: He adopted a policy designed to achieve total independence for Egypt.

On 26 January 1947, the prime minister broke off discussions with the British government and announced his intention to place the Anglo-Egyptian dispute before the United Nations. In the course of the next six months Egyptian political strategists debated among themselves the precise nature of their national demands and whether to address their appeal to the Security Council or to the General Assembly. The first indication of the case that Cairo would make before the United Nations appeared on 3 March, when al-Nuqrashi Pasha issued a statement explaining his refusal to continue the negotiations that Sidqi Pasha had started. The prime minister affirmed that:

> the final breaking off of these arduous negotiations may be attributed only to the inability of Egypt to obtain satisfaction on the two essential points which are unanimously claimed by the Egyptian people.
>
> These two points are as follows: (1) The evacuation of British troops from Egypt. This evacuation must be immediate, complete, and not conditioned by the treaty. (2) The maintenance of the unity of Egypt and the Sudan, self-government for the Sudanese, and the restoration to Egypt of her rights in the administration of the Sudan in order to further the preparation of the Sudanese for self-government. The unity of Egypt and the Sudan is the will of both Egyptians and Sudanese alike, whereas British policy is directed to inciting the Sudanese to secede from Egypt. . . .
>
> The two preceding points are a fair application of the principles of the United Nations Charter. For that reason, after exceptionally prolonged negotiations the Egyptian Government, regretfully convinced that direct discussions held no hope

of success, decided to appeal to the Security Council. This decision has received the enthusiastic endorsement of the entire Egyptian people. Egypt has abiding faith in the Untied Nations. . . . [1]

With this statement, the Egyptian government announced that, from its point of view, the Bevin–Sidqi formula had died and would never be resurrected.

Indeed, when Cairo formally addressed its appeal to the United Nations in July 1947, it left no doubt that tinkering with the terms of the 1936 treaty had ceased to be an option. By that point, strategists in Cairo had settled, after much deliberation, on the Security Council as the appropriate body to hear their appeal. In his letter to the Secretary General, Prime Minister al-Nuqrashi stated that "British troops are maintained in Egyptian territories against the unanimous will of the people. The presence of foreign troops within the territory of a Member of the United Nations . . . is contrary to the letter and spirit of the United Nations Charter. . . ." He requested that the Security Council oversee the "total and immediate evacuation of troops from Egypt, including the Sudan; and the termination of the present administrative regime in the Sudan."[2] Furthermore, when al-Nuqrashi appeared personally before the council in August, he stated that the alliance established by the treaty "masks a relationship that is both unbalanced and undignified. It ties Egypt to the British economy; it subjects Egypt to the vagaries of British diplomacy; and it imprisons Egypt within the orbit of British imperial power."[3] Thus, for the first time since 1936 the Egyptian government had staked out a position that expressed a complete refusal to compromise with Britain.

Indeed, as a result of the new policy a kind of cold-war mentality gripped both Cairo and London. The British ambassador immediately argued that the abandonment of the Bevin–Sidqi formula by the Egyptian authorities compelled the British government to hunker down. He advised London that, in order to avoid being "driven from pillar to post until we are driven out of the Middle East," Britain had no choice but "to stiffen" its whole attitude toward Egypt.[4]

In this regard, the thinking of the ambassador mirrored the dominant opinion of the Foreign Office, which concluded that the string of concessions made to Egyptian nationalist sensibilities in 1946 had failed to buy any goodwill for Britain.[5] Cairo, so the thinking went, read these concessions as signs of obvious weakness. In order, therefore, to dispel this conception and to restore the prestige of Britain, the ambassador argued that London must no longer appear solicitous of Cairo. It must take a firm stand on the basis of the 1936 treaty, until, at least, the Egyptian authorities softened their position. He suggested to his superiors that they gird themselves for a long struggle. The first order of business was to prepare a detailed case designed to sway the United Nations in favor of Britain— both on the issue of the Sudan and on the strategic interests of Britain in Egypt. In addition, he urged the Foreign Office to lobby the United States government for support.

In short, the embassy in Cairo believed that London must temporarily abandon its policy designed to secure a new treaty. If an agreement were reached with Cairo under the current circumstances, it would not be worth the paper on which it was written. The British government, the ambassador cabled, would be making "a great mistake" if it assumed that an understanding along the lines of the Bevin–Sidqi Agreement would inaugurate "a period of calm and unclouded relations." He continued:

> We should have to expect that the opposition would raise a clamourous agitation against the treaty and against us, who had signed a treaty with their political enemies; for at the basis of all present clamour is a constitutional struggle. This agitation . . . might lead to sporadic disturbance, and would almost certainly bedevil the amicable and satisfactory solution of any question left over by the treaty for ulterior settlement (e.g., Egypt's role in the Sudan or military cooperation). Indeed, it would be unwise to exclude the possibility that the opposition agitation might be such as to nullify the treaty. The government, on its side, would still be obliged to follow an extreme nationalistic policy and guard against anything which could be interpreted as concessions to us. The result might be that the king would be forced to call to power a government either resting on a platform of definite opposition to any treaty, or pledged only to accept one which should embody further concessions from us. . . . [6]

Following these considerations, the ambassador briefly played devil's advocate, raising a number of objections to his basic line of thinking. Then, however, he concluded as follows:

> But it would be most rash not to take into account the possibility that our position in Egypt, and perhaps the whole Middle East, would have been weakened by the conclusion of a treaty with the present Governmental set-up in Egypt (because it would almost inevitably be a bad one), and that when the Opposition came to power further concessions would be required for a treaty settlement with them—which, if granted, would weaken our position further. . . .

In the view of the embassy in Cairo, a nationalist whirlwind had engulfed the Egyptian political system. Britain had no choice but to dig in and ride out the storm.

The advice of the ambassador found a ready reception in London. Thus, from the spring of 1947, when al-Nuqrashi announced his new policy, until the autumn, when the United Nations had completed its examination of the Anglo-Egyptian dispute, London and Cairo remained at loggerheads. In fact, it is hardly an exaggeration to say that, as a result of the policy line adopted by al-Nuqrashi Pasha in March 1947, Anglo-Egyptian relations remained deadlocked until July 1952, if not longer. In an attempt to save themselves, the authorities in Cairo had climbed so high up on the nationalist platform that it was nearly impossible for them, or for any successor government, to climb back down.

The call for complete independence by al-Nuqrashi Pasha marks a major, yet unrecognized, turning point—certainly in Egyptian foreign policy, but also in modern Middle Eastern history in general. The adoption of a policy designed to extricate Egypt from the British sphere of influence planted the seeds for an international revolution in the region. These seeds would not fully blossom until the mid-1950s, but nonetheless they sprouted, albeit slowly, over the years that followed al-Nuqrashi's speech of March 1947. It is a major goal of this book to demonstrate that the decision to break with Britain, foisted on the Egyptian elite by their nationalist crisis, cast its shadow over every major arena of Egyptian policy, and over Middle Eastern politics in general. As will be argued in later chapters, even the policy of Cairo toward the 1948 war with Israel cannot be understood properly without being viewed against the background of the Anglo-Egyptian conflict.

International Repercussions

The new policy of al-Nuqrashi Pasha certainly had its roots in a domestic struggle for power; it was designed, first and foremost, to shelter the Egyptian government and the palace from their enemies at home. Its domestic origins notwithstanding, the decision to oust the British from Egypt had a profound effect on the politics of the entire region. Moreover, nothing about the manner in which the Egyptian authorities pursued their policy in 1947 suggests that they designed it as a purely symbolic maneuver. They were not, for instance, simply buying time by focusing the attention of the nation on the Security Council; they were also attempting to liquidate British interests. Thus, for instance, in the view of the American embassy in Cairo, al-Nuqrashi's "motivating ambition is to go down in history as the man who got the British out of Egypt."[7] The prime minister, informed observers believed, was deadly serious.

The earnestness of the rejection of Britain expressed itself on all levels of official Egyptian policy, not to mention in popular attitudes on the streets. The government, for instance, immediately dispensed with the services of the British Military Liaison Mission (discussed later in this chapter). In order to intensify its anti-British propaganda campaign, it canceled the contract, held by a British company, for running the Egyptian State Broadcasting system. These official actions were accompanied by a move, sponsored by the Independent Wafdist Bloc, to close the Anglo-Egyptian Union, a club in which prominent Egyptians and Britons associated.[8] Meanwhile, the Muslim Brothers and the Young Egypt Party had called for a boycott of everything British—a campaign that included, among other things, the burning of books written in English.

These activities, taken together, constituted for London a very worrying trend in Anglo-Egyptian relations. Of particular concern to the Foreign Office, however, was the concerted attempt of Cairo to marshal the support of the other Arab states for its anti-British policy. This regional component of the Anglo-Egyptian struggle will be analyzed in detail in the next chapter. For the purposes of the present argument, it is sufficient to point out that the 3 March speech by al-Nuqrashi Pasha exacerbated a preexisting conflict in the Middle East between those regimes wishing to shore up the British security system and those who sought to replace it with an indigenous organization. Turkey, Iraq, and Jordan comprised the first group; Egypt, Syria, and Saudi Arabia the second. For the sake of convenience, we will refer to the pro-British bloc as the Turco-Hashimite Entente, and to its opponent as the Triangle Alliance.

In this struggle between the two regional blocs, the British Empire's antagonists in the Arab world held a distinct advantage over its friends, because, among other reasons, they espoused an anti-imperial ideology that tapped into powerful political currents throughout the region. The Hashimite states, Iraq and Jordan, found it extremely difficult to oppose the call by the Triangle Alliance for a diminished British role in Egypt. Thus throughout 1946 Cairo had sought, and received, the support of the Arab League against Britain. While this state of affairs certainly did not please the authorities in London, they were not unduly alarmed, since Sidqi Pasha had not intended to take Egypt completely out of the British sphere of interest.

However, when al-Nuqrashi broke off negotiations at the end of January, British officials became fearful. At that time, Cairo initiated an aggressively anti-British propaganda campaign in the Arab world and attempted to force the Hashimite states to support the policy of Egypt in the Anglo-Egyptian conflict.[9] The ambassador in Cairo, therefore, issued a grave warning:

> There is every indication that King Farouk, and [the Secretary General of the Arab League Abd al-Rahman] Azzam are endeavouring to undermine friendly Hashemite rulers in Iraq and Trans-Jordan; thus the Egyptian influence is being used to alienate Arab states generally from Great Britain. . . . It seems to me that an essential condition of maintaining our positions in the Middle East is that we should show firmness, by which both friends and enemies will realise that we are not going to allow ourselves to be driven out of the Middle East by Egypt and that our patience and conciliatory attitude during negotiations does not mean we can be driven to any position the Egyptians choose.[10]

The alarm sounded by the ambassador was in no way exaggerated. The new Egyptian policy, and the mood in the country in general, posed a serious threat to Britain as the predominant power in the Middle East. The international order in the region rested on the British system of defense, which itself was centered around the Suez Canal Zone. Therefore, the Egyptian demand for a complete, immediate, and unconditional withdrawal of British troops amounted to an effort to break the spine of the Empire in the region. Moreover, if al-Nuqrashi Pasha were to score even a moderate success against Britain, the legitimacy of the alliances between Britain and other Arab countries would suffer. In Iraq especially, nationalists watched the Anglo-Egyptian conflict with great interest.

Not surprisingly, then, the Foreign Office took the warnings of the British ambassador to heart. For instance, one official commented in a representative fashion:

> The question of opposition in Egypt has, of course, repercussions on our position in all the other Middle East countries. To allow ourselves to be pushed out of Egypt without a treaty and to be forced to retreat from our pledge to the Sudanese will have disastrous effects on our prestige in the whole of this area.[11]

Another official stated:

> Our position in Egypt is the keystone to our position in the whole area and there can be no doubt that the recent developments in Egypt, coupled with our difficulties in Palestine, have seriously affected our prestige right through the Arab world. The recent proceedings of the Arab League have shown that the Arab countries are

coming to feel that they prefer to ignore our views rather than give offence to Egypt.[12]

Therefore, the new policy of al-Nuqrashi Pasha led immediately to a struggle between London and Cairo over the alignment of the other Arab states. Since Britain could not take lightly the challenge to its predominant position in the Middle East, one might ask why Cairo was willing to engage in this risky cold war with London. Without doubt, the constitutional crisis in Egypt goes very far toward explaining the appeal of the new policy to strategists in Cairo. Nevertheless, an analysis based purely on a consideration of domestic politics cannot account fully for the thinking of the political elite. Officials in Cairo gave both the British and the Americans the impression not just that they were the servants of popular nationalism but also that they actually believed it was possible to capture the advantage in the Anglo-Egyptian struggle. The Egyptian authorities certainly considered their anti-British stance to be a vital necessity for protecting themselves from their domestic enemies; in addition, however, they also considered it to be practical politics.

The decision, then, to seek a complete break with Britain reflected serious thought about the international system. If the 3 March 1947 appeal to the Security Council marked a significant change in the claims of Egypt against the Empire, it also signaled the beginning of a new era in terms of the mechanics of negotiation between the two antagonists. Al-Nuqrashi Pasha had announced that his government, in contrast to its predecessors, would not fight alone in the ring with the British. Whereas Sidqi Pasha had believed that direct negotiations with London constituted the only means of achieving their nationalist demands, al-Nuqrashi Pasha assumed that the Security Council would function, if not as an ally, at least as a referee.

Like the new policy itself, this attitude was in part foisted on the government by public opinion. At the same time, however, it also reflected an appreciation by the political elite of the massive shifts in the balance of international power— an appreciation, that is, of the potential benefits for Egypt brought by the weakness of Britain and by the advent of the Cold War.

The British Empire in Crisis

Strategists in Cairo undoubtedly thought they had a chance to oust the British because during the first half of 1947 the decline of the Empire expressed itself dramatically in the play of global and regional events. Small states everywhere were breaking out of the orbit of Britain.

For instance, on 20 December 1946, Prime Minister Attlee announced that Burma would receive independence; on 16 February 1947, London referred the Palestine question to the United Nations; on 21 February, it renounced responsibility for the defense of Greece and Turkey; on 3 June, London proclaimed its intention to partition India. If the British were to be forced out of India, the greatest symbol of imperial power, then leaders in Cairo no doubt asked why they should continue to guard the route to India through the Suez Canal. In Egypt itself, on 31 March, the British army completed its unilateral evacuation from Cairo and Alexandria to the Canal Zone. Local opinion regarded this policy as a sign of weakness: "the withdrawal of British troops from Cairo and the Delta," an informed eyewitness later observed, "far from satisfying national aspirations, had made anti-British agitators bolder because they felt more secure and thought they had got us on the run."[13]

Economic stagnation strengthened the impression of imperial weakness. Reports appeared daily about a host of traumas that were rocking the British economy: lengthy strikes, low productivity, rationing, scarce capital, and energy shortages exacerbated by the cold winter of 1946–1947. It can certainly be no accident that the Egyptian government first adopted an uncompromising position regarding the military alliance with the British close on the heels of a three-week cessation of British industrial production caused by the need to conserve electricity.[14] The February 1947 energy crisis was an unprecedented event in British industrial history. Overnight it raised the number on the unemployment rolls from 400,000 to 2.3 million. In Britain the crisis fostered pessimism about the chances of a postwar economic recovery, while abroad it raised doubts about the possibility of Britain continuing to shoulder its international responsibilities.[15]

In the Foreign Office, officials took it as axiomatic that the crisis had emboldened the Egyptian authorities. In order to avoid be driven out of the Middle East, one official wrote as follows:

> We must take a stand in Egypt. Events in India and Burma and Palestine and our domestic crisis are not conducive to inspire among Egyptians the only emotion which might move them to behave reasonably towards us, namely, respect, whether deriving from admiration or fear. Energetic and firm action will be necessary to stop our position from rotting away.[16]

When al-Nuqrashi Pasha announced his new policy in early March, the sun certainly appeared to be setting on the British Empire.

By contrast, the American star was in the ascendant. The British economic crisis and the renunciation of responsibility for Greece and Turkey prompted the pronouncement of the Truman Doctrine. On 12 March President Truman appeared before the U.S. Congress to declare the need to extend economic and military aid to the government of Greece, which was threatened by Communist insurrection, and of Turkey, which was subjected to pressure from the Soviet Union. The American government, awash in cash in comparison with the British, clearly had the means to fill the vacuum: Congress immediately appropriated $350,000,000 for distribution to Athens and Ankara.

Although it was trouble in the eastern Mediterranean that compelled the Americans to act, they conceived of their struggle against the Soviet Union in global terms. "At the present moment in world history," Truman stated, "every nation must choose between alternative ways of life. . . . It must be the policy of the United States to support free people who are resisting attempted subjugation by armed minorities or by outside pressure."[17] For regional powers such as Egypt, the Truman Doctrine spelled a remarkable transformation of the international system. Cairo, therefore, examined American policy to see whether the massive power generated by the Cold War could be harnessed in support of Egyptian national goals.

The economic and military resources of the United States offered particular advantages to regional powers. In preparation for this global struggle, the Americans began filling their war chest in order to aid "free people." In the course of 1947 Washington displayed a new obsession with the institutions of war: the National Military Establishment Act, which Congress began to debate in July, retooled the military and ancillary organs by establishing a permanent Joint Chiefs of Staff, appointing a single secretary of defense, separating the Air Force from the other services, and creating the Central Intelligence Agency. But the military was not the only object of obsession; preparation for the contest with the Soviet Union extended far beyond the expansion of warlike institutions. The global struggle also had a large economic component: In addition to the Truman Doctrine, on 5 June Secretary of State Marshall, responding in part to the British economic crisis, called for a comprehensive program of foreign aid to help the European states recover from the postwar economic malaise that threatened the stability of the existing order. Could some of these resources be diverted to Cairo?

The Greek and Turkish Models

While all these developments in Washington demonstrated intentions of phenomenal scope, in the eyes of the political and military authorities in Cairo the changing of the guard in the eastern Mediterranean no doubt provided the most exciting spectacle of all. The simultaneous British withdrawal from Greece, Turkey, and Palestine raised the question, "What new order will arise in the Middle East?"

Whatever the process by which this question would be resolved, one thing seemed certain: the United States would have a powerful influence over developments. To sway Washington against Britain became the first priority of the Egyptian government. By appealing to the Security Council, Cairo effectively made an offer to the United States to establish, through an alliance with Egypt, a new order in the Middle East.

The full extent of Egypt's regional ambitions can be appreciated only after considering that the demand of Cairo for the British to evacuate the Sudan and the Canal Zone appeared simultaneously with the virtual collapse of the Palestine Mandate.[18] The timing was no mere coincidence. The Egyptian government did not simply observe British distress in Palestine; it worked to exacerbate it. The adamant refusal of the Arab League, led by Egypt, to help London extricate itself from the Palestine morass had played an immediate and significant role in compelling the Attlee government to refer the mandate to the United Nations. In the Palestine arena, as in Anglo-Egyptian relations, Egypt staked out an inflexible position, demanding that the British establish an Arab successor state and then quit the country altogether. In July 1947, while al-Nuqrashi Pasha was addressing his appeal to the Security Council to nullify the 1936 treaty, the United Nations

Special Committee on Palestine was beginning its hearings on the future of Palestine. Thus, Egyptian policy toward every major issue in the Middle East was uniformly anti-British: While conducting a hostile propaganda campaign against the allies of Britain in Iraq and Jordan, the Egyptian government simultaneously called for breaking of the ties between the Empire and the Sudan, Egypt, and Palestine.

Even a partial success of the Egyptian policy hinged on the support of the United States. Viewed in retrospect, a request for American help in scuttling the British Empire in the Middle East would seem to have been the product of poor political judgment. We are, quite rightly, accustomed to conceiving of 1947 as the year in which the United States government resolved to prop up the British Empire, especially by means of the Marshall Plan. Indeed, by the end of the year the government in Cairo would learn that Washington was not, in fact, willing to help it dismantle the British strategic edifice in Egypt. In February and March 1947, however, when Egyptian strategists first formulated their new policy, the international system was in a state of flux, and it was by no means obvious where Washington would finally stand on the question of the new order in the Middle East.

In early 1947, an informed Middle Eastern observer had very good material from which to support the argument that the rise of the United States spelled the end of the British Empire. For some time Cairo had been paying particularly close attention to the policies of Washington toward imperialism. It had not escaped notice in Egypt that the Americans had for several years refrained from wholeheartedly supporting the policies of France, Britain, Belgium, and Holland toward the non-European possessions of the European powers. Therefore, according to an Egyptian diplomat who represented his country at the San Francisco Conference (which established the United Nations), Cairo believed that "the United States had been working along with the states that opposed imperialism in order to free the colonies."[19]

Moreover, by the time al-Nuqrashi Pasha addressed his letter to the Secretary General, the Egyptians had before them several local examples of American behavior to guide them in formulating an approach to Washington. The attitude of the Truman administration toward Greece and Turkey gave particular cause for optimism. The support that the United States extended to Athens revealed its profound fear of insurrections likely to benefit the Soviet Union. The treatment of Turkey provided the first example in the Cold War of the American attitude toward a regional power, like Egypt, occupying a position of geostrategic significance. In sharp contrast to the pattern at work in Anglo-Egyptian relations, however, Turkey received military and economic aid from the United States without being forced to provide onerous base rights, without being compelled to compromise on the principle of complete independence. Turkey was wooed. The brute nature of her Soviet suitor made her an easy mark, but she was wooed nonetheless.[20]

This new basis for Turkish-American relations provided leaders in Cairo with additional coordinates for charting the broad historical trajectory away from the age of empire and special treaties. The struggle between the United States and the Soviet Union, unlike previous struggles between global empires, would be not so much a competition for physical control of territory but rather for influence over sovereign powers. Small states everywhere were spinning out of the imperial orbit; the Americans were boldly proclaiming the global struggle of free peoples; and the Soviet Union was championing its own concepts of national liberation. Under such circumstances, how much longer could Britain hold the Egyptian government hostage in its own home?

A Counterweight to Britain: In Arabia

In order to understand why, in March 1947, American involvement in Greece and Turkey seemed likely to work against the continuation of the British presence in Egypt, one must examine the policies of the United States toward the Middle East in the five years that preceded the Truman Doctrine. It is impossible to write a definitive account of the Egyptian perception of the American penetration of the region, due to the inaccessibility of the Egyptian diplomatic archives. The question, however, is too important to be passed over, regardless of the lack of sources. We must, therefore, work on the basis of an informed hypothesis. It is certainly reasonable to assume that, given the Egyptian national dilemma, the first question that statesmen in Cairo asked regarding American policy was, "Will Washington help or hinder us in the struggle with Britain?"

In the years before the Egyptian appeal to the Security Council, the United States began to penetrate the affairs of the Arab world, where it displayed, in particular, great concern with Saudi Arabia and Palestine. In both cases, the Americans rode roughshod over the interests of the British Empire. In March 1947, therefore, if one reasoned from the assumption that the policy of the United States would continue along previously established lines, then the Truman Doctrine appeared, in power-political terms, not simply as a declaration of resolve to contain the Soviet Union but also as statement of intent to supplant Great Britain.

The American experiences in Palestine and Saudi Arabia have attracted the attention of a number of historians; the broad outlines of United States policy, therefore, are well known. While researchers have certainly examined these individual topics in great detail, few have studied them together. Nor have historians placed them in the context of the struggle for a new regional order—the question that stood at the top of the international agenda of Cairo. Since Egyptian strategists undoubtedly analyzed the activities of the Americans against the background of the Anglo-Egyptian conflict, it is worthwhile to review this rather familiar history while spotlighting the effect of United States policy on the status of Britain as the dominant power in the region.

In all likelihood, when the Egyptian archives one day open, researchers will find detailed reports on the hostile American attitude toward British influence in Saudi Arabia. These documents will reveal particular interest in the powerful economic forces in the United States that enjoyed considerable support from the State Department and from the military, and that, as early as 1943, were working to eradicate British interests in Riyadh.

The attitude of Washington toward Saudi Arabia is particularly relevant to the study of Egyptian policy; from the founding of the Arab League until the Suez Crisis, Riyadh was Cairo's staunchest ally in the Arab world. Together the two formed the hard core of the Triangle Alliance, which also included Syria. Egypt and Saudi Arabia strongly supported the republican regime in Damascus headed by Shukri al-Quwatli, whose position was threatened by the expansionist ambitions of Iraq and Jordan. Both Amman and Baghdad, which had cooperated on regional matters, harbored plans for creating a Fertile Crescent Federation under Hashimite rule. Prior to the American penetration of the region, the Saudi regime had no choice but to adopt a very friendly attitude toward London, in order to ensure that the British government contained its Hashimite clients. Nonetheless, Riyadh shared with Cairo a desire to weaken the allies of Britain—a desire which, in effect, envisioned the weakening Britain herself. The more the United States encroached on the politics of the region, the more pronounced this aspect of Saudi policy became.

Although the American oil concession in Saudi Arabia dated back to the 1930s, the United States government did not become seriously involved with Ibn Saud's regime until World War II. Even as late as 1943, when Washington extended lend-lease aid to Riyadh, Britain still wielded considerable influence in the country, not least of all because London paid Ibn Saud an annual subsidy to help him through a period of financial hardship caused by the war. On one level, lend-lease simply preserved the status quo by replacing Saudi revenue lost as a result of the interruption of the Hajj traffic. On another level, however, it constituted a bid for a new international regime in the Arabian peninsula.[21]

The Americans had powerful selfish motives for extending aid to the Saudi economy. A State Department official wrote:

> Since commencement of the war, the [Saudi Arabian Government] has been completely indigent, and has been kept on its feet by large subsidies from the British Government and advances from the oil company. The possibility that after the war the British may demand a *quid pro quo* at the expense of this important American interest has been very much on our minds.[22]

Thus, during what is otherwise considered the finest hour of Anglo-American cooperation, Washington cast fearful glances at its greatest ally in the war against the Nazis.

A powerful group of officials in the Near Eastern Division of the State Department regarded British influence in Riyadh as nothing less than sinister.[23] These men initiated a campaign to freeze out the British and to bring the Saudi government firmly into the American orbit. The early stages of this effort included an extremely crude and unsuccessful attempt to force London to recall the British ambassador—the mastermind of British perfidy—from Riyadh.[24] Failure, however, did not put an end to the anti-British campaign, which simply became more sophisticated.

World War II brought home to American statesmen the importance of Middle Eastern oil; military strategists in particular regarded control of the Saudi fields as a vital United States interest. Thus, the views of the oil companies and the anti-British officials in the State Department received strong support from, among others, the defense establishment.[25] As a result of these powerful interests, the effort to eliminate British influence in Saudi Arabia continued despite the clumsy maneuvering of the war years. Victories in the campaign to pull Saudi Arabia under the American umbrella included the granting of a large loan to Riyadh upon the cancellation of the lend-lease program, and the construction of an American air base at Dhahran.

Originally planned as a refueling station for planes transporting American soldiers from the European to the Pacific theaters, the base had yet to be constructed when the war ended. Nonetheless, the project continued. Faced with the difficulty of convincing a pro-Zionist Congress to approve further grants and loans for Saudi Arabia, the air base provided the State Department and the military with a means of extending economic aid while avoiding a frustrating debate with elected officials.[26]

From the point of view of strategists in Washington, by far the most significant component of the effort to pull Saudi Arabia into the American orbit was the Trans-Arabian pipeline (Tapline).[27] Although plans for an oil pipeline from the Persian Gulf to the Mediterranean had first emerged before the end of the war, no pipe was actually laid until late 1947, when agreement was finally reached with the transporting states—Jordan, Syria, and Lebanon. For the American oil companies, the pipeline delivered oil to the Mediterranean at a considerable savings over tanker transport through the Suez Canal. For Washington, it tightened the ties with Riyadh while extending a finger of American influence across the Fertile Crescent. For the Saudis, the pipeline, in addition to its obvious economic functions, also served as a useful lever of influence over Jordan and Syria, the first states in history to receive a transport fee for every barrel of oil piped across their territory.

If the Egyptian government regretted losing the revenue from oil tankers that, in the absence of Tapline, would have paid heavy Suez Canal dues, its sense of loss no doubt dissipated at the sight of Saudi and American influence flowing, together with the oil, across the Fertile Crescent. From the Egyptian point of view, the American attitude toward British power in Riyadh would have been welcome by itself. The penetration of Arabia by the United States, however, did much more than simply pry a single desert capital away from the British Empire. The special ties that quickly developed between Riyadh and Washington shifted the balance of power in the region in a manner detrimental to the expansionist plans of Iraq and Jordan. Since Saudi wariness of the British and hostility toward the expansion of Hashimite influence in Syria and Palestine dovetailed with Egyptian policies, Riyadh now functioned as a significant force pressing the United States to work in favor of the Triangle Alliance.[28]

Thus, simply by taking a powerful interest in the affairs of the Saudi government, the United States significantly changed the pattern of regional politics. The construction of Tapline funneled United States–Saudi influence directly to Syria, the most unstable point in the Triangle Alliance and the area most vulnerable to Hashimite expansion. Cairo and Riyadh could now expect that the voice of the most powerful state on earth would echo their own expressions of hostility toward Hashimite plans to absorb Syria.

American influence spread across the Fertile Crescent simultaneously with the growing involvement of the United States in Greece and in Turkey. At the very moment when the Egyptians were directing their appeal to the United Nations, representatives of American oil companies were conducting negotiations with the Syrian government over the extension of Tapline to the Mediterranean, while United States aid was flowing into Athens and Ankara. When access is finally gained to official Egyptian documents, it would certainly be surprising to learn that, under these circumstances, officials in Cairo did not believe that the United States stood poised to replace Britain as the dominant power in the Middle East.

A Counterweight to Britain: In Palestine

Postwar developments in Palestine also revealed a pattern of hostility to British interests.[29] During the period 1945–1947, the future of the policy set out in the 1939 White Paper—which severely restricted Jewish immigration to Palestine—formed the central issue in the struggle between the Jews and the Arabs. For their part, the Zionists demanded that the British abolish the immigration quotas in order to allow Jewish survivors in Europe to settle in Palestine, where (in their eyes) a Jewish state should have been immediately established. Throughout 1946, the Jewish community in Palestine (*yishuv*) remained in a state of semirebellion that included the organization of illegal immigration, sabotage, and attacks against British soldiers garrisoned throughout the country. By contrast, the Palestinian Arabs, supported by the Arab League, demanded that Britain continue to police the quotas set by the 1939 White Paper and then prepare the way for the establishment of an Arab state in Palestine.

The uncompromising demands of the two sides placed Britain in an untenable situation. Neither the Arabs nor the Zionists would accept compromise solutions, such as the creation of a binational state or the establishment of a loose federation composed of Arab and Jewish cantons. In reality, therefore, the British had three choices: to endorse a pro-Arab solution and suppress Jewish opposition; to endorse a pro-Zionist position and suppress Arab opposition; or to renounce responsibility.

All vital British interests in the Middle East militated in favor of supporting a pro-Arab solution. Massive investment in Arab oil, the character of the region as the crossroads of the British Empire, its location on the southern border of the Soviet Union and on the southeastern flank of Europe—all these factors and more compelled political, economic, and military planners in London to regard the continuation of the British presence in the Middle East as imperative. But, given the prevailing political winds, Britain could maintain its position in the region only with the active support of the Arab states. Since all patriotic Arabs already equated the establishment and support of a Jewish National Home in

Palestine with the ugliest forms of European colonialism, strategists in London believed that an endorsement by Britain of even the moderate Zionist program would permanently alienate the Arab world.

Despite the crushing power of the arguments in favor of supporting a pro-Arab position, Britain could not afford to create an Arab state in Palestine. The total rejection of the Zionist program would have sparked a full-scale uprising of the *yishuv*, the suppression of which would have come at a cost of thousands, perhaps tens of thousands, of Jewish dead and maimed. Even in the unlikely event of the British government mustering the legitimacy at home to conduct such a grizzly war in the immediate aftermath of the Holocaust, London could never have convinced the American public of the righteousness of its cause.

The Zionist lobby in Washington constituted a great obstacle to any British attempt to adopt an uncompromisingly pro-Arab policy. The desperate need of London for American financial aid during the first years following the war made Zionist influence in Congress a particularly potent means of dissuading the British military from conducting an unbridled assault on Jewish nationalism. For instance, in 1946 London negotiated, among other financial agreements, a $3.75 billion loan from Washington. Thus, it was no coincidence that during the Congressional debate over the loan the British military in Palestine discontinued an aggressive campaign designed to halt illegal Jewish immigration and to disarm the forces rebelling against the White Paper policy.

During the period 1945–1947 Britain stood in Palestine with one arm held behind its back by the Arabs, the other by the Jews. Against this background, the Americans aggressively entered the picture. Harry Truman, an unpopular and nonelected president during his first term in office, formulated his policy with great concern for its popularity among the American Jewish electorate; he displayed little concern for its effects on the British position in Palestine. The thinking of the State Department tended to run parallel to that of the Foreign Office with regard to the importance of Arab goodwill in preserving the economic, political, and military interests of the West. But time and again Truman ignored his diplomats, issuing statements broadly supportive of Zionist aims.

The 1939 White Paper policy on immigration caused the sharpest friction between London and Washington. Soon after the war, Truman called for the British to open up the gates of Palestine to the immigration of 100,000 Jewish Holocaust survivors who were at that time still residing in camps in Europe. Unwilling to risk provoking Arab unrest in Palestine, the British refused to honor Truman's call. In order to lessen the American pressure that threatened to undermine the British position, Ernest Bevin embarked on a policy designed to bring the United States into the Palestine arena as the partners of the British. The British attempt to bring the Americans on board fostered, first, the Anglo-American Committee of Inquiry, which produced a plan for a binational state, and, second, the Morrison–Grady scheme, which advocated provincial autonomy as the solution to the deadlock between the Arabs and Jews.

These plans both failed to win support in the Middle East. Moreover, neither succeeded in actually bringing into existence an Anglo-American consensus. Truman still advocated the immediate immigration of the 100,000 displaced European Jews while the British stood adamant in their refusal to comply. The political and economic costs of garrisoning Palestine became more than the British system could tolerate during the severe crisis of winter 1946–1947. In February 1947, therefore, the Labor government endorsed the third option in Palestine—withdrawal.

In contrast to its behavior in Saudi Arabia, Washington certainly did not display an aggressive interest in ousting the British from Palestine. Yet the Americans did in fact exhibit a flagrant disregard for the interests of the Empire. From the point of view of anti-British powers such as the Egyptians, the case of Palestine demonstrated yet again the very real limits of Anglo-American cooperation in the Middle East. When viewed as part of a pattern of involvement in Greece, Turkey, and Saudi Arabia, the American attitude suggested that under the right conditions the power of Washington could be brought into play against the British.

Unfortunately, however, for the leaders in Cairo, Egypt had neither the spectacular oil wealth of the Saudi deserts nor the sophisticated political lobby of the Zionists. As they watched British power receding from nearly everywhere in the Middle East except Egypt, policy planners in Cairo searched for a means of influencing the Americans.

The Appeal to Washington

The Egyptian prime minister arrived in the United States in August to make two separate but related appeals: One before the United Nations, the other before the bureaucracies in Washington. When al-Nuqrashi Pasha appeared before the Security Council, in support of his call for the annulment of the 1936 Anglo-Egyptian Agreement, he presented a legal argument and a historical justification. From the legal point of view, the Egyptian prime minister maintained that the 1936 Anglo-Egyptian Agreement had been contracted under special circumstances that no longer obtained. Because the Egyptian government did not accept the terms of the Anglo-Egyptian alliance and the Sudan Condominium (the agreement, signed in 1899, according to which Britain and Egypt shared power in the Sudan), and because international conditions had changed radically since 1936, he argued that both the alliance and the Condominium had lost their validity.

From the historical point of view, al-Nuqrashi portrayed his government as the representative of a subject people fighting for its legitimate rights to self-determination and complete sovereignty. "In all frankness," al-Nuqrashi Pasha stated, "we are here to challenge the basic assumptions of nineteenth-century imperialism. We ask the Security Council to affirm that in the twentieth century the world has moved on."[30]

The Egyptian government realized that the legal claim was weak and had little chance of swaying the Security Council. Cairo pinned its hopes instead on the United States government. Washington, the authorities in Cairo gambled, would exert its influence in the United Nations in order to prevent the Soviet Union from using the Egyptian case to characterize the Anglo-American alliance as the enemy of self-determination for non-Western peoples.[31] In private diplomatic discussions with American officials, Egyptian officials dispensed with references to the legalities of the matter, preferring instead to focus on the prerogatives of American power. As early as mid-April, the Egyptian government, through its ambassador in Moscow, had informed the Americans that it expected their support in the Security Council debate.[32]

Al-Nuqrashi Pasha reiterated this expectation at a number of meetings that he held with top American officials during his extended stay in the United States. In his first meeting with top State Department representatives, the prime minister stated that "Egypt looked to the United States for support, for without such support Egypt could not win."[33] During a later meeting, when the Americans had already displayed a reluctance to oppose their British allies, he stated baldly "that the influence and power of the United States was such that it could accomplish anything it desired in the Security Council."[34]

The Egyptian authorities regarded the United Nations as the stage on which their case would be settled. The actors in the drama, however, would be directed from behind the scenes—from within the halls of Washington bureaucracies. In his conversations with American officials, al-Nuqrashi Pasha revealed how Cairo perceived the relationship between American power and the Anglo-Egyptian dispute.[35] While calling for the support of the United States, the prime minister emphasized the basic compatibility between Egyptian and United States interests, stressing that "Egypt had attempted to formulate her policies generally in accordance with those of the United States."[36] Al-Nuqrashi said that if Washington would help the Egyptian government to expand its armed forces, "Egypt would be able to take her rightful place among the nations." Building up the military would strengthen the defense of the Middle East in general and would contribute to the security of the "democratic bloc." While cooperation with Egypt would work to the advantage of the Americans in the Cold War, failure to oust the British unconditionally would redound to the detriment of the West in its struggle with the Soviet Union. The prime minister stated that, as Muslims, the Egyptian people harbored deep suspicions regarding Communism:

> [but] if British troops were not removed from Egypt and Egypt was unable to develop her own forces, a feeling of discontent would arise among the masses. This would inevitably lead to the spread of Communist propaganda and Egypt would thus afford a fertile field of Communist infiltration.[37]

Failure

The Security Council debated the Egyptian appeal between 5 August and 10 September 1947. The United States representative refrained from wholeheartedly supporting the British position; in addition, he even made sympathetic noises regarding the desire of the Egyptians for complete independence.[38] But when the Brazilian delegate tabled a resolution calling for Egypt and Britain to return to direct negotiations, his American colleague, much to the chagrin of Cairo, expressed the strong support of the United States government. Despite the support of Washington, however, the Brazilian draft did not pass. As a result of the opposition of Poland, the Soviet Union, Syria, and Colombia, the Brazilian resolution failed. Thus, in the end the Council took no action, preferring instead to shelve the Egyptian appeal.

No doubt just as al-Nuqrashi Pasha had planned, the East-bloc delegates strongly supported the Egyptian position against Britain. The attempt by al-Nuqrashi to play on the American fear of Soviet power obviously reflected how the Turkish and Greek models of relations with the United States held sway over the political imagination of the Egyptian elite. Unfortunately for strategists in Cairo, Egypt did not suffer from a Communist insurrection in the manner of Greece, nor from overt Soviet encroachments in the manner of Turkey. The only threat to the peace in Egypt, as British officials repeatedly stressed, would come as a result of a decision by the Egyptian government to attack the British forces in the Canal Zone.[39] Thus the Soviet and Polish support for Egypt, though worrying to Washington, hardly constituted an immediate threat to the West in the Cold War.

Nonetheless, when Cairo invoked the Communist threat American officials listened intently. In fact, Washington displayed genuine concern regarding the nationalist dilemma facing the Egyptian leadership. Traditional American anti-imperialism, not to mention the belief that success in the Cold War required the goodwill of the Arab world, predisposed many in Washington to regard the Anglo-Egyptian conflict as a threat to the security of the West. Even if the rhetoric of al-Nuqrashi Pasha did not appear particularly persuasive in August and September 1947, the political conundrum that gave rise to it greatly troubled the American mind.

Officials at the State Department responsible for Middle Eastern affairs formed the circle in Washington most receptive to the message of the Egyptian prime minister. In power-political terms, the Office of Near Eastern and African Affairs may legitimately be considered as the lobby in Washington for the Triangle Alliance. Out of concern for furthering American interests and fostering good relations with the Arab world, this department led the movement to eliminate British influence in Riyadh, as already discussed; it championed the support for the Saudi government and the construction of Tapline; it consistently worked to counter the influence of the Zionist lobby in Congress; and it opposed the expansion of Hashimite influence in Syria.

Moreover, it also argued in favor of support for the Egyptian claim against Britain. On 28 August, during the debate in the Security Council, the Office of Near Eastern and African Affairs circulated an influential memorandum recommending "that our Government urge the British to indicate at once to the Egyptian Government that they are prepared to announce their intention unconditionally to withdraw all British troops from Egypt by a definite date."[40] The Office certainly did not consider itself to be the representative of Egypt and her allies; nonetheless, it consistently advocated policies that dovetailed with the interests of the Triangle Alliance. It is inconceivable that Cairo had no awareness of the support that it received from the State Department.

The Egyptian government, therefore, could make its case in Washington with the expectation that its demands would, at the very least, receive serious consideration. Nevertheless, the Office of Near Eastern and African Affairs did not by itself determine the policy of the United States. Cairo, moreover, could not hope to muster influence in domestic American politics to the same extent as the Saudis (thanks to their oil wealth) or as the Zionists (thanks to their clout in Congress). In order to drive a wedge between Washington and London, Cairo needed the support of more than just one bureau of the State Department. As a result of the strategic importance of Egypt, the success of al-Nuqrashi Pasha's appeal to the Americans ultimately required the support of the United States military, which, unfortunately for Cairo, regarded the British bases in the Canal Zone as vital to the defense of the West against the Soviet Union. As long as the American military establishment remained supportive of the British position in Canal Zone, the aspirations nurtured in Cairo would face formidable obstacles in Washington.

When al-Nuqrashi Pasha spoke of the need to expand the size of the Egyptian military and the role of Egypt in the defense of the Middle East, he tacitly recognized the fundamental obstacle that Egyptian policy faced in Washington. Given the state of the Egyptian armed forces and economy, the country could not plausibly present itself as a successor to the British in the area of Middle Eastern defense, and yet it was precisely this area that concerned the Americans the most. The Egyptian call for Britain's immediate and unconditional evacuation of the Canal Zone amounted to a call for a precipitous dismantling of the British security system in the Middle East.

Therefore, al-Nuqrashi Pasha in effect requested that the Americans immediately disassemble the British regional security system, and that they build a new network based on Egyptian power. Even if the Americans were to have embraced wholeheartedly the Egyptian proposal, the task of building a new framework for regional defense as powerful as the one already in place would have required years of effort, thus creating a temporary power vacuum and costing millions of dollars. Since the Cold War fostered a desire among the Americans for stability and predictability in Middle Eastern affairs, the appeal by Cairo was inherently weak, being based on potential power rather than existing capability. Thus the Egyptian state confronted the difficulty of transforming its size and power—"its natural role" in al-Nuqrashi's words—into international clout.

The Military and Economic Orbit of America

The record of Egyptian action suggests that the elite in Cairo possessed a keen understanding of their dilemma. The decision to appeal to the United Nations coincided with significant developments in Egyptian military policy. On 2 March, the day before al-Nuqrashi Pasha announced his decision to lay the Egyptian case before the Security Council, his government informed London that it intended to send home immediately many men serving in the British Military Liasion Mission; the remaining members were to be disbanded entirely by the end of the year.[41] The mission, composed of British military advisors, symbolized to leaders in Cairo one of the most onerous aspects of the 1936 Anglo-Egyptian Treaty, which obliged the Egyptian military to use equipment of the same type as the British, to purchase it from Britain, and to select foreign military instructors only from among British subjects.

In effect, then, Britain held the development of the Egyptian military in a stranglehold. Under the regime established by the 1936 treaty, any decision taken by Cairo to expand the armed forces effectively required the consent of London. This monopoly over supply and training gave the British government one of its most powerful instruments of control, not just over the military but over the alignment of the Egyptian state in general. The penetration of the region by the United States, however, now gave Cairo alternatives to Britain.

Having dispensed with many of the British advisors and having given notice to the rest, the Egyptians quickly set about establishing ties with the American military. By mid-April the Egyptian chief of staff and a group of high-ranking officers arrived in the United States for the purpose of visiting "various American military establishments and factories in order to acquaint themselves with the manner in which these establishments were being conducted and with various types of modern weapons of war."[42] By 25 June the Egyptian government made known its desire to engage American military instructors.

After six months of preparation the way was now paved to press the Americans for a concrete commitment. On 5 September, al-Nuqrashi Pasha met with the acting secretary of state and the secretary of war "to present a request on behalf of the Egyptian Government for military advisers for the Egyptian army and air force and for assistance in developing a small arms and munitions industry."[43] The acting secretary of state stalled the Egyptian prime minister, explaining that Congress was currently considering legislation governing the engagement of United States advisers by foreign armies.

Cairo did not restrict its efforts to move into the American orbit to the military sphere. In the realm of economics, the Egyptian government made similar efforts that achieved similar results. During his discussions with top officials in Washington, al-Nuqrashi made an oblique bid for economic aid, stating that he was "sure that the United States favored industrialization as a means of developing friendly relations among the peoples of the world," and he affirmed that "Egypt was on the verge of an industrialization program." This rather vague request had, however, been preceded by a more specific proposal. In April, apparently, the Egyptian government had unsuccessfully sought a large loan from the United States.[44]

The most dramatic attempt to develop economic ties with the United States, however, took place in June, when the Egyptian government opted to leave the Sterling Bloc—a group of countries that deposited most of their foreign exchange reserves at the Bank of England and followed monetary policy compatible with the economic policies of Great Britain. Such close ties to the British economy limited the ability of the Egyptian state to develop economic ties with the United States, because the pound was not freely convertible and, moreover, the Sterling Bloc suffered from a chronic shortage of dollars. In addition, the United States government formulated its policies toward members of the bloc with a keen eye to their effect on the British economy, which Washington, in principle, sought to strengthen. Egyptian participation in the Sterling Bloc, therefore, spelled economic subservience to Britain.

Cairo appeared to gain a significant measure of economic freedom when, on 30 June, it reached an interim agreement with London regarding the payment to Egypt of £450 million that Britain owed Egypt.[45] The British military had borrowed large sums during the war in order to pay for local goods and services. The poor state of the British economy, however, had made prompt repayment of this debt impossible. Moreover, London owed large sums to other countries, such as Iraq and India; the Bank of England, therefore, simply did not have enough money in reserve in order to pay its debts. Cairo had no choice but to bargain with London over the terms by which Egypt would be repaid.

Egyptian officials struck an agreement by which they promised, in order not to deplete the sterling reserves of Britain, to leave the bulk of the money owed to them in the Bank of England in the form of an investment. That is, they agreed not to draw the money out of Britain and not to convert it to dollars. In return, London agreed to make periodic payments into an account from which the Egyptian government could draw freely. Moreover, Cairo would be free to trade the money from this second account for dollars, because Britain had been forced by the United States to make sterling convertible starting 15 July 1947. Thus, the second account established by the Anglo-Egyptian financial agreement would effectively function as a large dollar pool for Egypt, which would facilitate economic relations with America.

Unfortunately for Cairo, the British found themselves unable to withstand the strains that convertibility placed on their currency. In mid-August, therefore, London felt compelled to renege on its commitment to trade sterling freely. By extension, then, London also reneged on the Anglo-Egyptian financial agreement—by forbidding the Egyptian government to convert to dollars the pounds paid into the second account. As a consequence, al-Nuqrashi Pasha denounced, in the most bitter terms, the British financial authorities to the American ambassador. On 1 October, the prime minister stated that the failure of London to abide by the 30 June agreement damaged the Egyptian economy.[46] When, two days later, the British even further restricted the Egyptian ability to gain access to foreign currency, the United States ambassador in Cairo wired Washington, strongly urging that the "presentation of the Egyptian dollar problem would be sympathetically considered."[47] The State Department responded with a general statement of goodwill.

In practical terms, however, the Egyptian economy remained tied to Britain to an extent that humiliated Cairo. Although the Egyptian government had succeeded in leaving the Sterling Bloc, it still found itself without dollars.

A Failed Policy?

On 1 October the State Department had its final say on the question of the Egyptian appeal to the Security Council. It wired to the United States ambassador information "for use if desired in conversations with officials," declaring that the United States government regarded the disagreement between London and Cairo to be relatively minor, and that the Egyptian case was "not sufficiently convincing" to require action by the Security Council.[48] With that, Washington signaled that it still regarded the Bevin–Sidqi framework as the best basis for a settlement of the Anglo-Egyptian conflict, and it attempted to force Cairo back to the negotiating table opposite Britain. Clearly, Washington refused to accept the Egyptian interpretation of the Anglo-Egyptian conflict.

Two months after this announcement, the policy of Cairo took yet another blow from the United States when the Truman administration supported the United Nations resolution to partition Palestine. The support for a Jewish state provided yet another indication that Cairo had little influence over the United States government. As a result of the partition resolution, leaders in Cairo stood before some of the hardest choices of their careers. As the founder of the Arab League and the leader of the Triangle Alliance, the Egyptian state had, for the last three years, been the most influential power championing the view that the only just solution to the Palestine question lay in the establishment of an independent Arab state. Time and again Cairo had staked its reputation on this bold moral position. On the basis of the principle of Palestinian self-determination, however, many in the Arab world now called for intervention by the regular Arab armies. Consequently, Egyptian leaders had to choose between, on the one hand, honoring their public commitments to the Palestinians by entering a war for which they were largely unprepared, and, on the other, attempting to find a compromise solution.

In the autumn and winter of 1947, then, Egyptian policy received three major blows: in the Security Council, in the General Assembly, and in Washington. By the beginning of 1948, Egyptian policy appeared in a shambles. The year 1947 had opened with the British Empire suffering a crisis on a global scale; by the end of the year, however, London had weathered the worst of the storm and now stood on the road to recovery, thanks to in large measure to the Marshall Plan. The American government had, despite trends elsewhere in the Middle East, backed the British in Egypt. Although the British were in fact withdrawing from Palestine, this positive development was canceled by the international forces that were lining up against the Egyptian position on Palestine. Whereas the example of American military and economic aid to Greece and Turkey had seemed to hold out great promise, by the end of 1947 the Egyptians remained shackled within the British orbit, both economically and militarily.

The involvement of the Americans in the politics of the region had certainly developed along lines disappointing to the Egyptian government. Nonetheless, the Middle East had changed significantly in the course of 1947—precisely because it had fallen under the shadow of American power. The transformation, though in many ways frustrating, had created options for Cairo that never existed in the past. Prior to 1947, the Egyptian government could not, for instance, have left the Sterling Bloc and dismissed the British Military Liaison Mission without being punished by Britain for insubordination. In the American era, London was not free to act without first considering how Washington would react. In short, an umpire now watched over the Anglo-Egyptian contest. To be sure, Cairo would have preferred a more sympathetic referee, but even a bad judge was better than no judge at all.

From March 1947 until the Suez Crisis, the foreign policy of Cairo, thanks to the Egyptian national crisis, remained focused on the conflict with Britain. During the nine years that followed the decision by al-Nuqrashi Pasha to sever the ties with the Empire, a very significant aspect of that conflict was the contest over the alignment of the United States. Driving a wedge between Washington and London was, of course, no simple matter for Cairo. But Egypt did, in fact, possess significant levers of influence over the Great Powers. It was the most influential Arab state and, therefore, the region could not be organized against the Soviet Union without its support. As shall be shown in the next chapter, Cairo fully understood the advantages of being the dominant Arab power, and it worked to maximize these advantages.

Egyptian policy might have been in a shambles, but Cairo hardly felt defeated. The failure in the Security Council simply meant that the Anglo-Egyptian struggle would be played out in other arenas of the Middle East.

THREE

The Keystone in the Arch

The *Wathba*

When Salih Jabir, the prime minister of Iraq, returned home from England on 26 January 1948, he was greeted in Baghdad by violent protests against him, his government, and the new Anglo-Iraqi Treaty that he and Ernest Bevin had signed eleven days earlier in Portsmouth. The demonstrations had first erupted as soon as details of the terms of the draft treaty reached Baghdad on 16 January, the day after the signing and many fateful days before Jabir, who was detained in London for yet another week, would board his return flight. The political elite in Baghdad, frightened by the public outcry, organized itself against the treaty even before the prime minister had a chance to defend his policy while standing on Iraqi soil.

Protests turned violent on 20 January; the next day, the regent, Abd al-Ilah, convened a meeting of leading politicians who all pressed for the rejection of Jabir's policy. The palace hurriedly broadcast a message over the radio criticizing the Portsmouth Treaty and conveying a promise by the regent to the Iraqi people "that no treaty whatever not ensuring the rights of the country and its national aspirations will be ratified."[1] Five days later Salih Jabir arrived in Baghdad dressed for battle, but his troops had deserted him.

It took little more than a week to slaughter and bury the Portsmouth Treaty, which Ernest Bevin, speaking before Parliament, described "as a model . . . for other Middle East defence arrangements."[2] Suppression of the demonstrations, which flared up with renewed intensity when Jabir returned to the capital, required the use of machine guns and armored cars: 100 people died and 300 were wounded. Outrage over the bloodbath toppled the cabinet; Jabir himself, fearing for his life, fled Baghdad in disguise, taking a circuitous route back to London. On 4 February the new prime minister, Muhammad al-Sadr, announced that his government rejected the Portsmouth Treaty, which, he said, conflicted with the aims of the nation. Thereafter, Iraqi politicians displayed a healthy reluctance to negotiate a bilateral agreement with the British, lest they be subjected to a repetition of the *Wathba*—"the Pouncing"—as the protesters' sudden leap at the government became known.

This episode did indeed conform to a model of relations between Britain and her Arab clients, though certainly one more appealing to Cairo than to London. The Egyptian and Iraqi experiences with treaty revision resemble two films based on similar scripts but set in different locations. The bare-bones scenario runs as follows. An Anglo-Arab treaty, due to expire in the mid-1950s, comes under attack by domestic Arab opposition as both a symbol and an instrument of domination by imperial Britain. London, though under no legal compulsion to negotiate, feels the pressure of Arab nationalism and, to a lesser degree, world— that is, American—opinion.[3] British diplomatists calculate that failure to pro- pitiate the embattled elite will strengthen the hand of the radical nationalists, who seek to abolish all military ties with the Empire.[4] A powerful but unpopular prime minister, believing that the opposition will buckle when strong-armed, travels to London, signs an agreement that perpetuates the alliance, and returns home only to find that his friends are few and his enemies legion. Violent street demonstra- tions force the lonely prime minister from office. The new government imme- diately renounces the draft treaty, which thereafter serves as an example for suc- cessor governments of that which must be avoided at all costs. The British withdraw behind their rights as spelled out in the old treaty which, though hated by the nationalists, still retains international legal force. Strategists in London wait for circumstances to produce a new government willing to accept—or too weak to reject—a renewal of the alliance.

Leaders in Cairo certainly noticed that a new model had been established for Anglo-Arab relations, and they rejoiced, regarding it as a stunning victory for Egypt.

The Egyptian Response

On 9 February, five days after the new Iraqi government drove the final nail into the coffin of the Portsmouth Treaty, King Faruq summoned the British ambas- sador for a discussion regarding regional defense. Referring to the events in Bagh- dad, the King criticized the British for attempting to strike a separate deal with Iraq: It was pointless, he said, to attempt to establish a coordinated defense of the Middle East by making treaties with the Arab countries in a "piecemeal" fashion.[5] The British had merely harmed their own interests by attempting to circumvent Egypt, which was "the keystone in the arch, the nation to whom the others looked for leadership." To create a regional security system that did not offend the nationalist sensibilities of the Arab states, the British "would now be well advised to take a step toward conferring some sort of recognition upon the Arab League, because . . . the only way of making progress . . . with the nations constituting the Arab League was . . . to come to an overall understanding with these nations *en bloc*." King Faruq skirted the issue of the precise relationship between the British and the proposed Arab defense organization, but he did emphasize the continued Egyptian demand for a complete withdrawal of British troops from the Canal Zone; the Arab bloc, therefore, would not accord per- manent base rights in Egypt to the British.

King Faruq stated that many responsible leaders in Cairo and other Arab capitals had begun to think along parallel lines, but he also claimed that his endorsement of the Arab-bloc idea was the result of long personal cogitation that he had yet to share with anyone else. This assertion was undoubtedly false. On

6 February, three days before this conversation, Shaykh Hafiz Wahba, the Saudi minister in London who was passing through Egypt, and Abd al-Rahman Azzam Pasha, the secretary general of the Arab League, had made proposals to British officials in Cairo along lines so similar as to leave no doubt regarding the coordination between the Saudis, the Egyptians, and the Arab League—all three of whom had, in any case, coordinated their regional policies for over two years.[6]

The Saudi representative and the secretary general had also stressed the folly of the British attempt to sign a separate treaty with the Iraqis; the British, Azzam Pasha said, "seemed to have treaties on the brain," and these were worthless "unless rooted in the goodwill of the people bound together by them." London could solve its problem by supporting the creation of an Arab alliance. The secretary general displayed a greater willingness than the king to discuss the nature of the British association with the Arab organization: No new special treaties or bases would be necessary in order to create a system of regional defense. The British, he said:

> still had a treaty of alliance containing military clauses with Transjordan. . . . Let that treaty stand. . . . It was sufficient to link [Britain] to the Arab world. If Transjordan were a party to an Arab regional defensive alliance and if one of the participating states were involved in a war which in its turn involved the other participating states, including Transjordan, Britain would automatically through the link with Transjordan be at war too.

In other words, the existing security system had outlived its usefulness: British troops would remain in the Middle East only in Jordan, a country that could not possibly serve as the foundation of a regionwide defense network.

For his part, Shaykh Hafiz Wahba reminded the British that in recent years the Iraqis had tended to club together with the Jordanians; the new government in Baghdad, however, would not follow such a policy. Therefore, London would be wise to exploit the growing responsiveness in Baghdad to the interests of Riyadh and Cairo by pressing "the Arab nations to form themselves together in a defensive alliance." To initiate the plan, London might propose to the Egyptians, the Syrians, and the Saudis that they form the nucleus of an Arab defense organization; this small group would then convince the others to join. "He added," the British ambassador reported to London, "that we should be well advised to let it be known that the Americans were in close touch with us." Although the support that the United States gave for the partition of Palestine caused much anger in the Middle East, "the Arabs well knew what colossal resources and power the Americans had and that their action would be decisive in the end in any future war."

A host of unspoken assumptions informed these conversations, which took for granted the existence of two contending power blocs within the Arab world, one composed of Jordan and Iraq, the other of Syria, Saudi Arabia, and Egypt (the latter association has been dubbed here as "the Triangle Alliance").[7] King Faruq and his allies presumed that the fall of the Jabir government constituted a victory for them in the struggle between these two blocs: The Triangle Alliance had frustrated an Iraqi attempt to conduct a policy on regional defense independent of Egypt. The violent power of anti-imperial forces in Baghdad had opened a sharp rift between Iraq and Great Britain, so that now both Egypt and Iraq—the two most powerful Arab states, and the two great anchors of the Empire in the region—had pronounced in favor of toppling Britain from its status as the paramount power in the Middle East.

The twin Egyptian and Iraqi rejections of a new British security system led to a stalemate. The government in London, had no means of creating a system of defense legitimate in the eyes of the most influential Arab governments; the opponents of the Empire did not have the power to oust the foreign troops from their entrenched positions. London still wielded significant influence, not just in Amman but also in powerful sectors of Baghdad and, importantly, in Washington. Nonetheless, the Egyptian palace had obviously concluded that the fall of the Iraqi government gave Cairo the upper hand in the battle over the regional defense system. When considered in the light of the British intention to remain the paramount power in the region, King Faruq's proposal constituted an offer of terms for surrender: The British, he implied, must renounce the special alliances with Iraq and Egypt; they must refrain from bypassing Cairo when making policy toward Middle Eastern security; and they must shift their primary allegiance from the Hashimites to the Triangle Alliance, the nucleus of the new order. In short, British power would become subordinate to the Arab League.

The Historical Significance of the Proposal

It should come as no surprise that London did not pause, even for a moment, to consider King Faruq's initiative. Despite the very real blow dealt by the *Wathba*, and despite being in the throes of an ignominious retreat from Palestine, London did not regard its position as dire enough to accept such onerous terms. The weakening of the Empire in 1947 and, in particular, the withdrawal from Palestine actually prompted the British to redouble their efforts to retain base rights in Egypt and to remain the preponderant power in the Middle East.[8] Consequently, nothing came of this Arab-bloc initiative, which would have been erased from all memory had it not been preserved on a few sheets of paper in the Public Record Office in London.

The failure of the proposal and the meager paper trail it left behind notwithstanding, the call for the creation of an indigenous Arab defense organization deserves closer attention.

The initiative offers a window onto the thinking of the elite in Cairo: It conveys the Egyptian palace's answer to the question, "What new order should arise in the Middle East?" For nearly a year, ever since al-Nuqrashi announced his intention to appeal to the Security Council, Egyptian policy had been directed toward destroying the British military position in Egypt. This policy, recognizing the importance to the Empire of the bases along the Suez Canal Zone, entailed toppling the British from their status as the dominant power in the Middle East. Successfully destroying the British regional security network would radically transform the political landscape of the entire area, and strategists in Cairo must have been keenly aware of the character and scope of this transformation. Yet, despite the regionwide implications of Egyptian policy, prior to the Arab-bloc initiative it is difficult to find hard evidence of a regionwide plan, although such a thing may well have sat on the drawing boards of Egyptian planners in 1947.

The Arab-bloc initiative is certainly of intrinsic interest, but the timing of King Faruq's approach also adds to its historical importance. The Palace's decision to launch a proposal for a new regional order during the civil war in Palestine suggests a connection between the initiative for an Arab League defense organization and the end of the British Mandate. At the very least, the plan casts some light on the geostrategic considerations of the Egyptian elite as it stood on the brink of a war that marked a turning point in the history of the modern Middle East.

First and foremost, the idea of creating an Arab bloc commands attention because immediately after the Palestine war the Egyptians did, in fact, establish an Arab League Defense Pact. Moreover, during the period 1949–1954, when the Western powers would again turn their attention to Middle Eastern security, Cairo would consistently argue in favor of establishing a regional defense system on the foundation of that Pact. King Faruq's trial balloon, therefore, did not simply pop and vanish: It signaled the imminent rise to prominence of a doctrine that, from 1949 to 1955, formed the basis of an Egyptian regional strategy.

Historians have devoted little if any attention to this policy; their lack of interest, no doubt, stems from the faint trace it has left in the Western diplomatic archives, which are organized according to the priorities and perceptions of Great Britain and the United States. Since neither of these powers—both of which sought to perpetuate the British defense system—had any interest in grafting a security organization onto the Arab League, their diplomatic papers do not accord significance to the Arab Pact. In Washington and London, diplomatic archives today house reams of documents devoted to negotiations with the Egyptians during the 1940s and 1950s. One could literally spend years poring over reports devoted to regional defense matters—reports regarding conversations, (formal and informal) about the renewal of British base rights in Egypt, regarding the renewal of various other Anglo-Arab alliances, regarding the Middle Eastern Command, the Middle Eastern Defense Organization, and, finally, the Baghdad Pact. With one notable exception, all these attempts by the Western powers to establish a new regional organization failed, and every failure resulted directly from adamant Egyptian opposition. True, the Baghdad Pact, the lone bud on this desiccated vine, did eventually bloom, but only to wither and die as a result of the storm of protest issuing from Cairo.

But the historical importance of a Middle Eastern phenomenon cannot be calculated according to the number of documents it has generated in Western archives. The American and British planners of the 1940s and 1950s, therefore, must not be permitted to play—simply thanks to the length of their paper trail—the role of protohistorian in the 1990s. Their lack of interest in the Arab Pact should not deflect our attention from that policy as the best window, in the absence of official Egyptian documents, onto the thinking of Cairo about regional order. That thinking, moreover, played as important a role in the shaping of the modern Middle East as did all the prodigious intelligence that went into the planning of the failed defense organizations. The enormity of the failure of Western policy itself offers the greatest proof of the importance of mounting an excavation in search of the lost Egyptian policy that first surfaced in February 1948.

In one sense, the Arab-pact orientation did not emerge in 1948, but rather it reemerged. The ideas animating King Faruq's proposal bear a strong family resemblance to those informing the Alexandria Protocol, the document which, in much diluted form, became the Covenant of the Arab League.[9] The protocol (which embodied the principle that individual Arab states should be held responsible to the will of the majority) and the pact (which called for the creation of an Arab bloc in matters of defense) were not altogether the same beast, but they did serve the same master. Both drew strength from an ideological climate dominated by anti-imperialism and by the popular doctrine that Arab states owed greater allegiance to each other than to non-Arab states. Though different in form, both had the same regional political purpose: They served the Egyptians as tools for imposing an anti-British discipline on the Hashimite states.

The Two Strategies

The course of Egyptian foreign policy during the period 1944–1948 can be profitably conceptualized as the product of an elite debate dominated by two currents of thought, which, for the sake of convenience, will be called here the Arab-League and the Insular-Egypt Strategies. Both sought the expansion of independence and the extension of sovereignty over the Sudan; they differed, however, in their attitudes toward the future role of the British, in Egypt and in the region as a whole.

The Arab-League Strategy, originally the brainchild of the Wafd, envisioned the creation of a new Middle East. In place of the system based on British predominance, Egypt and her allies would establish a bloc of Arab states, completely independent of Western power, thus presenting a common front to the outside world, especially in the realm of defense. The League strategy looked to Washington for support. Although the idea of an Arab bloc had little appeal to the British, Cairo hoped that the Americans, after realizing the fallacy of their pro-British position, might yet find it appealing, especially in the absence of a British alternative. No doubt, as Hafiz Wahba suggested, the Americans, with all their "colossal resources and power" would be encouraged to support the Arab Bloc, just as they were supporting the Turks and the Greeks—that is, from afar and with great generosity.[10]

In contrast to the uncompromising anti-imperialism of the Arab-League orientation, the Insular-Egypt Strategy, which guided Ismail Sidqi's abortive policies, attempted to solve the nationalist dilemma of the Egyptian elite by carving out the greatest possible degree of autonomy for Egypt without actually challenging the position of Britain as the preponderating power in the Middle East. Recognizing the overwhelming importance to the Empire of the Egyptian bases and of the Suez Canal, Sidqi Pasha regarded as hopeless any attempt to force the British to renounce completely their claim on Egyptian facilities and territory. Seeing no possibility of prying Egypt completely loose from the grip of the Empire, he sought instead to reduce and regulate British power, to create a legal and institutional framework of alliance that would safeguard Egyptian independence in time of peace and minimize the extent of British interference in domestic affairs in time of war. His policy, then, simply took the logic of the 1936 treaty one step further.

In the negotiations leading to the Bevin–Sidqi Agreement, the political necessity of reducing British interference in Egyptian life translated into two practical problems: restricting the size of the British military presence in time of peace, and limiting the circumstances under which the British would be permitted to occupy the Egyptian bases in the event of war. An examination of the attitude of Sidqi Pasha toward the second issue, the question of wartime use of the bases, reveals how the Insular-Egypt Strategy influenced regional policy.

After long and arduous negotiations over the question of reoccupation, London and Cairo arrived at an understanding whereby the British military would automatically return to Egyptian bases in the event of an attack on neighboring countries (presumably Palestine, Libya and the Sudan).[11] One principle, proximity to Egypt, informed the selection of these countries; strikingly absent from this formula is any suggestion that the Egyptian government owed a special commitment to the members of the Arab League, which, in 1946, did not even include the Sudan and Libya. Such a commitment would have required, at the very least, a symbolic nod toward the offer of aid to Lebanon, Syria, Saudi Arabia, and Yemen. The omission of Iraq and Jordan is even more surprising, given the membership of both countries in the Arab League and their role in the British security system. Thus the Sidqi policy cannot justly be termed a commitment to regional—that is, Middle Eastern—security, whether defined in terms of Arabism or of the British defense network; rather, it was a policy as close to neutrality as one could get under the circumstances.

The conspicuous absence from Sidqi's policy of the principle of Arabism, if only on a symbolic level, did not go unchallenged. By his own admission, members of the Egyptian delegation dedicated to Arab unity protested this disregard for the Arab League, arguing that Arab nationalism required Egypt to place its bases at the service of all member states.[12] London, too, would have liked to expand the radius of the automatic-reentry clause. Since the Canal Zone bases formed the nerve center of their regional system, the British had originally fought for the right to reoccupy the base in the event of war being declared against *any* state in the region, including Turkey.

Sidqi Pasha resisted the pressure from London and from the moderate pan-Arabists; he remained true to his policy of weaving around Egypt a legal cocoon that would insulate it from the vicissitudes of world politics. The Insular-Egypt Strategy sought to insure that every crisis in the world for Britain did not become a crisis for Egypt. By restricting the radius of automatic reentry to include only states in the immediate neighborhood, Sidqi Pasha hoped to convince the Egyptian public that their country would no longer function as the playing field of empires; that only when events obviously threatened Egyptian—not British—

security would the bases be turned over to foreign forces. In theory, at least, the British would be true allies, friends who came to the aid of the country only when it was in danger; Britain would never again pull Egypt into fights that were not her own.[13]

For its part, the Wafd continued while in opposition to champion the Arab-League Strategy, which had considerably more ideological purchase than the policy of Sidqi Pasha, because it extended the principles of pan-Arabism and anti-imperialism to their pure, logical conclusion.[14] According to al-Nahhas, Egypt must indeed play a regional role: It should lead the Arab world to total independence. The Wafd denounced the reentry formulas of the Bevin–Sidqi Agreement as not just a betrayal of Egyptian national principles but, in addition, as treachery to the other Arab states, whom it consigned through neglect to permanent domination by the British. The logic of the attacks based on the Arab-League Strategy dictated that if Sidqi Pasha had actually endorsed the view of the moderate pan-Arabists, if he had pressed to extend the radius of the automatic-reentry clause to include all members of the Arab League, then the Wafd would have responded with an even stronger claim that he had packaged and delivered the entire Arab world to the British.

The ideological power of the Arab-League Strategy illustrates the difficulty that faced any Egyptian leader who might have considered following a policy based solely upon the welfare of Egypt (or of the proposed Egyptian–Sudanese union). The Insular-Egypt Strategy could never be presented as a fulfillment of national aspirations not only because it sought a compromise with the British but also because the logic on which it was based had been discredited by the events of World War II. The 1936 treaty had in its day supposedly created a legal cocoon that would protect Egyptian sovereignty, yet all of the fine rhetoric of equality had not prevented Lampson from encircling the palace and forcing King Faruq to install al-Nahhas Pasha. Nor had it insulated Egyptian society from the pernicious influence of hundreds of thousands of foreign troops. With anger over British behavior running high in the streets, the acceptance of any reentry formula whatsoever would appear to many as a treacherous act. Therefore, domestic politics steadily pressed the Egyptian government toward denying reentry under any conditions.

The nature of the regional pattern of power, however, dictated that once the Egyptian government decided to deny the Empire the right to use the Canal Zone bases, it had no choice but to oppose the British everywhere in the region. There were three reasons for this situation. First, opposition to the continuation of the Anglo-Egyptian alliance translated automatically into complete rejection of the British security system, simply because the Canal Zone played a pivotal role in imperial defense. Second, as long as the British remained ensconced in bases spread across the Middle East, they would enjoy the international support—from the United States and from the regional allies of Britain—necessary to demand that the Canal Zone function as a component in the imperial defense system. Third, the Suez Canal, and Egypt in general, had such strategic and economic importance to the British that in time of war they could be expected to seek physical control over Egypt, regardless of legalities. Recent history was replete with examples of the occupation of nonbelligerent countries—including Iraq and Syria during World War II—simply in order to deny them to an enemy. Complete security for Egypt from the British threat, therefore, required the elimination of Britain as a Middle Eastern power.

The Rising Importance of the Arab League

Thus, the exigencies of Egyptian domestic politics alone militated in favor of adopting the Arab-League Strategy, if only as a means of organizing and leading all the forces in the region opposed to British imperialism. Had the Insular-Egypt Strategy succeeded, Cairo could have sat on the sidelines and observed with relative equanimity developments in, say, Anglo-Iraqi relations, because the Egyptian commitment to Britain would not have extended beyond the Palestinian–Jordanian border. Once the decision had been made to rid Egypt altogether of British influence, however, relations between London and the other Arab capitals impinged directly on the vital interests of Cairo.

Although the importance of the Arab League to Egypt increased significantly after the failure of the negotiations, Sidqi Pasha himself had not been blind to the value of the organization as a tool for pressuring the British. True, the Insular-Egypt Strategy did *imply* the relegation of the Arab League to a secondary status in Egyptian foreign affairs, but while the negotiations were still in progress the League proved useful as a mechanism for forcing a pro-Egyptian line on the Arab capitals. For instance, on the eve of serious negotiation with the British, Cairo pushed the League to support the claim that the entire Arab world stood with Egypt against Britain. When the League Council met in late March 1946, it passed a resolution affirming "Egypt's national demands" and expressing an expectation of "the withdrawal of British forces from Egyptian territory at an early date."[15] Three months later, in June, when the negotiations had reached an impasse, Cairo again turned to the League and received a similar resolution, but this time the resolution also included a statement of regret regarding the interruption of the talks, as well as a reference to the unity of the Nile Valley. Azzam Pasha capped this resolution by threatening that "the continued existence of the Arab League depends upon the attainment of Egyptian independence."[16]

The ability of the Egyptians to receive, on demand, support for anti-British resolutions from the Hashimite regimes, both of which relied on Britain for their security, if not survival, represented a rather worrying development for London, Baghdad, and Amman alike. In 1946, however, this worry did not give cause for panic, due to the rather vague nature of the resolutions (which, for instance, did not call for a total withdrawal of troops and did not set a final date for their evacuation). Moreover, at this stage Egyptian policy still aimed at the revision, not the complete abrogation, of the alliance with Britain; therefore, Iraqi and Jordanian endorsement of League resolutions did not constitute utterly self-destructive behavior. Amman and Baghdad could still console themselves with the expectation that Britain would remain the preponderant power in the region.

One year later, on 3 March 1947, the Egyptians created a radically new situation: Al-Nuqrashi publicly expressed his hostility to any alliance with the British and revealed his plan to place the Anglo-Egyptian dispute before the United Nations. The British intention, announced several weeks earlier, to lay the Palestine question before the General Assembly, increased the perception that the imperial order in the Arab world had begun to crumble; doubt regarding the continued preeminence of Great Britain grew stronger in the face of the British domestic crisis and the decisions to evacuate from Burma, India, Turkey, and Greece.

With an ordinary session of the League Council due to convene in mid-March, a struggle to influence the proceedings immediately broke out between Cairo and London. Due to the precarious state of the Empire in February–March 1947, and the sudden rise to prominence in the Middle East of the United States, much was riding on the outcome of the League session. With both London and Cairo now competing for the favor of Washington, a vote in the League for the Egyptian position would send a message to the Americans that the entire Arab world had reached a consensus against the continuation of the British security system. Moreover, the vote in the Arab world would have an immediate effect on the domestic position of Arab leaders willing to cooperate with the British.

During the two weeks between al-Nuqrashi's policy statement and the Council session, London and Cairo worked behind the scenes lobbying Arab representatives. However, despite making every effort to prevent a vote favorable to Egypt, the British suffered a resounding diplomatic defeat that must be considered a turning point in the history of Arab nationalism. For the first time the Egyptians, by drawing power from the anti-imperialist mood pervading the Arab world, forced the clients of Britain to toe the line on a policy that menaced their most vital interests. The influence of Cairo in the region now rivaled the influence of London.

In the maneuvering behind the scenes, the British targeted Iraq (pro-British and the second most powerful Arab country) and Saudi Arabia (West-leaning and the joint leader of the Triangle Alliance) as the two regimes most likely to persuade the Egyptians and the other Arab states to avoid building an anti-British platform from which Arab leaders would find it impossible to climb down.[17] On the eve of the vote, Whitehall was reasonably confident of its position. In the event, however, the actual vote shocked Foreign Office officials, whose powers of persuasion had apparently worked more magic on their own thinking than on the opinions of the Saudis and the Iraqis. On 23 March the League issued a communiqué stating that "whereas the Egyptian government has proclaimed its decision to submit its case to the United Nations Organization, the League Council take the opportunity . . . to reiterate once again the absolute support of the Arab powers for Egypt in her national claims, namely immediate and total evacuation and permanent unity of the Nile Valley under the Egyptian Crown."[18] In sharp contrast to the previous votes, the Arab states moved away from vague endorsements: They underscored their support by specifying that the evacuation be immediate and total.

The View from Baghdad

To the extent that the League established the norms of nationalist politics, this vote set a standard of uncompromising anti-imperialism to which future governments in the region would inevitably be held. For the Iraqi regime, which suffered from a legitimacy problem at home, endorsing such a standard was pure folly, as the *Wathba* would demonstrate less than a year later. How, for instance, could the Iraqi elite justify to their own anti-imperialist public their desire to maintain the Anglo-Iraqi alliance after they had already supported, in principle, the dismantling of the British system of defense? Would they not appear, in such an event, as the puppets of an anachronistic imperialism, as men who championed the British connection not for the defense of Iraq from external aggression but for the defense of a corrupt order from overthrow?

Iraqi leaders, of course, had no illusions about their predicament; they knew full well that they had been backed into a corner, that they stood before their own public bereft of ideological resources with which to combat the anti-imperialism of Cairo. Just three months after the vote in the Arab League, Prime Minister Jabir candidly admitted to the British that the power of anti-imperial feeling in Iraq led directly to the subordination of Iraqi policy to Egyptian will. Faced with an unstable political situation at home, the Iraqis could not be expected to function as the stalking horse of the British in the Arab world; if London had an Arab problem, it would have to solve it on its own. During secret military talks with the British, Jabir gave the following impromptu speech:

> The defence of Iraq cannot be separated from the strategic defence of the Middle East. The Middle East forms one united bloc and its plans must be co-ordinated as such. For this reason, I mentioned again and again that air bases in Habbaniyah and Shaiba, or air bases anywhere else, are matters which must be discussed by all the Middle Eastern States. It may be decided to move the present bases and it may be decided to have additional ones, but the whole subject must be decided by the Arabs—it does not concern Iraq alone. The Arab states must study the subject between themselves and Great Britain; Iraq cannot take the responsibility alone and neglect the views of the other Arabs. In any case the . . . members of the Arab League are bound by the rules of that League not to negotiate individually. For this reason I beg Britain to study this important subject and to prepare all the Arab States [that are] refusing to participate in the defence of the Middle East and [that are] leaving Iraq alone to do it; then it will not be impossible for us to provide these facilities for joint defence and for Iraq to offer help against any foreign aggression. The present situation in Iraq is not the same as when the treaty was signed with Britain. . . . The present treaty is not popular with the nation. If we force the people to continue to accept it, we will be preparing the way for a growing hostility to Great Britain which we would both want to avoid.[19]

A comparison of these words with the keystone-in-the-arch thesis presented by King Faruq reveals that both men had an identical grasp of the mechanics governing the power triangle linking Baghdad, Cairo, and London. The Egyptian king and the Iraqi prime minister agreed that the Iraqis, due to their legitimacy crisis at home, could not afford to lead the pack in pursuit of good relations with the British. The government in London, therefore, had no choice but, first, to settle alone its differences with Cairo and, only then, to negotiate a new treaty with Baghdad.[20]

Although it was some eight months after this speech that King Faruq claimed for Egypt the status of keystone in the arch, the Egyptians realized the extent of the power that they wielded over the Iraqis long before the *Wathba*, and even long before the March 1947 vote in the Arab League. As the earlier resolutions demonstrate, Cairo, with the aid of Secretary General Azzam Pasha, had throughout 1946 captured anti-imperial feeling in the region and harnessed it in the service of Egyptian interests.[21] The weakness of the Iraqis did not, in the light of events, gradually dawn on the Egyptians; on the contrary, the weakness was—at least in part—created by them.

In December 1946, immediately after the collapse of the Bevin–Sidqi Agreement, Azzam Pasha initiated a stridently anti-British propaganda campaign that enraged both London and its Hashimite clients.[22] In addition, the Egyptian media, singing in harmony with the Arab League Secretariat, portrayed the Hashimite states as the puppets of imperialism. Nuri al-Said, the *éminence grise* of Iraqi politics and the architect of the pro-imperial orientation of the regime, came in for particular vituperation, being accused, for instance, of "suffocating the liberties of the people" and "using Iraq for the military purposes of Great Britain."[23] It is tempting to call this coordination between the Arab League Secretariat and the Egyptian government an "open secret," but even this faint suggestion of clandestinity would be misleading: "naked threat" would more accurately describe the anti-Iraqi coordination between the two.

Azzam Pasha bragged openly about his pro-Egyptian orientation. In late 1947, for instance, the secretary general attended an informal social gathering at the house of a former Iraqi prime minister in Baghdad, and he gave the guests (one of whom recorded the evening's conversation in his diary) a summary of his recent activities in support of Egypt in her dispute with Britain.[24] In the course of this survey, he recounted to the gathering the details of a past episode in the relations between the Iraqi government and the Arab League: After Azzam delivered a speech, in early 1946, in which he called for putting an end to British bases everywhere in the Middle East, Hamdi al-Pachachi, the Iraqi prime minister, wrote a letter of rebuke, accusing Azzam of exceeding his authority.[25] Al-Pachachi argued that the position of secretary general of the Arab League entailed a responsibility not just to Egypt but to all Arab states, some of whom had close relations with the British.

Azzam described to his fellow guests the spirit of the letter that he wrote to al-Pachachi in reply. The Arab League, he told them, could not exist without Egypt; and, if the Arab countries failed to support Cairo against the British, Egypt would leave the League. Commitment to Arabism, therefore, required supporting Cairo wholeheartedly in its struggle with Britain. With regard to his fiery anti-imperialist speeches, Azzam explained that "it was his duty to strengthen the youth of the Arabs. When letters of protest reached him, he would rip them up and throw them in the trash, because he does not occupy his post thanks to governments but rather thanks to the aid of Arab public opinion."[26]

In Azzam's own eyes, then, the position of secretary general of the Arab League entailed a responsibility to a higher authority, to pan-Arabism, which, as he understood it, dictated complete obedience to Cairo in the Anglo-Egyptian conflict, regardless of the consequences for the Iraqi regime. Azzam concluded his story by telling his fellow guests in Baghdad that, after the Iraqi cabinet fell in early 1946, he sent al-Pachachi's letter of rebuke, together with a copy of his own defiant response, to the new Iraqi prime minister, thus informing him of the futility of attempting to influence the policy of the Arab League. The new prime minister who had received the letters from Azzam was Tawfiq al-Suwaydi, the same man who was hosting, in his own home, the gathering at which Azzam was telling the story.

No doubt Tawfiq al-Suwaydi sympathized to some extent, perhaps even to a great extent, with the policies of Azzam Pasha; he may even have seen the Arab League and the Triangle Alliance not as the enemies of Iraq but, rather, as the allies of Iraqi pan-Arabists against the likes of Nuri al-Said and Salih Jabir, who promoted the pro-British orientation in foreign policy. One thing, however, is certainly clear: If al-Suwaydi felt any unease about listening, while relaxing in his own home, to the secretary general of the Arab League brag about weakening the position of the Iraqi government, he was not going to show it.

The Roots of Hashimite Impotence

In late 1946 and early 1947 the British Foreign Office, greatly troubled by Azzam's activities, debated the merits of arranging his ouster; the debate reveals much regarding the inter-Arab balance of power during the period when Egypt and Britain squared off in a struggle for the alignment of the Arab states. In response to the question of whether the secretary general should be deposed, Sir Alec Kirkbride, the minister in Amman, wrote:

> No representations on my part are needed to bring home to the Transjordan Government the undesirable nature of some of the activities of the secretary general of the Arab League and no one would be better pleased at his supersession than King Abdullah. Azzam, however, has identified himself with the anti-Hashimite bloc which exists in fact, although not admitted in the Council of the League and he is, therefore, safe from any attempt to unseat him on the part of the Hashimite States.[27]

As a minority of two, the Hashimites could not counter the influence of the Triangle Alliance in the halls of the League. The Cairo–Riyadh–Damascus constellation could always count on the support, or the benevolent neutralism, of the Lebanese and Yemeni governments, leaving Iraq and Jordan in the wilderness.

But the roots of the problem went far deeper than the constitutional mechanisms of the League Council. As al-Suwaydi's attitude toward Azzam's policy demonstrates, the Egyptians, by using the Arab League Secretariat as their de facto ministry of propaganda, had captured the moral high ground in inter-Arab relations. Any attempt to topple them would, therefore, appear as treason to a certain segment of politically conscious Iraqis. The drone of criticism against the

Hashimites and their British patrons cowed those Iraqis who supported the continuation of the British connection, making them reluctant to swim directly against the anti-imperial current flowing from Cairo. For instance, when the British ambassador protested the Iraqi failure to bloc the decisive vote in the Arab League, Nuri al-Said, the strongman of Baghdad, meekly replied that the Iraqis "could not be expected to stand alone in face of Azzam, Yasin [the Saudi delegate], Farouk, and the whole of the Egyptian press."[28] His words echo the speech by Salih Jabir regarding the inability of the Iraqi government to proselytize in the Arab world for Britain. Both statements together indicate that, years before Abd al-Nasser's "Voice of the Arabs" radio broadcasts, the Egyptian government—aided by its media power, its control over the Arab League, and its Saudi and Syrian allies—had already imposed a pan-Arab, anti-imperial discipline on Iraq by appealing over the heads of leaders in Baghdad to opposition elements in the street, and to that section of the elite that supported, for whatever reason, the anti-imperial position of Egypt.

Given the ideological resources fueling Egyptian policy, Baghdad refused to mount a campaign against Azzam, who could easily portray any Iraqi move against him as the desperate attempt of puppets to protect their masters. In keeping with the penchant of the Iraqis for avoiding confrontation with the Egyptians, Foreign Minister Fadil Jamali suggested, when the British ambassador raised the possibility of mounting an attack on Azzam, that London should take care of the problem itself.[29] In an apparent effort to mollify the British, however, the Iraqis claimed to have hatched a clandestine plot to unseat Azzam; of course, nothing tangible ever emerged from this murky operation.[30]

For their part, the British also felt pinned down by Azzam's ideological power. The ambassador in Cairo wrote that "it would be unwise" to actively seek the dismissal of Azzam. If, in fact, he were successfully ousted, "the Arab League would at once become labeled as an instrument of British policy. This would provide an additional theme for anti-British propaganda in the Arab countries, and would undermine the League and probably lead to its disintegration." If, on the other hand, the attempt failed, Britain would suffer an intolerable loss of prestige.[31]

A Hashimite break with the League was also out of the question. In the case of Iraq, such a move would, just as in the manner of an attack on Azzam, damage the legitimacy of the government in the eyes of Iraqi pan-Arabists. Moreover, the British themselves did not want to destroy the organization, as the ambassador's fear of a disintegrating League demonstrates. Despite the evidence to the contrary, they still had hopes that the Egyptians would strike a compromise with them, and that the League would ultimately form the political basis for an Anglo-Arab alliance. A powerful current of pan-Arab thought ran through the Foreign Office, which, searching for a policy that would be broadly acceptable to all Arab states, had pinned great hopes on the Arab League.

Thus, for instance, London repeatedly worked to prevent the Jordanian government (which in contrast to the Iraqis had no domestic enemies to appease) from abandoning the organization. When requested by the Foreign Office to rebuke King Abdallah for voting in favor of the pro-Egyptian resolution in March,

Kirkbride cabled from Amman that a protest from Britain would provoke the immediate suggestion from the Jordanians that they should secede. He wrote:

> As you know, I have had on more than one occasion in the past to dissuade the Transjordanian authorities from withdrawal from the League, and if I now appear to reproach them for conforming with the majority of that institution, their reaction, as anticipated, would not be illogical.[32]

By seceding, King Abdallah, who was considered a British stooge by the other Arab states, would call down on the Empire the harsh criticism that it was conducting a policy of divide and rule among the Arabs. Ironically, then, Foreign Office pan-Arabism, especially in the case of Jordan, helped the Egyptians to tighten the Arab ranks against the imperial defense system.

The Turco-Hashimite Entente

Mobilizing the Arab League Secretariat in order to foster the principles of Arab solidarity and anti-imperialism served Egyptian interests, then, in two ways. First, it conjured up a pan-Arab consensus hostile to London's attitude on the Anglo-Egyptian dispute, and, second, it weakened British influence in Iraq, the only potential rival to Egypt in the League. These two objectives flowed directly from the decision to oust the British from Egypt, which was taken on the basis of domestic political considerations. They were not, however, the only advantages to Cairo of a pan-Arab policy. During 1945–1947, a number of regional political trends worked to magnify the role that the Arab League played in Egyptian foreign policy; these trends pushed the Egyptian leadership further toward adopting the Arab-League Strategy, in all its aspects.

The promotion, through the League, of Arab solidarity and independence also helped the Triangle Alliance restrict the expansion of Turkish influence in the Fertile Crescent. The alliance could thus also frustrate plans for increased cooperation between the Hashimite regimes, which, as Hafiz Wahba observed, had tended to club together in the years prior to the Portsmouth Treaty. From the perspective of Cairo, Damascus, and Riyadh, the clannishness of Baghdad and Amman appeared all the more menacing for coinciding with the development of a Turco-Hashimite entente. In 1945–1947, Turkey stood out conspicuously—thanks to its size, stability, and geostrategic importance—as the potential hub of a regional power bloc destined to pursue interests radically opposed to those of the Triangle Alliance. At the same time, therefore, just as the Arab League proved useful in dividing the British from their Arab allies, the League also helped prevent the Hashimites from uniting and moving into the orbit of Turkey.

The first sign in the postwar era of Turkish concern about Arab affairs emerged against the background of the Kurdish question, which Soviet support for the Republic of Mahabad, together with the simultaneous unrest in Iraqi Kurdistan, had successfully elevated from the status of a parochial issue to a matter of geopolitical significance.[33] Ankara and Baghdad shared a common interest in suppressing Kurdish nationalism and in limiting Soviet influence; they moved rapidly to close ranks. In September 1945, the Iraqi regent Abd al-Ilah, en route home from the United States, stopped briefly in Ankara for discussions with the Turkish government; the following February, Nuri al-Said traveled to Turkey; one month later, in March 1946, representatives of the two countries signed a draft treaty of friendship and *bon voisinage*.[34] The Iraqi parliament did eventually ratify the agreement, but only after much criticism, and, even then, not until June 1947, following the formation of the Salih Jabir Cabinet.[35]

The Turkish government's interest in developments beyond its southern border was not restricted to Iraq; in October 1946 the foreign minister stated publicly that Turkey wished to establish an alliance with *all* Arab states: "We have," he said, "concluded an alliance with Iraq and we wish to conclude similar treaties with Syria, Egypt, and the other Arab countries."[36] Not surprisingly, however, this proposal met with stiff resistance from Syria, Egypt, and Saudi Arabia.[37] By contrast, King Abdallah immediately responded favorably. Having just (in March 1946) achieved independence for Jordan, he jumped at the opportunity to strengthen the international position of his country at a moment when the future of his British patron was in jeopardy. The formalities of the rapprochement between Ankara and Amman unfolded rapidly. The following month a delegation from the Turkish foreign ministry visited Amman; then, in January 1947, Abdallah traveled to Ankara and concluded a treaty that was, if the storm of protest it provoked is any indication, as menacing to the Triangle Alliance as it was platitudinous in content.[38]

While the Hashimite regimes tilted in the direction of Ankara, they also embarked on an ambitious plan for an Iraqi–Jordanian federation. The scheme, however, progressed slowly, meeting in the Iraqi parliament the same cool reception that greeted the Turco-Iraqi Treaty. Representatives of the two governments first raised the issue of a union in November 1945, but real momentum did not develop until after Abdallah's coronation in May 1946. In September, one month before the Turkish foreign minister's controversial statement regarding a Turco-Arab alliance, King Abdallah and the regent of Iraq reportedly drafted a blueprint for a Hashimite federation. The plan was never published, but press reports indicated that it called for a unified policy in matters of defense, foreign relations, and customs, all of which would be directed by a joint Hashimite political council meeting alternately in Baghdad and Amman.[39] The scheme sparked off loud opposition from both the Triangle Alliance and Iraqi opposition groups, and as a result it became diluted, appearing before the public only in April 1947 as the "Treaty of Brotherhood and Alliance."[40] Though not nearly as bold an experiment in unity as first conceived, the treaty nonetheless contained, in contrast to the benign Turco-Jordanian agreement, provisions of serious political import, including an article providing for cooperation in the event of rebellion within one of the countries. This clause suggested, in a sign not lost on the Iraqi opposition, that the experience of the Rashid Ali Revolt, and the vital role of Transjordanian troops in quelling it, continued to play on the minds of leaders in Baghdad.[41]

The Triangle Alliance under Threat

Thus, between late 1945 and spring 1947 Amman, Baghdad, and Ankara established the rudiments of a regional bloc. Egypt, Syria, and Saudi Arabia protested vigorously against this new network of cooperation, because it threatened each at its most vulnerable point.

From the perspective of Damascus, the most alarming aspect of the recent developments stemmed from the renewal, in May 1946, of King Abdallah's agitation in support of his Greater Syria Project.[42] The new republican regime headed by Shukri al-Quwatli suffered from a severe legitimacy crisis and it lacked a Great-Power patron; it had, therefore, few political, economic, or ideological weapons with which to combat the efforts, directed from Amman, at organizing a movement in favor of the unification of Jordan and Syria under the Hashimite monarchy.[43] Actually, Damascus stood even weaker in relation to Amman than Baghdad stood in relation to Cairo, with the important caveat that the British restrained King Abdallah while no one restrained the Egyptians. The analogy is not frivolous: just as Cairo called over the heads of Iraqi leaders to elements opposed to the status quo, so King Abdallah called over the head of President al-Quwatli to a host of groups opposed to his ruling clique.

The plan for a Jordanian–Iraqi union appeared particularly menacing to Damascus. It raised the possibility that, in contrast to the experience of the past, Amman and Baghdad might actually succeed in formulating a unified Syrian policy. On paper, the Iraqi Fertile Crescent Unity Plan and the Jordanian Greater Syria Project were compatible; in practice, however, the Hashimite regimes had never cooperated in this sphere. With real unity now on the agenda, the countries bordering Jordan and Iraq could not but contemplate the threat of a powerful movement designed to bring the entire Fertile Crescent into a Hashimite federation. Even if the Iraqi government showed few signs at the moment of wishing to absorb Syria, how much time would pass before elements in Baghdad sympathetic to Abdallah's project rose to power?

The new Arab orientation in Turkish foreign policy compounded the sense of danger to Syria. The dispute over Alexandretta strained relations between Ankara and Damascus, which had never recognized the Turco-French agreement of 1938 that had separated this port from Syria and thus paved the way for its eventual annexation by Turkey. Iraq had a strong interest in promoting good relations between Turkey and Syria, which had yet to exchange formal representatives; in 1946, Nuri al-Said brokered a deal between his neighbors whereby Ankara refrained from demanding that Syria recognize the annexation and, in return, Damascus agreed not to pursue its protest formally.[44] While this compromise allowed the two countries to establish diplomatic relations, it could hardly erase the fear from minds in Damascus that Turkey might rid itself of all irritation by supporting, in return for complete satisfaction on the Alexandretta issue, a bid by Abdallah—or by a Hashimite federation—to absorb Syria. Damascus was, in a word, surrounded.

Although the Saudis, in contrast to the Syrians, enjoyed the staunch support of a Great Power, they too were troubled by developments in the northern Arab world. The Saudi–Hashimite dynastic rivalry, never completely laid to rest, had played a considerable role in the lives of many of the prominent men in Riyadh, Baghdad, and Amman; King Abdallah's continuous celebration of the Hashimite House as the greatest instrument of Arabism naturally revived memories of real battles fought between the two families. Regardless of the dynastic tensions, Riyadh had no interest in seeing a large federated state develop on its borders, simply because such a political unit would be bigger and stronger than Saudi Arabia. In addition, little imagination was required to foresee that forces within such an amalgamation would undoubtedly represent the new state as the realization of Arab nationalist dreams. Saudi reluctance to join the federation would thus appear as a betrayal of core nationalist values motivated by the greed of Riyadh to monopolize the oil wealth of the Arabian peninsula. Other voices in the federation would claim that the holy places of Islam, the property of all Muslims, belonged to the authentic representative of the Arab people as a whole. Under such circumstances Saudi Arabia would, in a manner similar to Syria, find itself largely isolated.

The close relations developing between the United States and Turkey may well have contributed to the visible sense of unease in Riyadh.[45] Prior to the Soviet advances on Turkish territory, Saudi Arabia had enjoyed the status of being the sole Middle Eastern client of the greatest power in the world; that Washington now perceived its own vital interests to be inextricably tied to the potential hub of a pro-Hashimite bloc could not please policy makers in Riyadh. They responded to the renewal of the Greater Syria Project and the movement for a Hashimite unity by lobbying London and Washington against the policies of Abdallah, and by their traditional anti-Hashimite tactic of resuscitating their dormant claim to Aqaba and Ma'an.[46] In addition, they may have laid claim, for the first time, to a corridor running from Saudi Arabia to Syria, as part of an attempt to place a territorial obstacle in the way of a Hashimite Federation.[47]

Both Syria and Saudi Arabia turned for help to Egypt, which had its own reasons for opposing the consolidation of the northern Middle East. From the point of view of Cairo, the most severe threat posed by this development resided in the favorable attitude of Turkey, Iraq, and Jordan to the British security system; a Turco-Hashimite bloc would function as an international pressure group working to maintain the British military bases in the region. Through the association of Turkey, such a bloc would have an especially strong voice in the United States, the only power capable of forcing the British to evacuate the Canal Zone. On a deeper, power-political level, the Egyptians opposed the formation of a northern bloc because Ankara constituted the only serious rival to Cairo as a political center for the region. If the Egyptians could convince the Western powers, by whatever means, to treat Egypt and not Turkey as the keystone in the arch, as the primary intermediary between the Middle East and the outside world, then the power of the Egyptian voice in international affairs would be considerably enhanced, be it with regard to the British security system or any other international issue.

Fear of British intentions, and concern over the erosion of the Arab League as a foundation for regional political predominance, are clearly perceptible even in the public attitudes expressed in Egypt toward the northern entente. The Cairo press regarded the Arab policy of Turkey as an attempt to revitalize the Saadabad Pact, an agreement signed in 1937 between Turkey, Iraq, Iran, and Afghanistan: "It is the aim of British politicians," one article claimed, "to form an Eastern Bloc that would include Turkey, Iraq, and Transjordan. . . . Britain is tired of the Arab League and now aims at dividing the Arab countries."[48] This tendency to draw a connection between the Arab policy of Ankara in 1946 and the Saadabad Pact of 1937 was not limited to the Egyptian press; the Soviet and Turkish media also played with the idea. In Moscow, the party line supported the propaganda of the Triangle Alliance, asserting that the Turco-Hashimite entente was part of "a British sponsored plot to bring the Hashimite monarchies closer to Turkey in an anti-Soviet bloc, thereby also disrupting the Arab movement toward national unity."[49] In Ankara, the press was more supportive, some papers going so far as to propose a Turco-Arab federation: "journalists are writing a great deal," a British report stated, "to the effect that the Turks are linked with the Arabs by 'ties of kinship, religion, and interests and for that reason, they will live in one state.' "[50]

Geopolitics and the Anglo-Egyptian Conflict

The Egyptian fear of the Saadabad Pact, fueled by the Turkish and Soviet press, had a firm grounding in geopolitical realities. The pact had expanded the regional influence of Turkey in the uneasy period just prior to World War II, when Great Power discord, together with unstable regional politics, opened doors to potentially hostile powers, such as the Italians and the Soviets, who were casting about (or were feared by Ankara to be casting about) for a foothold in the region.[51] A decade later in 1946–1947, as the Cold War developed in the Middle East, similar conditions existed. From the point of view of Ankara, the successful destruction of the British security system in the Arab world would create a power vacuum, which, if exploited by the Soviets, would cause Turkey to be sandwiched between simultaneous threats directed against her northern and southern flanks.

But the salience of the Egyptian comparison between the Turco-Hashimite entente and the Saadabad Pact extended beyond the logic of just Turkish policy. When the war was drawing to a close, and planners in London began to envision a postwar order, one current of opinion had championed a two-tiered—northern and southern—approach to Middle Eastern defense. For instance, a semiofficial study of British security conducted in 1944–1945 stated that "it would seem logical to encourage the further development of the League of Arab States and to follow this up by the revival or expansion of the Saadabad Pact."[52] With the British desire to create a regionwide security system a matter of public knowledge, it required no leap of fancy for the Egyptians to expect, especially after they had set themselves completely against British strategic predominance, that London would begin to think in terms of using the Turco-Hashimite grouping as a stem onto which a regional defense organization could be grafted. This, of course, was no doubt what Abdallah had in mind when he visited Turkey; it certainly informed Nuri al-Said's policies; and, in addition, it was exactly the direction that

British policy would eventually take—but not until 1954–1955, when London worked to establish the Baghdad Pact.[53]

The structure of power in the region and the fundamental interests of the British Empire gave London no choice, in the light of Egyptian policy, but to circumvent Cairo altogether and to adopt a northern, Turco-Hashimite orientation. As the Egyptian fears regarding the resurrection of the Saadabad Pact demonstrate, sensitive observers could read the writing on the wall already in 1946. The first suggestion from a British official that London should base its policy squarely on Hashimite power came, in early 1947, from Sir Walter Smart, the oriental counsellor (the political officer, in American parlance) at the embassy in Cairo. Intelligent, conversant in Arabic, and deeply experienced in Middle Eastern affairs, Smart perceived clearly the stark options before the British at a time when the Foreign Office, imbued with a pan-Arab ethos, still searched for a policy that would attract the support of all Arab states.[54]

The oriental counsellor, more alive than his associates in London to the great chasm separating vital Egyptian and British interests, politely nudged the Foreign Office toward abandoning the assumption that Egyptian anti-imperialism, amplified by the new radicalism of the Arab League, was simply an exercise in bargaining tactics: "the Arab League, under the direction of Azzam, is tending to liquidate us from the Middle East. In our empirical way we must no doubt adjust ourselves to this development."[55]

Adjusting to realities required, in Smart's view, a new policy characterized by a closer association with the true allies of Britain in the region. In this context, he pointed to the recent agreements creating a proto-bloc in the north, which "reflect a growing tendency of the Hashemite States to strengthen themselves against Egyptian hegemony in the Arab League. Azzam's disastrous policy of trying to run the Arab League in the narrower interests of Egypt is no doubt encouraging this tendency." Until now, Smart claimed, British policy had wisely avoided taking sides in the controversy over the Turco-Hashimite entente. But the division of the Arab world into two blocs, largely defined by their attitude toward the British security system, gave London no choice but to actively support the northern powers:

> This state of affairs is bound gradually to affect the orientation of our policy in the Arab world, unless Egypt pulls up in time. We are not interested in encouraging anything which will strengthen Egyptian predominance, which is being used against Great Britain in the Middle East.

What policy, then, would weaken the Egyptian position?

Given the geostrategic realities, the only tool available for undermining the influence of Cairo in the Arab world was Hashimite power. If Britain, however, were to abandon its policy of seeking an accommodation with the Arabs *en bloc*, if it were to throw its support unreservedly behind the Turco-Hashimite entente, a storm would ensue: Syria, Lebanon, Saudi Arabia, and Palestinian nationalists loyal to the Mufti would all draw closer to Egypt. Implicitly addressing this state of affairs, Smart argued that the support Cairo received in the Arab League from Syria, Saudi Arabia, and Lebanon derived not from their opposition to British policy per se but, rather, from their fear of King Abdallah's Greater Syria Project. In return for staunch guarantees from Britain of their security, Lebanon and Saudi Arabia could be detached from Egypt, thus crippling the Triangle Alliance. As for the republican regime in Damascus and the followers of the Mufti, they would necessarily fall victim to Greater Syria:

> The Partition of Palestine might add to Transjordan the truncated Arab–Palestine State, and the gradual strengthening of the Hashimite States might strengthen the Monarchist Movement in Syria, which, although it appears to have lost some ground in the last few months, is still strong in that country.

Of course, the expansion of Jordan would, as Smart well knew, inevitably destabilize Syria. The Greater Syria Project, however, was unpopular in Whitehall; no doubt Smart presented his comprehensive plan for a new British order in the Middle East in the manner of a detached survey of international forces—in order to coax the Foreign Office toward support for Greater Syria without appearing as a partisan of the scheme. With regard to King Abdallah's plan, therefore, Smart's memorandum ends on a slightly tentative note, but his view of the implications for Britain of the split in the Arab world are clear nonetheless:

> Obviously, if we are not to allow ourselves to be turned out of the Middle East, we must get together with those States which are prepared and desirous to keep us in the Middle East, namely Turkey, the Hashemite States, Saudi Arabia, the Lebanon, and perhaps later a Hashemite Syria. We shall then have little difficulty in dealing with a recalcitrant Egypt, but we must not give her time to get away with her present designs to consolidate the Arab world against us.

This power-political analysis, implicitly calling for a policy designed to cripple the League, vitiated the intellectual basis of every major component of British policy toward the Middle East. It did not, therefore, enjoy a ready reception. Ambassador Campbell forwarded the memorandum to London with the following disclaimer:

> With all the respect due to Smart's infinitely greater knowledge and experience, I would not myself have said that Egypt had taken a definite decision to consolidate the Arab world against us as a long-term policy, though I would think she might well do so, if things go really badly. But she is certainly trying to do so for the purposes of getting the sort of treaty with us which would be agreeable to her (and which with at least part of her mind and sentiment she wants).

The Egyptians, apparently, could still be reconciled with the imperial presence. Officials in London agreed with the ambassador; Britain, regardless of what the press in Cairo was saying, had yet to tire of the Arab League.

By the very logic inherent in the motion of regional power constellations, however, British policy did shift in the direction of the Turco-Hashimite entente. Two days after the ambassador had penned his polite reservations regarding the oriental counsellor's analysis, al-Nuqrashi Pasha broke off all talks with the British; then, on 3 March 1947, he announced his commitment to liberate Egypt completely. Ambassador Campbell changed his tune:

Nokrashi's statement makes it most undesirable if not futile for us to pursue any
longer the task of getting the Egyptians to reopen treaty negotiations. Efforts by His
Majesty's Government to this end would only be regarded as indicating a degree of
weakness on our part which must encourage those Egyptians who are so minded
to go further and further towards destruction of our positions not only in Egypt
but also in the Middle East. I think therefore the time has come to stiffen our whole
attitude to Egypt as long as the present situation continues.[56]

The vote in the Arab League in favor of the intransigent policy of Egypt,
coming only a few days after this cable, instilled in Whitehall a sense of urgency
regarding the future of the British position in Iraq; this concern, in turn, forced
London to tilt toward the Turco-Hashimite Entente.[57] Additional evidence
strongly suggests that, in addition to circumventing Cairo by negotiating directly
with Baghdad, London also attempted to hobble the Triangle Alliance by driving
a wedge between Riyadh and Cairo. The Foreign Office sought to co-opt Saudi
Arabia by negotiating a treaty of alliance with Riyadh.[58]

The course that the British adopted following the vote in the Arab League,
therefore, appears to have been a compromise between the Smart plan and the
traditional Egypt-centered orientation of the Foreign Office. The new policy envisioned placing the Egyptians before a fait accompli: London would corral both
Iraq and Saudi Arabia into a revitalized defense system; when Cairo realized that
the other Arab countries, despite their previous support for the Egyptian resolutions in the Arab League, had by their actions voted in favor of the British
security system, it would retreat from its recalcitrant position. Whereas Smart
had argued in favor of full-blown containment, the new policy was directed at
discrediting the policies of, in the words of the ambassador, "those Egyptians
who are so minded to go further and further towards destruction of our positions." The new policy, that is, still held out hope that the Egyptians, once en-
countering firmness, would turn soft.

The Greater Syria Project Moves to Center Stage

Although the Smart plan for reordering the Fertile Crescent did not, apparently,
form the basis for the new Foreign Office thinking, the power realities analyzed
in the oriental counsellor's memorandum did have a decisive influence over Foreign Office action. Regardless of the conceptual framework in which the British
understood their new policy, in power-political terms it signaled a decided tilt
toward the Turco-Hashimite entente. As such, it sent profound shock waves
across the region. In particular, the new orientation, while not consciously endorsing Hashimite revisionism, gave a fillip to the Greater Syria Project. Since a
kind of cold war had developed between the Triangle Alliance and the British,
the assumption, always present in any case, gained acceptance that London would
support the aspirations of Amman in order strike a blow against the Arab enemies
of the Empire.

Prior to March 1947 the position of London toward the Greater Syria Project is best described as "neutral against." British policy sought to reconcile conflicting interests. On the one hand, the Foreign Office wished to avoid needlessly provoking the Egyptians, Syrians, Saudis, Lebanese, Americans, French, and Russians—all of whom opposed the project with varying degrees of vehemence; on the other hand, it had no desire to weaken a staunch ally. Therefore, the British publicly espoused a neutral policy. But, in actuality, they had shown no interest in placing Abdallah on the throne in Damascus; at times London had gone so far as to quietly but firmly pressure Amman to curb its meddling in Syrian affairs, which conflicted with policies designed to sell the British Empire to the entire Arab world.

From the point of view of the Triangle Alliance, however, the policy of the British appeared much more like "neutral for" than "neutral against." Everyone in the region remembered that the abortive 1937 Peel Plan had called for the partition of Palestine between a Jewish state and Transjordan. In fact, prior to the November 1947 resolution in the General Assembly, the Peel Plan had functioned as *the* model for a partition solution to the Palestine question.[59] Since the breakdown in Anglo-Egyptian relations coincided with the crisis of the Mandate's regime in Palestine, an air of uncertainty hung over the western Fertile Crescent, whose borders were guaranteed, ultimately, by the force of British arms. With the future presence of British troops having been thrown into doubt by Egyptian policy, and with the Mandate crumbling in Palestine, regional powers tended to see Greater Syria (just as Smart had suggested) as the logical means for the British to escape simultaneously from their twin dilemmas of the Palestine morass and the Egyptian opposition to imperial defense plans.

Moreover, the Triangle powers had always assumed that the British secretly supported Greater Syria, because King Abdallah, with an army run by British officers and paid for completely by British money, appeared to be the puppet of London. They assumed that if he raised a ruckus over his plan to unify Syria, then he had been ordered, or at least permitted, to do so by his masters.

Rather than attempting to correct these widespread assumptions, King Abdallah astutely manipulated them in the service of his own interests. For instance, immediately following the adoption by Britain of its new, stiff orientation toward Egypt, he embarked upon the most aggressive campaign ever in favor of Greater Syria. This effort included the publication of a book in Arabic, entitled *Greater Syria: The Jordanian White Paper*, a compendium of documents recording the consistent and impressive efforts that he had exerted, for more than twenty years, to unify the Syrian lands (Transjordan, Palestine, Syria, and Lebanon).[60] Included among these documents, to the anger of the British, were a number of private communications exchanged during the war between them and King (then Emir) Abdallah, who had at that time repeatedly urged London to allow him to replace the French regime in Syria. While the British never endorsed any of his specific proposals, they avoided harshly rebuffing the king, preferring to console him at the end of each communication with ambiguous assurances, such as, "you can rest assured that his Majesty's government will safeguard the legitimate interests of Transjordan at the appropriate time."[61] The British attitude, then, did not appear to the Triangle Alliance as a policy objectively characterized as "neutral against"; rather, it appeared more like an alternative plan tucked away for a rainy day. The crisis of British power in 1947 gave rise to the belief that if, in fact, there would ever be an "appropriate time" for the alternative, then it had surely arrived.

Thus, in March 1947 King Abdallah began his most aggressive efforts ever to unite Syria, provoking a storm of outrage from the members of the Triangle Alliance and Lebanon. In contrast to the wobbly Iraqis, King Abdallah had no compunction about giving the Saudis and the Egyptians a dose of their own medicine. In March, an Egyptian paper published a false report of Jordanian troop concentrations on the Syrian border, eliciting a new round of anti-Abdallah invective from hostile capitals. In response to the clamor, King Abdallah gave an interview to a Lebanese journalist, in which he affirmed that he intended to unify Syria, Lebanon, Palestine, and Transjordan. He then displayed contempt for the Triangle Alliance:

> They talked of Transjordan troop concentration[s] on [the] frontier and said [that my] army wished to execute the Greater Syria Project by force. This is a lie; the army is but [the Syrians'] own army, and its sons are their own sons. I do not wish one single drop of blood sacrificed for the realization of this project for which we have struggled. Let them be reassured there will be no concentration[s], because [the] age of troop concentrations has passed; we are now in [an] age of surprise occupation: my army is able to do it and has proved [that] it is the strongest army. I went to Turkey and they said I had conceded Alexandretta to Turkey, as if Alexandretta were part of my possessions, [as if I] offered it to Turkey as a present on [the] occasion of [that] visit. [But the] sons of King Ibn Saud travel [to] Washington, to London, and then [back to] Riyadh, and you publish details of their visits and receptions; and [you publish pictures of them] in America, and [pictures of them] with Americans in Dhahran—yes, Americans in Dhahran, Americans in Taif, Americans in Riyadh, and in Hajijah. Their presence in the Holy Land never [upsets] you; [on the contrary], you [applaud] it, even though their president has promised to admit 100,000 Jews to Palestine—to Arab Holy Land! You ask me what the Arab League has done. [I'll tell you] what the Arab League has done up till now. It is merely a toy devised by Nahhas Pasha to serve [particularistic] purposes.[62]

Here King Abdallah astutely turned the tables on the anti-Hashimite propaganda of the Egyptians and the Arab League, which portrayed the Triangle Alliance as the authentic representative of the purest national values (unity and independence), while painting the Hashimites as the lackeys of the imperialists and the sowers of disunity. Plus, the king played on the contradiction between the claim of the League to represent the popular aspiration for Arab unity and its actual policy of maintaining the borders established by the imperial powers; he stated, in effect, that he represented the authentic spirit of Arabism because he truly sought to eliminate the illogical borders. Moreover, he implied that he had the power to carry out his program of unification, not despite but rather *because of* the British connection, which guaranteed him the most powerful army in the Arab world. As for the claim that the Hashimites served foreign powers—imperial as well as non-Arab—King Abdallah pointed to the cozy relationship between the Saudis and the Americans, underscoring the hypocrisy of the Triangle Alliance, whose domination of the League served the particularistic interests of Egypt. By setting one core Arab nationalist value (unity) against another (anti-imperialism), while at the same time casting doubt on the claim of the Triangle Alliance to represent authentic anti-imperialism, Abdallah scored a number of significant propaganda points, to which the great uproar his statement provoked amply testifies.[63]

This new wave of agitation for the Greater Syria Project enjoyed, behind the scenes, the support of Nuri al-Said, who was, of course, as threatened by the Egyptian attempt to oust the British from the Middle East as he was incapable of admitting it. In mid-April, Kirkbride informed London that on a recent visit to Amman, the Iraqi statesman had "been mischievous on the subject of Greater Syria," by suggesting to the King that "an attempt should be made to create a state of chaos in the Syrian territory adjacent to Transjordan and Iraq by stirring up the Druze and the Euphrates tribes, and then for the armed forces of Trans-jordan and Iraq to intervene in order to 'restore order.' "[64] Kirkbride doubted the good faith of Nuri, suspecting that the Iraqis would not employ their own armed forces in the scheme, but would be quite happy if the Jordanian army could be duped into both occupying Syria and taking the criticism for it. None-theless, the proposal resonated with King Abdallah; on the heels of Nuri's visit, he raised the issue with Kirkbride, subjecting him to "a tirade about the pro-Russian and anti-British attitude of the . . . authorities in Syria, who were now working with Egypt in a scheme to eliminate the British from the Middle East." The king, without disclosing the content of his discussion with Nuri al-Said, presented the invasion plot as a scheme of his own devising, while pressing the British, in words that echo the Smart memorandum, to "encourage their true friends, Turkey and Transjordan, to deal with this sore spot in the Arab world and unify Syria once more." Kirkbride threw cold water on the plan.

Although the British remained "neutral against" Greater Syria throughout 1947, one nonetheless detects a change in their tone. Amid the storms of protest that accompanied King Abdallah's renewed campaign, the Foreign Office debated the merits of issuing a statement against the Greater Syria plan. The embassy in Cairo, though traditionally the core of Foreign Office pan-Arabism, protested:

> Before committing ourselves to such a declaration . . . , we should bear in mind that [it] would strengthen the Egyptian domination of the Arab League—a domination which we have no interest in maintaining so long as Egypt remains hostile to us and the present regime pursues a course of conduct which seems already designed to drive Great Britain not only out of Egypt but out of the whole of the Middle East.[65]

The British remained, in their own minds, neutral, but they had learned once again—as they had previously learned during World War II, particularly at the time of the Rashid Ali coup—that Jordan was the only regime in the Arab world willing to function as the stalking horse of their empire. The pan-Arabists in the Foreign Office, traditionally embarrassed by Greater Syria, were discovering that allies were more useful than enemies; the Egyptians, aware of the support in Baghdad for the scheme, had always feared the Foreign Office would realize this.[66]

As the Mandate's regime in Palestine collapsed, the British discovery and the Egyptian fear, feeding off one another, would significantly influence the course of modern Arab history.

Conclusion: A Grand Strategy in Embryo

In March 1947 the Egyptian government, as a result of domestic pressure to end the Anglo-Egyptian alliance, set itself against the continued presence of British troops on Egyptian soil. In the course of the ensuing year, Egypt and Britain faced off in a regional cold war. In September and October, the British gradually gained the upper hand when the Security Council refused to support the Egyptian demand for the annulment of the 1936 treaty; the position of Cairo deteriorated further when the Americans—remaining aloof not just at the United Nations but in all regards—refrained from taking serious action to alleviate the Egyptian dollar crisis. By far the most serious threat to Cairo, however, issued from the British decisions to draw Iraq and Saudi Arabia into a new defense agreement, and to stand on the sidelines when King Abdallah began to rattle his saber. The new British policy, if carried to its logical conclusion, would have undermined the influence of Cairo in the Arab world—an influence, that is, which otherwise guaranteed the Egyptian state a significant voice in international affairs. It might even have resulted in a reordering of the Fertile Crescent.

The *Wathba*, therefore, shifted the balance of power in favor of Egypt. It took only a few weeks of rioting in Baghdad on behalf of Arab solidarity and complete Iraqi independence to destroy the latest British attempt to revitalize the imperial defense system and to circumvent Egypt. The rioters also succeeded in putting an end to the British effort to detach Saudi Arabia from the Triangle Alliance. While not consciously working for the interests of Egypt, the Iraqi protesters, regardless of their political hue, performed a great service for Cairo.

The same currents of opinion in Baghdad that laid waste to the Portsmouth Treaty also stymied, during the period 1946–1947, the development of stronger ties between Turkey, Iraq, and Jordan. Through their influence in parliament, anti-imperialist and pan-Arab groups succeeded in forcing the Iraqi government to back away from the original, detailed plan for Hashimite unity, and to substitute in its place the anodyne Treaty of Friendship and Brotherhood.[67] The Iraqi opposition, in harmony with Egyptian propaganda, painted King Abdallah as the tool of imperialism, arguing that Iraqi–Jordanian unity would increase British influence in Baghdad. The role that British bases in Transjordan and that Transjordanian troops had played in toppling Rashid Ali in 1941 provided the opposition with a concrete example of the pernicious regional influence of Amman.

The Turco-Iraqi Treaty had, likewise, a strong imperial odor: It too received the criticism, from both the Triangle Alliance and the Iraqi opposition, of being in violation of the Arab League Covenant and of serving the British plot to destroy the Arab League. The Suwaydi government, on whom Nuri al-Said had originally foisted it, found the treaty embarrassing and avoided actively supporting it; Jabir, immediately upon taking office, drove the stalled bill through parliament, displaying a cavalier attitude toward anti-imperialist opinion. Less than a year later the same trait cost him his career.

Despite the absence of strong anti-imperial forces in Jordan, even King Abdallah refrained from moving too close to Turkey. This uncharacteristic display of deference to his opposition arose, no doubt, from the king's desire to court public opinion in Syria—a project that required stressing the authenticity of his Arabism in order to combat the stigma adhering to his close relations with Britain. King Abdallah, therefore, drafted the text of the treaty with great care to insure that none of its provisions would appear to contradict the spirit of Arab solidarity expressed by the Arab League Covenant.[68]

The Iraqi opposition to the Portsmouth Treaty had its roots in the exceedingly complex domestic politics of Iraq, and it would appear that no direct ties had been established between the Iraqi protesters in Baghdad and the Egyptian diplomats in Cairo. Nonetheless, Salih Jabir, King Faruq, and the Foreign Office all agreed that Egypt, Great Britain, and Iraq were linked together within a power triangle. Developments in Anglo-Egyptian relations had a direct and immediate effect on the relations, on the one hand, between the Iraqi regime and its opposition, and, on the other hand, between Baghdad and London.

Well aware of this connection, and of the power that devolved on Cairo as a result of it, the Egyptians actively worked to create a political atmosphere in the Arab world which would be hostile to imperialism and hostile to the interests of the Hashimite regimes, and to foster an environment in which a separate deal between Iraq and Britain would appear as treachery in the eyes of significant groups in Iraqi politics. Since many diverse political groups shared a common aversion to granting the British continued base rights, the Egyptians needed only to raise the possibility of expelling the British in order to create a climate in Iraq that shifted the balance of power in Egypt's favor.

By commanding a majority of the members in the Arab League, which was itself built on the strength of anti-Hashimite feeling in Syria, Lebanon, and Saudi Arabia, the Egyptians were better equipped than the Iraqis and the Jordanians in disguising their parochial interest in ousting the British as a commitment to the broader Arab nationalist values of anti-imperialism and Arab unity. In fact, by dint of Egypt's special place as the linchpin in the structure of imperial defense, their domestic political concerns corresponded directly to the interests of every group in the Middle East that sought to expel Britain from the region. The ideological strength of the anti-imperial message, however, cannot alone explain the cohesion of the Triangle Alliance. Anti-British feeling did not run as deep in Syria and Saudi Arabia as it did in Egypt. Damascus and Riyadh, due to their fear of Hashimite expansion, needed the support of Egypt primarily to balance the power of Iraq and Jordan; however, they shed no tears over the distress that Egyptian policy caused the patron of their enemies.

Ousting the British from the region, and combating the efforts of Turkey and the Hashimite States to form an international pressure group, conspired to increase the importance to Cairo of the Arab League—which is correctly understood not as the representative of the common will of the Arab states but, rather, as the propaganda department of the Triangle Alliance. It was not until February

1948 that a member of the Egyptian elite first acknowledged to the representative of a Western power that Cairo considered the League as the basis for a new order in the region. But a close examination of Egyptian behavior throughout 1947 demonstrates that the organization had already begun to function as an instrument for ordering the Arab world as soon as Cairo decided on a policy designed to terminate the Anglo-Egyptian Alliance.

The Arab-League orientation, therefore, had all the earmarks of a grand strategy: It bound together in one overarching framework the most vital Egyptian policies, both foreign and domestic; it presupposed a set of relationships with all the major actors in the Middle East, Arab and non-Arab alike; and it sought to guide the development of those relations in a manner that would punish the enemies of Egypt and reward her friends. The Arab-League Strategy, therefore, while having its roots in a domestic crisis, took on its precise contours in connection with the deep structures of Middle Eastern politics.

The fundamental interests of Egypt and Great Britain were diametrically opposed. The Egyptians, in order to achieve complete independence—a prerequisite for solving their domestic crisis—had no choice but to seek to expel the British from the entire region. For their part, the British, in order to maintain the status of a Great Power, had no choice but to remain strategically paramount in the Middle East. From this basic divergence flowed all of the other major relationships subsumed under the nascent Arab-League Strategy of Cairo—hostility to Turkey and the Hashimite powers; friendship with the enemies of the Hashimites, namely, Syria and Saudi Arabia; and a desire to bring American power into the Middle East in support of the Triangle Alliance. The need to court the United States, the only power capable of peacefully dismantling the British security system, underscored the importance of becoming the keystone in the arch—a status which, in any case, entailed many benefits.

As a result of the *Wathba*, King Faruq proposed his keystone-in-the-arch thesis to Ambassador Campbell in a triumphal manner. But the very act of making the proposal constituted a tacit acknowledgment that the thesis was faulty—that Egypt, in fact, was not the keystone in the arch. Had the fall of the Iraqi government actually proved the claim, then Cairo could have circumvented London and dealt directly with Washington, just as the British, when they negotiated the Portsmouth Treaty, had attempted to circumvent the Egyptians altogether. Egypt, however, could not in good faith claim to be, in the words of King Faruq, "the nation to whom the others looked for leadership," because Jordan defiantly ridiculed the Egyptian claim to preeminence. King Faruq had no choice but to make his proposal to the British, because only they could apply the leverage necessary to slide Jordan into its designated place as a stone in the arch; only the British, despite their weakness, could place Egypt at the pinnacle of the structure.

After a year of being battered by Cairo, however, London was in no mood to deliver up an ally to an enemy. With just one stone missing, even the strongest arch collapses.

FOUR

Palestine between the Regional Blocs

Lord Moyne's Assassins

When Eliyahu Hakim and Eliyahu Ben-Zuri stood before an Egyptian court for the assassination of Lord Moyne, the British minister of state whom they had gunned down in Cairo in November 1944, they benefited from the aid of very impressive lawyers.[1] Two prominent Egyptians led the defense team: Tawfiq Dus Pasha, a Senator and former minister of communications, and Abd al-Fattah al-Said, a former president of the Court of Cassation, which was the highest legal office in Egypt. The accused, Jews from Palestine (and confessed killers), were indeed fortunate to have procured the services of attorneys with such elevated reputations, especially since the young assassins had shot Lord Moyne while in the service of the Stern Gang, the most extreme Zionist organization.

Although Eliyahu Hakim and Eliyahu Ben-Zuri both received a sentence of death, contemporary observers nonetheless praised the Egyptian lawyers for their efforts. For instance, *Haboker*, a Hebrew daily paper published in Tel Aviv, suggested that the performance of Tawfiq Dus Pasha and Abd al-Fattah al-Said had transformed the trial into one of the greatest moments in legal history:

> Among the sad winds blowing from the banks of the Nile, we can distinguish one fresh wind: The good wind of the Egyptian counsel for the defense. . . . We must praise those advocates who took upon themselves to defend the accused. They were not just official advocates who fulfilled their duty imposed upon them by the law. We could perceive in their words the feeling, the participation in the pain and the thoughts [that are aroused by] every great political trial. It would be no exaggeration to say that the defense in the Cairo trial raised the court to the level of a great court. . . .[2]

The treatment of Jews in Arab courtrooms rarely receives praise in Hebrew newspapers; the Egyptian lawyers won a standing ovation from a demanding audience.

Undoubtedly this loud applause expressed appreciation not for the arguments that the attorneys advanced in defense of the individuals accused of the assassination, but rather for the arguments they advanced in defense of the Zionist movement in general. For the Egyptian lawyers did not waste their time assessing the legal merits of the case against the killers: They staked the fate of their clients on a naked appeal for political sympathy. For instance, Tawfiq Dus Pasha delivered a lecture on the sufferings of the Jewish people in Europe, while his colleague traced for the court the connection between European anti-Semitism and recent developments in Anglo-Zionist relations.[3] Abd al-Fattah al-Said demanded clemency for the accused, arguing that the assassination of Lord Moyne was a forgivable action if considered against the background of the unjust reversals that had characterized British policy toward Zionism. He explained that the British government, by issuing the Balfour Declaration in 1918, had raised Jewish hopes of escaping from oppression in Europe; then, two decades later, London dashed those hopes with the 1939 White Paper, which had restricted Jewish immigration to Palestine. By promising the Jews a National Home and then forbidding them to populate it, the British government, Abd al-Fattah al-Said suggested, simply invited violent attacks against its representatives.

The Egyptian lawyers presented to the court a view of history that they may well have lifted directly from the literature of the Jewish Agency. Wherever they gathered their material, one thing is certain: They did not cull it from the Arabic press. According to popular Arab nationalist perspectives on modern history, the sufferings of the Jews at the hands of the Europeans did not justify Zionist claims to a state in Palestine; what is more, the Balfour Declaration had violated the Palestinian Arabs' right to self-determination. Although the Arab states had, just like the Jewish Agency, tended to oppose the 1939 White Paper, the rationale behind this rejection had nothing in common with Zionist thinking. Whereas the Jews (and the two Egyptian lawyers) railed against the restrictions on Jewish immigration, the Arab states criticized the White Paper for being soft on Zionism, for failing to eliminate it altogether.

The endorsement of a Zionist view of modern history by Tawfiq Dus Pasha and Abd al-Fattah al-Said is all the more striking for its having been designed to sway the opinion of Egyptian judges, who, it seems safe to assume, were not crypto-Zionists.[4] The lawyers cast Zionism in a sympathetic light in order, it would appear, to play on the patriotism of the court. They implicitly invited the judges to draw a direct parallel between the Jewish and Egyptian struggles against British imperialism. Tawfiq Dus Pasha, in particular, developed the theme of the understandable excesses of youth, presenting the killers as decent young men who had been swept up by the violent wind of nationalism. Undoubtedly he assumed that the Egyptian judges would liken the case of Eliyahu Hakim and Eliyahu Ben-Zuri to the many cases of decent young Egyptian men who had also been drawn to commit acts of violence against Britain. In short, the implicit messages that the lawyers sent to the Egyptian judges could not have been simpler: Opposition to the British Empire was not a serious crime; Zionism and Egyptian nationalism were cousins.

Britain's Misfortune, Egypt's Opportunity

That two Egyptians with political reputations to protect chose to champion publicly a Zionist view of history raises serious questions regarding the popular depth of the Egyptian commitment to Palestinian nationalism in the postwar period. The behavior in court of Tawfiq Dus Pasha and Abd al-Fattah al-Said strongly suggests that the principle of anti-imperialism tapped into deeper political emotions in Egypt than did the principle of Arab solidarity. Indeed, much evidence reinforces this assertion. For instance, in late 1946 and early 1947 the considered view of the British Foreign Office held that the Egyptian elite subordinated its Palestine policy to its policy toward the Anglo-Egyptian conflict. An authoritative summary of Foreign Office thinking stated the matter as follows:

> In Egypt, the growing spirit of nationalism is essentially local and Egyptian, rather than Arab, and in normal circumstances, a solution of the Palestine question unfavourable to the Arabs might not arouse strong feeling. There is, however, a strong tendency to support the cause of the Palestine Arabs for prestige reasons, to justify Egypt's claim to be the leading Arab state.... Passions have, moreover, been aroused in Egypt over the protracted treaty negotiations, and unfriendly politicians are ready to exploit for their own purposes any issue which can be turned to the disadvantage of Great Britain. It must be expected that they would seize for this purpose on any unfavourable solution of the Palestine question.[5]

If one were inclined by nature to cast doubt on the views of the Foreign Office, one might argue that the ruling class of Egypt—among whom the British diplomats circulated—had lost touch with new currents of pan-Arabism that were purportedly coursing through the Egyptian body politic. After all, for a decade and a half the Egyptian public, under the influence of groups such as the Muslim Brotherhood, had grown increasingly conscious of the cultural, religious, and political ties that bound Egypt to the other Arab states; this increased awareness of the Arab and Islamic components of Egyptian national identity no doubt had a direct bearing on the popular perception of the Palestine question.[6] Taking this observation as a starting point, one might then spin the line of reasoning out to the conclusion that the Egyptian elite expressed the fossilized views of a decaying generation—the generation of 1919 that had struggled on behalf of Egyptian patriotism rather than Arab nationalism. By contrast, so the argument would proceed, the generation of 1936 marched to the beat of a pan-Arab drummer.

Before endorsing such an understanding of Egyptian attitudes, however, it is worth pausing to consult *The Philosophy of the Revolution*, Gamal Abd al-Nasser's concerted attempt to express to the Egyptian people the political values of the Free Officers. The emergence of Abd al-Nasser from the lower-middle class, and his leadership of the movement that toppled the Pashas, have led many to regard him as the figure most representative of the generation of 1936. Yet when addressing the Egyptian public, he, too, gave precedence to the Anglo-Egyptian conflict over the question of Palestine. Moreover, he, too, drew a direct parallel between the Zionist and Egyptian struggles against Britain.

In the opening pages of his informative tract, Abd al-Nasser stresses at length the narrow Egyptian roots of the Free Officers' movement, which, he claims, emerged from the mainstream of Egyptian patriotism, the sources of which extended back to Urabi Pasha. He and his colleagues, he explains, took the reins of power in order to liberate Egypt from imperialism. Their thinking did not focus on Zionism. He writes:

> It is not true that the revolution started because of the war in Palestine.... We were fighting in Palestine but all our dreams were about Egypt. We aimed our bullets at

the enemy positioned before us in the trenches, but our hearts hovered over our distant homeland, which we had left to the wolves for safe keeping. . . .

In Palestine, Free Officer cells would meet, study, and teach in the trenches and in the command posts.

In Palestine, Sallah Salim, and Zakariya Muhiy al-Din penetrated the siege of Faluja and came to me. We sat without knowing how or when the siege would end, but nonetheless we spoke of nothing but our country and our duty to rescue it.

In Palestine, Kamal al-Din al-Husayn once sat beside me. With a faraway look in his eyes, he said to me in earnest, "Do you know what Ahmad Abd al-Aziz said to me before he died?"

"What did he say?" I asked.

Kamal al-Din al-Husayn, staring into the distance, raised his voice and quoted [the dead man]: "Kamal, listen, the battlefield of the greatest Jihad is in Egypt."

. . . It was not only with friends in Palestine that I discussed the future of our homeland. . . . The enemy also played a role in reminding us of our homeland and its problems.

A few months ago I read some articles written by an Israeli officer named Yohanan [?] Cohen and published in the *Jewish Observer*. In these articles the Jewish officer relates how he met me during talks and contacts concerning the armistice. "The subject that Gamal Abd al-Nasser always raised with me," he states, "was Israel's struggle against the English—how we organized our underground resistance in Palestine and how we succeeded in mobilizing world public opinion behind us in our struggle against them."[7]

In the rhetoric of this passage, Abd al-Nasser employs the refrain "in Palestine" in order to spotlight the Egypt-centered nature of his political thinking. The Free Officers, he explains, though besieged and killed by Jewish forces in distant Palestine, thought exclusively in terms of ousting the British from Egypt. Clearly, Abd al-Nasser presumed that his public expected him to give priority to the liberation of Egypt. In addition, he assumed that his people would applaud his perception of the Zionist campaign against Britain as a model for liberating their homeland.

As evidence of Egyptocentrism, the value of this passage increases when considering that it was written *after* the 1948 war—that is, after the Israeli army had inflicted defeat simultaneously on the Palestinians and the regular Arab armies. Given the pan-Arab nature of the war, Abd al-Nasser, who emerged from the battlefield a hero, had potent material with which to portray his revolution as a movement designed to free all Arabs, not just the Egyptians. He chose, however, to stress the specifically Egyptian concerns of his revolution, which constituted, in his words, "the realization of the great hope that has enchanted the Egyptian people ever since it began, in modern times, to imagine that power could be held in the hands of its own sons."[8]

These views of Abd al-Nasser—not to mention the arguments of the Egyptian defense lawyers and the reports from British diplomats—give us good reason to pause and reconsider the attitude of the Egyptian state toward Palestinian nationalism. To call for such a reappraisal is not to suggest that popular concern for the Palestinian Arabs did not exist in Egypt. Many, no doubt most, Egyptians sympathized with the nationalist aspirations of their fellow Arabs; the Muslim

Brotherhood, among others, certainly advocated a commitment to anti-Zionism. Nevertheless, we must also admit that the Egyptians tended to view the Palestine question through the prism of their own national dilemma. Politics is a parochial profession. In Cairo during the postwar period, the careers of politicians flourished or floundered primarily against the background of one issue: Anglo-Egyptian relations. As a result of this national obsession, the overdetermining attitude of the men who ran the Egyptian state is perhaps best summed up by the dictum, "Britain's misfortune is Egypt's opportunity." Unless we remain keenly aware of this dictum, we can never successfully map the course of Egyptian policy toward Palestine.

Partition

Eliyahu Hakim, Eliyahu Ben-Zuri, and their defense lawyers were not the only Zionists and Egyptians thrown together by the assassination of Lord Moyne. In order to prevent further acts of pro-Zionist violence on Egyptian soil, the Jewish Agency and the Egyptian authorities opened a conduit for the direct exchange of information. On its side of the border, Cairo appointed as it liaison officer an Egyptian police official who remains anonymous in the available documents. By virtue of his regularized contacts with the Zionists, this official quickly found that his role had expanded beyond routine police duties: In no time at all he became an intermediary in triangular negotiations between the British, the Egyptians, and the Zionists.

In August 1946, Eliyahu Sasson, the chief expert on Arab Affairs in the Jewish Agency, made at least two trips to Cairo, where, with the aid of the anonymous policeman, he met with members of the Egyptian political elite.[9] Sasson lobbied the leadership in Cairo in favor of partition as the best basis for a settlement of the Palestine question. For their part, the Egyptians gave the Zionist representative a surprisingly warm welcome: He met with numerous politicians and officials, including, among others, the prime minister, the foreign minister, and the secretary-general of the Arab League. Although neither King Faruq nor his immediate advisors met with Sasson, the palace received reports on the talks and did nothing to scuttle them.[10]

These contacts formed part of the political maneuvering in the weeks prior to the opening of the London Conference on Palestine, to which Ernest Bevin had invited representatives of the Jewish Agency and the Arab States. The framework of the conference perturbed Arab and Jew alike. Without consulting the parties to the conflict, the British government set the agenda to suit itself, announcing that the talks would focus on the Morrison–Grady Plan. The withered fruit of protracted negotiations between London and Washington, the plan envisioned settling the Palestine question by establishing autonomous Arab and Jewish provinces that would operate within the framework of a federal government. Since the Jewish Agency sought to establish an independent state, in all or in part of Palestine, it shunned the conference. For their part, the Arab states accepted the invitation of Ernest Bevin. But they, too, rejected the provincial autonomy scheme, because they opposed granting the Jews communal political rights. On the face of it, then, the gulf between the two sides precluded direct discussions between Cairo and Tel Aviv.

The Jewish Agency, however, suggested something that aroused the keen interest of the Egyptian leadership: A plan for ousting the British from the Suez Canal Zone. During Sasson's talks in Cairo, he advanced the view that the Anglo-Egyptian conflict and the Palestine question were inextricably linked. The British, he said, would remain ensconced in Egypt as long as they had no other place in the Middle East to which they could transfer the bases and facilities located in the Suez Canal Zone. Were it not for the conflict between Arab and Jew, Palestine would present itself as a viable alternative. It, like Egypt, had much to offer British strategists: outlets to both the Mediterranean and the Indian Ocean; supplies of fresh water; port facilities; a developed infrastructure; a close political association to Britain; and proximity to the Suez Canal. Unfortunately, however, the perpetual turmoil there prevented the British from developing the country as a strategic alternative to Egypt. Plus, the possibility of a complete breakdown of order in Palestine gave London yet one more reason to garrison troops in the Canal Zone.

Sasson argued that if a solution acceptable to both Arabs and Jews could be found, then the British could be persuaded to move their bases—that is, to evacuate Egypt completely. He proposed a deal: Cairo would convince the Arab states to accept partition; in return, the Jewish Agency would use its clout in Washington and in London on behalf of the Egyptians. More specifically, the Zionists would persuade the British to transfer the Canal Zone bases to the new Jewish state.

Despite their traditional rejection of partition as a basis for solving the Palestine conflict, the Egyptians responded favorably. To be sure, they explained that their commitments to the other Arab states would complicate the radical reversal of policy that partition entailed. Nonetheless, Abd al-Rahman Azzam, who was in a position to know, felt certain that with the help of London the Egyptians could overcome the opposition of the other Arab states. Sasson reported to the Jewish Agency:

> In his [Azzam's] view there is only one solution and that is: partition. But collective debates and discussions are required in order to arrive at this solution. As the Secretary of the Arab League, he cannot appear before the Arabs as the initiator of this suggestion. His position is very delicate. He is married to seven wives (that is, he is the Secretary of seven Arab states), each one fearing her fellow wife, competing with her and trying to undermine her. He can see fit to support partition on two conditions: If one of the Arab states will find the strength and the courage to take the initiative and to propose the matter at a meeting of the League, and if the British will request that he follow this line.[11]

Azzam Pasha's claim to represent all Arab states notwithstanding, one detects in his two conditions a desire to embarrass the Hashimites: If the British would endorse partition, he implied, and if they would induce the Iraqi and Jordanian governments to incur the onus of selling out the Palestinians, then Egypt would also ratify a compromise with the Zionists.

Sidqi Pasha also expressed support for a solution based on partition. With regard to the views of the prime minister, however, Sasson recorded no mention of concern for the attitudes of the other Arab states. Sidqi Pasha was, first and foremost, an Egyptian patriot. According to Sasson's report, the prime minister "repeatedly stressed that he is a businessman. He is neither pro-Jewish nor pro-Arab. He looks out for the welfare of Egypt. If that dictates Jewish–Arab understanding, so be it."[12] As one would expect from a businessman, Sidqi demanded to know how the Jews would reward his support for partition. The prime minister explained to Sasson that he viewed the Palestine question within the context of Anglo-Egyptian relations:

> Ismail Sidqi . . . understands: The English will not leave Egypt as long as the Palestine question remains unresolved and continues to serve as a source of instability that threatens the entire Arab East; the English hope that Palestine will be a safe haven for the British army in the East.
> Within this framework he is willing to listen to our claims and our demands and to try to help as best he can. But in order to commit himself he must know: How much are we willing to concede? A Jewish state covering all of Palestine is no basis for discussion; partition, a binational state, a federal state—these certainly are. In addition he must know the extent of the aid that we can give him in England and in America toward the success of the Anglo-Egyptian negotiations; he must know the extent of the economic aid that we can give to the Arab world.[13]

Sidqi, like Azzam before him, suggested that the British must come to him and ask for his help in solving the Palestine question. Sasson reported that the prime minister "cannot understand the English. Why don't they request that he intervene? Couldn't we, the Jews, do something in this regard?"[14] Indeed, the Jews jumped at the opportunity.

Acting on the Egyptian suggestion, the Zionists immediately informed the British Foreign Office, at the highest levels, that the Egyptians would, under certain conditions, support partition.[15] In order, no doubt, to lend credence to the Zionist initiative, Sidqi Pasha apparently dispatched the anonymous police official to report discretely to the British on the discussions between the Jewish Agency and the Egyptian leadership.[16] The Foreign Office responded quickly; it rejected any attempt to tie the question of Palestine to the Anglo-Egyptian negotiations. The plan, therefore, died a quick death.

The Consensus Position

From the foundation of the Arab League until 1977 the Egyptian government, along with most other Arab regimes, publicly espoused a commitment to Palestinian self-determination. It is an understatement, however, to characterize the pan-Arab position as an endorsement of Palestinian nationalism. Such a description fails to highlight the uncompromising aspects of the policy, which called for the creation of a Palestinian Arab state with sovereignty over every inch of Palestinian territory. Thus the Arab League rejected the proposals that envisioned the establishment of Jewish and Arab cantons within the framework of a single state; it considered the creation of a federal state of any kind as anathema; and, above all, it branded partition as the worst of many evil plots hatched against the Palestinians by the international community. The consensus position also rejected the right of Jews who had recently immigrated to Palestine to remain in the country. According to the Arab League, the only legitimate solution to the Palestine question called for the establishment of an independent state that would be dominated by the Arab majority. Certainly this Arab state would adopt a tolerant attitude toward Jews as individuals, but it would reduce the number of Jewish citizens to manageable proportions and deny them communal political rights.[17]

This position enjoyed no support from the non-Arab parties to the Palestine conflict. The Zionists, of course, called for the creation of a Jewish state. The Great Powers, in their search for a compromise between the Arab and Jewish positions, proposed, at one time or another, a variety of solutions. However, all of these recognized, to some extent, the communal rights of the Jews in Palestine; all, therefore, met with rejection from the Arab League. When viewed from the point of view of the moderate Zionists and the Western powers, the Arab League position seemed irrational. Arab politics, from this vantage point, appeared rife with a disease called "rejectionism." When, however, approached from the angle of its own premises and not correlated to ideas foreign to it, the consensus position was coherent and principled, though idealistic. It extended the principle of Palestinian self-determination to its logical conclusion: if the Balfour Declaration constituted the theft of national property, the logic ran, then the stolen property must be restored to its rightful owners, the Palestinian people. This attitude, of course, made no concession to the realities of international relations or, for that matter, of Jewish power on the ground. The adherence of the Arab states to it, therefore, placed them in a poor position from which to gain non-Arab allies.

Out of deference to the pure logic of this policy, for the sake of convenience it may be dubbed the Consensus Position on Palestine. In public, Cairo consistently supported it. Behind the scenes, however, the Egyptian state displayed a flexibility that, among the Arab countries, was only matched by the attitude of the Jordanian regime, which actively sought a compromise with the Zionists. It would be wrongheaded to ask which position—the public support for the Consensus Position or the secret willingness to compromise—constituted the true Egyptian attitude. That is, we must avoid the temptation to shed the outer layers in search of the essential core: the Palestine policy of Cairo, like an onion, was composed only of layers. We gain the deepest insight by examining how all the layers fit together.

The willingness of Ismail Sidqi to abandon the Consensus Position arose from the nature of the Insular-Egypt Strategy that drove his foreign policy. Within this framework, Cairo sought ultimately to reach a compromise with London: In return for the withdrawal of imperial troops from the Canal Zone and a guarantee of near neutrality for Egypt, the Egyptian government would allow Britain to continue to play its role as the predominant power in the Middle East.[18] In order to gain leverage over Britain in the short term, however, Cairo used its leading position in the Arab League to impose an anti-British discipline on the Arab states. In order to succeed as the union organizer of the Arab world, the Egyptian government had no choice but to espouse principles that it would ultimately abandon. Cairo preached Arab solidarity today, in order to withdraw from the Arab world tomorrow. It appealed to anti-imperial elements in neighboring states in order to cut a deal with Britain that would leave those states within a British-dominated order. The contradiction, then, between public and private positions on Palestine fit a general pattern that governed Sidqi Pasha's foreign policy.

Although nothing came of the Sasson initiative, it cannot be dismissed as irrelevant to the study of Egyptian foreign policy, for it betrays much regarding the intellectual framework in which the Egyptian elite approached the problem of Palestine.[19] The failure of the proposal does not diminish the significance of Sidqi's willingness to compromise on the Consensus Position. After all, this episode cannot be characterized as a trial balloon launched by a few individuals. Sasson met with officials from every bureaucracy that played a role in foreign policy; the conditional acceptance of partition, therefore, represented, for a time, the covert policy of the Egyptian *state*.

The proposal of the Jewish Agency met with a wide welcome, because it arrived when the attacks of the domestic opposition on Sidqi Pasha had begun to bite. The government saw in the Sasson initiative a possible means for extricating itself from the damaging concessions it had made to Britain: renewing the Anglo-Egyptian Alliance, granting a continuation of base rights on Egyptian soil, and establishing the Joint Defense Board.[20] If Cairo, instead of entering into an ignominious agreement with Britain, could convince London to shift the center of its security system to Palestine, then Sidqi and his associates would place themselves before their own population as the men who had finally ended the British occupation. Realizing the dream that, according to Abd al-Nasser, had enchanted Egyptians for generations would without doubt have been attractive to any Egyptian leader—regardless of the consequences for Palestine.

Given the attractive qualities of the Sasson proposals, why did Prime Minister Sidqi resist approaching the British directly? Why did he and Azzam Pasha both emphasize the need for London to take the initiative with Cairo? Sidqi Pasha, as he insisted to Sasson, thought as a businessman: Every merchant knows that it is better to receive requests than to solicit them.[21] Assigning the Jewish Agency the task of lobbying the British for partition made good negotiating sense, because it maximized the power of Cairo over London. The Egyptians had no cause to waste precious bargaining capital in an effort to change British thinking, especially when the Jewish Agency itself would willingly take on the task. All that was needed from Cairo was a nod to the British affirming that the path to which the Jews were pointing did in fact exist.[22] Moreover, if London needed a hand in getting out of the Palestine swamp, the Egyptians had no intention of running to their aid; the British government would have to beg for help. Thus, a British diplomat summed up Sidqi's attitude as follows: "He does not wish to pull our chestnuts out of the fire in Palestine unless he can get a quid pro quo over the treaty negotiations."[23]

In 1946 the Egyptian government had no interest in making life easy for Britain in Palestine; it is in the light of this elementary fact that we must view the support of Cairo for the Consensus Position. Faithful adherence to the consensus by all Arab governments placed London in an untenable position. On one side, the Zionists were engaged in a violent anti-British rebellion in Palestine; on the other side, the Arab states threatened Britain with retribution if London caved in to Jewish demands. The true popularity of the Consensus Position in the Arab world made it impossible for the British—who aspired to project an image friendly to Arab national aspirations—to force partition on the Palestinians against their will and in open defiance of the Arab League. At the same time, however, the dependence of Britain on the United States, where the Zionists had considerable support, also made it impossible to pound the Jews into submission. As long as the Arab League endorsed the Consensus Position, therefore, the British had no hope of finding an Arab interlocutor. More specifically, the policy of the Arab League blocked King Abdallah from making a separate peace.[24] This situation suited the Egyptian state well--not because it opposed compromise in principle but rather because only Egypt possessed the ability to extricate Britain from the swamp.[25]

In the ideological arena, the commitment of Cairo to the Consensus Position pitted the Egyptians against the Jewish campaign for statehood. In the arena of power politics, however, the reality was not so simple. The Egyptian endorsement of the Consensus Position did not prevent Cairo from recognizing a kind of tacit ally in Zionism. Historians do not tend to regard the Egyptians and the Zionists as united against Britain; indeed, in a formal sense the two groups certainly were not. But it would be a grave mistake to assume that Cairo did not understand that the Zionists, while pursuing their own goals, also provided the Egyptian state with leverage over Britain. The bombings by Jews of British facilities, the attacks against imperial soldiers, the stream of illegal Jewish immigration, and the lobbying of Washington—all these Zionist activities created great difficulty for London and, therefore, considerable opportunity for Cairo. The wide reception that Sasson received proves that the Egyptians understood well the value to them of the Jewish revolt.

Thus, the sympathetic portrayal of Zionism by the Egyptian lawyers who defended the assassins of Lord Moyne should not be seen as a bizarre footnote to the history of the Arab–Israeli conflict: it should, rather, be understood as a by-product of the workings of the balance of power.

Militant Iraq, Moderate Egypt

The failure of the London Conference to bridge the gulf between the Zionist demands for statehood and the Arab support for the Consensus Position forced the British government, in early February 1947, to announce its intention to refer the Palestine question to the General Assembly. This decision set off a long series of international events that, having been narrated countless times, needs no retelling here. Suffice it to say, that, in the debate at the United Nations, the Egyptians, together with the other members of the Arab League, consistently advocated the Consensus Position as the only legitimate solution. Behind this thin veneer of unanimity, however, the Palestine question functioned as an arena of conflict between the Arab states. This is not at all surprising, given that these powers were divided between two regional blocs—the Triangle Alliance and the Turco-Hashimite Entente.

The basic contours of the inter-Arab debate over the Palestine question crystallized at the March 1947 meeting of the Arab League. This was the session, analyzed in the last chapter, during which the Egyptians coerced the Iraqis and the Jordanians into supporting their nationalist demands against Britain. The simultaneous treatment by the League of two such momentous issues made it inevitable that the Egyptian struggle against Britain and her regional allies would find reflection in the inter-Arab debate over Palestine.

As the representatives of the Arab states assembled in March, they faced the problem of how to respond to the announcement by London of its decision to refer the Mandate to the United Nations. Although the British had proclaimed their intentions in February, they had not yet taken any decisive steps. The League, therefore, deliberated over a simple question: Would treatment of the Palestine question by the General Assembly further the cause of the Consensus Solution? The Iraqi foreign minister, Fadil al-Jamali, set the terms of debate: He answered the question with a resounding "no," tabling a resolution proposing that the Arab states should block the British government from referring the future of the Mandate to the United Nations. Dr. al-Jamali argued—correctly as it would turn out—that an appeal to the General Assembly "was undesirable because the pro-Zionist views of the United States would probably prevail. He considered that every possible step should be taken to bring Great Britain and America to direct negotiations with the Arab States."[26] The Iraqi proposal had a solid basis in earlier League decisions, namely, the pseudosecret Bludan resolutions that called for, among other things, ceasing oil shipments to the Western powers if they denied the Arab League satisfaction on the Palestine question. Thus armed with a strong precedent, the Iraqi foreign minister argued that the Arab states must engage the Western powers in direct negotiations. He proposed issuing a stern ultimatum to Washington and London: Either they immediately support the establishment of an independent Arab state in Palestine, or the Arab countries would sever diplomatic and economic relations with them.

The representatives of the other Arab states flatly rejected the proposal, arguing that the Arab League should permit the British to proceed to the United Nations. When word reached Baghdad that the foreign ministers had refused to take direct action to save Palestine, Nuri al-Said immediately convened an extraordinary session of both houses of the Iraqi Parliament. The regent, Abd al-Ilah, also attended the session, thereby investing it with great political significance. Thus, while the Arab foreign ministers were still assembled in Cairo, the Iraqi prime minister appeared before the political elite of his country and reported on the refusal of the Arab League to adopt the Iraqi proposal. He then drove through Parliament a special resolution calling on the Council of the Arab League to adopt a policy strikingly similar to the one that had just been rejected.[27] In his zealous speech, Nuri al-Said stated that if the Arab states again failed to meet his demand, then the Iraqi government would consider itself "absolved of all responsibility" toward them. Tearing a page from the Egyptian book, he broke out bitterly: "Either the League shall save Palestine, or there shall be no League!"[28] Following this performance, al-Jamali received instructions to inform the other foreign ministers of the unanimous vote and of the ultimatum. A short debate ensued in the League Council, but the Arab states again rejected the Iraqi proposal.

This rebuff caused Nuri al-Said no embarrassment, because he fully expected it. The Iraqi government foisted the proposal on the League purely in order to force the Egyptians and the Saudis to demonstrate that their good relations with Washington took precedence over defeating Zionism. Since the press of the Triangle Alliance regularly described the Iraqi regime as the creature of British imperialism, Baghdad now sought to discredit the League in the eyes of the Iraqi political elite by unmasking it as the tool of particularistic Saudi and Egyptian interests. Weakening the status of the League would provide Nuri al-Said and his protégés with greater room to maneuver; it might even pave the way for a pseudoprincipled Iraqi withdrawal from the organization.[29] No doubt Nuri al-Said, as he addressed Parliament, drew in his mind an explicit connection between his speech and the impending negotiations with Britain over the renewal of the Anglo-Iraqi alliance. By discrediting the people who championed the notion of Arab solidarity—such as the Egyptians and the domestic Iraqi pan-Arabists—Nuri and his supporters created a reserve, so to speak, of ideological resources. They anticipated the inevitable claims of the opposition that, by negotiating independently with London, the regime had stabbed the League in the back. Nuri and his protégés now possessed the ready reply that the refusal of the League to act in favor of Palestine proved that it had no legitimate claim to speak for the general Arab interest.

The motives of Nuri al-Said notwithstanding, the refusal by Cairo to endorse his demand for direct action on Palestine certainly did demonstrate that the Egyptian government placed, at that moment, a priority on relations with Washington, where the fate of the Anglo-Egyptian conflict hung in the balance.

Indeed, in the course of 1947 the major developments in the Palestine question unfolded simultaneously with the major developments in the Anglo-Egyptian arena. In late January 1947, al-Nuqrashi Pasha announced his intention to refer the Anglo-Egyptian dispute to the United Nations; two weeks later, on 14 February, the British stated that they, too, would internationalize the Palestine question. In April, London requested the convening of the emergency meeting of the General Assembly that established the United Nations Special Committee on Palestine (UNSCOP); in July, just as UNSCOP began its hearings, Cairo formally appealed to the Security Council regarding the Anglo-Egyptian conflict. On 31 August, UNSCOP recommended the partition of Palestine; in early September, the Security Council began its proceedings on the Anglo-Egyptian conflict. In mid-October the debate over the Egyptian appeal reached an impasse; on 29 November 1947 the General Assembly voted for partition.

This simultaneity forced the Egyptian leaders to view their policy toward Palestine with regard to the effect it would have on their first priority, the attempt to convince the Americans to support the ouster of the British from the Canal Zone. With the question of the Anglo-Egyptian alliance also en route to the United Nations, it would be unfortunate (in Egyptians' eyes) if the deliberations in New York would be overshadowed by the Palestine question, or if pressure developed to link the two problems, Egypt and Palestine, in an undesirable fashion. In the best of all possible worlds, therefore, Cairo undoubtedly preferred to place the Palestine question in a kind of diplomatic holding pattern—at least until after the Americans had reached a verdict on the Egyptian appeal against Britain. Just as Nuri al-Said had expected, Cairo steered the League away from decisive action and toward a policy that supported the legitimacy of the Consensus Position yet required no immediate sacrifices of the Arab states. Thus the Egyptian government avoided making any concession to Zionism while continuing to benefit from the Zionist revolt, which did much to weaken the status of Britain in Washington.

In mid-March 1947, Cairo could confidently expect to keep the fire on a low boil under the British Mandate. At the time of the Arab League Council meeting, no observer could have predicted that in early April London would call for the convening of an *emergency* session of the General Assembly in order to treat the crisis in Palestine. In February, when the British Labor government first proclaimed its intention to refer the Mandate to the United Nations, everyone, including the Attlee cabinet itself, assumed that the next regular session of the General Assembly, which was scheduled to convene in September, would conduct a lengthy and no doubt inconclusive debate.[30] The decision in favor of an emergency session arose suddenly, in response to criticism from the domestic opposition of the Attlee government, which previously had proclaimed its intention to remain in Palestine.[31] For instance, on 25 February, Colonial Secretary Creech-Jones had explained in Parliament that "we are not going to the United Nations to surrender the Mandate. We are going to the United Nations setting out the problem and asking for their advice. . . . If the Mandate cannot be administered in its present form we are asking how it can be amended."[32] According to its own understanding of its policy, then, the British government sought to restructure the Mandate, not to surrender it.

If the attitude of the Foreign Office is any indication, then the relative moderation of Cairo served it well in its relations with the Great Powers. Abd al-Rahman Azzam's role in restraining Baghdad struck some in London as a pro-British stance; after all, Cairo had actively supported the decision of Britain to refer Palestine to the United Nations. By dampening the ardor of Iraq, the secretary-general of the Arab League won the heart, in particular, of Harold Beeley, the chief architect of British policy toward Palestine. Beeley defended Azzam Pasha against his detractors in the Foreign Office. As shown in the last chapter, many in London considered the secretary-general of the Arab League to be anti-British—with good reason, since he had just orchestrated the new League policy that demanded the immediate and unconditional withdrawal of British troops from Egypt and the Sudan. During the debate over the merits of deposing the secretary-general, however, Beeley described Azzam as "impulsive and volatile" yet fundamentally friendly. "I am not convinced," he wrote, "that his mind is, at present, set in an anti-British mould."[33] The Egyptian effort to save the Western powers from economic sanctions undoubtedly had a similarly beneficial effect on thinking in Washington, where opinion mattered most to Cairo.

In all of the anxiety surrounding the Iraqi call for an activist policy, officials such as Beeley failed to notice a slight but significant shift in the policy of the Arab League toward Palestine. In March 1947, for the first time the League Council called on Britain to quit Palestine. The following month, it reaffirmed this policy at an extraordinary session in Damascus, where it demanded "the independence of Palestine, the abolition of the Mandate, and the immediate prohibition of [Jewish] immigration."[34] Although the Arab states had traditionally envisioned that, at some point, Britain would grant the country independence, they had avoided demanding an immediate withdrawal. This new policy, of course, ran parallel to the call for Britain to quit Egypt and the Sudan. It dovetailed, therefore, with the Egyptian attempt to convince the Americans to create a new system of regional defense. The perceptions of Harold Beeley notwithstanding, the policy of the Egyptian government toward British power everywhere in the Middle East expressed a consistent hostility to the predominant position of the Empire. This consistency did not arise by chance: When representatives of the Triangle Alliance argued down al-Jamali's proposal to block the British from placing the Palestine question before the General Assembly, they advanced the reasoning that "it would be illogical for the Arab states to oppose the reference of the Palestine problem to the United Nations at a time when Egypt was appealing to that organisation against Great Britain."[35]

The Jordanian Threat

Because the Mandate in Palestine began to crumble during a period of cold war between Cairo and London, the Triangle Alliance faced the threat of Britain using the disorder in Palestine as an opportunity for extending the power of the Turco-Hashimite Entente. The basic scenario ran as follows: A deal might be struck, along the lines of the Peel Commission Report of 1937, whereby Jordan and the new Jewish state would partition Palestine. The regional partners to this agreement would each accord base rights to the British; each would suppress Palestinian nationalism in its own territory. As the Egyptians knew from their own negotiations with the Zionists, the Jewish state would not, in principle, be opposed to granting the British strategic facilities on its territory. Thus Palestine, when partitioned between Jordan and the Jewish Agency, would cease to function as a great generator of anti-imperial forces. Moreover, Cairo, Riyadh, and Damascus also had to ask themselves what attitude the new Tel-Aviv–Amman axis would adopt toward the issue of Greater Syria. Would the partition of Palestine simply constitute the first stage in a radical Hashimite reorganization of the Fertile Crescent?

King Abdallah, for one, certainly had such a plan in mind. In August 1946, he also met with Eliyahu Sasson. Amman, like Cairo, supported partition; by way of contrast, however, it supported the kind of partition that would strengthen the Turco-Hashimite Entente. Sasson reported home:

> In the course of the conversation, the Emir revealed that the Iraqis had a hand in creating and formulating the proposed "Federal Plan" [the Morrison–Grady Plan that Bevin made the basis for discussion at the upcoming London Conference]. He himself prefers partition and attaching the Arab part to Transjordan. . . . I asked him to go into details. He requested that I not reveal them to anyone but our policy makers. Then he launched into it, saying that he aspires to expand the borders of Transjordan and to create a single Hashimite Kingdom, great and powerful, that will ally with Britain and Turkey and guard the English line of defense in the East. His plan is to be carried out in several stages: (a) partition of Palestine and attaching the Arab part to Transjordan; (b) attaching Syria to Transjordan; (c) uniting the expanded Transjordan in a federation with Iraq; (d) uniting the Jewish part of Palestine in the federation or in an alliance with the Transjordanian-Iraqi federation.
>
> With regard to Lebanon—she will be given the choice of joining the bloc or remaining on her own.
>
> When I asked whether England knows about this plan and agrees to it, the Emir responded that, in the past, he and the Iraqis had discussed the plan with the English. But the British believe that it is best to postpone these discussions until after solving the Palestine question on the basis of the "Federal Plan." They have their reasons: They are taking into consideration the position of the rest of the Arab states. They are not interested at this moment in allowing the Saudi–Hashimite, or the Egyptian–Hashimite disputes to rise up and confuse matters even more in the Arab East. . . . [36]

Although King Abdallah requested that Sasson keep his blueprint for a new order secret, it was taken as axiomatic in Arab politics that the Jordanians and Iraqis were conspiring to cut a deal with the Jews in order to create a Greater Syrian Federation under the Hashimite monarchy. Consider, for instance, the demand by Baghdad to present the Western powers with an ultimatum over Palestine. Iraqis who sympathized with the Triangle Alliance did not regard Nuri al-Said's dramatic speech before the special session of Parliament as a sign of zealous commitment to Palestinian rights. They suspected, rather, that the Greater Syria Project lurked somewhere in the shadows. For instance, after the Iraqi demand for immediate action on Palestine, Taha al-Hashimi, an ex-Iraqi prime minister, recorded in his diary the interpretation of events given to him by a friend, a certain Ali Mumtaz:

> Apparently this emergency meeting, the secret session, the appearance of the regent in the Parliament and the adopting of extraordinary resolutions . . . were all part of a stratagem decided upon between King Abdallah and the Regent of Iraq. This appears to be the case because the president of King Abdallah's Court, followed by his palace manager, recently came to Iraq. After attaining the consent of the British, they rushed to get the decision [from the League regarding the issuance of an ultimatum to the Great Powers over Palestine], believing that Ibn Saud would not agree to cut relations with the United States. In that case, Iraq would be absolved from responsibility from the decisions of the League. A gap would, therefore, appear: Iraq and Jordan would withdraw from the League. Then the air would be

purified for Abdallah, and he would use Iraq to further his ambitions: He would proceed with his plan to stir things up in Syria and obtain the [Syrian] crown that he covets.[37]

Ali Mumtaz's understanding of King Abdallah's purportedly secret plan is accurate—so accurate that, with nothing else to go by, one might assume that he had accompanied Sasson to discuss partition with the Jordanian monarch.

While Ali Mumtaz's appraisal of Jordanian politics is solid, the remaining components of his interpretation resemble, on the face of it, the conspiratorial delusions of a paranoid mind. The appearance is misleading. In fact, a cogent power-political logic informs his thinking. In addition to the reasons recorded in the diary entry for assuming a conspiracy between Amman and Baghdad, Ali Mumtaz's understanding of events was undoubtedly influenced by the recent rise in tension between Jordan and Syria, and by the behavior of Amman during the proceedings of the Arab League. Just prior to the convening of the League Council, relations between Syria and Jordan had deteriorated to the extent that Damascus broke off diplomatic relations, in retaliation for the continued agitation by King Abdallah for the unification of the two countries. Then, while the Arab states were debating whether to block the referral of the Palestine question to the United Nations, the Jordanian monarch claimed for the Jordanian army, on the basis of his proximity to the Zionist threat, the right of independent action—independent not just of the United Nations, of which Jordan was not a member, but of the Arab League as well.[38] Thus while Nuri al-Said was proclaiming "Either the League shall save Palestine, or there shall be no League!" his ally in Amman was proclaiming that the authority of the Arab League did not extend to the actions of his army. No doubt this twin attack on the legitimacy of the Arab League, combined with the hint of military action, struck Ali Mumtaz as a signal that Iraq and Jordan intended to unleash the forces of King Abdallah on Syria.

The subsequent behavior of Nuri al-Said indicates that when he belittled the Arab League for its inaction over Palestine he did, in fact, intend to pave the way for the reorganization of the Fertile Crescent. Chapter 3 already discussed how in April 1947—only three weeks after his speech before Parliament—he traveled to Amman and urged King Abdallah to create a pretext for invading Syria. He proposed, it will be recalled, that the Iraqis and the Jordanians should stir up the Euphrates tribes and then, while intervening to restore order, occupy Damascus and proclaim Abdallah King of Greater Syria.[39] To be sure, these actions, by taking place after Nuri al-Said's ultimatum to the League, certainly do not prove Ali Mumtaz's claim that Amman and Baghdad colluded *before* Nuri presented his ulitmatum to the League. The British archives, however, do contain evidence that strongly buttresses this assertion as well.[40]

The Triangle Alliance, then, faced the very real threat that Amman, in collusion with Baghdad, would exploit the Palestine question so that Jordan might annex parts or all of Palestine and Syria. Fortunately for Cairo, Riyadh, and Damascus, the British, as King Abdallah had explained to Sasson, did not wish to antagonize the Arab League. Indeed, London thwarted the plot by Nuri al-Said to occupy Syria. This British component of the Greater Syria equation did not go unnoticed by the enemies of Hashimite expansionism. For instance, Taha al-Hashimi, in contrast to his friend Ali Mumtaz, did not believe that Nuri al-Said's speech signaled the imminent march on Damascus of the Arab Legion—not because he imputed different motives to Amman and Baghdad, but rather because all the pieces necessary for the success of the Greater Syria Project had not, in his eyes, fallen into alignment:

> With regard to the claim that Nuri is hostile to the League, that is a certainty: He is not able to withstand the criticism of him in the Egyptian and Syrian newspapers, nor the appearance on the scene of [the secretary-general of the Arab League Abd al-Rahman] Azzam. With regard to Abdallah, he is waiting for an opportunity to destroy the League. He already spoke frankly to a magazine correspondent who asked him his opinion of the League. His answer came after thinking for a long time. Abdallah made a gesture of disdain with his hand and said: "The League is the plaything of Mr. Eden and of al-Nahhas, a game with which past foreign ministers have amused themselves, a pretext for throwing parties, for organizing banquets at which they eat tasty food."
>
> But Ali Mumtaz was rash in his conclusions, as if the matter had already been decided—as if the League had been destroyed, the English supported its destruction, Abdallah would occupy Syria by the force of his army, and so on, and so forth.[41]

Thus the Hashimite threat to Palestine and Syria, though very real, nonetheless lay dormant. In March 1947, when Taha al-Hashimi penned this entry in his diary, nobody knew that on 4 April London would call for an emergency session of the General Assembly: nobody knew, that is, that the Mandate would soon come crashing to the ground. Naturally, then, as it collapsed, and a power vacuum developed in Palestine, fear of Jordanian expansionism would seize the opponents of King Abdallah.

Moral Authority

When Cairo and Baghdad locked horns at the Arab League in March 1947, the Egyptians demonstrated a striking advantage over the Iraqis in the arena of ideological battle. When al-Nuqrashi, with the loyal aid of Azzam Pasha, captured the moral high ground of anti-imperialism, he forced Nuri al-Said to endorse an uncompromisingly anti-British policy that furthered the interests of Cairo but manifestly harmed the interests of the Hashimite regimes. By contrast, when Nuri al-Said captured the moral high ground of anti-Zionism, the Egyptians shrugged off the Iraqi ultimatum. Together with their Syrian and Saudi allies, the Egyptians refused to adopt a forward policy on Palestine; moreover, this rejection entailed no political penalty. This imbalance, of course, resulted from the presence inside Iraq of powerful groups that supported the policies of the Arab League over the policies of their own government. In 1947 there existed no Egyptian equivalent of Taha al-Hashimi. Whereas he, an ex-Iraqi prime minister, would write of Nuri al-Said's inability "to withstand the criticism . . . in the Egyptian and Syrian newspapers," no commentator in Cairo would ever have discussed the domestic political damage done to, say, al-Nuqrashi Pasha as a result of attacks on him in *foreign* newspapers. In short, the Egyptian political system spun on its own axis.

Moreover, the Egyptians derived great advantage in inter-Arab relations from the authenticity of their anti-imperial politics. They genuinely sought to oust the British from the Canal Zone, if not the region, and the call to send the imperialists home had a resonance that reverberated everywhere in the Arab world. Although anti-Zionism certainly struck a resounding chord in Arab political culture, the Iraqi demand for an aggressive policy on Palestine appeared, as Taha al-Hashimi's diary indicates, as a ruse. Perceptive observers regarded it as a manifest attempt by Nuri al-Said to strike back at the Egyptians, precisely because their anti-imperialism punished him with devastating effect. In addition, the Iraqi state had close dynastic relations with King Abdallah, who was known to be hostile to the Consensus Position. Consequently, the Iraqi policy inspired little conviction even in those charged with conducting it. For instance, when the other Arab foreign ministers rejected the demand to hand the Western powers an ultimatum over Palestine, the Iraqi foreign minister only put up a halfhearted defense of the proposal. Dr. Fadil Jamali, according to the Jordanian representative at the session, "finally admitted defeat and made it clear that his personal feeling on the subject did not coincide with his instructions."[42]

Thus by dint of its ideological resources and its domination of the majority bloc in the Arab League, the Egyptian government wielded considerable leverage over Baghdad while remaining impervious to Iraqi counterattacks. The ability of Cairo to harass Nuri al-Said, however, did not give the Triangle Alliance a decisive advantage over the Turco-Hashimite Entente, because the Egyptian ideological weaponry did little damage to King Abdallah. In contrast to Iraq, Jordan harbored few pan-Arab and anti-imperial constituencies to which the Egyptian leadership and the Arab League might have appealed. A comparison of the politics of treaty revision in, on the one hand, Jordan and, on the other, Iraq and Egypt demonstrates the point. Whereas angry mobs confronted both Salih Jabir and Ismail Sidqi when they proposed to renew their respective alliances with Britain, King Abdallah negotiated the Anglo-Jordanian Treaty of 1946 with remarkable ease.[43]

Jordan, quite literally, provided no fertile soil for the cultivation of political opposition. In socioeconomic terms, the East Bank of the river Jordan, with the exception of the Ajlun, may fruitfully be conceptualized as the northern extension of Arabia rather than the southern extension of Syria. With little land suitable for farming, Jordan, in contrast to Iraq and Egypt, produced no latifundia and, therefore, no class of great landowners, no social distinctions that bred political resentment. Tribal egalitarianism rather than class resentment informed the attitudes of the common citizen toward the political elite. Reporting on this subject, Alec Kirkbride, who was fluent in Arabic and who had been deeply involved in Jordanian politics for thirty years, observed that "while there are good and bad years, generally speaking everyone prospers or suffers together."[44]

The Jordanian political system, then, was to an extent sealed from the influence of the Triangle Alliance. It did not, however, spin on its own axis: Britain had influence over Amman. The Arab Legion, of course, constituted the greatest conduit for this influence; British soldiers dominated its officer corps, and the British government paid for it, to the extent that no revenue raised in Jordan went to the Jordanian army. As a result of these close ties, however, the other Arab states held London accountable for the actions of the Arab Legion. Since the Foreign Office strove to formulate a regional defense policy acceptable to all Arab states, the British restrained King Abdallah in his aspiration to extend Jordanian sovereignty over Syria. The Triangle Alliance's opposition to the expansion of Jordan did, therefore, make itself felt in Amman, albeit indirectly.

But because the Mandate in Palestine faltered during a period of Anglo-Egyptian conflict, the absence of Egyptian influence in Amman combined with the abundance of British influence to precipitate a severe threat to the Triangle Alliance: the Greater Syria Project. One might assume that, since he was a political anachronism, King Abdallah had no following in Syria. This, however, was not the case; the Jordanian monarch did, in fact, benefit from the support of a number of politically significant groups in Damascus. But to quibble over the extent of the support that King Abdallah enjoyed is to miss the point. In the final analysis the Hashimite threat to Syria was based on military power. Recent history had conspired to leave the Triangle Alliance little defense against Hashimite expansionism—the legacy of French rule had insured that the Syrian army was simply no match for the Arab Legion. Under the Mandate, the authorities had filled the ranks of the army with soldiers drawn from the communities of compact minorities. As a consequence, when the Sunni notables of Damascus took power from the French, they tended to distrust their own military. Thus, partially from fear of sowing the seeds of their own destruction, partially from lack of resources, they neglected their armed forces.[45] When viewed from the angle of Cairo, the weakness of Shukri al-Quwatli's regime created a rather absurd situation: Jordan, a desert kingdom containing a population perhaps one-thirtieth the size of Egypt, possessed a fighting force capable of crippling the Triangle Alliance by annexing Syria. The threat, however, was no less real for being absurd.

The veteran Syrian politician Khalid al-Azm tells a story in his memoirs that epitomizes the Syrian dilemma. At 2:00 in the morning on the night of the coup d'état led by Husni al-Zaim, soldiers burst into al-Azm's house, rousted him from his bed, bundled him into a car, and, without a word of explanation, whisked him away to the headquarters of the military police. After marching him inside the building, an officer gave al-Azm a cigarette and locked him alone in a room. Having been dragged around in the darkness without his glasses, al-Azm suffered confusion. Now, however:

> the cigarette smoke influenced my thinking and my grasp of matters. I began to think clearly. For I had believed, prior to my entrance into the military police headquarters, that the officer was a Jordanian, because his headgear looked just like a Faisal cap. I thought that King Abdallah had attacked Damascus with his soldiers and occupied it.[46]

Thus, the Syrian leadership lived with the sense that, at any minute, they might fall prey to a Jordanian blitzkrieg.

As the Palestine Mandate came to an end, two Arab blocs contested the right to determine the position of the Arab side in the conflict with Zionism. One bloc, the Triangle Alliance, wielded tremendous moral authority by virtue of its ability to project its interests in terms of core nationalist values: Arab unity, anti-imperialism, and the Consensus Position on Palestine. The other bloc, composed of the Arab members of the Turco-Hashimite Entente, possessed limited ideological resources but, by way of compensation, had powerful friends and controlled an efficient army—an army, moreover, that was already in Palestine, where it supported the British forces.

The Plan to Buy the Arab Legion

The Egyptians first bent their minds around the problem posed by King Abdallah's army in October 1947, just after the announcement by the British of their plans to abandon the Mandate. Freshly returned from the United States, al-Nuqrashi Pasha attended a meeting of the Council of the Arab League in Lebanon, where the representatives of the Arab states gathered to study the military dimension of the Palestine problem. A committee of experts, appointed by the Arab League Secretariat, presented a report stating that the Jews had amassed considerable power in Palestine—so much power that the defeat of Zionism would require action by the regular militaries of the Arab states.[47]

After the Arab representatives received this depressing news, al-Nuqrashi Pasha dropped another bombshell. As he later described it himself, he explained to the representatives of the Arab states that "Egypt is in the midst of a conflict with Great Britain, and the soldiers of Britain are still stationed on her soil. She cannot, therefore, become engaged in any military entanglement as long as that situation persists."[48] However, the prime minister continued, the inability of Egypt to commit troops to Palestine did not mean that the Arab cause was lost. The Egyptian army would not participate in a war against Zionism, but there did exist another force that could save the Palestinians: the Jordanian army. The Arab Legion, al-Nuqrashi explained, had much to offer the Arabs: For one thing, it was already serving in Palestine, where, he said, "it is aiding the English in preserving order. This army is well-trained, well-armed, and experienced. Its bravery is common knowledge." Given this state of affairs, the Egyptian prime minister proposed to the members of the Arab League that, in the light of Egyptian non-intervention, the League itself should assume from Britain the total cost of maintaining the Jordanian army, which then could function as the guardian of Palestine on behalf of the Arab League.

Al-Nuqrashi's plan had obvious attractions to the Triangle Alliance. Immediately, the Arab Legion would be transformed from a tool of British imperialism into the expeditionary force of the Arab League. Thus the scheme suggested a means of diminishing the influence of Britain over the Jordanian army. If Azzam Pasha were to take hold of the purse strings of the Jordanian army, King Abdallah would become accountable to the Arab consensus. He would, that is, be charged with implementing the Consensus Solution to the Palestine problem. In one swift move the influence of Cairo in the Palestine conflict would be secure; the threat of the Greater Syria Project would disappear; the influence of the British in the Middle East would diminish; and the domination of the Triangle Alliance over all territorial changes would be guaranteed.

The proposal, however, caused considerable consternation in Damascus, where it seemed like a silly fantasy. Taha al-Hashimi recorded in his diary the following discussion on the subject with the Syrian prime minister, Shukri al-Quwatli:

> Then I told [Shukri al-Quwatli] what Azzam had said to me about Egypt being ready to pay a subsidy to Transjordan if Abdallah would break with the British. Shukri responded: "It is not Egypt alone that will pay the subsidy; rather, the idea is that the Arab states [collectively] will assume payment of the subsidy. Al-Nuqrashi came to Syria, and he met with me while holding in his hand the draft of an agreed statement on the matter, which he asked me to sign. I did not agree to it. I said that the Jordanian army is an English army, subject to the authority of England alone. Were the Arabs to purchase this army with money, they would be buying nothing but an army that is English in its heart and soul. Abdallah says that the English pay him a subsidy per year of 2,300,000 pounds sterling, while he demands [from us] 3,000,000 pounds—that is, [even] more than the English support. Surely all that this means is that he will use the extra money on the army, the subsidy, and on his efforts to establish Greater Syria. Furthermore, the English are determined to leave Palestine, and they will transfer their bases to Transjordan. This army, therefore, will come under their command; it will budge only according to their will." In the end, the plan failed—the plan of the Arab governments to buy the Jordanian army.[49]

It is a common occurrence in international affairs for states to extend aid to allies, but as the Syrian prime minister lectured, they rarely work to expand the war-potential of their rivals. The seeming failure of the Egyptian prime minister to remember that success in politics springs from supporting friends and punishing enemies might prompt us to view the plan to buy the Arab Legion as an indication of Egyptian naiveté concerning the depth of antagonism between Syria and Jordan. Indeed, the exasperated tone of the Syrian prime minister certainly lends credence to such an interpretation.

It would, however, be irresponsible for the historian to assume ignorance on the part of the Egyptian leadership. After all, Cairo had been deeply involved in Arab affairs for years. Some insight into the seriousness of the thinking that informed this proposal can be gained by considering an episode that took place some nine years after Shukri al-Quwatli scuttled this Egyptian initiative. In 1956, the Egyptian, Syrian, and Saudi governments did, in fact, succeed in driving a wedge between Amman and London—precisely by proposing to buy the Arab Legion from Britain. In January and February of that year, when the question of Jordanian participation in the Baghdad Pact stood on the inter-Arab agenda, the Triangle Alliance, which opposed the pact, announced over the radio its intention to assume from Britain payment for the Jordanian army. Cairo, Riyadh, and Damascus, of course, presented their offer as a magnanimous gesture of Arab solidarity designed to release Amman from dependence on the imperialists. This proposal, aimed at exciting the imagination of the Palestinian refugees who now populated Jordan, embarrassed Amman. It placed King Husayn in the position of having to choose publicly between the call to Arab solidarity and fidelity to Britain. As a result of this pressure, the Hashimite monarch, seeking to prove that he was no puppet of London, summarily dismissed Glubb Pasha and the other British officers in the Legion. Without doubt, the same lines of thought that gave rise to the proposal in 1956 undoubtedly inspired the unsuccessful plan of 1947.

Although the scheme to buy the Arab Legion had failed, Cairo did not abandon the basic assumption that capturing the high ground of pan-Arab solidarity provided the key to containing Jordan. Faced with no means of establishing direct control over the Jordanian army, the Egyptians fell back on the Arab League Secretariat as the second best instrument for extending the authority of Cairo over Amman. Some three weeks after al-Nuqrashi Pasha attempted to sell his plan to the Syrians, Azzam Pasha traveled to Jordan. In the wake of the trip, he bragged to friends about his success at subduing King Abdallah:

> Concerning the chant about Greater Syria that issues now and then from Abdallah, Azzam believes that were it not for the supportive position of the Iraqis, Abdallah would not dare to raise the matter. When he went to him a few days ago, Azzam sought to win him over. Thus Azzam let Abdallah talk, all the while encouraging him by saying "you're right, and time will guarantee the implementation [Greater Syria], but the Palestine problem takes precedence over every other problem; we must abandon all that until after we settle the Palestine question." At that point Abdallah asked him, "What, then, will be the fate of Palestine?" [i.e., "Who will rule Palestine?"] Azzam said to him, "Saladin's kingdom came to an end after he saved Palestine from the Crusaders, but his name has remained glorious for a thousand years. Kingship does not endure, but one's name lives on forever." And with that Azzam avoided committing himself. When Abdallah asked who would be entrusted with the General Command, Azzam said to him, "This is the last thing that we have to think about. It would be inappropriate now to debate the matter or raise the issue." Then Abdallah presented him with a note containing several articles. Azzam took it, read it, and told Abdallah that it pleased him. Azzam encouraged Abdallah to join with the Arab governments in the Jihad and in saving Palestine, claiming falsely that Egypt would extend economic aid to the army.[50]

Thus Cairo persisted in its policy of attempting to co-opt King Abdallah, to rope him into a pan-Arab alliance that would harness the power of his military to the policies of the Arab League while simultaneously eviscerating his Greater Syria project.

It would seem that the pleasing note King Abdallah passed to the secretary-general contained a promise to desist from agitation on behalf of Syrian unification. On 3 November 1947, at the very moment when the secretary-general of the Arab League was regaling his friends with this account of his trip to Amman, King Abdallah was delivering a speech. In it he stated that the Palestine problem took precedence over all other matters, including the question of Greater Syria.[51] This pronouncement, coming on the heels of the visit by the secretary-general, revealed the inability of King Abdallah to maintain freedom of action from the Arab League. It represented, therefore, a significant shift in the balance of power away from Amman and toward Cairo. After all, only two months before this meeting the Jordanian monarch had released a manifesto inviting the represen- tatives from the constituent parts of Greater Syria to convene a conference in order to draft the constitution for a federal government. The manifesto, which propelled the perpetually bad relations between Amman and Damascus to an all- time low, avowed that Jordan would never cease to work for a unified Arab state.[52] In his own mind, no doubt, King Abdallah had not renounced his aspirations. Certainly, however, he had set them aside. Even worse, from his point of view, was that every political observer in the region had seen him retreat under pressure from the Arab League. King Abdallah had been disciplined.

The balance did shift in favor of Egypt, yet the Jordanian reversal did not signal total subservience to Cairo. Amman conceded nothing in connection with two crucial questions: "What should be the political goal of military action?", and "Who should command the Arab armies?" When King Abdallah addressed the issue of unification between Palestine and Jordan, the secretary-general, through his reference to Saladin, signaled the complete rejection of the Jordanian plan. But in view of the Jordanian army's independence from the Arab League, it would remain to be seen whether Azzam Pasha, who had no military might behind him, would have the power to impose his will on King Abdallah. Given the Syrian refusal to buy the Arab Legion—a proposal that implied the estab- lishment of a unified Arab command—Azzam had no pretext for demanding control of the Jordanian military. The secretary-general temporized when King Abdallah, coveting the role of Supreme Commander, asked who should lead the unified Arab forces. Thus, though certainly weakened by the visit of Azzam, King Abdallah was still the proud owner of the Jordanian army. This ownership would guarantee Amman an important say in whatever political settlement followed Arab military action in Palestine.

War in Palestine: Syrian Fears

The vote by the United Nations on 29 November 1947 to partition Palestine ignited a civil war between the Jewish and Arab inhabitants of the country. This violence injected urgency into the debate among the Arab governments over the best means of saving the Palestinian Arabs. The basic tenets of the Consensus Position monopolized the terms of this debate. Although the language of Arab consensus constituted the only medium in which the Arab states justified their actions, it did not constitute the only factor (or even the dominant factor) that actually determined their policies. After all, the question, "What political au- thority should replace the British Mandate in Palestine?" had momentous im- plications for every regime. No leader could have answered this question without first considering a number of issues other than the dictates of ideology. Of these, by far the most significant was the struggle between the Triangle Alliance and the Turco-Hashimite Entente. Since the contest between these two blocs struck at the security of every Arab regime, no leader adopted a policy toward Palestine without first evaluating the effect it would have on the balance of power in the Middle East as a whole. As a result, therefore, the shape of the conflict within Palestine itself was, to a significant degree, molded by the conflict between the two regional blocs.

When, in early December, delegates assembled in Cairo to attend a meeting of the Arab League, they faced the immediate problem of extending aid to the Palestinians. The Triangle Alliance, in particular, found itself in a quandary: It had scant military resources to devote to the struggle against Zionism. Cairo, with a view to internal unrest and the Anglo-Egyptian conflict, still refused to commit its regular troops to Palestine. For its part, Riyadh had few troops to send, and was in any case separated from the battlefield by Jordan. Only Damascus possessed some limited means for intervention, but its military was no match for that of Jordan, much less the combined power of both Hashimite armies. Given the military advantage enjoyed by the Arab Legion, units of which were already stationed in Palestine, it should have been no surprise that Amman argued against guerrilla warfare and in favor of saving Palestine with regular armies. In addition, the Jordanian government advocated postponing intervention until after the expiration of the Mandate on 15 May, when the British military presence would no longer restrain the Arab states. In other words, in the eyes of Amman the best settlement of the problem was a solution that would almost inevitably result in the aggrandizement of Jordan.

Notwithstanding the obvious self-interest that colored the Jordanian reasoning, the proposal did carry the force of logic. Even had all Arab states been willing to intervene directly in Palestine, no leader could contemplate the deployment of his regular army prior to 15 May. Such a course of action would have provoked a lethal response from the retreating British forces, who remained responsible to the United Nations for keeping order in Palestine. Under the circumstances, then, it made sense—at least in theory—to preserve resources until the international political context would permit a coordinated Arab occupation. By contrast, Hajj Amin al-Husayni, distrustful of Jordanian intentions, called on the Arab states for immediate support of a purely Palestinian effort to defeat Zionism.

The Arab League, being dominated by the Triangle Alliance, rejected the Jordanian position. At the same time, however, it stopped short of wholeheartedly endorsing the Mufti's program, which it preferred to tailor to the interests of Cairo, Riyadh, and Damascus. The League somehow arrived at a two-pronged strategy. On the diplomatic level, the League worked between December and April to compel the international community to reverse the decision to create a Jewish state. This effort would actually enjoy considerable success: It produced the startling—though ultimately disappointing—retreat from the policy of partition by the American government, which became suddenly fearful of losing the support of the Arab world in the Cold War.[53]

In the military arena, under pressure from the Syrian government, the League extended aid to the Palestinians by organizing a force of irregulars. The League Secretariat formed a special military commission that directed a training camp for volunteers at Qatana, twelve miles southwest of Damascus; it dubbed the new force the Army of Liberation.[54] After a short period of instruction, the irregulars stole into Palestine, where they harassed Jewish settlements and disrupted lines of communication. Infiltration began seriously in mid-January; by early March, Fawzi al-Qawuqji, the commander of the army, had established a field head-quarters in the Nablus region.

On the face of it, the Army of Liberation was a pan-Arab force in spirit as well as composition. It presented itself before the world as the institutional expression of the collective Arab resolve to defeat Zionism. Indeed, the rank and file, though dominated in numbers by Syrians and Iraqis, volunteered from a variety of Arab countries. Moreover, the special military commission also projected an image of Arab unity: Being led by two Iraqis (Taha al-Hashimi, a former prime minister, and Ismail Safwat, a general), it suggested by its very composition that, in the face of the Zionist threat, the al-Quwatli regime and Baghdad had overcome the bitterness that separated Syrian republicans and Hashimite royalists.

These appearances, however, were illusory. The political will to establish the Army of Liberation came, primarily, from the Syrian government and, second-arily, from its Saudi and Egyptian allies; in the final analysis it served the interests of the Triangle Alliance. A look beneath the surface reveals machinery made exclusively in Damascus: for instance, Fawzi al-Qawuqji was himself a Syrian; the office of Taha al-Hashimi was located in the Syrian Ministry of Defense; the force had very close, if not organic, links to the Syrian army.[55] True, the Iraqi presence was tangible. The prevalence of Iraqi personnel, however, did not, in the end, dilute the Syrian substance of the project. Although Damascus and Baghdad did indeed cooperate to a surprising extent, the character of the Iraqis who directed the project functioned as a guarantee to Damascus that Syrian interests would predominate.[56] Ismail Safwat and Taha al-Hashimi were pan-Arabists; their po-litical views corresponded more closely to the positions of the Triangle Alliance than to the attitudes of, say, Nuri al-Said and the Iraqi regent. The al-Quwatli regime trusted them implicitly; they served the regime loyally.[57]

At the outset, the Jordanians struck a pose of indifference toward the project; later, however, they placed a representative on the military commission in order to keep a finger on the pulse of decision-making in Damascus.[58] The coldness of feeling in Amman toward the Army of Liberation is easy to understand. After all, the Syrians, who had broken off diplomatic relations with Jordan the previous year, fashioned the army to function as an anti-Zionist weapon that would also check the ambitions of King Abdallah. In his memoirs, Fawzi al-Qawuqji de-scribes the inter-Arab political climate that spawned the Army of Liberation, highlighting the anti-Jordanian intentions of Damascus:

> But perhaps King Abdallah was [actually] determined to realize his Greater Syria Project by means of Palestine. This possibility more than any other troubled the Syrian government. And as for Iraq, which would send its army to the field of battle in Palestine by passing through Transjordan, how might it possibly act? Would it aid Jordan in the realization of the project? And as for Abd al-Aziz bin Saud, how would he react? He had to be prepared to act when the real intentions [of King Abdallah] became clear.

His Excellency President al-Quwatli one day asked me, "What are the steps that must and can be taken to prevent the occurrence of this grave danger?" I answered that the Army of Liberation in Palestine can prevent that, because it will prevent a war between the Arab states. It will enable you to take the precautions that you consider necessary without those precautions influencing the course of the war between us and between the Jews in Palestine. So the president immediately gave the order to send a division of the Syrian army to the Palestinian–Jordanian border, where it remained frozen in place.

His Highness Abd al-Aziz bin Saud demanded that some territory be allocated to him in Transjordan, where he could concentrate his forces in preparation for the intervention in Palestine. But what if these forces would not be there in order to prepare for an attack on Palestine? King Abdallah feared the request and avoided complying with it. He believed the real intention behind the request was to occupy Transjordan on the basis of a conspiracy between President al-Quwatli and King Ibn Saud, according to which the northern section would go to Syria and the southern section, including Aqaba, to Ibn Saud. With urgent insistence, King Abdallah demanded from the Iraqi government that it immediately send a force to Transjordan in order to thwart any Saudi–Syrian conspiracy. An Iraqi brigade, comprised of mechanized artillery and infantry, arrived in Transjordan; as a result His Highness King Abdallah regained his confidence and relaxed. Egypt favored the Saudi–Syrian camp, and promised to supply it with aid. But this camp was not overly reliant on that aid.

Each Arab state feared its so-called sister state; each coveted the territory of its sister, and conspired with others against its sister. At one of the meetings of the Arab League Council in October 1947, the Egyptian prime minister, Mahmud Fahmi al-Nuqrashi Pasha, made a declaration in which he reported that Egypt would participate with the other Arab states in providing "military support" on behalf of Palestine; these states, however, must be informed beforehand that the Egyptian army would not participate in combat. That decision resulted solely from considerations of domestic Egyptian affairs, and the Arab states should make their calculations on that basis. As I mentioned above, each Arab state feared its sister state: this was the situation in which the Arab states found themselves as they prepared to save Palestine; and this, first and foremost, is what troubled them. Only after this, very far after this, came the problem of Palestine itself.[59]

Damascus supported the Army of Liberation, then, in order to protect itself against the Jordanian threat. At issue for the al-Quwatli regime was a simple question: Who, on the Arab side, will have the say in creating a new order in Palestine, the Triangle Alliance or the Hashimite armies? In this context, directing a pan-Arab military effort plausibly designed to realize the principle of Palestinian self-determination provided the Syrian government with the best means of focusing the attention of Egypt and Saudi Arabia on the military aspects of the Palestine problem—while, at the same time, thwarting King Abdallah's expansionist intentions.

This anti-Jordanian character of the Army of Liberation expressed itself in the logistics of its campaign. Certainly it was the desire to diminish the influence of Jordan that drove Fawzi al-Qawuqji to locate his base of operations in the Nablus region—that is, in the area of Palestine where King Abdallah enjoyed the strongest political support.[60] With his headquarters in the northern West Bank, al-

Qawuqji stood watch, as it were, against the incorporation of the area into the Jordanian kingdom. The Triangle Alliance—and the Syrians most of all—had an especially strong interest in maintaining a political presence in the West Bank, because units of the Jordanian army, which aided the British in their withdrawal, were already deployed in a number of Palestinian cities.

To assert that the Syrians regarded the Army of Liberation as an anti-Jordanian tool is not to suggest that they ever ordered it to attack the Arab Legion. Rather, they used it to stake a claim; it provided Damascus with a *locus standi* in the resolution of the Palestine question. For Fawzi al-Qawuqji, therefore, success simply meant showing up—until, that is, the Great Powers and the Arab states finally sorted matters out.[61] This task did not preclude correct relations with King Abdallah, or, for that matter, with the Arab Legion. Nor did it preclude negotiating directly with the Zionists, with whom al-Qawuqji may have struck an agreement that gave the Jews a free hand against the followers of Hajj Amin al-Husayni.[62]

The Army of Liberation, therefore, had egregious relations with the Mufti and his militia, which operated in the Jerusalem area.[63] Fawzi al-Qawuqji had in any case a long history of personal conflict with Hajj Amin; by directing the Syrian attempt to dominate the Palestinian scene, he certainly did not improve relations. Ultimately, however, the split between Syria and the Mufti did not compare to the divide between Damascus and Amman, or, for that matter, between King Abdallah and Hajj Amin al-Husayni. Whereas the Triangle Alliance wanted to control Palestinian nationalism, the Jordanians sought to eliminate it. Whatever the differences, therefore, between President al-Quwatli and Hajj Amin al-Husayni, they both shared a total opposition to the expansion of Jordan. Thus an informed Palestinian observer such as Musa al-Alami believed that, in the event of a Jordanian occupation of Arab Palestine, the Mufti and the Syrians "would sink their differences in order to present a common front against King Abdulla."[64]

Fawzi al-Qawuqji may well have been an adventurer loyal only to himself; his organization, at any rate, certainly did not function as an effective mechanism for destroying Zionism. The Army of Liberation, however, served the Triangle Alliance most effectively not in the military but in the political sphere; by upholding the valuable fiction of a unified Arab effort, the army rendered independent action by Jordan illegitimate. However poor its performance, and whatever the personal failings of its commander, its mere existence kept legitimate military activity in Palestine squarely under the authority of the Arab League. In other words, the Army of Liberation fostered a political climate that forced Jordan and its supporters to respect the tenets of the Consensus Position. Any independent move by King Abdallah would be greeted by a resounding chorus of denunciation; the Arab states would accuse Amman of breaking the League consensus and stabbing the other Arab states in the back.

Instructive in this regard are the attitudes expressed by Taha al-Hashimi and Ali Mumtaz in March 1947, when Nuri al-Said proclaimed, "Either the League shall save Palestine or there shall be no League!" At that time, al-Hashimi and his friend had perceived the Iraqi prime minister's militant stance as a maneuver designed to embarrass the League, as an attempt to clear, in their words, an ideological "gap" into which King Abdallah's army would waltz. Now, when serving as the inspector-general of the Army of Liberation, Taha al-Hashimi undoubtedly took it upon himself to plug all the gaps that King Abdallah might have found inviting.[65]

The Hashimite Threat Reveals Itself

Made from memory without the help of documents and dates, the description by Fawzi al-Qawuqji of the climate of distrust among the Arab states has an imprecise quality that suggests exaggeration. Moreover, given al-Qawuqji's abject failure on the field of battle, one expects him to search for scapegoats, to pin his disastrous military record on internecine Arab conflict. British diplomatic correspondence from the months of January and February 1948, however, substantially supports his characterization of inter-Arab relations. While one could quibble with al-Qawuqji over details, and while one should certainly discount his personal claims to ideological purity, his general depiction of the diplomatic arena is nonetheless accurate, as the following discussion demonstrates.

By late January, public order in Arab Palestine stood on the verge of collapse. By himself, Fawzi al-Qawuqji could not hope to restore order, and his arrival no doubt increased the sense of chaos for many Arab residents.[66] The development of this vacuum in Palestine forced London, Amman, and Baghdad to discuss in earnest the new order in Arab Palestine that would replace the Mandate. Of all the contacts in this regard, the conversation of greatest historical significance took place in London, on 7 February 1948, between the British foreign minister, Ernest Bevin, and the Jordanian prime minister, Tawfiq Abu'l-Huda. The meeting was brief and highly secretive; Glubb Pasha acted as interpreter; Tawfiq Abu'l-Huda did almost all the talking. To put it crudely, he informed Bevin that upon the expiration of the Mandate the Jordanians intended to swallow as much of Arab Palestine as they could digest. Bevin responded, according to Glubb, by stating: "It seems the obvious thing to do."[67]

The Jordanian prime minister displayed a subtle understanding of the political pressures operating on the British, who were worried lest Amman become embroiled with either the United Nations or the Arab League. The intricate ties between the Jordanian army and the British government meant that, in the eyes of the international community, London would be held responsible for the actions of the Arab Legion in Palestine. Britain wished to appear before the world as if it respected, to the extent that its vital interests allowed, both international law and the collective aspirations of the Arab people. Therefore, Abu'l-Huda attempted to reassure Bevin that Jordan would not conduct itself in a manner embarrassing to the British internationally. He explained that Amman would pay due respect to the United Nations but would not allow its policy to be dictated by that organization. The only available record of the conversation paraphrases the Jordanian prime minister as follows:

The presence of the Arab Legion in Palestine would not prevent the execution of any United Nations decision which might ultimately be taken, but would enable such a decision to be more easily enforced. If . . . some solution was ultimately adopted involving a modification of the present arrangements [the Jewish and Arab states envisioned by the 29 November partition resolution] in favor of the Arabs, the Arab Legion would be able to help enforce such a solution. Even if, on the other hand, the United Nations tried to enforce the present decision, the presence of the Arab Legion would limit the ensuing chaos and not increase it. Tewfik Pasha thought it was possible that the Jews would find that they had opened their mouths too wide and that the United Nations would come to a similar conclusion, but, however this might be, the Arab Legion could not wait for the prior permission of the United Nations to enter the Arab areas of Palestine.[68]

Thus the British and the Jordanians, while guarding their freedom of action in a fluid political context, entered into a loose agreement to modify the partition plan of the United Nations. Instead of Palestine being shared between independent Arab and Jewish states, Jordan would annex much of the Arab areas; the Jews would get whatever they could grab, an amount that would likely be less than what the United Nations had promised them.

While London and Amman were striking their informal understanding, minds in Baghdad were also planning for the future of Palestine. The new foreign minister, Hamdi al-Pachachi, suggested to the British that they should immediately (that is, before the expiration of the Mandate) transfer power in Palestine to a joint Jordanian–Iraqi force, thus presenting both the Jews and their American supporters with a fait accompli.[69] Such a solution, from the Iraqi point of view, had the merits of defeating Zionism while trumping the Triangle Alliance. By blocking the rise of a Jewish state it would insulate the Hashimite regimes from the accusation of colluding with Zionism and the West against the Palestinians. At the same time, however, it would also give Amman and Baghdad the greatest say in creating the new order in the Fertile Crescent. Iraqi and Jordanian influence would reach the shores of the Mediterranean, thereby diminishing the stature of the Triangle Alliance; Syria would become a Hashimite satellite, perhaps even a province.[70]

Though admittedly attractive, the plan was fanciful. The Foreign Office disliked the Iraqi scheme, because, in contrast to the Jordanian plan, it displayed no concern for British sensitivities over the attitude of the United Nations.[71] The absence of this consideration in al-Pachachi's thinking resulted from the impact of pan-Arab forces on the Iraqi government. Indeed, many of the pressures operating on Baghdad worked counter to the pressures on London. The Foreign Office, though conniving in secret to modify the United Nations partition plan, aspired to appear in public as a nation that respected international law.[72] By contrast, the Iraqi regime looked to satisfy a citizenry that viewed the partition resolution as a crime against the Arabs. Baghdad could not, therefore, allow itself so much as to appear as if it honored the lines that the United Nations had drawn on the map of Palestine. The Iraqis feared the propaganda attacks of the Triangle Alliance, and they feared their own public. Their fright would force them to attack the Jewish state ostentatiously.

While the British deflected Baghdad from the proposal to transfer power in Palestine to the Hashimite armies, they did nothing to discourage planning for Jordanian–Iraqi military cooperation after the expiration of the Mandate. On the contrary, the records of the Foreign Office in February 1948 clearly reflect the assumption that a joint Jordanian–Iraqi intervention would be the most likely determinant of the future of Arab Palestine. In effect, London left it up to the Iraqis to work out with the Jordanians the steps that the two Hashimite armies would take when the Mandate ended.[73] Thus, the problem of restraining the aspirations of Iraqi pan-Arabism devolved upon the Jordanian leaders, and upon their friends and family in Baghdad.

In the contacts between London, Amman, and Baghdad during February 1948, there took shape something approaching the nightmare scenario of the Triangle Alliance: the Hashimite regimes, with British diplomatic support, cleared the way for unfettered military action in Palestine. However, the vulnerability of the Iraqi government to pan-Arab appeals gave Cairo, Riyadh, and Damascus some leverage over the embryonic Hashimite coalition. In addition, Iraqi military involvement in Palestine would destroy the possibility of a rapprochement between Amman and Tel Aviv, because the compulsive need of Baghdad to establish its pan-Arab credentials would force Jordan into an alliance designed to breach the United Nations frontiers. Thus, Shukri al-Quwatli's greatest fear—that the Jews would ally with King Abdallah and work toward the creation of Greater Syria— had no prospect of materializing. Nonetheless, simply the prospect of Jordan annexing Arab Palestine profoundly threatened the republican regime in Syria.

War in Palestine: Saudi Fears

Damascus, of course, was not the only Arab capital that feared Jordanian intentions; the Saudi Arabian government, which had got wind of King Abdallah's plan, also raised a shrill voice of protest. Riyadh reacted to the Jordanian threat on several planes at once: it protested to London; it sought a security guarantee from Washington; it delivered rifles and money to the Palestinian enemies of King Abdallah; and it threatened to attack Jordan if it annexed Arab Palestine.[74]

In late January rumors reached London, Baghdad, and Amman that the Saudi Arabian government had begun organizing tribesman from the Najd with the intention of sending them across southern Jordan, ostensibly to fight in Palestine.[75] On 3 February, the British representative in Jedda received confirmation of the rumors from Shaykh Hafiz Wahba, the Saudi ambassador to London, who had returned home for consultations with King Ibn Saud. As Fawzi al-Qawuqji states in his memoirs, the Jordanians interpreted this maneuver as a hostile act—a natural reaction when considering that the Saudi government claimed sovereignty over southern Jordan.[76] King Abdallah, therefore, answered the threat by despatching units of the Arab Legion to Maan and Aqaba.[77] Meanwhile, the Foreign Office itself weighed the merits of a military display; it briefly considered placing units of the Royal Air Force, normally stationed in the Amman area, along the Saudi border.[78] In the event, however, the British opted for diplomacy as the best means of deterrence: they redoubled their efforts to reconcile Riyadh and Amman.[79]

If we take Ibn Saud at his word, war between the two kingdoms was a real possibility. While Tawfiq Abu'l-Huda was in London planning the Jordanian annexation of Arab Palestine, Shaykh Hafiz Wahba was in Cairo discussing the same subject, but in a very different tone. The Saudi ambassador to London, who had just arrived in Egypt in order to attend a meeting of the Arab League, put the position of his government to the British Ambassador in plain terms:

> King Ibn Saud had several times last week at Riyadh mentioned to him reports that
> . . . King Abdallah of Transjordan was intending, on the withdrawal of British forces,
> to try and seize and occupy in his own name the Arab parts of Palestine. King Ibn
> Saud did not know whether or not the British were behind such a plan. He suspected
> that they might be. He was very uneasy indeed about it all. Sheik Hafiz said it was
> a very serious matter, for Ibn Saud would never agree to such an arrangement and
> would do everything in his power, even in the last resort go to war, to prevent it.
> If it should appear that Britain was in fact backing the scheme, Ibn Saud's confidence
> in us would suffer a fatal blow.[80]

The true goal, then, of threatening to send men across Jordan into Palestine had little to do with fighting the Jews; rather, the Saudi government intended to use the threat of dispatching forces in order to pressure both London and Amman to abandon their plans to cede Arab Palestine to Jordan.

In the event of real hostilities, it is unlikely that Najdi tribesmen would have been any match for the Arab Legion. Nonetheless, simply by threatening to act, the Saudis placed considerable pressure on London. For one thing, if King Ibn Saud had actually decided to introduce men into Palestine, by whatever route, it would have proven embarrassing to Britain. More important, however, was the effect that the rift between Jordan and Saudi Arabia was having on London's attempt, in January and February 1948, to rope Riyadh into the British defense system, and to detach it from Cairo.[81] Under the circumstances, the British could scarcely afford to witness a severe deterioration between King Abdallah, their closest Arab ally, and Ibn Saud, who was playing an increasingly powerful role in the region (and who had the ear of Washington). In short, a breakdown in relations between the kingdoms would simply drive Riyadh closer to Cairo, and it would vastly complicate the Palestine question. As it happened, the immediate Saudi threat subsided, perhaps because King Ibn Saud received an unconditional guarantee of his security from Washington.[82] American support against potential attacks from either Iraq or Jordan, however, did not reconcile Riyadh to the Jordanian annexation of Arab Palestine; nor did it detach the Saudis from Egypt. It simply eliminated the immediate signs of friction.

Cairo Answers the Call for Help

Chapter 3 briefly focused the spotlight on Shaykh Hafiz Wahba's trip to Cairo in early February. It was during this visit that he, in coordination with King Faruq and Azzam Pasha, championed the creation of a regional system of collective security based on the Triangle Alliance and the Arab League.[83] Thus, at the exact moment when Shaykh Hafiz Wahba was protesting to British representatives regarding Jordanian aspirations in Palestine, he was also pitching a plan to London regarding the establishment of an Arab bloc. On the face of it, then, a trace of schizophrenia ran through Saudi policy—after all, King Ibn Saud was threatening war against Jordan while proposing the establishment an alliance that would bind Riyadh closely to Amman. If, as Shaykh Hafiz Wahba stated, his government feared both Britain's and Jordan's intentions toward Palestine, and if, in fact, Saudi Arabia was indeed willing to resort to arms, then what sense was there in proposing a system of collective security that would, among other things, require Saudi Arabia to defend Jordan?

Chapter 3 analyzed this scheme for strengthening the League as an episode in the struggle between the Turco-Hashimite Entente and the Triangle Alliance— that is, as an attempt by the Egyptians and the Saudis to capitalize on the *Wathba*, which had foiled the British circumvention of Egypt, the would-be keystone in the arch. The timing, however, of the Saudi and Egyptian proposal to create a new Middle Eastern security network suggests that other considerations were also at work in the minds of King Faruq, Shaykh Hafiz Wahba, and Abd al-Rahman Azzam Pasha. Specifically, it suggests that Palestine loomed large in their calculations. One question strikes at the heart of the matter: Was it simply by chance that the proposal to graft a regional defense organization onto the Arab League coincided with the trip to London of the Jordanian prime minister?

Many historians have studied the famous conversation between Ernest Bevin and Tawfiq Abu'l-Huda. Most, however, have failed to note a significant aspect of the encounter: The Cairo press accurately reported the content of this purportedly secret understanding.[84] As the Saudi protests to London also indicate, reliable information regarding Jordan's plans circulated freely in the capitals of the Middle East in early February. As far as the Arab opponents of King Abdallah were concerned, the understanding over Palestine between Ernest Bevin and Tawfiq Abu'l-Huda had been brokered in broad daylight before a large audience.

The deep suspicion that the British had endorsed the Jordanian annexation of the West Bank limited to two the number of options that stood before Cairo, Riyadh and Damascus. On the one hand, they could acquiesce in a Hashimite solution to the Palestine question—that is, a solution that entailed the partition of the country between Jordan and the emergent Jewish state, with perhaps the Western Galilee being absorbed by Syria.[85] On the other hand, they could attempt to manipulate the Jordanian army, to extend the authority of the League over the Arab Legion, and to force King Abdallah to fight the Jews in order to create a Palestinian national state allied to the Triangle Alliance. Despite the refusal of the Egyptian government to commit its regular army to Palestine, the Alliance never entertained the first option. It is, therefore, in the light of the second option that we must analyze the proposal on regional defense made by King Faruq, Hafiz Wahba, and Abd al-Rahman Azzam.

Behind the Arab-bloc plan we witness the resurfacing of the calculations that, in October 1947, had informed the proposal to buy the Jordanian army. Just as then the Egyptians had not lost sight of the basic principles of power politics, the Saudis did not now suffer from schizophrenia. On the contrary, their very sane logic ran as follows: If King Abdallah could be gripped in a pan-Arab bear hug, then his army could be harnessed to the political goals of the Triangle Alliance. Since the convulsions in Iraq had left King Abdallah with no Arab allies capable of endorsing his plans in Palestine, the Triangle Alliance could capture the reins of the Arab Legion, by mobilizing the moral authority of the League. Although the logic driving the Arab-bloc proposal was identical to the logic informing the plan to buy the Arab Legion, the tactics were different. Whereas the earlier plan had envisioned driving a pan-Arab wedge between London and Amman, the Saudis and the Egyptians now approached London directly, in effect requesting that it share control. Previously Cairo had schemed to capture the puppet; now it sought to seduce the puppeteer.

It was Abd al-Rahman Azzam who explicitly raised the status of Jordan in connection with the Arab-bloc proposal. During his conversation with a British diplomat, he asserted that the *Wathba* had proven that the Arabs rejected the idea of special treaties proposed by the British Empire. The only solution to the problem of regional defense, therefore, lay in creating an alliance between the Arab League and the British. This alliance, however, would not entail special base rights in Egypt and Iraq. The close ties that London enjoyed with Amman would satisfy its need for a connection to the Arab states. Britain, he said,

> still had a treaty of alliance containing military clauses with Transjordan. . . . Let that treaty stand. . . . It was sufficient to link [Britain] to the Arab world. If Trans-jordan were a party to an Arab regional defensive alliance and if one of the partic-ipating states were involved in a war which, in its turn, involved the other partic-ipating states, including Transjordan, Britain would automatically through the link with Transjordan be at war too.[86]

In other words, according to the Arab-bloc plan, the Arab League Secretariat would enter into a partnership with London. Such an arrangement, of course, would inevitably restrict the ability of King Abdallah to act independently in Palestine—or, for that matter, anywhere else. In effect it would grant the Arab League the power of veto over any scheme hatched between London and Amman. True, in this conversation with the British diplomat, Azzam Pasha only *implied* that the Arab League Secretariat deserved the authority to regulate relations be-tween the British government and its Arab clients, and to control the action of Arab militaries. However, when considered in context, there can be no doubt regarding the intent behind his words. Given years of hostile propaganda against the Hashimite states, given the proposal to build the regional organization around a nucleus containing Egypt, Syria, and Saudi Arabia, given the pan-Arab nature of the *Wathba*, and given the Saudi protests over Jordanian intentions in Pales-tine, it is clear that Azzam Pasha searched for leverage over Jordan.

Certainly, at this time the air was thick with plans to expand the power of the Arab League, to give it the authority to regulate the relations between London and the Arab governments, and to create a unified Arab command. For instance, in early February reports reached Baghdad stating that Azzam Pasha intended to foist on the League Council a new regulation stipulating that "no member of the League will negotiate [a] separate treaty with a foreign state without prior consultation with the League which will be constituted as [the] supreme regional authority."[87] In the event, it fell to the Syrian prime minister, Jamil Mardam, to table the proposal, which the Iraqi foreign minister successfully resisted, presumably with the aid of his Jordanian colleague.[88] While assigning to the Syrians the task of pursuing the issue of relations between the Arab states and the Great Powers, the secretary-general himself floated publicly the idea of creating an Arab League military authority. According to the British embassy in Cairo, on 7 February Azzam Pasha stated at a press conference:

> that the British had denied any intention of concluding a treaty with the Arab League, but the Arab countries are being pushed by their peoples towards the formation of an Arab bloc. The League had set up a military commission to defend Palestine, purchase arms, and collect funds which would lead to the formation of a common defence force. The Charter of the Arab League contained no article concerning the defence of Arab countries in the case of aggression against any one of them. . . . Consequently it had become necessary to modify the pact of the Arab League to remedy the omission.[89]

If the Triangle Alliance had gotten its way, the powers of the commission directing the Army of Liberation, led by Taha al-Hashimi and Ismail Safwat, would expand. The staff of the Army of Liberation, working under Abd al-Rahman Azzam, would form the nucleus of an Arab organization that would prefigure NATO. In short, it would become a unified regional command.

The idea of a unified command, of course, did not originate with Abd al-Rahman Azzam; nor did it first arise at this moment. In early November 1947, it will be recalled, King Abdallah had raised with Azzam Pasha the matter of setting up a unified command. In response, the secretary-general claimed that the time for such a discussion was not ripe; he preferred, instead, to discuss topics such as Saladin, to postpone the matter indefinitely. If the urgent necessity of controlling Jordan was not the reason, then what was it that convinced Azzam Pasha that 7 February 1948 was the appropriate day to discuss the issue of a unified Arab command? What was it that moved Hafiz Wahba to choose 6 February for threatening war against Jordan while proposing the creation of an Arab bloc? What was it, then, that led the Syrians, within days, to call for a strengthening of the League, and that compelled King Faruq, on 9 February, to proclaim the status of Egypt as the keystone in the arch?

The Bevin–Abu'l-Huda meeting of 7 February 1948 awakened diverse fears, all of which centered on the threat posed by the power and independence of the Jordanian army. The Triangle Alliance responded to the threat with its most potent weapon: The call to Arab unity.

FIVE

The Decision to Intervene

Sidqi Takes a Stand

Four days before the expiration of the Palestine Mandate, the Egyptian Senate met in secret. The prime minister, Mahmud Fahmi al-Nuqrashi, convened this closed session in order to announce the likelihood that the army would intervene in Palestine, and to request from the Parliament four million pounds to finance the planned operations. Prior to this appearance, al-Nuqrashi Pasha had opposed the use of the regular army. Thus, in order to justify his new position, he appealed, first, to the national and humanitarian sentiments of the senators:

> Honored Senators! 15 May is at hand! Great Britain will abandon the Mandate and its responsibilities. Thus all the Arab inhabitants of Palestine are subject to the mercy of these three gangs [the Stern Gang, the Irgun, and the Hagana]. Is it possible that we will remain as spectators fixed at a standstill? [Voices: No!] I felt that I—I, who for many reasons did not in any way promote [the view] that our forces should become embroiled [in this conflict]—must come before you in your capacity as the representatives of the nation . . . and I must say: If the killing is not stopped in a manner that will grant the Arabs peace, then there is no choice but for the Egyptian forces to set about establishing security in Palestine![1]

After stressing the necessity of halting the suffering of the Palestinians, al-Nuqrashi Pasha also told the senators that the government had no choice but to honor prior commitments to the Arab League. "There is a duty," he stated, "that is most important. It is [the principle] that if . . . Egypt says it will do something, then it does it; if it makes a promise, then it carries it out." Thus, both morality and state interest dictated intervention. The Senate strongly supported his claims; it unanimously authorized the decision to go to war.[2]

Although nobody voted against al-Nuqrashi, his arguments did not convince at least one prominent Egyptian: The former prime minister, Ismail Sidqi, who left the Senate without casting a vote.[3] Before he walked out, however, he attacked the decision to go to war by posing fourteen thorny questions to the prime minister. When considered as a whole, these questions, together with the observations that accompanied them, comprise a cogent exposition of the intellectual framework—the Insular-Egypt Strategy—that had given structure to Egyptian foreign policy during the premiership of Sidqi Pasha in 1946.

In the ex-prime minister's view, the Egyptian state occupied a unique position among the Arab countries. Although Egypt was the largest Arab power and the leader of the Arab League, and although it contributed the most money to the fight against Zionism, "we cannot say that she is the country that has the greatest interest in the Palestine conflict."[4] A "vast desert" separates Palestine from Egypt, a land which, "though counted among the Arab countries," was nonetheless "considered distant." Dialect, culture, geography—all these ties bound the other Arab societies more closely to Palestine, making them, in contrast to Egypt, "particularly interested" in developments there.

Being the most influential member of the Arab League and yet being somewhat removed from the Palestine question, Egypt occupied, in Sidqi Pasha's view, the swing position among the Arab states. A decision by Cairo to prepare for war would tip the balance in favor of the hawks in the Arab camp, making violence inevitable. However, Egypt also had the option of throwing her weight decisively behind a policy seeking to compromise with Zionism. While it is true, he said, that Arabism "has great value . . . , it is also true that other considerations contradict and weaken it."[5] Therefore, he dared the prime minister to claim in good faith that he had "completely exhausted all means of achieving an understanding between the two ethnic groups, the Arabs and the Jews." He called on al-Nuqrashi Pasha to adopt the role of mediator, directing his attention to files in the foreign ministry archive that, he claimed, proved that the two groups inhabiting Palestine can live together with "ties of mutual benefit."[6] Ismail Sidqi insisted that, after making exceptions for "the aggressive activities of some gentlemen on both sides," one could not help but see that "war is easy to avoid."

While claiming that Egypt enjoyed a special standing that rendered her capable of mediating between the Jews and the Arabs, the former-prime minister also raised a number of practical issues that militated against intervention. The armed forces, he claimed, were ill-prepared. When he had left power a year and a half before, the state of the Egyptian army "did not induce a sense of security," and he questioned whether the deficiencies had been remedied.[7] Did the Egyptian military possess sufficient ammunition? Was it true, he asked, "that the tank corps is almost nonexistent, and that the air force is good for nothing?" Air power had considerable importance, he explained, because according to recent reports the enemy stood on the verge of acquiring planes from one of the Great Powers—by which he presumably meant the Soviet Union, which allowed Czechoslovakia to arm the emergent Israel. Largely absent from the air, the Egyptian military also had, according to Sidqi Pasha, insufficient power on the ground. Observing that the army commanded only 50,000 soldiers, he cast doubt on its ability to prosecute the war in Palestine while simultaneously conducting its duties at home. Moreover, recent events indicated that the other Arab armies would not be capable of performing at the level necessary for defeating Zionism.

In addition to these practical military concerns, the elderly politician warned that going to war in Palestine would embroil Egypt with the Great Powers. In his worst-case scenario, the struggle against Zionism might spark a world war. In support of this view, he cited an earlier statement by Prime Minister al-Nuqrashi, who had informed the foreign affairs committee of the Senate that a "war between the two blocs struggling for world domination is not a fanciful danger."[8] Given this state of affairs, the involvement of the Egyptian army in the Palestine conflict would certainly serve the interests of the Soviet Union; moreover, it might produce the sparks that would ignite a war between the blocs.

Even if such a catastrophe did not occur, Egyptian intervention would nonetheless cause friction between, on the one hand, Egypt and, on the other, Britain, the United States, and the United Nations. This, in turn, would lead to an embargo of arms and ammunition, of which Egypt was in sore need. In addition, the Great Powers might punish Cairo with economic sanctions. The experience of World War II had taught that the Egyptian economy was particularly vulnerable with regard to vital imports—including cereals, chemical fertilizers, and petroleum-based products—the absence of which would be "crippling to the war effort."[9]

Behind these statements stood a conception of the relations between the West and Egypt that ran counter both to the anti-imperialist policy that Cairo had conducted since March 1947, and to a campaign in favor of neutralism that the Egyptian press was currently waging. About a month before the Senate debate on intervention in Palestine, Ismail Sidqi had called implicitly for a reconciliation with Britain, admonishing as unrealistic those who believed that Egypt had any alternative other than to ally itself with the West. Both in a press interview and at an earlier appearance before the foreign relations committee of the Senate, he had stressed that "it was illusory . . . to practice a policy of neutrality between the Western and Eastern blocs, because in the event of war Egypt would certainly be invaded." Instead, he recommended an alliance with a strong power or group of powers.[10] In the secret session of the Senate on 11 May, the former prime minister did not raise these issues explicitly, but they generated an atmosphere that influenced the statements of both sides in the debate.

The last issue Ismail Sidqi raised regarding intervention in Palestine was the social cost of war. The Egyptian state, he said, stood prepared to embark on a project of socioeconomic reforms that would be endangered by a lengthy and costly conflict. He claimed that a war against Zionism would exacerbate social tensions and rob the authorities of the means to alleviate them. A brief survey of events in April and May 1948 proves that, by expressing these social concerns, Ismail Sidqi was not simply spouting antiwar rhetoric. On 5 and 6 April, the country had suffered a strike by policemen for higher wages, which in Alexandria led to a complete breakdown of order, forcing the government to call the army out onto the streets. In Cairo, a strike by hospital attendants, who were also demanding higher wages from the government, turned violent. In addition, a strike by transportation workers in the capital was narrowly averted. Although all was quiet in the textile mills of Mahallat al-Kubra, a perennial center of labor agitation, this good fortune no doubt resulted from the inauguration by King Faruq of a project that included housing and social amenities for the workers. The authorities intended this action to demonstrate their commitment to the welfare of the workers. This small success by the government on the labor front was offset by continued signs of a struggle between the security services and radical organizations. Just before May Day, for instance, the police rounded up scores of Communists in order to prevent a violent demonstration on behalf of workers' rights. The labor movements, of course, were not the only agents of political violence. Anonymous assailants, presumably tied to the Muslim Brotherhood, made at least two attempts, one quite serious, to blow up the house of al-Nahhas Pasha. Presumably the Muslim Brothers had a hand in these attacks, which took place amid statements of concern by the government concerning the rising tide of paramilitary activity. They also coincided with the well-publicized trial of the assassins of Amin Osman, who was killed as retribution for his pro-British sympathies.[11]

The conflicts *within* Egyptian society proceeded along their well-established trajectories, largely unaffected by the crisis in Palestine. Thus, Sidqi Pasha based his policy on the perception that Egypt, though predominantly Muslim and Arabic-speaking, was to a certain extent a world unto itself. He gave first priority, therefore, to the development of the Egyptian economy and to the alleviation of social tensions. In his view, leading the struggle against imperialism and championing the values of Arabism would prevent Egypt from solving her deepest problems.

Despite the manifest seriousness of Sidqi's arguments, they found no other champions in the Senate, though silent supporters of them did undoubtedly exist. Al-Nuqrashi Pasha's extremely late conversion to the prowar camp suggests that the elite in Cairo did not unanimously approve of the decision to intervene. Nevertheless, no one dared to stand at the side of the elderly former prime minister, who withdrew in defeat. Thus, his failure marked not just the beginning of the Egyptian intervention in Palestine but, in addition, a mortal blow to his Insular-Egypt Strategy. On 11 May 1948 the Egyptian state decided to cross the Sinai desert and plant roots in the Arab world on a scale unknown for a century. This bold experiment, though destined to last thirty years, would ultimately prove as unsuccessful as the northward expansion of Muhammad Ali in the nineteenth century. Sidqi Pasha, for one, had perceived the dangers, but a fly cannot stop a wheel from spinning.

Public Opinion

As reports reached Egypt about the distress of the Palestinians, a rising chorus demanded direct intervention. The supporters of an activist policy included the Muslim Brotherhood and a number of political parties, plus King Faruq and the Egyptian press.[12] With powerful political movements, the palace, and the papers all in support of a hawkish policy, it would hardly seem necessary to ask why the prime minister abandoned his position against intervention. On the face of it, the easiest explanation for the Egyptian entry into the conflict would be that al-Nuqrashi Pasha buckled under pressure from an enraged public, for whose support both the palace and the politicians competed. Such an interpretation has the merit of explaining not just the decision to intervene but also the disastrous outcome of the war. Our awareness of conflict among the elite before the war, and our knowledge of the subsequent failure on the battlefield provides the elements of a coherent narrative: A weak government bowed to the pressure of an enraged public and threw an unprepared army into battle against an unknown and powerful enemy.

While this interpretation contains perhaps a grain of truth, it is decidedly one-dimensional. It directs attention away from issues that were just as important as public opinion in compelling the government to intervene in Palestine. In particular, it ignores the strategic dimension of decision-making. What effect, in the eyes of al-Nuqrashi Pasha and the king, would intervention in Palestine have on relations with the Great Powers? What was the connection between the place of Egypt in inter-Arab alignments and the decision to go to war? Would the fight against Zionism aid or hinder the struggle for independence from Britain? The blind-blunder explanation of Egyptian behavior declares these crucial questions irrelevant. Moreover, since historians tend to assign King Faruq an important role in undermining the policy of detachment that al-Nuqrashi Pasha had previously advocated, a consideration of strategy seems particular relevant.[13] After all, the monarch had a long record of concern with such matters. It will be recalled that in the early weeks of February 1948, the palace displayed serious concern regarding the regional and international status of Egypt. Did the calculations that had then motivated King Faruq to unveil his plan for an Arab bloc now inform his decision to intervene?

Even if we assume, for the sake of argument, that domestic factors *alone* drove the government to declare war, we would not have completed a serious investigation of the major determinants of the Palestine policy of Cairo. The strategic dimension of Egyptian thinking would, in any case, still require analysis. Regardless of whether public opinion played a significant role in compelling the elite in Cairo to take action, the Egyptian state did not, simply by going to war, shed the fundamental attributes of its political personality. Its place in inter-Arab relations, for instance, did not change when the Egyptian army crossed the border into Palestine. If those relations had been important to the authorities in Cairo before the decision to intervene, then they continued to be important afterwards. Moreover, it is in the nature of the world that decisions taken by a handful of people, especially in matters of war, influence the lives of millions. As a consequence, we ignore at our own peril the structure of the Palestine problem as it appeared before the eyes of the Egyptian elite.

Power Politics: The Setting

In April 1948, the Palestinian resistance to Zionism all but collapsed. The fall of Tiberias and the expulsion of its Arab population, the Deir Yassin massacre, together with the mounting threat to Haifa, Jaffa, Jerusalem, and Safed, brought home the realization that neither the British military nor the Arab partisans in Palestine could protect the Arab population from the Jewish forces. This recognition led to a slump in the morale of the Triangle Alliance.[14]

During the second week of April, the political committee of the Arab League met in Cairo, where it heard yet another depressing report from General Ismail

Safwat, the chairman of the military commission of the League. Having repeatedly warned the Arab states about the military power of the *yishuv*, and yet never having received much of the money and weapons promised to him, Safwat stood on the verge of resignation. During one appearance before the political committee, he described the inadequacy of Arab weaponry in comparison with that of the enemy, causing Khalid Qarqani, the Saudi representative, to weep. At another meeting, after outlining the situation in the region of Safed, where the Arabs were outgunned by the Jews, Safwat said, "I am adamant about resigning, because my requests are not honored. But I do not want to shirk my responsibilities. I say to you, therefore, that if my requests are not carried out within a short period of time, then I will resign." At this point, Azzam Pasha stood and reminded the members of the committee of the embarrassment to them that the departure of the general would cause. "Without doubt," he said, "you appreciate the significance of the resignation of Safwat Pasha, who will not be quiet, but rather will tell what he knows."[15]

Given the refusal of the Egyptians to commit their regular army, given the weakness of the Syrian and Lebanese forces, and given the distance and lack of interest of the Saudis in the conflict, in order to save Palestine the enemies of King Abdallah had no choice but to call on him for help. Amman, of course, had long foreseen the dependence of the Arab League on the Jordanian army, and it moved quickly to exploit developments to its advantage. While Safwat was explaining the dire situation to the political committee, therefore, King Abdallah sent a message offering to rescue Palestine with his army.[16]

This Jordanian offer created friction between, on the one hand, the Egyptians and, on the other, the Syrians and Hajj Amin al-Husayni, who was also in attendance at the meeting of the political committee. The Egyptian government, represented by Abd al-Rahman Azzam and Mahmud Fahmi al-Nuqrashi, argued in favor of sanctioning the operations of the Jordanian army in Palestine, under the aegis of the Arab League. By contrast, the Syrians and (especially) the Mufti lived in such fear of King Abdallah that they argued against accepting the Jordanian proposal. This attitude enraged al-Nuqrashi, who "accused them of being willing to sacrifice Palestine to their personal jealousies."[17] During an emotional moment in the debate, the Egyptian prime minister "screamed in the Mufti's face: 'Hajj Amin, please! Our dignity and our honor are hanging in the balance, and our lives are in danger!' "[18] In the event, the dependence of the Syrians and the Palestinians on Cairo gave them no choice but to acquiesce before the will of al-Nuqrashi Pasha. Thus, Abd al-Rahman Azzam dispatched General Safwat to Amman, entrusting him with a letter, a favorable but cautious reply to King Abdallah's offer to save Palestine.

This clash between the members of the Triangle Alliance did not in any way represent significant differences in attitude toward King Abdallah or his Greater Syria project. The Egyptians, Syrians, and Palestinians (and, of course, the Saudis) all competed in their hostility to the annexation of Arab Palestine by Jordan. This unanimity notwithstanding, they strongly disagreed about whether the League was an instrument sufficiently powerful to discipline King Abdallah. Thus, the debate among the enemies of Amman in April 1948 followed directly along the lines first established in October 1947, when al-Nuqrashi Pasha had proposed, to the horror of the Syrians, that the Arab states should buy the Jordanian army. The idea that the League should lend its authority to Jordanian military action seemed to Damascus as threatening now as it had seemed ludicrous then.

By contrast, the Egyptians believed, as they always had, that the Arab League, by virtue of its ability to mold public opinion, possessed an efficient mechanism for harnessing the Jordanian Army to the wagon of the Triangle Alliance. Thus, in a discussion with the friends of Egypt in Damascus, Abd al-Rahman Azzam stated that he distrusted the Jordanian monarch; he went on to say, however, that "if the treachery of King Abdallah is confirmed, then we will announce it to the Arab world so that it will see the evil of his actions."[19] And thus, on 13 May, only two days before the regular Arab armies intervened in Palestine, Azzam Pasha explained to Taha al-Hashimi that he "still smells a rat in the policy of King Abdallah. So he [Azzam] will go to him and spur him on, saying to him, 'Either you will attack the Jews like Saladin attacked the Crusaders, or the curse of the world will fall upon you.' "[20]

As part of their tactic of pinning Jordan under the moral weight of Arab unity, the Egyptians worked to create an ideological environment inimical to the plans of Amman to accept the partition of Palestine and to absorb the Arab areas. For instance, when King Faruq received the political committee of the Arab League on 12 April, he issued a statement affirming that "if the Arab armies intervene in Palestine to save it, then their action will be regarded as a temporary expedient, devoid of any character of occupation or partition; after its liberation Palestine must be handed back to its owners, so that they may rule it as they please."[21] All observers, including foreign diplomats and the local press, read this directive as a shrill warning to King Abdallah against the annexation of Arab Palestine and against negotiating with the Zionists.[22]

Amman got the message. The next day, King Abdallah appeared before a delegation of Palestinian refugees and said:

> I swear to you before God that I do not aspire to rule over Palestine, and I do not seek to annex any part of it to my country; I will intervene with the rest of the Arab states in order to save this noble Arab country. After we have accomplished that, we will leave to you the task of deciding what [form of government] you consider to be fitting and appropriate.

The Jordanian monarch did not, however, let the matter rest with this statement. After all, for three years he had been playing cat-and-mouse with the Arab League over his Greater Syria project. By now, therefore, he had honed to a fine art the skill of paying deference to the Consensus Position while still guarding his freedom of action. Thus, he also told the refugees the following:

> But if you determine that your interests dictate uniting with us, then we welcome you with open arms. I give you my complete assurance on this policy, because there does not exist a single Jordanian under the shadow of my rule who would approve of taking unlawful possession of Palestine.[23]

The tension between King Faruq and King Abdallah that produced these dueling statements expressed itself more ominously in the negotiations between the

Arab League and Amman that followed the Jordanian proposal to liberate Palestine. When Ismail Safwat delivered to King Abdallah the letter from Azzam Pasha authorizing the Jordanian intervention, he initiated a three-week tug-of-war between the Triangle Alliance and the Jordanian government over the command of the Arab armies. For their part, Cairo, Riyadh, Damascus, and Beirut all sought to elevate the status of the military commission in Damascus, transforming it into the staff of a unified Arab command, with Ismail Safwat receiving the position of supreme commander. The idea, it will be recalled, had first been proposed in February, when the Egyptians and Saudis, fearing a deal between Amman and London, had made their Arab-bloc proposal to the British.

Naturally, of course, King Abdallah had other ideas. Thus, no sooner had General Safwat arrived in Amman than he received a stern lesson in power politics: The Arab state possessing the strongest army sets the terms for liberating Palestine. King Abdallah insisted, among other things, that he himself deserved to be the supreme commander; in addition, he demanded that the League pay him a subsidy in order to cover the extra expenses of combat in Palestine.[24]

The news that Amman refused to hand its army over to the League threatened the Triangle Alliance, which perceived sinister intentions behind King Abdallah's desire to guard his freedom of action. After completing a round of negotiations in Amman, Ismail Safwat traveled to Damascus, where he informed Shukri al-Quwatli of King Abdallah's troublesome attitude. Taha al-Hashimi, who attended the meeting between the two men, quotes in his diary the account given by General Safwat to President al-Quwatli:

> Then I traveled with the [Iraqi] regent [Abd al-Ilah] to Amman, where we found that Riyad al-Sulh [prime minister of Lebanon] . . . had preceded us. Some meetings took place, and I learned that King Abdallah, in exchange for the participation of his army, had imposed the conditions that he receive the Supreme Command, and that he be paid money. I asked Riyadh al-Sulh to apprise me of the true attitude of King Abdallah. He responded by saying that he is sure that the Arab Legion will participate [in the war effort], because he contacted [the Jordanian prime minister] Tawfiq Abu'l-Huda and asked him, "Is it true that all the forces of the Jordanian army will participate?"
> "Yes," he said.
> "Do the British support that?"
> "Yes," he said.

Given the rising power of the Jewish forces, given the collapse of the Arab partisans in Palestine, and given the weakness of the Syrian military, one might have expected that the Jordanian and British support for intervention would have come as something of a relief to the president, notwithstanding the annoying demands of the king. In actual fact, however, this information struck the Syrian leader like a mortal blow:

> At that point Shukri al-Quwatli exploded, in a manner I had never witnessed before, displaying extreme emotion and using strong language. Among other things he said, "King Abdallah wants to deceive [us] and the British are exploiting the opportunity to impose a treaty on our country, because our independence is a thorn in their

eyes. They want our army to move first, so that it will be destroyed. Then they will pretend to come to our aid, but in exchange they will demand the price of our enslavement. They want to pave the way for Abdallah to spread his influence in Palestine and Syria. This is a trick that I will not allow them to play on me, because my respect for my homeland is great. I will sacrifice everything for its independence. Syria alone is the fortress of Arabism, and she is proud of her independence. We have done the greatest things on behalf of Palestine, but I do not want to risk [destroying] the army, because it will protect our country from these plots and intrigues. So if King Abdallah wants to advance [on the Jews] with his army, then let him advance, and I will obey him. But if he wants the [Syrian] army alone [to defend] Palestine, then that will never happen.[25]

Shukri al-Quwatli read in King Abdallah's desire for autonomy a plot to destroy the republican regime in Damascus and to extend the terms of the Anglo-Jordanian alliance over all of Syria. The Jordanians, according to this scenario, sought to lure the paltry Syrian army into a battle with superior Jewish forces, which would annihilate it. In prior agreement with the emergent Israel and with the British, King Abdallah would then direct his attention toward the north and implement his Greater Syria project.

These fears drove the negotiations between King Abdallah and his rivals over the command structure that would guide the Arab military operations. Two very different sets of concerns defined the attitude of the Triangle Alliance toward these talks: the desire to strengthen the Arab side against the Jews, and the need to contain, if not weaken, the Turco-Hashimite Entente. The Triangle Alliance, therefore, wished to control the moves of the Jordanian army in order to prevent King Abdallah from annexing Arab Palestine, from cutting a deal with the new Jewish state, and from leaving the other Arab armies alone on the battlefield opposite superior enemy forces. In addition, however, the Palestine crisis also offered Egypt, Syria, Saudi Arabia, and Lebanon an opportunity to emasculate Jordan. It provided them with a pretext for stripping King Abdallah of the source of his power and influence in the region, thereby putting an end to the threat of his Greater Syria project and weakening the power of Britain in the Middle East.

The knife of suspicion cuts with a double edge; since the distrust between Amman and the Triangle Alliance was total, Shukri al-Quwatli's fears of King Abdallah were returned in kind. What guarantee did the Jordanian monarch have that the League would not leave *his* army alone on the battlefield? If one compares the difference between, on the one hand, the depiction of King Abdallah during this period by the British Minister in Amman and, on the other, the depiction of him by the representatives of the Triangle Alliance, then the magnitude of the distrust separating the Arab countries becomes apparent. According to Kirkbride, the decision by the League to endorse the Jordanian intervention did not have the expected effect on the king, who, "having got what he has always demanded, freedom to act, is losing his nerve." King Abdallah, in the eyes of the British representative, was a man in distress; while facing a military threat from the Jews, he was almost totally isolated among the Arab states.

The Syrians and their friends were short on empathy. In the talks that followed the Jordanian offer to liberate Palestine, Riyad al-Sulh, the prime minister of

Lebanon, played the role of intermediary between the Triangle Alliance and Amman. After one meeting with King Abdallah, he briefed the Syrian Prime Minister Jamil Mardam, who, in turn, reported to Damascus that:

> King Abdallah is playing the game of a stage actor: thus he cried, pretended to cry, and tried to make Riyad al-Sulh cry. Finally, he said that his army is small, not exceeding eight thousand men. As a result it is necessary for the Syrian army to begin first by taking the Hula region.[26]

Whereas Kirkbride recorded signs of real distress in the behavior of King Abdallah, the Lebanese prime minister and the Syrians saw nothing but a false show of emotion designed to trap them. Perceiving an attempt to lure the Syrian army out into the open, Damascus kept up the pressure to strip King Abdallah of his military.

Given the fears of the Triangle Alliance, it should hardly come as a surprise that, in the negotiations with King Abdallah, the League adopted the principled position that the duty to Arabism required Amman to hand over command of its army to the military commission of the League. During one session of talks, General Safwat explained to the king that specifically Jordanian security concerns had no legitimate place in planning the war effort. Thus, the general reported to Shukri al-Quwatli that King Abdallah, after hearing a summary of the invasion plan that the military commission had drawn up, "demanded that I change it in accordance with his views. I responded that private considerations would complicate the progress of the operations."[27] Although Jordan was contributing by far the most powerful army to the Arab coalition, the Triangle Alliance believed that Amman should have no say regarding the deployment of forces.

Behind the struggle over the Supreme Command stood four related but separate questions:

- What would be the plan of operations?
- When would the intervention begin?
- What would be the fate of the irregular forces—the Mufti's militia and the Army of Liberation?
- What would be the relationship between the Iraqi and Jordanian armies?

The difference between the answers that Jordan and the Triangle Alliance gave to these questions arose as a result of the conflict between the two Arab blocs.

Safwat's military commission, being fundamentally the creature of Damascus, favored a plan that focused on the north of Palestine, where it would provide Syria with the greatest protection.[28] The operations would begin early, about two weeks before the expiration of the Mandate. The irregular forces would remain operational and separate from the unified command so that, in the event of a truce, they could continue to press the fight home to the Jews without the unified command being held responsible by the international community.[29] In addition, the Triangle Alliance calculated that the irregulars would constitute a Palestinian *political* presence independent of King Abdallah's authority. With regard to the Iraqi and Jordanian armies, the Supreme Commander would control each separately, thus preventing collusion between the Hashimite states.

By contrast, King Abdallah pressed for a plan of action that focused operations on central Palestine—that is, the areas closest to Jordan, where the concentration of his forces would ensure the security of his regime. Circumstances permitting, this course of action would also allow Amman to annex the Arab areas of Palestine. The operation would begin only after 15 May, thus preventing friction between, on the one hand, Jordan and, on the other, Britain and the United Nations. Abdallah demanded that the League disband the irregular forces, in order to pave the way politically for the annexation of Arab Palestine, but also in order to reduce the chaos created by all of the competing military organizations operating among the Arabs. Finally, he agreed to permit Iraqi troops to operate from Jordan, but only on the condition that he be given direct command of them, thereby insuring that groups hostile to him (both inside and outside Iraq) would not deploy the Iraqi forces in a manner detrimental to Jordanian interests.[30]

Since even moderate success against the Jewish forces required the power of the Jordanian army, in the end the Triangle Alliance had no choice but to acquiesce to King Abdallah's demands. Immediately before the war, therefore, the Egyptians caved in: They fired Safwat and recognized King Abdallah as the supreme commander of the unified forces. In addition, Azzam arrived in Amman with £250,000, which he described as a first installment of a sum of three million pounds that Jordan would receive from the League in order to raise additional forces needed to prosecute the war.[31]

This seemingly friendly behavior toward Jordan was, in reality, merely a grudging concession to the realities of power. The remainder of the money never arrived, its delivery, as will be shown in the next chapter, being tied to concessions that Amman found too onerous. In addition, the title of supreme commander was completely symbolic, devoid of all serious military significance, because the Arab armies had all agreed to fight separately. Given the distrust between Amman and the Triangle Alliance, no other solution was possible: Egypt, Syria, Saudi Arabia, and Lebanon were no more willing than Jordan to permit another, hostile power to control the movements of their armies in combat. Though militarily meaningless, conferring the empty title of supreme commander on King Abdallah did have serious political value. It served the interests of the Triangle Alliance by roping Amman into a coalition designed to implement the Consensus Position on Palestine rather than the Greater Syria project. King Abdallah had been swarmed by an agitated crowd, thrown up on its shoulders, and hailed as its leader. However, if he failed to remain loyal to its desires, then it would turn on him with the accusation of treachery—it would, that is, call down on his head "the curse of the world."

Power Politics: The Calculations

When exactly did the Egyptian government decide to go to war? The reports from Cairo of Jamil Mardam, the prime minister of Syria, provide a window onto the confusion in the Egyptian capital. In the course of the struggle between the Triangle Alliance and Amman over control of the Supreme Command, Prime Minister Mardam expended great efforts in Cairo to secure the aid of King Faruq against the "intrigues of King Abdallah and the tricks of the British."[32] Thus, he gave President al-Quwatli daily reports on the attitude of the palace and the ministers; summaries of some of these dispatches appear in the diary of Taha al-Hashimi, who himself received regular briefings from the Syrian president.

On 23 or 24 April Mardam reported to Damascus that he had met "with Azzam, who said . . . that the king had resolved to come to the aid of Palestine with the strength of his army, no matter whether al-Nuqrashi accepts or rejects the decision. If he does not agree, then the king will dismiss him, and the intervention of the army will be carried out in an unofficial manner."[33] A few days later the Syrian prime minister reported to his president that he had received, directly from the palace itself, confirmation of Azzam's assurances. Moreover, the Egyptian foreign minister, Ahmad Khashaba Pasha, told him "that al-Nuqrashi agrees to the participation of the Egyptian army; he is, in fact, enthusiastic about the matter." Mardam reported that "orders had been transmitted to the army. Its forces began to advance to the border. . . . The heads of the General Staff will meet within two days to deliberate."[34]

While there is no reason to doubt the veracity of these dispatches, it is striking nonetheless that al-Nuqrashi Pasha delayed (until 11 May) going to the Senate in search of authorization for the intervention. Moreover, Muhammad Husayn Haykal, the president of the Senate, describes in his memoirs the surprise he experienced when the prime minister requested that a secret session be convened.[35] If, therefore, Jamil Mardam was correct in his claim that on 25 April the Egyptian prime minister had already decided to go to war, then al-Nuqrashi kept his decision a secret for nearly three weeks. This secrecy may have been dictated by the need to keep the enemy guessing, or it may have reflected second thoughts. At present, we have no way of determining. Thus, as a consequence of the confusion and secrecy that reigned in Cairo during the countdown to war, it is impossible to say with certainty when and how the decision to intervene was made.

Although the politics in Cairo during late April and early May 1948 remain shrouded in a thick fog, a few prominent landmarks do stand out above the mist: The Egyptian authorities reached a consensus in favor of war at a moment when they were locked in negotiations with King Abdallah over control of the Jordanian army, when their allies were begging them for aid against Amman, when Abd al-Rahman Azzam repeatedly acknowledged the threat posed by Hashimite expansionism, and when King Faruq issued a public statement warning Jordan away from a policy of territorial aggrandizement. It is inconceivable, therefore, that the problem of Jordanian power did not weigh heavily on the minds of both King Faruq and al-Nuqrashi Pasha as they calculated their moves in the Palestine arena.

Moreover, circumstantial evidence suggests that, especially in the case of King Faruq, the threat posed by King Abdallah's Greater Syria project constituted the *primary* consideration leading him to champion direct intervention.[36] As recently as February, he had displayed concern over the status of Egypt as the keystone in the arch. The king, together with Azzam and Hafiz Wahba, had advanced the Arab-bloc formula for regional defense—a proposal designed, at one and the same moment, to contain Jordan, permanently diminish the international status of Iraq, and advance the interests of Egypt in the Anglo-Egyptian struggle. Thus, the record suggests that King Faruq supported intervention in order to preserve the interests of the Triangle Alliance and to diminish the power of the Turco-Hashimite Entente.

Indeed, when King Abdallah refused to relinquish his army to the Arab League, he left no choice to the leaders in Cairo: In order to retain their influence in the Fertile Crescent, they had to go to war in Palestine. If the Egyptian government had failed to join the battle, then the freedom of action that Jordan enjoyed in the military arena would have inevitably translated itself into freedom of action in the political arena as well. Given the proclivities of King Abdallah, the peace conference following hostilities would have resulted in the partition of Palestine between the new Jewish state and Jordan—that is, it would have resulted in the worst-case scenario of the Triangle Alliance. Such a settlement would have fostered the creation of a Jordanian–Israeli axis potentially dedicated to the demolition of the republican regime in Damascus. As we have seen, President al-Quwatli and his advisors operated under the assumption that, in fact, King Abdallah intended to use the Palestine war to topple them from power. In addition, Azzam Pasha, the primary architect of the Egyptian policy toward Palestine, shared the fears of the Syrians, whom he comforted by promising the support of the Arab League against Amman.

Since the power of the League was based entirely on moral authority, it would evaporate the moment the Egyptians allowed the Jordanian army to enter the battlefield alone. For how, in the event of Egyptian nonintervention, could Cairo ever call down "the curse of the world" upon the head of King Abdallah? If the Egyptian state had refused to sacrifice a single soldier in order to save Palestine, then it would have had no legitimate basis on which to accuse the Jordanians of treachery. One cannot meaningfully accuse another of breaking a consensus unless it has actually been established. In order, therefore, for Cairo to control the actions of Jordan in the political arena, it had no choice but to enter the fray.

As Sidqi Pasha understood, the Palestine crisis in April–May 1948 placed a stark choice before the Egyptian state: Either it could beat a retreat out of Asia and hide behind the Sinai desert, or it could pursue the leadership of the Arab world. The prime minister, wavering between the two, held the decisive vote. Despite the signs of uncertainty in the behavior of al-Nuqrashi Pasha, his decision to reject the Insular-Egypt Strategy would appear to have been a foregone conclusion. When Cairo set itself, in March 1947, against the continued presence of British troops on Egyptian soil, its only hope of achieving that goal lay in organizing a bloc of like-minded Arab states against the British security system. Leadership of the Triangle Alliance was the primary source of Egyptian power in international affairs, the greatest weapon that Cairo wielded against London. Failure to protect the alliance, therefore, would have eliminated the possibility of achieving the national aims. In the case of nonintervention, the Egyptian authorities would, as Sidqi Pasha suggested, be forced to accept a compromise with the West. That is, they would be forced to allow Britain to retain base rights in the Middle East.

By April 1948 the Egyptian state, together with its allies, stood for anti-imperialism and anti-Zionism. In theory, the two issues were separate. Political realities, however, tied them together inextricably. Egyptian policy toward Palestine was the result of the following syllogism: (1) the Anglo-Egyptian conflict dictated a policy designed to protect the Triangle Alliance, which was under threat from Jordanian expansion; (2) the only method of containing Jordan lay in aggressively supporting the Consensus Position on Palestine; (3) therefore, the Anglo-Egyptian conflict dictated aggressively supporting the Consensus Position. Since, by contrast, the Insular-Egypt Strategy of Ismail Sidqi allowed for compromise with British power, it also opened the door to compromise with Zionism. Thus, when the former prime minister appeared before the Senate, he called for moderation on all fronts.

The decision to intervene in Palestine, then, struck at the fundamental international orientation of the Egyptian state. The reluctance of al-Nuqrashi Pasha to commit troops to Palestine represented a final, thin cord tying the Egyptian state to the Insular-Egypt Strategy of Ismail Sidqi. Failure to intervene would have amounted to a renunciation of Arab Leadership—by turning the resolution of the Palestine question into the exclusive concern of the Hashimite powers, the new Jewish state, and the West, it would have spelled the abandonment of the Triangle Alliance. Al-Nuqrashi Pasha, in keeping with the trajectory of the foreign policy that he had established in March 1947, cut the cord of isolationism and set Egypt loose on a pan-Arab odyssey.

Feasibility: Hashimite Policy

At the eleventh hour Cairo cobbled together a very shaky alliance. The weakness of the Arab side arose from the problem of Jordanian power. While Amman was contributing the most impressive military force to this coalition, and while King Abdallah had been anointed supreme commander of the unified Arab armies, relations between Jordan and the other members of the alliance could hardly have been worse. Saudi Arabia, which in any case was sending only a token force, had extremely bad relations with Jordan, against whom it had threatened war just three months before. Trust between the two would remain impossible as long as Riyadh claimed sovereignty over the southern part of Jordan and Amman claimed sovereignty over the Hijaz.

Syrian–Jordanian relations were no better. The official ideologies of both Amman and Damascus claimed that Jordan and Syria were constituent parts of a unitary Arab country—a land which in the eyes of King Abdallah should have been ruled by an enlarged Hashimite monarchy; in the eyes of President Shukri al-Quwatli, by a Greater Syrian Republic. For its part, the Egyptian government had, for more than a year, structured its foreign policy around the goal of destroying the British system of regional defense—the system that accounted for the very existence of the Jordanian army and, therefore, the health of the Jordanian state itself. Egypt, then, could hardly be regarded as a power friendly to Jordan. Only in Baghdad did one find significant political forces that supported the interests of Amman. After the *Wathba*, however, these were to a certain extent checked by the anti-imperialist groups in Iraqi politics who, like everyone else, regarded King Abdallah as a British stooge.

Since only a very thin and brittle shell of Arab unity covered this rotten core, why did Cairo pin the fate of its army on the Arab coalition? A serious answer to this question requires an analysis of the geopolitical context in which the Egyptian authorities made the decision to intervene. At least three basic factors must be considered: the perception by the Egyptian authorities of relations within the alliance, the attitudes of the Great Powers, and the military balance between the Jews and the Arabs.

With regard to the central political problem that plagued the coalition—that is, the threat of Hashimite expansionism—Cairo believed that it could manage both Baghdad and Amman. This belief was founded on a very sound basis. After all, the military alliance drew its strength from a broad Arab consensus in favor of united action designed to liberate an Arab land that had, first, been detached from its sister lands by the imperialists and, then, settled by a foreign people. The Hashimite rulers, therefore, could not swim directly against the ideological current that Cairo was channeling against them.

In the case of Baghdad, the regime felt so threatened by popular pan-Arab forces that it bent over backwards to appease Cairo. Militant anti-Zionism had in any case always played a greater role in Iraq than in the other Arab states. But the *Wathba*, which had been immediately preceded by large and violent demonstrations on Palestine, now made the atmosphere in Baghdad particularly dangerous for the Hashimite House.[37] As a result of the shaky legitimacy of the regime, and of the ideological connection between anti-imperialism and anti-Zionism, the regent, Abd al-Ilah, had one overriding political goal in the conflict with the Jews: To avoid the appearance of being soft on Zionism or antagonistic toward the Arab League. Thus on 25 April, during the negotiations between the Triangle Alliance and King Abdallah, he flew to Cairo, where, in a somewhat mysterious meeting with King Faruq, he pressed the Egyptians to intervene in Palestine.[38]

The British minister in Amman met with the regent just before he flew to Cairo: Kirkbride, a sensitive observer, gained the impression that Abd al-Ilah's "main objective was to calm public opinion in Iraq rather than to save Arab Palestine."[39] Since the Iraqi regent was widely regarded as a British henchman, Iraqi nationalists scrutinized his every move for signs of treachery. Abd al-Ilah, therefore, sought Egyptian participation in the war in order to create the appearance of fraternal cooperation among the Arab states. He worked to secure collective Arab responsibility for developments in Palestine in order to shelter the Iraqi government from the claim that it followed a policy hostile to the Arab League. Thus, although the exact content of the meeting between King Faruq and the regent remains secret, the basic direction of Iraqi politics is easy enough for us to glean, as it was for the Egyptians at the time. As early as February 1948, the

Triangle Alliance had noted that the *Wathba* would force Iraq to distance itself from Jordan.[40] Cairo knew it had the advantage over Baghdad.

The weakness of Iraq diminished the strength of Jordan. Since the regent was loath to appear as the antagonist of the Triangle Alliance during the Palestine crisis, King Abdallah had no strong allies in the Arab arena. Consequently, his political room to maneuver had narrowed considerably. It is striking, in this regard, that one of the first requests that General Safwat made to King Abdallah was that Amman should allow an Iraqi mechanized brigade to establish a forward position in Jordan in preparation for war in Palestine. Since the regime in Baghdad was held hostage by a public that endorsed a policy of no compromise with Zionism, the intervention of the Iraqis would place additional pressure on Amman to respect the Consensus Position.

In addition to the international isolation of Jordan, the domestic political environment was in the throes of a momentous transformation, the Palestinian-ization of Jordanian society. Partially as a result of this change, the Triangle Alliance now possessed, in contrast with the past, the means to discipline King Abdallah. The anti-Zionist and anti-imperialist ideology that Cairo and its allies disseminated began to bite deeply into the Jordanian body politic. For instance, Kirkbride reported on 25 April that:

> tremendous public pressure is being brought to bear on the king and on the regent to intervene with troops in Palestine immediately. The fact that Amman is crowded out with Palestinian refugees and that reports are now coming in of a Jewish offensive in Jerusalem does not make matters any easier.[41]

The Palestinians were not the only ones who pressed for action. As early as February—that is, before the major Jewish victories—Jordanian leaders did not have the power to force the lower echelons in their bureaucracy to enforce orders that contradicted the policies of the Arab League.[42] More important, the younger ministers in Amman disliked the king's close ties with Britain and his hostility to the Arab League, to say nothing of his negotiations with the Jews.[43] As a result, they could not be trusted to keep his clandestine policies secret.

As powerful forces converged on the Jordanian monarch, he had no choice but to demonstrate his fidelity to the League. Consequently, his actions in April 1948 betray a newly found desire to prove that Jordan did indeed respect the Consensus Position. For instance, on 17 April the Jordanian palace released a statement "in order to quiet public opinion and to dispel all doubts." It noted that the Arab countries, while themselves rejecting partition, had been pressing for Jordan to declare its policy "in a manner beyond interpretation." For this purpose, the statement affirmed that Jordan "has the same duty as that of the other Arab countries," and that it "opposes vigorously partition and trusteeship." It considered the Jews to have declared war against all Arabs, including Jordan, as evidenced by the Deir Yassin massacre.[44] The defiance of the Arab League that had formerly characterized the official statements of Amman was totally absent.

So powerful was the pressure to conform to the will of the Triangle Alliance that, even when dealing with the Jews in secret, King Abdallah forced himself to behave in a manner consistent with his warlike statements. Things had been different only a few months earlier. Before the United Nations partition resolution, King Abdallah met frequently with representatives of the Jewish Agency. In early November he had even come to a strong verbal understanding with them regarding the partition of Palestine between a Jewish state and Jordan.[45] By April 1948, however, he had turned his back on the Jewish Agency, fearing that leaks regarding his relations with the enemy would harm not just his relations with his Arab rivals but also with some of his supporters at home.

During the diplomatic prelude to the war, therefore, the king refused, even in his covert diplomacy, to acknowledge the verbal agreement on partition that he had reached with the Jewish Agency.[46] For instance, after the palace in Amman issued a statement announcing that the best deal the Zionists would ever receive would be autonomy within an Arab state, the Jewish Agency responded with a protest telegram that Kirkbride characterized as "a judicious mix of menace and readiness to negotiate."[47] In response, King Abdallah sent a message that simply reiterated the terms of the public offer made the previous day. He explained to Kirkbride "that in view of the publicity attending these exchanges" an offer of autonomy within an Arab state "was as far as he could go. He did not expect the Jews to accept such terms but his purpose was to keep the door open for negotiations when both sides were in a more reasonable frame of mind."[48]

This tacit renunciation of the earlier agreement with the Jewish Agency, combined with a host of other signals, convinced the leadership of the emergent Israel that King Abdallah had become completely subservient to the Arab League. Indeed, they were correct in their assessment. True, he had succeeded in retaining the command of his army. Moreover, in his own mind he knew well that the Zionists were powerful, that the likelihood of an Arab victory over them was small, and that if Jordan could preserve its army intact, then it would be well placed when the dust had settled to seek an accommodation with the new Jewish state. This, of course, was the stuff of which Syrian fears were made. But who could say what would happen before the dust had settled? For the moment, at least, King Abdallah had no ability to act independently of the Triangle Alliance. Thus, while the Syrian leadership did have good reason to be wary, the Egyptian authorities were certainly not wrong about the persuasive power of the Arab League. Whether viewed from Cairo or Tel Aviv, King Abdallah was the League's servant—potentially rebellious, yes, but a servant nonetheless.

Feasibility: British Policy

On the eve of the war, therefore, the Egyptian leadership felt secure in its assumption that the Jordanian army could, in fact, be pressed into the service of the Triangle Alliance. The ability to manage both the Iraqis and the Jordanians led Cairo to the conclusion that it had achieved the coveted status of keystone in the arch. That is, having corralled all of the Arab governments behind the Consensus Position, the Egyptian government believed that it had automatically corralled London behind it as well. This attitude was already present in the proposal on regional defense that King Faruq and Azzam Pasha had floated in February. At that time the two great pillars of the Empire in the Arab world—Iraq and Egypt—had both refused to renew their alliances with Britain, and the recognition of this had infused the Egyptian authorities with a sense of power. They knew that Jordan alone could not possibly function as the foundation for a regional security system for the Empire, nor could it protect the vast oil interests in the Arab world. They reasoned, therefore, that if Britain wanted to retain any influence in the region, it would have no choice but to accommodate itself to the rising tide of nationalism—a tide consciously channeled by the Arab League.

Two officials who carried out the policies of the Arab League in 1948 attest to the belief by Cairo that control over the Jordanian army translated directly into control over Britain. Fawzi al-Qawuqji, the commander of the Arab Liberation army, writes:

> Among those Arabs who were too clever for their own good, the criterion for testing the validity of the British claims [to support the Arab side in the conflict] was the position of the Transjordanian state. When King Abdallah announced that he would intervene in Palestine as a combatant, the Arab states heaved a sigh of relief. They assumed, therefore, that the English were going to support the Arabs, otherwise King Abdallah would not have rushed to proclaim his determination to fight for Palestine.[49]

Although Fawzi al-Qawuqji does not specify the Egyptians by name, in the next paragraph he suggests that the Syrian government did not agree with this line of thinking, thereby leaving no doubt that when referring to "Arabs who were too clever for their own good" he meant the Egyptians and, perhaps, the Saudis.

Ahmad Farraj Tayi', who served as the Egyptian consul-general in Jerusalem during the war, corroborates the perception of al-Qawuqji, stating that "the reliance of the Arab leaders on the Jordanian Arab Army was based on the erroneous calculation that King Abdallah's having entered the war against the Jews meant that the British had agreed that he should participate in it."[50] The accounts of al-Qawuqji and Tayi', written with the benefit of hindsight, are colored by an awareness of the many ways in which Britain did not, in fact, live up to the high expectations of Cairo. Among other things, London had honored the United Nations arms embargo against the belligerents, refusing to supply the Arabs, including Jordan, with sorely needed ammunition and arms. Thus, Tayi', writing in an atmosphere defined by grave disappointment regarding British policy, depicts the Egyptian leadership as obtuse. He writes, for instance, that:

> Abd al-Rahman Azzam forgot that the most important Arab countries, those whose armies would play the primary role in preserving the Arabism of Palestine—that is, Egypt, Iraq, and Jordan—were at that time oppressed under the yoke of the British occupation. . . . Furthermore, he forgot that the weaponry and materiel of the Jordanian army came from Britain; that its soldiers and officers drew their pay from its treasury; that, what is more, the officers that led this army in battle were themselves British officers. All of this was absent from the calculations of Abd al-Rahman Azzam as he endeavored to make the Arab armies pursue a policy not just independent of the policy of the British government but, rather, completely opposed

to it. When he was reminded of the realities of the Jordanian army, he thought that he could enable this army to operate in freedom, independent of the will of the British government. Therefore, he suggested to the Arab states that they aid it with money.[51]

If this passage is compared with the lecture Shukri al-Quwatli gave to al-Nuqrashi Pasha in October 1947, when the Egyptians tabled the plan to buy the Arab Legion, then it almost appears as if the Egyptian consul-general exchanged notes with the Syrian president on the policies of Cairo.

Tayi' does not place all of the blame on Azzam Pasha. The prime minister also receives a thrashing:

> It was the duty of the late Mahmud Fahmi al-Nuqrashi to remember that in August 1947—that is, just a few months before the decision to enter the war—he had referred the Egyptian case against Britain to the Security Council, where he heaped abuse on the British. Was it reasonable to expect that the British would aid him against the Jews while the echo of his voice in the Security Council still rang in their ears?[52]

Buried under Tayi"s ridicule is the description of a policy. Of course, neither al-Nuqrashi Pasha nor Azzam Pasha "forgot" the extent of British influence in Jordan; nor did they fail to realize the bitterness that Egyptian anti-imperialism had created in London. Certainly it would be more accurate to say that they miscalculated: They overestimated the benefits of being the keystone in the arch. They simply discounted the possibility of British opposition to the Arab League.

The war would prove that Cairo had greatly exaggerated its power to corral Britain behind the policies of the Arab League. When viewed, however, in terms of the evidence available in April 1948, it cannot be denied that the Egyptian attitude toward Britain arose from a serious analysis of the dominant currents of thought in London. After all, for more than two years the British had refused to oppose the Consensus Position on Palestine, even when their policies provoked the United States, their most important ally. In addition, as Fawzi al-Qawuqji notes, Foreign Minister Bevin and other officials in London had repeatedly stressed that British self-interest required good relations with the Arabs. Under these circumstances, then, it was not at all unreasonable for Cairo to expect that Britain would persist in her attempts to cultivate a reputation as the Great Power most sympathetic to Arab nationalism. As long as the Egyptian government, together with her allies, enjoyed the ability to define the collective will of the Arab states, it had reason to believe that it could manipulate London.

Undoubtedly as a consequence of this line of thought, Cairo tilted toward Britain in the period immediately before the war. After rejecting the American trusteeship proposal, Azzam Pasha suggested to the British that they prolong the Mandate—an initiative predicated on the assumption that continued British rule would tip the balance to the advantage of the Palestinians, providing the Arab states with an opportunity to prepare for battle.[53] This kind of calculation also revealed itself in the negotiation with Jordan over the supreme command. Before bestowing the empty title on King Abdallah, the Egyptians first offered it to John

Bagot Glubb, the British commander of the Arab Legion. Kirkbride describes the episode in his memoirs:

> The next caller of note at Amman was Abder Rahman Azzam who probably came there with the express intention of making sure that the Jordanian authorities did not fail to play the part assigned to them in the plan drawn up by the Arab League. He had several talks with Glubb and, surprisingly enough, offered him the appointment by the League to the post of commander-in-chief of all the Arab forces in the field. Both Glubb and I were convinced that the offer was made in bad faith and that none of the other Arab governments would be prepared to permit their troops to be placed under the order of a British officer, even if he was technically a servant of the Jordanian Government. We suspected that the hidden idea behind the proposal was to provide a ready-made scapegoat for any future failures. Anyway, the suggestion was rejected with something approaching derision.[54]

Kirkbride and Glubb grasped the basic principle at work, if not the precise goal of the tactic. Abd al-Rahman Azzam calculated that, by associating a prominent British officer with the Arab war effort, he could co-opt London—precisely because the Foreign Office would fear the possibility of being made a scapegoat for failure. He reasoned that the British, with their own reputation for friendship toward the Arabs at stake, would have no choice but to support wholeheartedly the position of the League.

Feasibility: American Policy

In early May, the United States government worked feverishly for a truce in order to forestall the intervention of the Arab armies. This effort had been preceded by a dramatic shift in American policy away from support for the partition of Palestine and toward the idea of a United Nations trusteeship. By backing away from their previous endorsement for the creation of a Jewish state, the State Department intended to signal to the Arab world a policy more favorable to the Palestinians and less supportive of Zionism.[55] Even though the trusteeship plan had failed by late April, it nonetheless indicated a change in the priorities of Washington. It announced a tilt in American policy toward the Arab League. The violence in Palestine had awakened the fear that defeat of the Palestinians by the Jews would result in the refusal by the Arab states to cooperate with the West in the Cold War.

Though the authors of the trusteeship proposal intended to prevent hostilities, this sudden American solicitude toward the Arabs actually strengthened the hawks among the Egyptian elite. While Sidqi Pasha believed that by going to war the Egyptian government risked becoming embroiled with the Great Powers, others claimed that the obvious dependence of the Americans on Arab goodwill eliminated the risk that Washington would frustrate Egyptian goals.

This line of reasoning emerged in a very clear form during the secret session of the Egyptian Senate; it arose in the debate over Sidqi Pasha's assertion that

Egypt, if it wished, had the option of removing itself from the Palestine conflict. The prime minister and others responded that isolationism was impossible, because the expansive Jewish state, if given time to grow, would inevitably attack Egypt. Sidqi Pasha responded to this claim as follows:

> Anyone who possesses some familiarity with international politics knows the extent to which the countries comprising the Western bloc are concerned with [winning] the friendship of this area of the world, that is, the Arab area. It became apparent in what was said before—as it became apparent in the statement of the prime minister himself—that everything indicates there is a strong desire [among the Western Powers] not to oppress the Arabs and not to obstruct their activities. The Powers tried to avoid the [negative] consequences of the thorny problems that arose. The greatest proof of this is that the partition plan—which America had considered to be the best plan—was abandoned. Why? Was it not in order to keep the friendship of the Arabs? Do you think, Your Honors, that there exist Powers who will help that minority of the Jews living in Palestine to cross this desert [the Sinai], which neither the Turkish nor the German armies was capable of crossing?[56]

Al-Nuqrashi Pasha answered this reasoning by depicting Zionism as the tool of Western imperialism. He stated that "Zionist gangs" constituted "the spearhead of the invasion that is being planned against this region"; the Great Powers would, contrary to Sidqi Pasha's appraisal, support the gangs "in order to spread confusion and disturb the security" of the region.

The task of responding directly to the arguments of Sidqi Pasha fell to the influential Wafdist, Fuad Siraj al-Din Pasha, who explained how a policy of intervention would avoid damaging the relations between Egypt and the United States. Sidqi Pasha, he claimed:

> is certainly correct in his view that the Great Powers ... desire the friendship and goodwill of the Arabs. They fear that a war will break out in the Middle East because of the Palestine question. . . . This military intervention [by us] is precisely the thing that will force the Great Powers to change their policies in order to prevent a clash with the Arabs and to prevent a war in the Middle East, the scope of which God alone knows. Therefore, I say that the assumption of His Eminence Sidqi Pasha about [the Great Powers] desiring the friendship of the Arabs is correct. Indeed, this military intervention is the way to activate that desire [for friendship]. We can remain still and quiet, we can waste time in meetings held here and there, and in broadcasting declarations here and there, but these are activities on our side that, as long as the matter remains peaceful and quiet, will not stir the Powers that desire the goodwill of the Arabs. These activities do not have the results that they fear.[57]

The hawks among the Egyptian elite recognized that the United States had not truly respected the Consensus Position of the Arab League until violence had descended on Palestine. They reasoned, therefore, that further violence would force the hand of Washington and elicit even greater respect for the Arabs.

Thus, the advocates of war felt that the international political context, on balance, favored the Arab forces. Having roped Jordan into an Arab League coalition, Cairo considered itself to have secured the support of Great Britain, which would not allow the Jewish forces to destroy an Arab army led by British officers.

For their part, the Americans could not afford to alienate the Arab League because of its importance to them in the Cold War. The Egyptian government must have been well informed regarding the conflict between President Truman, who sought to win the favor of Jewish voters by supporting the establishment of a Jewish state, and the State Department, which tilted toward the Arab League out of fear of losing the support of the Arab world in the Cold War. Presumably, therefore, Cairo did not expect Washington to renounce completely its concern for Jewish interests in Palestine. No doubt, however, the Egyptian leadership felt reasonably confident that, as a result of its desire for Arab goodwill, Washington would never permit the rout of the Egyptian army that actually took place.

In the event, the thinking of men such as Fuad Siraj al-Din turned out to be completely in error. During the war, the balance of power in Washington actually shifted back toward Truman's Zionism.[58] The failure of Siraj al-Din to predict this shift, however, should not be attributed to ignorance. With regard to the Great Power arena, the advantage of Israel over the Arabs in 1948 stemmed from the simultaneous support that it received from the Eastern and Western blocs. While Washington took Israel under its wing at the United Nations, Moscow provided diplomatic support and, in addition, supplied the Jewish state indirectly with arms and ammunition. Since in May 1948 the Cold War was already in full swing, many sober observers of international affairs would not have predicted that both Washington and Moscow would work simultaneously against the policy of the Arab League. Thus, the calculation of Fuad Siraj al-Din that the blocs would vie for the goodwill of the Arabs, though totally wrong, was nonetheless based on sound reasoning. In fact, it prefigured the correct calculations in 1956 of Abd al-Nasser, who nationalized the Suez Canal Company with the assumption that Washington would not support Britain in a war against Egypt. The willingness to take that risk, of course, won Abd al-Nasser the adulation of the Arab world.

Feasibility: The Military Balance

The rout of the Egyptian army by the Israeli forces in 1948 fosters the impression that Cairo had a very poor grasp of the realities of the military balance. If they had known that the Israeli forces were more powerful, the reasoning goes, they never would have placed their men in harm's way. The evidence, however, will not completely support this view. Sidqi Pasha, for one, perceived the ill-preparedness of the Egyptian army, saw the military disaster coming, and did his utmost to avert it. In addition, the reluctance of al-Nuqrashi Pasha to join the war camp suggests that he, too, shared many of the doubts expressed in the Senate by the former prime minister.

Perhaps Cairo, though aware of its own forces' deficiencies, felt that they were still adequate for the job of vanquishing the "gangs," as al-Nuqrashi described the military force of Zionism. The evidence, however, will not support this hypothesis either. Since October 1947 the military commission of the Arab League, under the direction of General Safwat, had prepared numerous reports on the strength of the Zionist forces; all of these emphasized the power of the Jews. The first report set the tone for the rest, arriving at, among others, the following conclusions:

A. The Zionists in Palestine control political parties and military and administrative structures that are characterized by a very high level of organization. These institutions are capable of being converted immediately into a Zionist government that will possess all of the resources required by a state.
B. With regard to men, weapons, and supplies, the Jews control large forces. They also have large reserves of trained men, or men capable of being trained, who can be called up and organized within a very short period of time.
C. The Jews have huge sources of money both inside the country and abroad.
D. The Jews have a great potential for bringing, in very large quantities, reinforcements and equipment from overseas.[59]

This is the tune that Ismail Safwat sang from October 1947 to April 1948. The failure of the Arab states to organize themselves adequately to defend the Palestinians, it will be recalled, prompted him to threaten resignation when the Arab resistance reached the verge of collapse. Moreover, it was the consequent demoralization of the Triangle Alliance that forced the alliance, with some misgivings, to turn to Jordan for military aid. It is impossible, therefore, to argue that the Egyptian government did not know, in general terms at least, that it faced an enemy of some consequence in Palestine.

In addition, as we have seen, the opponents of Sidqi Pasha in the Senate argued down his isolationist position by stressing the *power* of the enemy. Thus, while Senator Abbas al-Jamal depicted the Jewish state as an insatiable, expansive force that would inevitably attack the Nile Valley itself, Fuad Siraj al-Din explained that the Jews controlled the world economy. To be sure, these arguments focused on the future power of the Jewish state rather than the immediate military balance, but they nonetheless represent a tendency to stress the strength rather than weakness of the Zionist movement.

If the authorities in Cairo did not minimize the power of their enemy, neither did they exaggerate the abilities of the Egyptian army. True, when addressing the Senate, al-Nuqrashi Pasha dismissed the doubts that Ismail Sidqi had raised regarding the preparedness of the military for battle. He categorically affirmed that, as the Egyptian army "stands on the verge of entering Palestine, its organization is more than adequate for combating the terrorist gangs." In addition, he denied any problems related to the supply of equipment and ammunition. There can be no doubt, however, that the prime minister lied through his teeth.

The views of Abd al-Rahman Azzam prove that the doubts of Sidqi Pasha regarding the preparedness of the Egyptian army were in fact widely shared by the elite in Cairo. On 11 May, the same day when the Egyptian prime minister assured the Senate regarding the state of the armed forces, Azzam Pasha found himself in Damascus. He confessed to his Syrian associates that the chiefs of the Arab militaries had concluded that the Arab forces were "insufficient."[60] Two days later, he told Taha al-Hashimi that the Arab states "do not possess ammunition sufficient for a war of long duration. . . . He said that Egypt had an inadequate store of rifle ammunition, and that it did not possess a factory for producing it."[61]

The Egyptian leadership, while worried about the preparedness its own military, had no confidence whatsoever in the combined power of the Syrian, Lebanese, and Saudi armies. Al-Nuqrashi Pasha responded to a query regarding the strength of the Arab side by stating that Syrian "resources are limited" because, he explained, "the period of time during which she has controlled the affairs of her army has been short, so that she has yet to complete her preparations."[62] The same considerations applied to Lebanon. As for the Saudi contribution, the prime minister at first forgot to mention it—an omission that spoke volumes. When a senator noted that al-Nuqrashi had skipped an ally, he responded vaguely: "I forgot to do that and I apologize, because I am in contact with the Saudi army. The Saudi state will send some forces that will play a great role."[63] In the event, the Saudi contribution to the war effort was purely symbolic.

The Egyptian evaluation of the Iraqi army on the eve of the war is difficult to ascertain. Given the great distance separating Iraq from Palestine, given the civil unrest in Baghdad, and given the tenuous hold of the government on Iraqi Kurdistan, it is most unlikely that Cairo expected the Iraqi army to respond to the crisis in Palestine with all of its resources.[64] In the event, the Iraqi forces displayed a marked lack of initiative in the war. According to one credible eyewitness, they arrived without proper supplies and with no maps of Palestine; a large contingent took up defensive positions in the Nablus region, far removed from the battle. When asked why they failed to advance, the Iraqi commanders responded with a refrain that became something of a joke among the local people: "*Maku awamir*"—"We have no orders," they said in Iraqi dialect.[65] This distaste for combat, which almost rivaled the prudence of the Syrian and Lebanese armies, may well have come as something of a surprise to Cairo. Under the circumstances, however, it could not have been completely unforeseen.

Any confidence, therefore, that the Egyptian authorities had in the strength of their coalition partners sprang from a consideration of the power of the Jordanian army. Thus, al-Nuqrashi Pasha began his survey of allied militaries by extolling the virtues of General Glubb's forces:

> You ask me now about the preparedness of Egypt and the preparedness of the Arab peoples. Let us place [the case of] Egypt to one side, and I will describe to you the power of the Arab states. The Arab Legion—as I said to you—is the army of Transjordan and it is powerful, well trained, and has experience in [Palestine], where it has served in preserving order. As I told you, the gangs will oppose the British forces, but when the Arab Legion is present they remain quiet. Its officers and men alike are well trained and they have the [necessary] equipment.
>
> [Question from a senator: How many men does it have?]
>
> I cannot cite the number, but you all know that the important thing is the striking power of the army, and the number of men is not important. The striking power of the Arab Legion is total.[66]

Al-Nuqrashi Pasha was certainly justified in his positive appraisal of the Jordanian army. The imbalance, however, between the military contributions of the Triangle

Alliance and of the Hashimite bloc undoubtedly gave rise to considerable apprehension in Cairo.

Indeed, if the attitude of the secretary-general of the Arab League is any indication, then on the eve of the war the Egyptian leadership was nothing if not nervous. On 11, 12, and 13 May, Abd al-Rahman Azzam Pasha fretted continuously—about the military balance, the policy of the Americans, and the intentions of King Abdallah. Taha al-Hashimi recorded a typical encounter with him:

> I met with Azzam at the Palace [of the Republic in Damascus]. It emerged from what he said that he is fearful of the results. He foresees a difficult resistance over a long period of time. I allayed his fears, saying to him that I believed the Jews were still weak when compared with the regular forces. Thanks to the excellence of their weaponry, their settlements, and their means of transport and communication, they are superior to the irregular forces, which are armed with [only] rifles and a few machine guns. But compared with the regular forces—provided these operate in unity and with mutual responsibility—well then there is no doubt that the position of the Jews will be difficult. *Therefore, the desirable thing is to eliminate the possibility of partition being carried out.* If the forces advance rapidly, taking control of the Galilee region and the Jezreel Valley, if they arrive at Afula, and if the Egyptians advance to the proximity of Jaffa, besieging Tel Aviv, then they can aim their cannons from their encampments. Then, the situation permitting, they will attack Tel Aviv. There is no doubt that the Powers will intervene after that and demand a truce.[67]

If we take this conversation as representative of opinion among the Egyptian and Syrian leadership on the eve of the war, then the optimists in the Triangle Alliance did in fact hope, albeit against their better judgment, to defeat Zionism.

Nonetheless, even Taha al-Hashimi's extremely rosy scenario—which he drew in order to calm his friend's nerves—did not envision total victory for the Arab forces, which, before destroying the resistance in Tel Aviv, would be compelled by the Great Powers to pull back. Indeed, in a different conversation with Taha al-Hashimi, Azzam Pasha took early intervention by the Great Powers as a strong possibility. On 12 May, during a discussion about whether the irregular forces should be placed under the control of the General Command, Azzam stated that

> he thinks that the organizations should remain as they are, so that they can continue to operate even if the truce is accepted. The armies will be stopped in their positions, but these organizations will continue to operate covertly, just as the Jewish terrorist groups operate. In that way, the Command [of the regular army] can renounce their activities.[68]

Thus, the Triangle Alliance, although it endorsed a public policy of no compromise with Zionism, was actually aware of the military limitations of the coalition. It may have overestimated its own strength, and it may have failed—despite Sidqi Pasha's predictions—to foresee the manner in which the arms embargo would work against the Arab side. Nonetheless, Cairo operated under the assumption that its resources were limited, perhaps even inadequate. The Egyptian authorities, therefore, planned for the possibility of being forced to stop short of total victory.

Given the limitations of the Arab side, the primary political goal of military action was the prevention of partition, as Taha al-Hashimi mentioned. In the political world of 1948—especially as viewed from Damascus—preventing partition meant only one thing: thwarting cooperation between Jordan and Israel. Total victory over the Jewish forces was certainly the best means of eliminating the threat of an Amman–Tel Aviv axis; it was not, however, essential to this project. The creation of a military and political climate that would drive a wedge between King Abdallah and the new Jewish state would serve, in the eyes of the Triangle Alliance, as an undesirable but nonetheless acceptable solution to the Palestine crisis.

The Goals of the Intervention

On 15 May the Egyptian state intervened in Palestine as the political leader of a military coalition ostensibly commanded by King Abdallah of Jordan. The public goals of this coalition were to restore order by suppressing the armed forces of the Jewish state and to turn Palestine over to its Arab inhabitants. Behind the scenes, however, Cairo harbored doubts about its ability to achieve these aims— because the Egyptian army was ill prepared, because sober voices regarded even the combined Arab forces as inadequate to the task, because the policies of the Great Powers might prevent it, and because the best Arab army belonged to Jordan—a country that sought to annex Arab Palestine. Since the Egyptian authorities clearly perceived most of the factors that cast doubt about the attainment of the public goal of coalition, it is wrong to state that Cairo entered the war with the primary intention of destroying all of the Jewish forces, although such an outcome would certainly have served its purposes.

The Egyptian state intervened, first and foremost, in order to protect its position as the leader of the Triangle Alliance and as the dominant power in the Arab world. Preserving its status as the keystone in the arch was an essential prerequisite for success in the Anglo-Egyptian conflict, the primary concern of its foreign policy. In concrete political terms, retaining the leadership of the Arabs meant preventing the establishment of a Jordanian–Israeli alliance. An Amman– Tel Aviv axis would have spelled disaster for Cairo, because it would have inaugurated cooperation between the two most powerful military organizations in the Fertile Crescent; it also would have constituted a direct threat to the republican regime in Damascus. It would, therefore, have reduced to naught the influence of Egypt in the northern Arab world.

The flimsy alliance that the Egyptian authorities pretended to let King Abdallah lead into battle was, at one and the same moment, an anti-Israeli and an anti-Jordanian instrument. Cairo viewed the coalition not as a weapon for destroying Zionism but, rather, as a catapult designed to hurl the Jordanian army at the Israelis. The distinction between these two conceptions is indeed fine, but significant nonetheless. In military terms, the goal of the coalition was to liberate as much Palestinian territory as possible and to weaken, if not defeat, the enemy. In political terms, however, its purpose was to prevent the partition of Palestine between Israel and Jordan by forcing Amman, first, to make war against Zionism, and, second, to refrain from cutting a deal with the enemy without the author-ization of Cairo.

The task of catapulting the Arab Legion at the Israelis required harnessing to the coalition the tremendous weight of anti-imperialist and anti-Zionist senti-ment in the Arab world. In order to bring the full force of this weight to bear on the mechanism, the Egyptians had no choice but to go to war themselves. In addition, they had no choice but to capture the moral high ground of Arab politics by advocating a policy of no compromise, even though they realized that compromise would be a very likely outcome of the conflict. Calling for the lib-eration of Palestine, and behaving in a manner consistent with the call, were essential components of the Egyptian project, but they did not constitute its central objective.

Thus, partial failure on the battlefield would not constitute a failure of the entire operation, if the maneuver were to result in driving a wedge between King Abdallah and the Zionists. If Cairo stopped short of destroying Zionism and yet still succeeded, say, in creating a Palestinian state sandwiched on the West Bank between Jordan and Israel, then it would have achieved its fundamental goals of preventing the expansion of Jordan and thwarting the creation of an Amman–Tel Aviv axis.

The Egyptian leadership, despite the ill-preparedness of its army, did not en-vision an embarrassing defeat of the Arab forces, certainly not a complete rout. On the basis of the available evidence, the calculations of Cairo in 1948 appear to have been similar to its calculations in 1973. The Sadat regime, knowing that it could not destroy Israel, hoped that, by striking a blow powerful enough and by holding on to territory long enough, it could create an international political atmosphere more favorable to its interests. In 1948 the miscalculations of the Egyptian leadership did not result from a faulty understanding of the Arab arena, or from ignorance of the military balance but, rather, from the expectation that war in Palestine would force the Great Powers to respect the will of the Arab League. The authorities in Cairo erroneously assumed that the concern of the West—Britain, first and foremost—with maintaining the friendship of the Arab world would insulate the Arab armies from failure on the battlefield. In addition, the close ties of Britain to the Arab Legion would, they calculated, force London to support to the fullest the operations of the Jordanian army—operations that would be directed ultimately by the Triangle Alliance, not by King Abdallah.

The Egyptian government did not blunder into the war, it simply gambled and lost. When, on 11 May 1948, Ismail Sidqi stood before the Senate to oppose the military intervention, Abd al-Rahman Azzam was in Damascus planning for war. Hundreds of miles and a vast desert separated the two; nonetheless, the former prime minister's warnings somehow managed to reach the other man's ears:

> At a luncheon at the Palace of the Republic, Azzam turned to me with an embar-rassing question. He said that some of the military men consider the forces . . . to

be weak. . . . He said that if, in fact, our forces were not sufficient, then it would be best to accept the conditions of the truce, because the truce might still allow us to attain our rights, whereas failure in battle will strip us of all rights.[69]

After soberly calculating the odds, the Egyptian leadership turned a deaf ear to Ismail Sidqi and rolled the dice of war.

SIX

War and Containment

Let the Consequences Be Damned

The leaders of Jordan considered Egypt an irresponsible ally. They found particularly reprehensible the refusal of Cairo to renew the first cease-fire, which ex-
pired in early July 1948. Britain, the United States, and the Security Council had
all strongly urged the belligerents to prolong the truce; and the Israelis, for their
part, agreed to an extension. Thus, the Egyptian refusal both tested the goodwill
of the Great Powers and ushered in a disastrous round of fighting.[1]

At the decisive meeting of the Arab League, Amman argued against resuming
the war, pointing out that the Arab side was weaker than the Israelis and low on
ammunition. Cairo, however, argued on the basis of unassailable nationalist principles that the battle must be resumed. In response to the Jordanian complaints
regarding the weakness of the coalition and the lack of supplies, the proponents
of war explained that, in light of their deficiencies, the Arab armies would simply
have to remain on the defensive. The Jordanian prime minister, Tawfiq Abu'l-
Huda, felt powerless to defy his allies:

> I was a minority of one. All the others wanted to renew the fighting. If I had voted
> alone against it, we should only have been denounced as traitors, and the truce
> would not have been renewed. Jordan cannot refuse to fight if the other Arabs insist
> on fighting. Our own people here would not stand for that.[2]

The second round, of course, lasted only ten days and resulted in significant
Israeli advances, including the capture of Lydda and Ramleh, whose inhabitants—
numbering perhaps 30,000—the Israelis forcibly expelled. The Egyptian decision
particularly vexed the Jordanians, because when the truce first took effect, Cairo,
which had no illusions about the military balance, had indicated to Amman that
it would not open a second round.[3]

Referring to the Egyptian decision, John Bagot Glubb, the commander of the
Arab Legion, states in his memoirs that he "can recollect no precedent in history
for such irresponsible action on the part of those in power."[4] Indeed, in retrospect
it is clear that the resumption of combat marked the turning point in the war.
During the first round of fighting, the Arab armies held the initiative; in the
remaining rounds, however, they fought a purely defensive war, with the Israelis
choosing when and where to attack. Given the shorter Israeli lines of commu-

nication, and given the defensive posture of the Arab armies, the Israelis benefited from the ability to concentrate massive firepower at a single point. From Glubb's perspective, therefore, the failure to preserve the status quo in July harmed the Arabs both diplomatically and militarily. Had the truce been accepted, then the further expansion of Israel might have been prevented.

In trying to explain the decision by Cairo to resume a war that it knew it could not win, Glubb advances three explanations—one based on the peculiar mental makeup of the Egyptians, the other two based on their political calculations. With regard to the first, Glubb writes:

> The Western Arabs—the Egyptians, Palestinians, and Syrians—have that logical mentality which deals only in purely intellectual conceptions. Such people are incapable of compromise. To them it was unjust that the Jews should forcibly invade and conquer their country—and that was the end of it.
>
> Count Bernadotte [the United Nations special mediator] encountered this factor on at least two occasions in his negotiations with the Arabs—in Nokrashy Pasha and Abdul Rahman Pasha Azzam, secretary-general of the Arab League. When he pointed out that if the truce were not renewed, the Arabs might be defeated, they replied to the effect that this might be true, but that it was better to lose all than consent to a wrong.
>
> When the political committee of the Arab League met in Amman, immediately before the end of the mandate, I happened to be summoned to see King Abdulla. I was shown into his study immediately after the members of the committee had left.
>
> As I entered, he looked at me and shook his head.
>
> "If I were to drive into the desert and accost the first goatherd I saw, and consult him whether to make war on my enemies or not, he would say to me, "How many have you got and how many have they?" Yet here are these learned politicians, all of them with university degrees, and when I say to them, "The Jews are too strong—it is a mistake to make war," they cannot understand the point. They make long speeches about rights."
>
> King Abdulla never could see eye to eye with the Egyptians. Perhaps their differences were not solely due to a clash of interests, but also to some organic difference in their mental makeup. For King Abdulla was a practical man, always ready to make a bargain or consider a compromise.[5]

This passage does evoke powerfully the Jordanian sense of impotence before the Triangle Alliance, whose militancy had captured the moral high ground of anti-Zionism. But we can dismiss out of hand the organic explanation of Egyptian intransigence. For, as we shall see, only months after the Egyptian leaders professed a willingness to go down in flames, Cairo offered to cut a separate deal with the Israelis. Thus, the Egyptian authorities did, of course, possess the mental faculty that permits one to compromise on heartfelt principles.

Glubb himself did not really believe the organic explanation of Egyptian behavior, if only because al-Nuqrashi Pasha had told the Jordanian prime minister that Egypt would not seek to open a second round of fighting.[6] At some point, therefore, during the twenty-eight days of the first truce, the policy of Cairo had shifted from flexibility to intransigence. In order to account for this change, both Glubb Pasha and Prime Minister Tawfiq Abu'l-Huda concluded that the Egyptian government had been taken hostage by its own propaganda machine. Glubb writes:

> During the first period of fighting the Egyptian Press had daily announced the dazzling victories of the Egyptian army. The public were expecting an early end to the war, the occupation of Tel Aviv by the Egyptian army, and the surrender of Israel. Instead of that, they were told that a month's truce had been agreed to. The Egyptian people were incensed—they had been given to understand that complete victory was in their grasp.
>
> During the period of the truce, criticism of the government increased in Egypt. To silence this criticism, the Egyptian prime minister decided to start hostilities once more. The future of the Arabs of Palestine was sacrificed to Egyptian politics.[7]

Undoubtedly there is more substance to this argument than to the theory of a differences in mentality. Nonetheless, given the eventual willingness of Cairo to negotiate a deal, it is difficult to conceive of the Egyptian state as nothing more than a cork tossed about by the stormy waves of public opinion. Did Cairo simply abandon the rudder, forsaking any attempt to negotiate these waters? In addition, if al-Nuqrashi Pasha actually did decide to sacrifice the army in order to satisfy a public ignorant of the realities on the battlefield, one wonders how he convinced the military to open another round against the more powerful Israeli forces. Did the Egyptian generals simply offer up their battalions in sacrifice to the fickle crowd? Did not the government itself foresee *political* danger in the annihilation of the army—especially in the light of its misleading propaganda? These questions are worth pondering before adopting the "cork-on-the-waves" theory of Egyptian state policy.

Glubb Pasha also offers a third explanation, one that takes into consideration the attitudes of the Great Powers:

> Presumably the politicians hoped that they would regain their reputations for patriotism by refusing to renew the truce, and that the Security Council would then insist more forcibly. They could then bow to the inevitable, and explain to their constituents that they had done their best to destroy Israel, but that the Western Powers had compelled them to stop fighting.

This analysis appealed to Glubb, undoubtedly, because he had seen behavior of this sort in Amman. In early July, during the inter-Arab debate over the renewal of the truce, King Abdallah felt crushed between the hammer of Palestinian nationalism and the anvil of Arab League intransigence. As long as Cairo continued to raise the call of no compromise, the Jordanian authorities, in order to escape the charge of treachery, had no choice but to fight a losing battle. In desperation, therefore, they appealed—with the very motivations that Glubb ascribes to Cairo—to the United Nations and to the Great Powers.

Immediately after the Egyptian refusal to renew the truce, King Abdallah cabled the United Nations Special Mediator, Count Folke Bernadotte, who was based on the island of Rhodes, and urged him to come to Amman immediately.[8] Bernadotte's plane crossed the Palestine coast as the guns opened the second round of fighting. When he reached Amman, King Abdallah asked him:

to act quickly to change the situation. He had himself ordered the Arab Legion not to start hostilities . . . but only to answer Jewish fire and to repulse Jewish attacks. . . . It was, the king closed, necessary for the Security Council to take serious measures to prevent a renewal of the war. . . . The situation was strange indeed. Here I was sitting conferring with one of the leaders of the Arab world. And he demanded that I should try to induce the Security Council to intervene against the Arabs, his own kinsmen and allies, if they insisted in their refusal to prolong the truce—induce it to first use violent language against them and then, if nothing else helped, to apply sanctions.[9]

If the Great Powers were to have intervened forcefully, then they would have provided King Abdallah with a pretext for stopping before it was too late. By projecting similar motives onto the Egyptian leadership, Glubb assumes that they labored under a political burden similar to that oppressing the leadership in Amman. But is this assumption really justified?

The structure of the Palestine problem for Cairo was very different from what it was for Amman. Take, for instance, the relations between each government and the Arab League. This organization weighed heavily indeed on King Abdallah, who had little choice but to conform to its decisions. In contrast, the Egyptian authorities defined the policy of the League to a very significant degree; in many respects the League was an extension of their Foreign Ministry. Thus, with regard to the secretary-general of the Arab League, King Abdallah writes in his memoirs:

Azzam Pasha is a warrior in the Ottoman tradition, a fighter for Tripolitania and Libya, secretary-general of the Arab League, and at the same time an Egyptian by nationality. For Egypt's sake he would not hesitate to destroy anything, even his own son, which might stand in his way; such is the duty of every man who values his own and his country's security. As the saying goes, "Begin with thyself and then with thy brother."[10]

There is, as we have seen, considerable justification for this bitter judgment.

Had Cairo wished to establish a consensus among the Arab states in favor of prolonging the truce, it would have found the task easy, especially since the Jordanians, who wielded the most significant forces, opposed a resumption of the fighting. Certainly the Syrian and Saudi allies of Egypt, whose contribution to the war effort was not great, would have been in no position to criticize Egypt. From mid-February, the Iraqi regime had shown a strong desire to avoid running afoul of the Egyptian authorities, precisely because Cairo controlled the League machinery, not to mention the moral high ground of anti-imperialism.

With regard to its own public opinion, Cairo could have justified extending the truce by drawing attention to the policies of the Great Powers. Both the United States and the Soviet Union had immediately recognized Israel as a sovereign state, while the Soviet Bloc was providing it with weapons on a significant scale. Great Britain, which was the sole supplier of war materiel to the three most important Arab armies, had committed itself to respecting the international arms embargo voted by the United Nations in mid-June. It had, therefore, ceased to supply Iraq, Jordan, and Egypt with arms and ammunition. Since even an uneducated shepherd knows that it is self-destructive to make war against a more powerful enemy, the Arab League might have explained to the public that the Great Powers, against the collective will of the Arab people, had supported the establishment of Israel and then denied the Arab states the resources necessary to make war against it. Being rooted in the basic facts of the situation, this policy would have enjoyed the benefit of appealing to common sense, a faculty no less powerful among Egyptians than among Jordanians.

Largely absent from Glubb's analysis of the decision by Cairo to resume the fighting is the idea that internecine Arab relations might have played a role in Egyptian calculations. No doubt Glubb played down the question of inter-Arab conflict, because it constituted a sensitive subject for the British commander of the Jordanian army. After all, the major source of discord between the Egyptian and Jordanian authorities was not their irreconcilable organic natures but rather their diametrically opposed policies toward Britain. To discuss the real wedge that separated Amman from Cairo, Glubb would have had no choice but to admit that he himself stood at the center of the problem.

That a British officer commanded the most powerful Arab army was a fact that stuck in the craw of the Egyptian leadership—and the leadership of every other Arab state, with the possible exception of Iraq. A discussion of these issues would also have obliged Glubb to explore in greater depth the claim by the rest of the Arab countries that Jordan failed to fight seriously against the Israelis precisely *because* its army was led by a British soldier. This fundamental aspect of the political scene does crop up in Glubb's memoirs, which are often reliable and informative, but it does not play a prominent role in his analysis of Egyptian thinking.

Glubb's explanations notwithstanding, the anti-British and anti-Jordanian orientation of the Triangle Alliance directly influenced the decision to initiate a second round of fighting. The United Nations mediator, with the support of Washington and London, had proposed to settle the Palestine conflict by aggrandizing King Abdallah. If Count Bernadotte were to have had his way, Jordan would have absorbed all of Arab Palestine, while the Jewish state would have been incorporated into the expanded kingdom as an autonomous unit. Count Bernadotte published his ideas for settling the conflict on 28 June 1948. Nine days later the Egyptian guns opened fire again. If we wish to understand what happened between 11 June and 7 July to convince al-Nuqrashi Pasha to renew the fighting, then we must look to the Bernadotte proposals. We must examine the effect that their implementation would have had on the inter-Arab balance and, by extension, on the Anglo-Egyptian conflict, the main aspect of Egyptian foreign policy.

First, however, it is necessary to set the scene.

Before the Bernadotte Plan: A Pseudo-Alliance

From the outbreak of war until the Bernadotte proposals, Amman and the Triangle Alliance went through the motions of a honeymoon. Being dependent on the Jordanian army, Egypt, Syria, and Saudi Arabia briefly pretended to have friendly relations with Jordan. On 20 May, King Abdallah, together with Glubb and the Iraqi regent, held a summit meeting with President Shukri al-Quwatli of Syria and with Azzam Pasha—in Syria just by the Jordanian frontier.[11] Wartime conferences between heads of state are certainly not unusual occurrences. This meeting, however, drew special attention, because Syria and Jordan, though technically allies, did not enjoy formal diplomatic relations. President al-Quwatli had recalled his representative from Amman in 1947, in response to King Abdallah's efforts on behalf of Greater Syria.[12] The unusual encounter on the Syrian–Jordanian border was not the only apparent sign of a growing warmth in inter-Arab relations. During the first truce, King Abdallah traveled to Cairo and Riyadh, at (surprisingly) the invitation of the Egyptian and Saudi governments.

This appearance of a thaw between Amman and the Triangle Alliance ended with the publication of the Bernadotte plan. But even before the mediator had drafted his proposals for a settlement, the traditional distrust between Jordan and its putative allies continued to make itself felt. The performance of the Arab Legion apparently disappointed the Triangle Alliance, which claimed to have expected a faster advance.[13] The enemies of Jordan noted, in addition, that King Abdallah's army had failed to attack any areas allotted to the Jews by the United Nations partition resolution. Although the Arab Legion had engaged in the heaviest fighting of the war, its operations had been confined to Jerusalem, which the United Nations had sought to internationalize. Moreover, King Abdallah's Arab enemies believed, possibly with good reason, that even in Jerusalem the Arab Legion limited its actions to taking and defending the old city rather than attacking the new city.[14] In short, the leaders of the Triangle Alliance smelled treachery.

The underlying feelings of distrust and anger burst into the open during the Syrian–Jordanian summit meeting. At one point in the proceedings, Glubb Pasha explained to the Syrian leadership that the Jordanian army had no choice but to concentrate its attention on Jerusalem; it could not advance on the Jews in other areas until this front was secure. When King Abdallah chimed in to stress the power of the Israeli forces and the deficiencies of the Arab armies, Taha al-Hashimi, whom President al-Quwatli had invited to the meeting, lost his cool. The existing Arab forces, he said, were more than adequate to the task if only they were deployed in order to achieve military rather than political goals.

This accusation of collusion between the Jordanians and the Israelis sparked an explosion from King Abdallah. Referring derisively to al-Hashimi's position as the inspector-general of the Arab Liberation Army, he roared: "Oh, honorable Inspector of the volunteers, you have organized a motley crew and placed the Arab states in dire straits."[15] King Abdallah, then, threatened to withdraw his army from the conflict. Switching to Turkish so that only Taha al-Hashimi would understand, the king criticized him for abandoning his home in Iraq and taking up residence in Syria. Then, threatening to slap al-Hashimi's face, he demanded—and received—an apology.

Apparently nothing so dramatic as the encounter with Taha al-Hashimi occurred during King Abdallah's trips to Cairo and Riyadh, although there, too, he repeated his claims regarding the relative weakness of the Arabs.[16] Although the

Saudis and the Egyptians appear to have demonstrated greater control over their tongues than did Taha al-Hashimi, their policies toward Jordan suggest that they stood in total agreement with the inspector-general of the volunteers.

Although the Triangle Alliance was placing enormous pressure on Amman to assume the central role in the war against Israel, it took steps that actually weakened the ability of the Arab Legion to fight effectively. For instance, just before the first phase of fighting, the authorities in Cairo confiscated a large shipment of ammunition that was en route to Jordan. Alec Kirkbride, the British representative in Amman, explains:

> Both Glubb and I sensed that Azzam shared the hostility which the Egyptian authorities showed towards King Abdullah and his followers. Azzam was entirely unhelpful in the scandalous case when the Egyptian army seized a shipload of ammunition at Suez which was consigned by the British ordinance depot to the Arab Legion. This high-handed action was all the more reprehensible because the consignment in question proved to be the last opportunity for the Legion to replenish its stocks before the general embargo on the issue of supplies and money was imposed by Great Britain with regard to all the belligerents. The only explanation offered by the Egyptian Government for stealing the ammunition was that they were in urgent need of it themselves. Their needs could not have been greater than those of the Arab Legion, particularly as regards shell for twenty-five pounder guns which made up the bulk of the consignment. Azzam declined to intervene in the matter and the Egyptians refused to return the stores or to refund their value to the Jordanian government.[17]

While the Egyptian authorities stole the ammunition of the Jordanian army, the Arab League refused to pay the Jordanian government the balance of the three million pounds that Azzam Pasha had promised just before the war, when he had delivered the first installment.[18] These actions considerably burdened the authorities in Amman, because, as Kirkbride notes, the British government had suspended not just deliveries of ammunition and other war supplies but also payment of the regular subsidy to the Arab Legion.[19] Since the budget of the Jordanian army was drawn entirely from this source, the government in Amman was running up a very large debt.

The British stopped the payments in response to strong American criticism of the Arab Legion.[20] Supporters of Israel in the United States Congress questioned whether the American government could remain quiet while an army financed by Britain and led by British officers made war against the Jews. They claimed that, since the United States provided Great Britain with economic aid, American money was indirectly funding the operations of the Jordanian army. The attitude of Congress threatened to become a source of friction between London and Washington.

Seeking to shelter itself from American criticism, London not only suspended the payments to the Arab Legion, but it also committed itself to honoring the arms embargo. In addition, the Foreign Office solemnly pledged that it would withdraw from duty in Palestine all the British officers seconded to the Arab Legion. Kirkbride, however, circumvented this policy: He withdrew the officers long enough for London to state truthfully that no British soldiers were serving in Palestine, then he looked the other way as they returned to the battlefield.[21]

The Jordanian government did manage to keep its officer corps, but, nonetheless, it felt squeezed between a rock and a hard place. On one side, the British punished the Jordanian government for failing to remain strictly within the boundaries of the proposed Palestinian state. On the other side, the Arab League demanded that King Abdallah prove, by attacking territory that the United Nations had allotted to the Jews, that he had not cut a deal with the Israelis. Amman found an uneasy middle ground between these impossible demands by occupying and defending Jerusalem. While this policy did not satisfy anybody completely, it did place King Abdallah, for the time being, in a position that he could defend before the Arab world—especially since the heaviest fighting erupted in the struggle for Jerusalem.

Egypt and Jordan: The Military Dimension

Cairo intervened in Palestine in order to maintain the position of Egypt as the leader of the Triangle Alliance and as the dominant power in the Arab world. One rather optimistic scenario for attaining this goal was for the Arab coalition to liberate Palestine completely. After having destroyed all the Israeli forces, the Arab League, which Egypt and its allies controlled, would then oversee the creation of a new order in Palestine. Once all of the Arab armies converged on Tel Aviv, the Arab League would establish a provisional Palestinian government dominated by the enemies of Amman. The Triangle Alliance, in complete control of the League, would then bring tremendous political pressure to bear on Jordan in order to force it to relinquish authority over the Palestinian territories under the control of its army.

As shown in chapter 5, there is room for doubting that the Egyptian authorities ever believed that the Arab forces would actually vanquish the Jewish state. But, whatever their calculations might have been, immediately after the outbreak of the war it became abundantly clear that the necessary conditions for total victory had not been fulfilled. At a bare minimum, the defeat of Israel would have required a relentless advance by the Arab Legion and solid support from Britain. Lightning progress by the Arab Legion was essential, because it was the most powerful Arab army—the only first-rate force in the field—and because success required destroying Israel before international opposition to the Arabs could organize itself. The coalition needed Britain for three things: supplying it with arms and ammunition; balancing the power wielded in the Security Council by the patrons of Israel; and permitting the Jordanian army to perform the bulk of the fighting against the Jewish forces.

In the event, Britain sorely disappointed the Arab states by honoring the United Nations embargo and by urging restraint on Jordan. These obstructive policies, together with the failure of the Jordanian army to fight its way beyond Jerusalem, may have come as something of a disappointment to Cairo. But the

Egyptian authorities certainly knew the limitations of their own forces and were aware of the desire of King Abdallah to fashion a separate deal with Israel. They had no choice, therefore, but to prosecute the war in a manner that would place them in the best position to dominate the political arena in the event of a stalemate on the battlefield. Dominating the political arena, of course, meant driving a wedge between Amman and Tel Aviv.

An examination of the operations of the Egyptian army reveals a pattern of action consistent with the goal of containing Israel and Jordan simultaneously. The Egyptian forces invaded Palestine along two routes. In accordance with the Arab League plan, the main column drove straight up the coast toward Tel Aviv, stopping in the area of al-Majdal, which it reached sometime before 23 May. At the same time, other forces, including volunteer units of the Muslim Brothers, made their way north from Beersheba to the West Bank. Unexpectedly, from Amman's point of view, these Egyptian forces occupied Hebron and Bethlehem.[22] Once the reach of the army extended to these northernmost points, the Egyptians came to a halt. They then set about constructing defensive fortifications, an Egyptian Maginot Line, from Majdal on the coast to Hebron on the West Bank.

Thus, during the first week of fighting the Egyptian army (by overrunning largely empty territory) had placed itself in a position to stake a claim, before the Great Powers and the United Nations, over all of Palestine south of a line running from Hebron on the West Bank to Majdal on the coast. This area, of course, included all of the Negev, which had been allotted to the Jewish state by the United Nations partition plan. The Egyptian forces did not penetrate the coastal zone of Jewish settlement stretching south from Tel Aviv. Already in late May— that is, more than a week before the first cease-fire—the British Foreign Office believed that Cairo had no plans for an offensive that might have taken the battle into areas densely populated by Jews.[23]

While the Egyptian army avoided heavy casualties by stopping short of the Jewish zone of settlement, it also shied away from battle in the south. Rather than attack the Jewish settlements in the Negev, the Egyptian High Command chose to circumvent most of them. On the face of it, this tactic calls to mind to the island-hopping conducted by the American forces in the Pacific during World War II. That is, by avoiding costly struggles over strategically insignificant targets, the Egyptians, so it would appear, preserved their forces in order to use them in the big battles designed to cripple the Israeli war effort. However, the complete absence of a major Egyptian offensive casts doubt on this hypothesis. Stopping (or being stopped) outside the Jewish coastal zone, and dispatching forces to Hebron are actions inconsistent with a strategy designed to direct maximum firepower at the heart of the enemy. The major advance of the Egyptian army was, therefore, a land grab, an operation designed to acquire the greatest acreage at the cheapest cost.

Egyptian soldiers who participated in the war certainly believed that Cairo directed military operations in a manner designed to serve political rather than military goals. Gamal Abd al-Nasser, for one, writes in his memoir of the Palestine war that immediately upon his arrival at the front, he was struck by:

the leitmotif in the comments of the officers to the effect that the war was a "political" one. Much of what they saw around them seemed to fit in with and confirm
this interpretation. This could not be a serious war. There was no concentration of
forces, no accumulation of ammunition and equipment. There was no reconnais-
sance, no intelligence, no plans. Yet they were actually on the battlefield. The only
conclusion that could be drawn was that this was a political war. . . . [24]

Everything that Abd al-Nasser witnessed thereafter confirmed the prevalent view
that the commanders in the field carried out instructions from Cairo that had
no foundation in sound military thinking. It appeared to Abd al-Nasser that:

> the chief interest of our High Command . . . was to occupy the largest extent of
> territory possible. But the only result of this was that the four battalions [all the
> forces participating] were dispersed at the end of long lines of communication.
> They became so scattered that their main concern was to defend themselves and
> protect their lines of communication. Our High Command no longer had a reserve
> to use against the enemy. The commander of what had been a fighting force became
> virtually a commander with no troops to command, or at best a commander of a
> string of outposts scattered over a wide front. I could see that we had lost all power
> of initiative which, of our own free will, we had surrendered to the enemy.[25]

Everyone, including the lowest ranks, shared this perception. Although Abd al-
Nasser states that he was involved in a "political" war, he does not explain precisely what political motives drove the military action.

If, however, we view the operations of the Egyptian military against the background of the struggle between the Turco-Hashimite Entente and the Triangle
Alliance, then we can begin to make sense out of the behavior of the Egyptian
High Command. Cairo fought this "political war" in order to place its army in
the best position to ensure that the Jordanian authorities remained subject to the
will of the Arab League. By ordering its battalions to lurk on the perimeter of
the Jewish coastal zone, the Egyptian High Command turned its army into a
jackal poised to steal the kill of the Hashimite armies. In the unlikely event that
the Jordanian and Iraqi forces actually defeated the Israelis, then Egypt, together
with its allies, would be positioned to reap the greatest reward: The right to define
the new political order in Palestine. On the other hand, if Jordan and Iraq failed
to finish off the Israeli forces, then Egypt had a foothold on the West Bank, in
Hebron and Bethlehem, where it could work to prevent Jordan from annexing
the Palestinian territories under its control.

From the moment the Egyptian forces effected their unannounced arrival in
Hebron, there was political friction between Jordan and Egypt.[26] Cairo immediately installed an Egyptian military governor in the city, even though the Jordanian authorities had already appointed their own man to the post. According
to a contemporaneous British report, "the various factions in the town have taken
sides, and now part obey Transjordan orders and the rest Egyptian."[27] When
King Abdallah, the ostensible supreme commander of the unified armies, expressed a desire to review the Egyptian troops in the area, his request was refused.[28]

Thus, at the moment when the first truce went into effect, the Egyptians stood poised to lead the Arab coalition in the political negotiations with the United Nations. With one foot on the West Bank, Cairo possessed the ability to prevent the Jordanians from annexing Arab Palestine; with the other foot on the coast south of Tel Aviv it had the right to demand from the Great Powers that the borders of the Jewish state not extend south of the Majdal–Hebron line established by the Egyptian army.

The Bernadotte Proposals

On 30 June 1948, Count Bernadotte presented to the Arabs and the Israelis three short papers in which he outlined his "views and suggestions for a possible approach to peaceful adjustment of the future situation of Palestine."[29] The Mediator hoped to soften the harsh blow of his proposals by couching them in a convoluted and tentative language. Count Bernadotte suggested that "Palestine, as defined by the original mandate entrusted to the United Kingdom in 1922— that is, including Transjordan—might form a union comprising two members, one Arab and one Jewish." The borders of states envisioned by the United Nations partition resolution would be significantly amended: The Negev and Jerusalem would be integrated into the Arab territory of the United Palestine, while the Western Galilee would be given to the Jews.

Bernadotte's attempt to soften the blow with woolly language failed. In the view of all the belligerents except Jordan, the mediator's plan was a disaster; it appeared as if a British plot had been hatched in the Middle East.[30] Ben-Gurion, without doubt speaking for the Egyptians as well as for his own people, wrote in his diary: "Today the Count's suggestions were received. Whoever suspected that he was Bevin's agent did not do so entirely without reason."[31] To Tel Aviv, Cairo, Riyadh, Damascus, and Beirut, these proposals looked suspiciously like the first step toward the realization of King Abdallah's Greater Syria program.

As for the Israelis, unlike the Triangle Alliance they did not oppose the expansion of Jordan onto the West Bank. But they did object to having their claims to the Negev and to Jerusalem annulled. Most important, they vehemently rejected the assumption of the mediator that the status of Israel as an independent state was open to question. Tel Aviv insisted that the basis for negotiations should be the 29 November 1947 partition plan, which Bernadotte's proposals completely ignored.[32]

The official response from the Arab League closely followed the plan for a unitary Arab state submitted to the London conference in December 1946.[33] That is, it deemed unacceptable any solution other than the establishment of a unitary Palestinian Arab state sovereign over every inch of Palestinian territory. It was the rejection of the truce on this basis that struck Glubb as the most irresponsible act in history. After all, Count Bernadotte, with the full support of the United States and Great Britain, had proposed a plan that, if enacted, would have annulled the Jewish claim to the Negev, given the Arabs sovereignty over Jerusalem, and denied full statehood to Israel. True, given the strong Israeli opposition, even had the Arab states unanimously embraced the Bernadotte plan, it is extremely doubtful that all its clauses would have been fulfilled. Nonetheless, renewing the truce and engaging in the diplomatic process would have given the Arab League the means to enlist the Great Powers in an effort to contain Israel, whose army was growing more powerful by the day.

A report by the Central Intelligence Agency in late July, just after the second round of fighting had ended, summarized the situation:

> The truce resulted in so great an improvement in the Jewish capabilities that the Jews may now be strong enough to launch a full-scale offensive and drive the Arab forces out of Palestine. Events during the truce, and the enormous increase in Jewish strength resulting from them, considerably change the previously held estimate of the probable course of the war in Palestine. The Arabs' logistical position generally is very bad and their ammunition supply is exceedingly low.[34]

Given the rapid shift in the balance of power in favor of the Israelis, it is difficult to disagree with Glubb that the decision to resume the war was an act of monumental folly. This judgment, however, is only valid if one assumes that Cairo considered the containment of Israel to be its first priority. The assumption deserves reconsideration.

By recapitulating the pan-Arab consensus against partition, in early July 1948, Cairo no doubt intended (in part) to appease a domestic audience that believed, on the basis of misleading propaganda, that an Arab victory was inevitable. Even so, there is much more to the story than the fear of a political backlash at home. Undoubtedly the Egyptian authorities decided to resume the war after considering the impact that the extension of the truce would have on the status of Egypt as the dominant power in the Arab world.

From the moment the British first referred the Palestine question to the United Nations, the Triangle Alliance had feared the possibility that London and Amman would work to aggrandize Jordan at the expense of Arab Palestine. The Bernadotte plan was simply the fulfillment of a recurring nightmare. Thus, when speaking with representatives of the United States, the allies of Egypt did not hide the hostility they felt toward Jordan:

> Amir Faisal [the son of Ibn Saud] and [Syrian Prime Minister Jamil] Mardam . . . made it clear that the suggestions were unacceptable. Faisal declared that the suggestions denied to the Arabs everything that they sought and gave the Jews everything that they were seeking. Mardam declared that the suggestions were even worse than partition since, if accepted, they would make Transjordan a Jewish colony through the joint economic functions, and they would constitute an even greater menace to the Arab world. Both clearly indicated opposition to the aggrandizement of Abdullah.
>
> Amir Faisal declared that unless better suggestions would be forthcoming, the Arabs would have no choice but to resume fighting on July 9, notwithstanding the consequences to the Arabs through the inability to secure arms and through the possible United Nations sanctions—including the lifting of the arms embargo by the United States. He declared that recent events showed that the Jews were getting arms from the United States, and hence lifting the embargo would not greatly alter the situation. The United States must also be aware that the Arabs

could impose sanctions, including the cancellation of oil concessions. He said that the withdrawal of concessions did not mean that Saudi Arabia would not re-offer them . . . to Belgium, Italy, or even to Russia. The latter might lead to unfortunate results, but he cited an Arab proverb about how a "drowning man will grasp even a serpent."[35]

These statements reveal much regarding the decision by the Triangle Alliance to resume the fighting. First of all, they indicate that the Bernadotte proposals, although unacceptable in terms of what they gave to Israel, also threatened the balance *among* the Arab powers, because they strengthened King Abdullah. In short, the Bernadotte plan fostered the creation of a Tel Aviv–Amman Axis—the very threat that had compelled the Egyptian government to go to war in the first place. Second, the Triangle Alliance had no illusions regarding the military balance. It is certainly within the realm of possibility that they underestimated the full strength of the Israeli forces, but not to the extent that they believed victory to be imminent.[36] Third, by resuming the fighting, Egypt, Syria, and Saudi Arabia intended not to alter the situation on the battlefield, but rather to dismantle the political framework in which the Great Powers had placed the Arab–Israeli conflict. They fought, that is, in order to wipe the Bernadotte Plan off of the slate of the United Nations. Britain and America, they gambled, would then adopt a policy that tilted toward the interests of the Triangle Alliance and away from those of the Turco-Hashimite Entente.

Resuming the war against Israel functioned as a means of pressuring the Great Powers to respect the Triangle Alliance and as a means of weakening King Abdallah. The manifest desire of Cairo, Riyadh, and Damascus to cripple Amman raises doubt regarding the sincerity of the representatives of the Triangle Alliance, when they stated that the Arabs would rather go down in flames than compromise with the Israelis. These statements, though undoubtedly expressing a very real rage, are almost as empty as the Saudi threat to run to the Soviet Union. To be sure, all self-respecting Arab nationalists found the Zionist project repugnant, but this emotion was not the sole or even major determinant of *state policy*.

Saudi, Syrian, and Egyptian authorities could allow themselves the luxury of a principled indifference to the consequences of renewing the war, because they realized that the heaviest fighting would rage on the Jordanian front. Since the Arab Legion was the most powerful army in the field against the Israelis, the Triangle Alliance knew that as long as Amman could be forced into the fight, then the enemy would, by necessity, be obsessed with the eastern flank. During the last two weeks of the first round, the Israelis had demonstrated an overwhelming concern with Jerusalem and the approaches to it.[37] At that time, in late May and early June, the participation of Syria, Lebanon, and Saudi Arabia in the fighting had been so slight that these states felt comfortable giving the Egyptian government full powers to negotiate the terms of the truce for them.[38] For the time being, they had become spectators in the war that was taking place for Jerusalem. When, in July, they called for a resumption of the fighting, they undoubtedly—and correctly—assumed that the second phase of the war would take up where the first had left off.

The thinking, then, that informed the decision to resume the war simply followed along the same lines that had led to the original decision to intervene: The coalition functioned as a catapult designed to hurl the Jordanian army at the Israelis. From the point of view of the Triangle Alliance, the situation had a pleasing irony to it: The forces of Jordan—commanded by British officers and paid for by the British treasury—were being used in order to achieve political goals designed, ultimately, to weaken Jordan and Britain in the Middle East. No wonder Amman did not like its allies.

Lydda and Ramleh

The Egyptian army attacked an Israeli settlement in the Negev on 8 July, one day before the first truce was scheduled to end; the fighting continued until the second truce took effect on 18 July. In the intervening ten days, the Israelis, who maintained a constant offensive, made significant advances along the corridor to Jerusalem and along the central belt girding Tel Aviv. In the north, they took Nazareth from the forces of Fawzi al-Qawuqji. They achieved no sustainable gains, however, against the Syrian positions near the Sea of Galilee, against the Iraqi forces stationed on the northern West Bank, or against the Egyptian forces in the south. The Egyptian army, therefore, managed to hold its line of defense running from Majdal to Hebron; it maintained both its grip on all of southern Palestine and its foothold on the West Bank. Just as the Triangle Alliance had undoubtedly anticipated, the decision to resume the war did not in fact force Egypt, Syria, or Saudi Arabia to go down in flames.

On the Jordanian front, where the fighting was by far the heaviest, the Israelis took Lydda and Ramleh, which removed the threat of an Arab attack on Tel Aviv; this action also weakened the position of the Arab Legion in Latrun, the control of which had the greatest strategic importance to Jordan. When capturing these two towns, the Israelis expelled their populations, sending a stream of some 30,000 refugees eastward, thereby placing a huge administrative burden on the Jordanian authorities.

From the point of view of the Arabs, the fall of Lydda and Ramleh constituted one of the most traumatic events of the war. The blow fell particularly hard on Jordan. The capture of the two towns led to a severe crisis of legitimacy, because the Arab Legion had consciously chosen not to defend them in any way. When the Israelis actually struck, the Jordanian forces ignored the calls for help from the embattled residents. The failure of the Arab Legion to rescue Lydda and Ramleh prompted many refugees to assume that King Abdallah and his British officers had been complicit in their fate.

Glubb Pasha's decision to ignore the calls for help was based purely on strategic considerations. Because he had no reserves, he could send detachments to defend the towns only by denuding the garrison at Latrun, which was the position most vital to the Jordanian hold on the West Bank in general. Lydda and Ramleh sat on the coastal plain, where the troops of the Arab Legion would be exposed to an Israeli assault; in Glubb's eyes, therefore, any attempt to defend them would inevitably have failed. The troops sent to the rescue would have been lost, and the Israelis would been handed an opportunity to capture Latrun.

British diplomatic correspondence in fact confirms the sincerity of Glubb's explanation.[39] Nonetheless, the loss of Lydda and Ramleh provided the Triangle Alliance with potent material for its propaganda machine. Kirkbride writes:

> Up to that time, the press and radio services of the Arab world had been entirely optimistic about the progress of the war and its probable outcome. Now, the general euphoria generated by the inaccuracies of those media became counterproductive: When a major setback could no longer be concealed, it had to be explained away by accusing somebody else of treachery. Therefore, the otherwise inexplicable loss of the two towns was described as a sellout by the British with Mr. Ernest Bevin as the man principally responsible. King Abdallah, the friend and puppet of Great Britain, came next in the order of demerit with Glubb as runner-up. The refugees in Jordan seemed to make the unfortunate Glubb their particular target for abuse, and he and his men, from being popular heroes, turned almost overnight into the villains of the piece. Children spat at Glubb's armed convoy as he drove through the streets and my own car, flying a small union jack, attracted scowls and shaking fists.[40]

This propaganda barrage from Egypt and Syria caused severe tension between, on the one hand, the British commander of the Arab Legion and, on the other, King Abdallah and his ministers. Under the pressures of the moment, even *they* briefly entertained the notion that Glubb delivered Lydda and Ramleh to the Israelis.[41]

As a result of this tension, Glubb was forced to go on a holiday, lasting nearly two months, which he spent in Europe, far removed from the passions of the Middle East. He describes in his memoirs a scene that took place at Cairo airport, where he landed while in transit to London:

> On arrival at Cairo airport, we were surrounded by Egyptian journalists.
> "Why did you betray the Arab cause?" "Have you been dismissed?" "Why did you give Lydda and Ramle to the Jews?" "Is it true that you alone were responsible for the Arab defeats?"[42]

Undoubtedly Kirkbride is partially correct in asserting that the Triangle Alliance's need for a convenient scapegoat explains this intense concern on the part of the Egyptian media. Nonetheless, two other explanations for the interest of the press, which was subject to wartime censorship, are worthy of consideration. First, the authorities in Cairo and Damascus—not to mention the clutch of reporters that swarmed around Glubb—may well have believed that a sinister collusion had taken place at Lydda and Ramleh. Second, the human suffering provided the Triangle Alliance with powerful material with which to undermine the regional influence of both Jordan and Britain.

The perceptions of the Egyptian consul-general in Jerusalem are instructive. Ahmad Farraj Tayi', in his honest and revealing book on 1948, does in fact attribute the disaster of Lydda and Ramleh to the Egyptian decision to resume the battle. Al-Nuqrashi Pasha, he states, renewed the fighting even though King

Abdallah had informed the Egyptian prime minister about the weakness of the Arab military position. But, while Tayi' does not repeat the cant about King Abdallah's treachery, he still attributes to him partial blame for the disaster of Lydda and Ramleh:

> Nevertheless, the responsibility of King Abdallah for the fall of Lydda and Ramleh was also great. Although he had ordered his prime minister to refuse [the demand of the other Arab states] to resume the battle, nonetheless he should have commanded his army—he should have placed his army outside of Lydda and Ramleh in order to defend those two cities. It was his duty to take a determined and persistent position against General Glubb. Had he ordered his army to defend Lydda and Ramleh then they would not have fallen, and the situation would not have precipitously declined after that.
>
> I wrote to my government as follows about the fall of Lydda and Ramleh: "The people of Palestine attribute the fall of the two towns, first, to Jewish deception and, second, to the restraint of the Jordanian army. This is because the Jews entered Lydda and Ramleh while wearing the uniforms of the Jordanian army, and then they opened fire on the inhabitants. These people started defending themselves, and they called for help from the Jordanian army, which was within reach. The army, however, did not send them any aid. After Lydda fell, Ramleh surrendered without notable resistance."[43]

In this passage, Tayi' clearly regards King Abdallah as the tool of Glubb, who is, to use Kirkbride's phrase, "the villain of the piece." Although here the Egyptian consul-general does not analyze Glubb's motives, in other reports to Cairo he does in fact display a deep distrust of the British officers serving in Jordan—an attitude unsurprising in an Egyptian official.[44] Thus, Tayi' may well have believed that Glubb had ulterior motives for abandoning Lydda and Ramleh.

Whatever the true appraisal by Egyptian officials of Glubb's motives, this dispatch unquestionably reveals that Cairo received accurate reporting on the currents of opinion among the Palestinian refugees in Jordan. The Egyptian authorities, that is, may not have known exactly why Glubb failed to come to the rescue of Lydda and Ramleh, but they did know very well what the inhabitants of those towns themselves believed. Therefore, the propaganda campaign directed against Jordan deserves to be analyzed as an Egyptian way of calling over the head of King Abdallah to the Palestinian refugees. The failure to defend Lydda and Ramleh provided Cairo with a means of undermining Britain's influence in Jordan by inciting opinion against the British officers serving in the Arab Legion, and against the Jordanian authorities themselves. Thus, while the interest of the Egyptian media in the events of Lydda and Ramleh no doubt helped Cairo explain the Arab military failure to its own people, it also functioned as yet another volley in the regional struggle between the Triangle Alliance and the Turco-Hashimite Entente.

During the Lydda and Ramleh press campaign, a series of negotiations took place between King Abdallah and his Arab enemies. The demands made on Jordan by the Triangle Alliance reveal the motives behind the propaganda campaign. In his book , the Egyptian consul-general in Jerusalem includes a memo written by the Lebanese prime minister which provides us with a window onto the relations between Amman and the Triangle Alliance during this period. Riyad al-Sulh wrote the memo—copies of which he sent to the Iraqi prime minister and to Abd al-Rahman Azzam—after a long visit with King Abdallah and Tawfiq Abu'l-Huda on 4 August 1948. That is to say, he visited the Jordanian leaders during the propaganda campaign against Glubb, the British officers in the Legion, and King Abdallah himself.

According to Riyad al-Sulh, the Jordanian monarch and his prime minister immediately directed the conversation to "the stinginess of the Arab League toward Jordan, its failure to keep its promise to pay his Highness the agreed amount in order to conscript soldiers and buy weapons."[45] In addition, "King Abdallah complained bitterly about Egypt having taken the ammunition that was on its way to him." The Lebanese prime minister responded that the League would in fact make good on its promises, provided that the Jordanian government would fulfill three conditions: It must discontinue the British subsidy to the Arab Legion, expel the British officers, and resume combat against the Israelis. Riyad al-Sulh, whose minuscule army had barely reached the Palestine frontier, explained gravely that the reputation of King Abdallah had been severely tarnished by his desire to stop fighting.

The Jordanian monarch responded sensibly to the demands of the Arab League:

> His Majesty said to me that Transjordan cannot resume the battle unless the Arab nation [as a whole] concentrates its power and throws all its weight into the arena at once; he said that he cannot dismiss the British officers from his army. His argument for not resuming the battle is that such a course of action requires arms, ammunition, and sufficient preparation. With regard to his unwillingness to dismiss those officers, he advanced a number of arguments. First of all, he said that no treachery by them had been detected; second, that he cannot change the saddle of his horse in the middle of a battle; and third, that he does not have enough Arab officers with sufficient qualifications to take the place of the British officers. There is a forth argument, the importance of which he explained to me as follows: His Majesty is eager to preserve the martial spirit that reigns in his army. Sacking the British officers in response to the pressure caused by the grievances expressed against them, and as a result of the criticisms that have been directed at them, would ruin that spirit. In addition, he does not want his army to become like the army of Iraq, which meddles in matters of politics. If it were to shake off its British officers today, then it could just as well shake off King Abdallah tomorrow. . . . His Majesty pointed to Bakr Sidqi in Iraq as an example of this. After that, he described the political conditions of Transjordan, and its established foreign ties. In response, I asked His Majesty if it would be possible to transfer his army entirely to the Iraqi army, so that all of its affairs would be administered as if it were a part of the Iraqi army.[46]

These conditions set by the Triangle Alliance belong to a family of proposals, by now quite familiar, designed to take control of the Arab Legion. The first of these arose in October 1947, when Mahmud Fahmi al-Nuqrashi produced his plan to buy the Jordanian army. Next came King Faruq's scheme, in February 1948, to establish a regional defense system based on the Arab League. Finally, on the eve of the war, the Triangle Alliance had attempted to establish a unified Arab command over which Amman would have had minimal influence.

That the Triangle Alliance pursued Riyad al-Sulh's proposals with serious intent is confirmed by the arrival in Cairo of the Iraqi premier, Muzahim al-Pachachi, three weeks after this meeting. The Iraqi prime minister engaged in discussions with al-Nuqrashi Pasha on the unification of the Arab armies.[47] According to the Egyptian press, these talks centered on an Iraqi proposal to establish three separate commands—Iraq–Jordan, Syria–Lebanon, and Egypt–Saudi Arabia–Libya–Yemen. Each of these would then be made responsible to a supreme Egyptian commander.[48]

The nature of the evidence makes it difficult to ascertain the link between the proposals of Riyad al-Sulh and the Iraqi premier's trip to Cairo. The logic of the situation, however, suggests that Baghdad, embarrassed by the damage to the Hashimite House that the Lydda and Ramleh episode caused, hoped to shield itself from further disgrace by proving that the Jordanian army was not the plaything of the British and the Israelis. The Egyptian government would have been willing to entertain these proposals, of course, because their implementation would have severely weakened the ties between Great Britain and Jordan. By dominating the military sphere, Cairo would gain control over the political settlement that would follow the war. In the event, for reasons that are not yet clear, nothing came of these talks; Glubb Pasha returned from Europe in mid-September and resumed his duties.

That Amman came under such pressure in the middle of the war reveals much about Egyptian priorities. It is difficult to argue that the proposals floated by Riyad al-Sulh had any goals other than damaging King Abdallah, his army, and the British position in the Middle East. To decapitate the Arab Legion, the most powerful Arab army, in the middle of the war with Israel made no military sense whatsoever. To be sure, Riyad al-Sulh may well have demanded the ouster of the British officers as a negotiating tactic—say, as part of an attempt to pressure King Abdallah to give the Iraqi army a greater influence over the affairs of the Arab Legion. Nonetheless, the implementation of even his minimal demands could only have created turmoil among the Jordanian ranks. The interest of the Triangle Alliance in ousting the British officers in the middle of the war with Israel constitutes, therefore, strong evidence that its priorities lay not in the struggle against Israel, but rather in the struggle against Jordan.

With no military successes to the credit of the Lebanese forces, the ability of Riyad al-Sulh to demand that King Abdallah purge the officer corps of his army and resume the battle offers yet more testimony to the ideological power of the Triangle Alliance. The Lebanese prime minister could make such an outrageous proposal without King Abdallah threatening to slap his face, because behind him stood not just the influence of Egypt, Syria, and Saudi Arabia but also the power of the Lydda and Ramleh propaganda campaign that was making life difficult indeed for the Jordanian leadership.

Without doubt, all Arabs responded with shock and rage when learning of the fate of Lydda and Ramleh. It would, however, be a mistake to assume that nothing more than these genuine feelings accounts for the interest that the Egyptian media, which was under a regime of wartime censorship, took in the episode. Had Cairo wished to protect its ostensible ally from harsh criticism, it possessed the means to hush up the matter or to explain it away. However, the swarm of desperate refugees that the Israelis drove to Jordan provided the Triangle Alliance with a valuable weapon to be used against King Abdallah and the British.

The memo of Riyad al-Sulh is also instructive in this regard. He writes:

> As I see it, our political situation today is better than before the truce. On the one hand we have benefited from the refugees. For you know that the similar problem of refugees in Europe created a disposition [among people] in the world to be moved by matters such as these. Until today the Jews have built a considerable part of their case on the question of the displaced persons. By this means they sought to evoke the sympathy of the world for their case. We have the ability to exploit this situation greatly: If we do the work well and if we properly bring the matter to the attention of the world, then we will begin to feel a bit of sympathy from some international quarters. . . . [49]

In this memo, Riyad al-Sulh is obviously not referring to the use that the Triangle Alliance might make of the refugee problem against King Abdallah; instead, he is suggesting how it might provide a means of gaining influence over the West. Nonetheless, he certainly does perceive the plight of the refugees as a weapon—an attitude that, under the circumstances, is not all that surprising. Given the fundamental trajectory of Egyptian foreign policy, it would be equally unsurprising to learn that Cairo immediately saw the refugee problem as a resource in its struggle to oust the British from the Middle East.[50]

The All-Palestine Government

Until the second round of fighting, the Egyptian authorities could have confidently assumed that a decision by the Arab League to resume the war would also compel the Jordanian army to attack the Israelis. They could also have assumed that the balance of power would permit the Egyptian forces in the south to hold the line against their enemy. After the second round of fighting, however, neither of these assumptions was valid.

The Arab Legion was low on ammunition and had suffered more losses of men that it felt an army of its size could sustain; its forces were stretched to the limit, and it had no reserves on which to draw. Thus, as King Abdallah's statements to Riyad al-Sulh demonstrate, the Legion's participation in the battle could not be taken as a foregone conclusion. In addition, the Israeli army had strengthened considerably during the first truce. As the contemporaneous report of the Central Intelligence Agency claimed, it now had the power to drive all of the Arab armies out of Palestine. Therefore, even if the Arab Legion were to participate in the battle, Cairo could no longer assume that the Israelis were incapable of carrying out a victorious campaign on two fronts. Not surprisingly, then, the previous willingness of the Egyptian authorities to carry the fight to the bitter end disappeared completely. When faced with the possibility of losing control of the Negev, leaders in Cairo ceased to manifest the intransigent behavior that Glubb had attributed to their mental makeup. They began instead to talk in terms of a compromise solution.

The first signs of a change in the Egyptian attitude came on 3 August, the day before Riyad al-Sulh visited King Abdallah. In a meeting with Count Bernadotte, al-Nuqrashi Pasha outlined a new policy. He told the United Nations mediator that he realized "that the Arab hope of preventing the emergence of an independent Jewish state had been crushed."[51] At the same time, the creation of Israel was so repugnant to Arab sensibilities that no Arab government would establish relations with the Jewish state. The Egyptian prime minister said that "the Arabs intended to ignore the Jewish State altogether, that they would have nothing whatever to do with it." Thus, the Egyptian authorities intended to build a steel wall around Israel.

The idea of establishing a pan-Arab quarantine was the logical extension of the no-compromise policy that Egypt had followed consistently until the second round of fighting. As we have seen, the rigorous insistence by the Egyptian government that any concession to Zionism constituted treachery to the Arab nation functioned as the primary means by which the Triangle Alliance thwarted the establishment of a Tel Aviv–Amman axis. This policy had prevented King Abdallah from cutting a deal with the Jewish Agency during the last phase of the British Mandate; it had forced Jordan to join the Arab coalition in late April; and it had compelled King Abdallah to commit his forces again in July.

Now that the military strategy had shot its bolt, the quarantine policy provided the Egyptian authorities with the means to continue an ideologically pure policy without risking war. That is to say, it allowed them to accept the establishment of Israel as a fait accompli while at the same time maintaining the moral high ground in inter-Arab politics, a stance essential in order to prevent King Abdallah from making a separate peace with Israel.

Although the quarantine strategy had the benefit of creating an ideological climate inimical to a Jordanian–Israeli peace agreement, it had the drawback, unlike the war policy, of requiring the cooperation of the Western powers, whose influence was needed to restrain Israel. Thus, after the July round of fighting, the Egyptian authorities suddenly began to speak more openly to the Western powers regarding their true aims. For instance, Count Bernadotte records in his memoirs the following conversation, on 3 August, with al-Nuqrashi Pasha:

> [The Egyptian prime minister] considered that the wisest course would be to constitute the Arab part of Palestine a separate and independent State supported by the Arab League. *He would not wish to see Arab Palestine united, for example, with Transjordan, as that would upset the balance of power in the Arab world.* Nor could he agree to the partition of Arab Palestine among a number of Arab countries. Such a solution, he emphasised, would bring grist to the mill of the enemies of [the Arabs]: It would enable them to claim that Egypt, for example, had begun the war in order to make territorial conquests. When I expressed doubts as to whether the Palestine Arabs were in a position to manage an independent kingdom and pointed out that their achievements so far hardly suggested they were, Nokrashi Pasha replied that the committee that had already been set up to administer the Arab part of the country might possibly form an embryo from which a government might develop. Besides, the other Arab countries would certainly give the new State the benefit of their counsel and support.[52]

Only three weeks before al-Nuqrashi Pasha unveiled this plan to Count Bernadotte, the Egyptian authorities had justified the resumption of warfare on the
basis that no compromise was possible with Israel. The speed with which Cairo
produced the idea of creating a Palestinian ministate suggests that the plan existed
before the second round of fighting.

This passage represents the very practical realization on the part of Cairo that
Israel existed and that the Egyptian government had no power to change this
unpleasant fact. Its policy focused, therefore, on matters that it did in fact have
the power to change: the inter-Arab balance. The plan of the Egyptian authorities,
then, was to drive a Palestinian wedge between Jordan and a quarantined Israel.
The Palestinian state would be a satellite of the Triangle Alliance, which would
provide it with "counsel and support." Undoubtedly Egypt, which would enjoy
a common border with the West Bank state, would wield great influence in
Jerusalem, its capital—from whence the power of the Triangle Alliance would
radiate eastward across the river Jordan.

Al-Nuqrashi Pasha no doubt stretched the truth when he told Count Bernadotte that his objection to the partition of Arab Palestine was based on the use
that anti-Arab propagandists would make of it. Undoubtedly, his primary concern was not with the enemies of the Arabs but, rather, with Arab enemies—the
Jordanians first and foremost. If the Egyptian authorities were to consent to a
carving-up between the Arab states, they would undermine their own ability to
accuse King Abdallah of treachery and cynical self-interest. Maintaining the
moral high ground in inter-Arab affairs had a usefulness that extended far beyond checking the territorial expansion of Jordan. Palestinian nationalism functioned as one of the primary conduits through which Cairo projected its power
into the Fertile Crescent. Thus it had more uses than simply denying the West
Bank to Jordan. For instance, fomenting discord between the Palestinians and
the Jordanian authorities, as in the case of the Lydda and Ramleh propaganda
campaign, functioned as a powerful weapon in the Egyptian struggle to oust the
British from the Middle East. Indeed, during the decade that followed the 1948
War, the ability of Cairo to harness Palestinian resentment toward Great Britain
and the Hashimites would constitute its trump card in the contest for regional
domination.

On 22 September, seven weeks after the discussion between Count Bernadotte
and al-Nuqrashi Pasha, the Egyptian authorities did indeed establish a Palestinian
government based on the administration to which the Egyptian prime minister
had referred. This new authority was dubbed "The Government of All-Palestine,"
signifying that it stood for the rejection of the very notion of partition, and that
it claimed the right to rule over every inch of Palestinian territory, be it under
Israeli or Jordanian occupation.[53] Cairo installed the government in Gaza. All
around it the Egyptian military reigned supreme; the authority of the All-Palestine
government, therefore, did not extend beyond the lobby of the hotel in which it
held its cabinet meetings.

For the Egyptian leadership, this puppet government was an anti-Hashimite
instrument: Its purpose was to foster an inter-Arab consensus against the annex-

ation of the West Bank by Jordan. Thus, all of the officials in the government were either close associates of Hajj Amin al-Husayni or men who, for one reason or another, had become disaffected from King Abdallah. During the first week in October, the Mufti himself appeared in Gaza with the intention of leading the new government, but the Egyptian authorities unceremoniously bundled him up and carted him away to Cairo, where he was placed under house arrest.[54] Although the Egyptians sought to capitalize on Hajj Amin al-Husayni's organization and on his personal prestige, the man himself had so many enemies, both inside and outside the Arab world, that allowing him to lead the All-Palestine Government would have risked undermining its usefulness.[55]

As al-Nuqrashi Pasha's statements to Count Bernadotte indicate, Cairo had for some time been intending to establish a Palestinian government. The Egyptian authorities chose the third week of September to act on their intentions, because they needed the All-Palestine Government as a weapon in their struggle against the new peace plan of Count Bernadotte, which the United Nations had made public on 20 September. The announcement of the new proposals for a settlement coincided with the assassination of the mediator by the Stern Gang, who shared the feelings of the Egyptian government toward his proposals. Although Bernadotte himself was eliminated from the scene, his peace plan, now touted as his last will and testament, immediately became the basis on which the Western Powers discussed a settlement of the war.

Count Bernadotte's second plan, in contrast to the first, recognized Israel as a permanent part of the Middle Eastern landscape.[56] It called for the internationalization of Jerusalem. With regard to the question of frontiers, it recommended that the Galilee should be incorporated into the Jewish state, while the Negev should not. The southern frontier of Israel, therefore, would run along the line defined by Majdal–Faluja–Hebron—by, that is, the de facto border established by the Egyptian army. As to the fate of the Arab parts of Palestine, the second peace plan, like the first, still favored King Abdallah. But it did stop short of wholeheartedly endorsing the expansion of Jordan. The relevant passage read as follows:

> The disposition of the territory of Palestine not included within the boundaries of the Jewish State should be left to the Governments of the Arab States in full consultation with the Arab inhabitants of Palestine, with the recommendation, however, that in view of the historical connexion and common interests of Transjordan and Palestine, there would be compelling reasons for merging the Arab territory of Palestine with the territory of Transjordan, subject to such frontier rectifications regarding other Arabs States as may be found practicable and desirable.[57]

No doubt out of deference to the Triangle Alliance's opposition, Count Bernadotte retreated slightly from his concept of basing the entire settlement on Jordan. Nonetheless, his continued preference for the aggrandizement of King Abdallah forced Cairo to abandon even the thinnest pretense of cooperating with Amman.

The Egyptian government, therefore, established the All-Palestine Government in order to undermine the pro-Jordanian clauses of the second Bernadotte

proposal. The advent of the Gaza government nearly sparked off a violent rebellion against King Abdallah by the followers of Hajj Amin al-Husayni. Kirkbride describes the scene:

> At this time, doubtless on instructions from Cairo, the Mufti's supporters in Pal-
> estine adopted an attitude openly hostile to Jordan and commenced organising
> another armed force which they called the Holy War Army. One would have
> thought that there was already a sufficient variety of armies in the field but, when
> the new formation declined to play any part in the defence of Jerusalem, it became
> evident that it was going to be used for subversive purposes. Its growth was then
> nipped in the bud when orders were given by the Jordanian government that armed
> bodies operating in the areas controlled by the Arab Legion were either to be under
> their orders or be disbanded. The Holy War Army refused to submit to this direction
> and it was forcibly disbanded and dispersed on October 3rd. The plot had failed to
> achieve its objective but its authors, the Egyptians, had, typically enough, brought
> the Arabs within measurable distance of fighting amongst themselves whilst still
> facing an enemy who was growing in strength. A renewed Israeli offensive at that
> moment might have left the Arab Legion engaging them in front and being attacked
> from behind by the Mufti's men.[58]

In his characteristically laconic fashion, Kirkbride actually underplays the seriousness of the tension between, on the one hand, Jordan and, on the other, Egypt
and the organization of Hajj Amin al-Husayni.

Immediately following the establishment of the All-Palestine Government, the
Egyptian army transported to Bethlehem a convoy of trucks filled with small
arms, which it delivered to anti-Hashimite elements. At the same time, a band
of Palestinian irregulars established itself north of Jerusalem and, according to a
contemporary British report, began "operating in the 1936 style—levying money
and recruits from villages, and holding courts of justice, all in the Mufti's name.
A clear attempt seems to be in progress to disturb conditions in Palestine areas
occupied by Transjordan."[59] As part of this effort to weaken the regime, irregulars
loyal to Hajj Amin al-Husayni began (during the cease-fire) to attack both United
Nations officials and Israelis in the Latrun area. British observers took it as axiomatic that these raids, conducted from areas under tight control by the Arab
Legion, were designed to embarrass Jordan internationally and to provoke an
Israeli counterattack that would embroil the Arab Legion in battle.[60] In addition
to these operations, around this time at least two attempts were made on the life
of King Abdallah. A Syrian army officer, no doubt working for his government,
stood behind one of them.[61] Thus, the decision by the Jordanian authorities to
disband all irregular forces did indeed prevent serious turmoil in Jordanian-
occupied Palestine.

The pressure by the Triangle Alliance to decapitate the Arab Legion, the propaganda campaign that presented the fall of Lydda and Ramleh as a British–Jordanian–Israeli plot, the creation of the Gaza government, and the support for
militantly anti-Hashimite organizations—all of these activities combine to form
a pattern of behavior on the part of the Egyptian government that, as Kirkbride
suggests, was not consistent with the goal of confronting Israel effectively. On
the contrary, this pattern constitutes very solid evidence that the Egyptian gov-

ernment, under the cover of pan-Arabism, pursued a Palestine policy in the middle of 1948 that was subordinate to its struggle against Britain and the Hashimites.

These anti-Jordanian activities met with considerable success. King Abdallah informed Washington on 24 September that Amman, as a result of Arab League pressure, could not openly accept the new Bernadotte plan. He also stated, however, that if the United Nations were to pass a resolution forcing the plan on the Arabs, then Jordan would gladly allow the international community to twist its arm. He told an American diplomat that, unfortunately:

> he is surrounded by hostile elements in Syria, Lebanon, Egypt, and to a certain degree in Iraq. . . . These are seeking to destroy him and Transjordan, and they criticize every step that he makes which they consider not in concert with Arab League decisions. Therefore as an Arab leader he is obliged to . . . adopt the decisions made by the majority of the other Arab leaders.[62]

Kamil Riyad's Mission

On 21 September, the day before the Egyptian authorities announced the formation of the All-Palestine Government Kamil Riyad, an emissary of King Faruq, appeared in Paris at the hotel where Eliyahu Sasson, the leading expert on Arab affairs in the Israeli Foreign Ministry, was staying.[63] The two men ate dinner together and talked for four hours about the possibility of peace between Israel and Egypt. Sasson, apparently, had not had such meaningful contact with the Egyptian elite since the summer and autumn of 1946, when he had investigated the possibility of partition with the government of Ismail Sidqi. Riyad informed Sasson that King Faruq had arranged for him to accompany the Egyptian delegation to the United Nations General Assembly, which was meeting in Paris. The Egyptian legation in the French capital had received orders to give Riyad free use of its diplomatic pouch, but neither it nor the special delegation knew anything about his mission.

Riyad explained that he had come "in order to examine with [Sasson] the possibilities of a separate arrangement between Israel and Egypt."[64] He knew where to find the Israeli diplomat, because Sasson had sent a letter informing the Egyptian government that, during the Paris meeting of the General Assembly (for which Count Bernadotte had prepared his progress report), he would be stationed in the French capital. According to Riyad, Sasson's letter was not the only thing that had prompted King Faruq to arrange this secret mission; in addition, he said, "the fundamental clashes in perspective and ambition between Transjordan and Egypt, which came to light in the last meeting of the political committee of the Arab League, proved to the king and his supporters that the interest of Egypt dictates following a separate foreign policy, one that is outside the framework of the Arab League."[65]

Riyad came with no suggestions of his own; the palace had instructed him to collect information. He wanted to know what kind of peace Israel could offer—to

Egypt by itself or to the Arab world as a whole. In addition, he requested that Israel make two pledges: not to expand at the expense of neighboring states, and not to align with the Communist bloc.

During the long conversation, Riyad focused on three main subjects: Anglo-Egyptian relations; the responsibility of the British for the war between Israel and the Arabs; and the conflict between Egypt and the Hashimite states. First, he explained that a small group of British and Egyptian officials was about to open informal talks on the outstanding issues between the two countries. On the agenda, among other things, was the future of the Negev, which the British sought to attach to Jordan—something that Cairo hoped to prevent.

Next, Riyad launched into an analysis of the Arab–Israeli war, which he presented as the outcome of an elaborate conspiracy hatched in London. The British, who controlled the press in the Arab world, had directed public opinion toward their own ends. In addition, they had misled all the leaders of the Arab countries—by feeding them false information about Jewish conspiracies, and by assuring them that, if they intervened in Palestine, they would be richly rewarded. The promised gains included political advantage, territorial aggrandizement and, in some cases, money. The representative of King Faruq explained that a number of prominent officials, including the secretary-general of the Arab League, were on the British payroll.

Undoubtedly Riyad characterized the war as an elaborate British conspiracy in order to demonstrate goodwill. By speaking in this manner, he signaled that the war had been a big mistake, the fault of London. Had the Arab powers not been misled by Britain, then they would never have gotten involved in the first place. The conflict between Israel and Egypt, he implied, did not arise as a result of a clash of fundamental interests; it was, rather, a simple misunderstanding.

Now that a pleasant atmosphere had been created, Riyad got serious: He informed Sasson about the recent meeting of the political committee of the Arab League. Not a single representative of an Arab state had proposed resuming the conflict, although some of the Palestinians present had still demanded a fight to the bitter end. Despite the unwillingness of the Arabs to continue the war, the Israelis, Riyad said, should not expect a change in the Arab position at the meeting of the United Nations General Assembly, where opposition to the recognition of the Jewish state would continue to reign supreme.

At the meeting of the political committee, according to Riyad, a serious breach had opened up between, on the one hand, Egypt and Syria, and, on the other, Iraq and Jordan.[66] The two sides had clashed over the question of the Jordanian annexation of Arab Palestine. As a result of this conflict, he explained, Egypt was supporting the organization of Hajj Amin al-Husayni:

> He did not try to deny that his government is maintaining the Mufti and his people, and supporting their political plans. But it is not doing this out of a recognition of the effectiveness of this step, or out of a desire to trouble Israel but, rather, as part of the score it has [to settle] with the Hashimite bloc, "which proved in the war with Israel its superiority over every other Arab army." This bloc, if it annexes

the Arab part of Palestine plus the Negev will be capable of threatening the independence of Egypt—a situation that just a few months ago was impossible to imagine.[67]

Thus, according to Riyad, although Egypt supported an organization dedicated to the destruction of Israel, in fact it harbored no aggressive intentions toward the Jewish state.

Following this discussion, Sasson drew up, on the basis of standing instructions from Tel Aviv, a draft peace agreement between Egypt and Israel, which he then transmitted to Kamil Riyad. When the Israeli and Egyptian diplomat met again a week later, on 30 September, the character of the secret mission had become slightly more formal. After the receiving the draft peace agreement, the palace instructed Riyad to consult with three experts—one political and two military—attached to the Egyptian delegation to the General Assembly and loyal to the palace. Despite the growing number of officials involved in the mission, Riyad stressed to the Israelis that his government had definitely not entered into formal negotiations.

During the second encounter with Sasson, Riyad reported his impression that Cairo now considered his mission as "more serious than before." He also produced a document containing the reactions of the advisors who had examined the draft peace agreement.[68] On the basis of these and of Riyad's comments on them, it is clear that the Egyptians were "seriously considering the annexation of the Arab part of southern Palestine [the Negev] to themselves." Egypt needed this territory, according to Riyad, in order to protect itself in case of further war with Israel, and "in order to prevent its annexation to Jordan and its transformation into a British military base."[69] It was this consideration, he said, that led Cairo to establish the All-Palestine Government, which appeared in Gaza during the week that intervened between the two Riyad–Sasson meetings.

With regard to the disposition of the rest of Arab Palestine, Riyad did not commit himself. The issue arose only obliquely, in connection with an Egyptian demand that Haifa function as a free port for Palestinian territories, "whether they remain independent or become annexed to Transjordan."[70] The Egyptians justified this demand by explaining that since Egypt would annex Gaza—and thereby cut off the only route from the West Bank to the Mediterranean through Arab territory—it would need this concession from Israel in order to counter the claim that it had betrayed Arab national values.

The desire of Cairo to hold onto the Negev did not suit the plans of the Israeli Prime Minister David Ben-Gurion, who immediately began planning to oust the Egyptian forces from the south, before the policies of the Great Powers turned the Majdal–Faluja–Hebron border into a permanent frontier. On 15 October, the Israel Defense Forces launched a massive attack on the Egyptian military, striking a severe blow and, at the same time, bringing to a close this stage of the negotiations.

How do we make sense of this intriguing mission? Riyad's presentation of Egyptian motives contained a glaring internal contradiction. On the one hand, he claimed that the palace was contemplating a separate agreement with Tel Aviv, and in this regard was seriously contemplating the annexation of the Negev. On the other hand he also emphasized the hostility that Egypt harbored toward Jordan. As a consequence of that conflict, he explained that Cairo was bankrolling the organization of Hajj Amin al-Husayni. Hostility to Jordan and support for the All-Palestine Government, however, do not square with the intention of annexing the Negev and making peace with Israel. The Egyptian strategists could not have seriously contemplated a policy that would have been simultaneously pro-peace and anti-Hashimite, because cutting a deal with the Israel meant, by definition, compromising on core national values. In the event of an Egyptian–Israeli peace agreement, Cairo would have no moral position from which to criticize a separate agreement between Amman and Tel Aviv. If, moreover, Egypt annexed the Negev, on what grounds would it oppose the Jordanian absorption of the West Bank? As al-Nuqrashi Pasha had suggested to Count Bernadotte, people would say that Egypt had sold out the Arabs.

There are two possible explanations for this internal contradiction. First, we can take what Riyad said at face value: King Faruq contemplated a break with the League and wished to know what terms he could obtain from Israel. This explanation presupposes a sharp debate behind the scenes in Cairo. It suggests that, although Egyptian policy was set on a staunchly anti-Hashimite track, some voices were arguing that support for Palestinian nationalism and the struggle with the Hashimites had already cost Egypt too dearly. Perhaps the strength of the Israelis caused some officials to again advance the arguments of Ismail Sidqi against a pan-Arab policy.

The second interpretation of the mission starts with the observation that when Cairo established the All-Palestine Government it announced to the world that one item stood at the top of its agenda—thwarting the Jordanian annexation of the West Bank. Its covert actions, therefore, should be read against the background of that pressing goal. Putting the screws on King Abdallah required two things: a foothold on the West Bank, and international (especially inter-Arab) support for the establishment of a Palestinian ministate. Cairo could only secure both of these if it succeeded immediately in preventing the Israelis from resuming hostilities or from making a separate deal with Jordan.[71] According to this explanation, Kamil Riyad went to Paris in order to play for time.

By dangling before Tel Aviv the possibility of peace with the most influential Arab country, Cairo hoped to engage the Israelis in the negotiations that, although not leading anywhere themselves, would forestall an Israeli offensive. During the extra time that Cairo would gain by engaging Tel Aviv in the process of negotiation, it would work to establish international support for the Gaza government.

Apart from Israeli inaction, all that the Egyptian authorities really needed for their policy to succeed was to establish a pan-Arab consensus in favor of a Palestinian ministate. Such a consensus would have created a climate in the Arab world—and especially among the refugees—hostile to the annexation of the West Bank by Jordan. If Amman were denied the freedom to absorb Palestinian territory, or to cut a separate deal with the Israelis, then the negotiating power of

Cairo would increase considerably; the question of peace between the Arab world and Israel would, in that case, remain solely in the hands of Egypt, the master of the consensus. Both the Israelis and the Great Powers would have no choice but to route their peace policies through Cairo. The pro-Jordanian Bernadotte plan, for lack of takers, would be dead.

The two explanations for the Riyad mission are not mutually exclusive. It is certainly possible that while following an anti-Hashimite and pro-Palestinian policy, the Egyptian leadership contemplated a different course altogether. Whatever the case, Cairo desperately needed time.

Certainly the Egyptian interaction with the Americans at this stage suggests a desire to stall. While Kamil Riyad was meeting with Sasson, Mahmud Fawzi, an Egyptian member of the United Nations delegation in Paris, held discussions with an American diplomat, Henry Villard, regarding the debate in the General Assembly over the Bernadotte proposals. Villard stated in his report that he took "Fawzi to lunch in the country and spent the better part of the afternoon discussing Palestine."[72] Fawzi, who would later serve as Abd al-Nasser's first foreign minister, said that it would be a "fatal mistake" for the United States to remain wedded to the Bernadotte proposals as a package.

In his view, the recommendations of the slain mediator should be subjected to negotiation, item by item. Before placing the entire package before the General Assembly, he suggested the following procedure:

1. There should be a general discussion of the Bernadotte proposals in Committee 1, carefully steered by the Chairman in order to avoid pressure for an immediate decision.

2. At the proper moment a very small subcommittee should be appointed of carefully chosen nations to work for a negotiated settlement on basis of the Bernadotte proposals, under the leadership of one or more "neutral" states. Possibly Belgium might qualify in this respect, with the addition perhaps of certain states which had abstained on the partition vote, together with one which had voted for and one which had voted against partition.

3. The role of such a subcommittee would be to conciliate opposing viewpoints on the Arab and Jewish sides and to bring forth a solution which both sides could accept under the urging of other members of the General Assembly

It was pointed out by Fawzi Bey that both parties to the controversy have extremists in their midst and have publicly assumed positions from which they cannot officially retreat. Nevertheless, the possibility remains of finding a middle ground on which agreement could be reached without serious loss of face, particularly in the light of the overall General Assembly opinion. The best way of finding this ground would be outside of formal debates in the Assembly or in the heat of Committee 1 proceedings.[73]

By showing moderation and expressing a desire for a settlement, Mahmud Fawzi exhibited goodwill toward Washington, whose help Cairo needed at this point in order to prevent an Israeli offensive in the south. At the same time, however, he also outlined a procedure for establishing the terms for an agreement that would inevitably be long, legalistic, and ultimately inconclusive. Thus, while the issue was slowly buried in committee, Cairo would gain the time necessary to establish a pan-Arab consensus around the All-Palestine Government, and push the Americans in the direction of regarding the Majdal–Faluja–Hebron border as inviolate.

Compromises and More Compromises

As mentioned previously, on 14 October the Israelis, in an effort to vitiate the clauses of the Bernadotte proposals pertaining to the Negev, attacked in force along the Majdal–Hebron line. In a period of nine days, they punched a series of holes in the static defenses, thereby isolating a large portion of the Egyptian army in the Faluja pocket. The Israelis drove south to Beersheba, separating the Egyptian forces in the Hebron area from their comrades located around Gaza. Syrian, Iraqi, and Jordanian guns remained silent during the fighting. The Egyptian hold on the Negev weakened considerably.

These operations had an immediate impact on the Jordanian–Egyptian struggle over the West Bank. The Israeli offensive cleared Palestinian territory of nearly all the forces, political and military, dedicated to preventing King Abdallah from enlarging his kingdom. The Government of All-Palestine, fearing for its safety, scurried out of Gaza, heading straight for Cairo. At the same time, the position of the Egyptian units on the West Bank, who had lost all direct contact with the main army, became untenable.

The Arab Legion, having already disbanded the irregular forces of the Mufti, quickly moved units to the Hebron area in order both to defend it against the Israelis and to wrest it away from the Egyptians. Glubb wrote to one of his commanders:

> If we step in and occupy Hebron, we shall have no further political complications in the Hebron area! We shall appear as saviours, to rescue Hebron from the Jews when the Egyptians have run away.
>
> This Jewish offensive may have good and bad sides. It may finally knock out the Gaza government and give the gyppies [Egyptians] a lesson. On the other hand, it will make the Jews even more arrogant, and if they knock out the Egyptians, they may turn on us.
>
> Anyway, if we do send someone to Hebron, I don't think we can send the 8th Regiment! This may well mean business, and not be a mere political demonstration. . . . Presumably the gyppies cut off in Hebron would co-operate for what they are worth!
>
> I don't see how we could let the Jews occupy Hebron if we could prevent it. At the same time, if the Jews are going to have a private war with the Egyptians and the Gaza Government, we do not want to get involved. The gyppies and the Gaza Government are almost as hostile to us as the Jews![74]

The Hashimite grip tightened around the West Bank.

King Abdallah moved swiftly to fill the power vacuum in Arab Palestine. In defiance of all the Arab states, including Iraq, he began to encourage Palestinians loyal to him to call for unification with Jordan. Hashimite radio broadcasts gave prominence to reports about delegations from the West Bank arriving in the capital to pledge loyalty to the monarch. In early November, the palace initiated a new phase in this campaign by organizing in Amman a Palestinian pro-unification conference. Then, on 4 December, the Jordanian authorities, longing for a more impressive spectacle, organized a grand congress in Jericho. With a little stage-managing by Amman, this assembly proclaimed the union of Palestine and Jordan and recognized Abdallah as the king of the expanded realm.[75] The Jordanian parliament immediately voted unanimously in favor of the proclamation.

These proceedings provoked a storm of protest from the Triangle Alliance. King Faruq denounced King Abdallah's intention to annex the West Bank. For their part, Damascus and Riyadh immediately expressed their full agreement with the statement of the Egyptian monarch. The policy of Cairo received support from al-Azhar (the famous Islamic university in Cairo) where the clerics ruled that the decisions of the Jericho Congress contravened Islamic law. Naturally, the clerics in Jerusalem interpreted the law differently.[76] The wheels of the Egyptian propaganda machine turned rapidly. The press adopted a uniformly hostile attitude: A typical article, published in *Akhbar al-Yawm*, branded the Jericho Congress "a stab in the back for Arabism." It asked whether "Egypt and the Arab states sacrificed their funds as well as their sons in order that Palestine should become a British base under an Arab name—a base from which to jump upon Syria and to destroy her independence, humiliating all Arab countries?"[77] The newspapers accused King Abdallah of exploiting the misery of the refugees, and they denounced as traitors some individual Palestinians who had participated in the congress. Of course, the All-Palestine Government, now situated comfortably in Cairo, labeled the Jericho Congress a sham, proclaiming itself the legitimate representative of the Palestinian people.

While Amman and Cairo were locked in conflict over the future of Arab Palestine, the Egyptian government continued to pursue its secret contacts with the Israelis. In early November, Kamil Riyad transmitted to Eliyahu Sasson the Egyptian terms for an armistice agreement.[78] In addition, he demonstrated to the satisfaction of the Israelis that support in Cairo for his mission had expanded beyond the palace: al-Nuqrashi Pasha either endorsed the secret contacts with Tel Aviv, or knew of them and did nothing to stop them. Despite this sign that Cairo now took the path of direct negotiations with Israel more seriously, Riyad's new initiative failed to generate an agreement with Tel Aviv, which considered the Egyptian terms onerous.

In return for an armistice agreement, not a full-fledged peace treaty, Cairo demanded two things from the Israelis: That they withdraw from the territory conquered in the recent round of fighting; and that they concede to the Egyptians the right, which would be exercised at an unspecified date in the future, to annex two strips of territory. The first stretched down the coast from Ashdod, through Gaza, to the international frontier; the second ran along the frontier itself, starting at the coast and moving southeast. The Israeli government rejected these terms. It feared having the finger of Cairo as close to Tel Aviv as Ashdod; in addition, perhaps, it worried about antagonizing the Hashimite bloc, which still constituted the greatest military threat.

Unlike the previous suggestions floated by Kamil Riyad, these proposals were completely consistent with the intention of pursuing a staunchly anti-Hashimite policy. Thus, the Egyptian authorities sought an Israeli withdrawal from the Negev in order to provide a land link to the West Bank. By maintaining a border with Jordan, and a foothold in Hebron, the Egyptian authorities would be able to place the All-Palestine Government in the populous center of Palestine, where it could work to thwart the annexation of the West Bank by Amman. Since Cairo courted Palestinian irredentism in order to thwart the intentions of King Abdallah to cut a deal with Israel, it could not itself propose a full peace treaty. Thus, it offered Tel Aviv an armistice—a limited agreement that would allow Cairo to end the war and yet, in the Arab arena, continue to denounce any attempt by Amman to establish full relations with Tel Aviv.

Whereas Kamil Riyad had previously spoken to the Israelis about annexing all of the Negev, he now spoke only in terms of two strips of territory. Cairo no doubt sought to annex these for strategic reasons. There are two basic routes for an invasion of Sinai: One runs south along the coast from Gaza; the other goes south from al-Awja, a crossroads next to the international frontier, south of Beersheba. Both of these areas fall within the strips of territory demanded by Cairo. That the Egyptians asked for recognition of their *future* right to annex these areas suggests that Cairo envisioned the formal annexation as part of some later arrangement with the All-Palestine Government.

Cairo quickly learned that it had nothing to gain from direct contacts with the Israelis. Developments in the Great Power arena, however, provided some hope that international pressure might force the Israelis to disgorge the Negev. On 4 November the United States and Britain pushed a resolution through the Security Council in effect calling on Israel to return its forces to the positions that they had occupied prior to the latest offensive. Then, in late November, the British, who for their own reasons were set on rolling back the Israelis, put forth a resolution at the Political Committee of the General Assembly calling for the creation of a Conciliation Commission charged with implementing a settlement.

This resolution, as drafted by the British, failed in the end to pass. The Conciliation Commission did, in fact emerge, but in a considerably different form than originally envisioned by London; the British had sought to create an organization invested with the power *to impose* a settlement on the belligerents. Since the British government intended to push the Israeli forces back behind the Majdal–Faluja–Hebron line, and since the 4 November Security Council resolution in fact called on the Israelis to return to the positions that they occupied prior to their latest advance, the commission that the British sought to create would inevitably function as an instrument designed to clear the Israelis out of the Negev. Although the commission as envisioned by the British never came into existence, an examination of Egyptian diplomacy surrounding this issue reveals much about the priorities of Cairo.

Given the weakness of the Egyptians on the battlefield, and given their tenuous hold on Palestinian territory, the British draft resolution appeared particularly attractive to Cairo. Thus, the British delegation reported to London:

It is now evident that the Egyptian attitude on the Palestine question is very different from that of the other Arab delegations. The latter are still expressing, privately as well as publicly, their hostility to any resolution instructing the Conciliation Commission to work on the basis of partition. The Egyptians on the other hand are not only expressing satisfaction with the United Kingdom draft [resolution] but are even hinting that in their view a settlement less satisfactory than the Bernadotte plan would be better than no settlement at all.

This line was taken by [Foreign Minister] Khashaba [Pasha] in conversation with Beeley last night. He said the Arabs must recognise that they were not strong enough to give effect to their wishes in Palestine at present. They could not begin to strengthen themselves militarily and in other ways until the truce was over and a provisional settlement established. Therefore it was a great mistake to work, as some of the Arab delegates were working, for a postponement of any decision.[79]

Thus, in the middle of a war, the Egyptian state switched suddenly from behavior apparently based on complete fidelity to the tenets of pan-Arabism to a very practical attitude toward the realities of power. The speed and the totality of this switch casts doubt on the depth of the previous Egyptian commitment to the rhetoric of no compromise. At any rate, Cairo was now willing to work with the Great Powers in order to halt the Israeli advance.

Working with the British, however, posed a problem for the Egyptian authorities. Insofar as the Conciliation Commission, as the British originally conceived of it, would have forced the Israelis to withdraw, it was extremely attractive to Cairo. The commission, however, would have been charged with much more than just fixing the southern border of Israel: It would also decide the fate of Arab Palestine. Thus, from the point of view of Cairo the draft resolution had two major drawbacks: It was sponsored by Britain, the patron of King Abdallah; and it envisioned a settlement influenced by the Bernadotte proposals, which suggested giving Arab Palestine to Jordan.

The Egyptian authorities found themselves in an awkward bind. On the one hand, in order to secure the Majdal–Faluja–Hebron line—or for that matter any line that still gave them a considerable chunk of Arab Palestine—they needed the support of Britain and of the Bernadotte proposals. On the other hand, however, they remained staunchly opposed to the aggrandizement of Jordan, which was both sanctioned by the Bernadotte proposals and supported by Britain. Thus, Cairo needed to find a means of persuading the British to carry on with their intention of rolling back the Israelis but to abandon their support for Jordanian expansion.

The policy of the Foreign Office provided Cairo with no hope regarding the Jordanian question. London consistently took the line that Egypt and Jordan should work their differences out together. Thus, for instance, the British delegation to the United Nations General Assembly in Paris also reported to the Foreign Office that:

Beeley told Khashaba that in the event of a negotiated settlement [between the Arab states and Israel] His Majesty's Government would hope for a friendly agreement between Egypt and Transjordan concerning the division of the Arab areas. They could not disinterest themselves, and they hoped the Egyptian government would in no circumstances disinterest themselves, from the settlement of the frontier between the Jewish State and Transjordan.[80]

Behind this statement stood the British aim to foster a unified Arab stance—in order to prevent the Israelis from playing Egypt off against Jordan, and in order for London, Amman, and Cairo to present a common face to Washington. Unfortunately for Britain, however, a friendly agreement between Cairo and Amman presupposed completely different relations between Jordan and Egypt than actually existed.

Direct negotiations with Amman were unthinkable, because they would have required Cairo to compromise on fundamental interests. The moment the Egyptians would have sat opposite King Abdallah at the negotiating table, the wily monarch would have inevitably demanded, in exchange for an Egyptian foothold in the Negev, the approval of the Arab League for the Jordanian annexation of the West Bank. Moreover, as Kamil Riyad told the Israelis in September, the British favored placing the Negev in the hands of Jordan. Cairo, therefore, could look neither to Amman nor to London for help in subverting those clauses of the Bernadotte proposals that favored Jordan. Thus, the Egyptians projected a pleasant disposition toward the British, whom they needed in order to contain Israel; at the same time, however, they avoided discussing with them the disposition of Arab Palestine.

The attitude of Cairo toward Washington, however, was different. Whereas in conversations with British representatives the Egyptians spoke only about the Majdal–Faluja–Hebron border, with the Americans they went into elaborate details concerning the disposition of the Negev after the Israelis had been rolled back. Clearly, therefore, Cairo hoped to improve its negotiating power vis-à-vis London and Amman by pulling the Americans into the arena on its side. The Egyptians gambled that Washington would, first, force the Israelis to withdraw and, subsequently, support the Egyptian rather than the Jordanian vision of the postwar political order in Arab Palestine.

On 24 November, Mahmud Fawzi called on Phillip Jessup, an American representative at the Special Session of the General Assembly, in order to talk about the British draft resolution that called for creating a powerful Conciliation Commission. Fawzi expressed satisfaction with the resolution and with the American amendments to it, noting in particular that there existed an opportunity for "some flexibility" in the drafting of the terms that would govern a settlement with Israel. That is to say that the commission would not be saddled with the Bernadotte proposals as an inviolate package; it would, instead, have the power to draft its own terms for a settlement.

Fawzi then explained that he thought it would be wise to pass a resolution couched in general terms; it would "be a mistake for the General Assembly to attempt to make a definitive delineation of the boundaries."[81] After making this point, Fawzi delineated the boundaries that Egypt desired; and in order to drive home the point, two days later he returned with the precise map references—in terms of longitude and latitude. By extolling vagueness as a virtue in the general resolution that he advocated and then immediately discussing the boundaries that Egypt wanted, Fawzi tacitly admitted that vagueness was a laudable quality not because it created a good atmosphere for negotiation but, rather, because it provided Egypt with the opportunity to capture all of the Negev for herself and her puppet Palestinian state.

This kind of map-drawing, of course, smacked of partition—and, therefore, constituted a serious breach of the Egyptian commitment to pan-Arabism, especially since it took place without prior consultation of the other Arab states. Fawzi explained that although the official Arab position called for a unitary state, it was necessary to be practical. He favored the principle of geographic continuity: "Egypt could not be separated from other Arab states by the Jewish state."[82] When Jessup asked Fawzi if any real disagreement existed between Jordan and Egypt about boundaries, the Egyptian diplomat responded dishonestly that there was not: "These matters," he said, "could be settled if viewed realistically." Naturally, the "realistic" boundaries that Fawzi laid out to the Americans worked to the disadvantage of Jordan.

Fawzi's plan for the disposing of Arab Palestine was based on *two* principles: geographic continuity between the Arab states, and the containment of Jordan. He stated that "Egypt should have the portion of the Negev south of the line drawn through Majdal and Hebron"—on which Faluja was located. He said that Beersheba must be located in the Egyptian sphere. In addition to demanding for Egypt all of southern Palestine allotted to the Arabs by the Bernadotte plan, he refused to grant Jordan access to the Mediterranean. If Amman needed a corridor to the sea, he said, it could have one above the Majdal–Hebron line. Since this was the border in the process of being recognized by the United Nations, he implied that the Jordanians should look to the Israelis rather than the Egyptians for port facilities. The Americans assumed, without doubt correctly, that this attitude arose from a desire to diminish the Jordanian and British spheres of influence in the region.

While demonstrating a complete disregard for the economic life of Jordan, which had been severely damaged by the creation of Israel, Fawzi also revealed a cavalier attitude toward the other allies of Egypt: "When asked whether the Arab states would hold similar views to Egypt on the question of borders, Fawzi said that they were not in a position to do anything in the present situation so they would have to acquiesce."[83] Though not really very surprising, this attitude did completely contradict the principles of Arab unity and of collective responsibility for Palestine—principles the Egyptians constantly brandished against Amman.

For instance, shortly after this conversation, Karim Thabit, a close advisor of King Faruq, explained to the British that if King Abdallah were to accept the throne of Palestine, the Arab League would expel him. Thabit saw only "one chance" for Arab unity: Amman must request permission from the Arab League to annex the West Bank. The League, he admitted, would certainly reject the request, but Jordan could expect some territorial compensation.[84] As the dominant power in the Arab League and as the leader of the Triangle Alliance, Egypt enjoyed the luxury of following its own independent policy while simultaneously demanding that Jordan respect the Arab consensus.

Conclusion

At the heart of Egyptian policy toward Palestine stood one question: Would the final settlement work to the advantage of the Turco-Hashimite Entente or the Triangle Alliance? If the Egyptian demand for a border along the Majdal–Hebron line had been satisfied, then Cairo could have kept a foothold not just in the Negev but in the populous regions of Palestine as well. In this position, the Egyptian authorities would have been well situated to prevent the annexation of the West Bank by promoting the cause of the All-Palestine Government. Under such circumstances, Hebron would undoubtedly have become a center of anti-Hashimite political activity, a base for subverting the pro-British order in Jordan.

The diplomacy of Cairo following the July fighting conclusively disproves Glubb's thesis that public fervor over Palestine held Egyptian diplomacy hostage. In Cairo's policy during this period, we witness a state pursuing its interests according to the brutal logic of power. Mahmud Fawzi and Foreign Minister Khashaba Pasha—to say nothing of Kamil Riyad and King Faruq—all displayed a willingness, when the military balance had shifted against Egypt, to compromise on core principles. These were the same principles that they had advanced as a pretext for resuming the battle in July—when a fervent public commitment to them worked to the detriment of Jordan and functioned as a means of pressuring the Great Powers to respect the interests of the Triangle Alliance rather than those of the Hashimite bloc.

The analysis that Glubb advances in his memoirs is correct in one respect: Cairo did conduct an ideological policy. He is wrong, however, in asserting that the Egyptian authorities demonstrated an implacable commitment to principle simply in order to appease a domestic audience. Rather, they also sought to excite a foreign crowd—the Palestinians, who, by regarding their homeland as *terra irredenta*, pressured Jordan to fight on. Glubb also misses the mark when he characterizes the Egyptian leadership as unbending: Compromise, when it suited their interests, came naturally to them. As a consequence, Cairo had no difficulty adopting a realistic attitude toward the existence of a Jewish state.

But in this, too, Glubb was not completely mistaken. On one issue, the Egyptian authorities were, without exception, incapable of compromise—the expansion of Jordan. Thus, although Cairo found it possible to acquiesce in the creation of Israel, a close examination of Egyptian diplomacy reveals that it remained steadfast in its opposition to the expansion of King Abdallah's realm. This seeming paradox did not arise from some peculiar aspect of the Egyptian character. Rather, it resulted from the realities of power in the Middle East—realities of which Cairo had a cool and practical understanding.

Whereas the Egyptian state had few tools at its disposal for influencing the policies of Tel Aviv, it had tremendous influence in the Arab arena. Thanks to its size, geographical location, language, religion, and state tradition, Egypt held sway over nearly all that transpired in inter-Arab politics. Moreover, the continued ability of Egypt to cut a profile in global affairs was, to a considerable extent, predicated on its special status among the Arab states. Since the development of a Tel Aviv–Amman axis threatened that status, the priority of Cairo lay in driving a wedge between Israel and Jordan. Containing King Abdallah—by supporting Palestinian nationalism and by championing the creation of a West Bank state—constituted the best means that Cairo possessed for achieving this goal. Of course, from the moment they ordered the Egyptian army across the Palestinian frontier, leaders in Cairo had sought to prevent a rapprochement between Israel and Jordan. Until July, however, the true priorities of Cairo were not easy to discern. Once the military balance had shifted, however, all ambiguity dissapeared: The stronger the Jewish state grew, the more hostile Egypt became toward Jordan. As the Israeli forces achieved the capability of driving all the Arab armies from Palestine, the Egyptian authorities fomented rebellion in Jordan, conducted a propaganda campaign designed to undermine the cohesion of the Arab Legion, and pressed the Jordanian authorities to purge their army of its officer corps. No other motive can be found for this policy than to weaken King Abdallah and undermine the position of the British in the Middle East.

The refusal of the Egyptian government to make any concessions to the interests of Britain and Jordan dramatically expressed itself at the end of the year, during the final assault by the Israelis against the Egyptian forces. On 24 December, while the battle was at its height, the British ambassador had a discussion with Muhammad Haydar Pasha, the Egyptian minister of defense. Ronald Campbell developed a familiar theme: Egypt, Britain, and Jordan all sought to remove the Israelis from the Negev; if they could only agree among themselves then they would strengthen their position in international circles. According to the Ambassador:

> Haidar Pasha made it clear that he favoured and would support, both with the king and with the cabinet, an early and serious effort to come to agreement with Transjordan. He appreciated the fact that Great Britain, Egypt, and Transjordan had essential interests in common which were being sacrificed by lack of unity between us. Egypt could not however deal with Transjordan direct. Egypt would have to deal with us, and it would be for us to deal with Transjordan. The reason for this, at the back of his mind (though he did not say so in so many words), was that Abdallah was known to be ready to [negotiate direct?] with the Jews, and Egypt was not prepared either to do that or to give the appearance of so doing by too close [an] association with Abdallah. As ever in this part of the world, one's dignity, whether national or personal, ranks before the acceptance of realities.[85]

A strong sense of the balance of power would have served the ambassador much better than did either his confidence in his ability to read minds or his belief in the power of Arab honor.

Contrary to the assumptions of the ambassador, Haydar Pasha refused to support direct negotiations with King Abdallah because he was thinking in terms of narrow Egyptian rather than general Arab interests. He was thinking, that is, about the position of Egypt as the dominant power in the Arab world. He did not wish to negotiate on the basis of terms set by Great Britain, because such terms would force Egypt to make concessions to Jordan. If, by contrast, Cairo were to lay before the British government its own conditions for a settlement, and if Britain were to deliver up King Abdallah, then Egypt would never have to compromise.

Haydar Pasha further qualified his support for negotiations by stating that no attempt to come to terms with King Abdallah, even if brokered by Britain, was possible during the current military emergency. "The Egyptians," he said, "must not be made to appear to be seeking an agreement with Abdallah about dividing up the Negev simply because they were being knocked about by the Jews."

No threat from Israel was great enough to force the Egyptians to cooperate with Jordan.

Conclusion

DURING the period July to December 1948, the Egyptian government had sought to retain, with the aid of the Great Powers, control of the Negev and a foothold on the West Bank. However, the Israeli offensive at the end of the year, which coincided with the assassination of the Egyptian prime minister, convinced Cairo to accept the best terms that it could obtain directly from Tel Aviv. In February 1949, therefore, Egypt became the first Arab power to sign an armistice with the Jewish state. When negotiating this agreement, the Egyptian representatives displayed a complete disregard for the principle of Arab solidarity. In an effort to achieve the best deal for Egypt, they demanded that the other Arab states refrain from negotiating their own armistice agreements until after the conclusion of the Israeli–Egyptian agreement.

This refusal to bargain collectively had disastrous results for Jordan. Within days of the Egyptian agreement, the Israelis—having effectively detached Egypt from the conflict—dispatched troops to the Gulf of Aqaba. They quickly drove detachments of Arab Legion from this area, which was destined to become the port of Eilat. The Egyptian diplomatic withdrawal also led indirectly to Israel's gain of territory further north. The posture of Cairo allowed the Iraqi government to quit the fight without being branded a traitor to the pan-Arab cause. For the purposes of domestic consumption, Baghdad took the pseudoprincipled line that it would never stoop so low as to sign an armistice agreement—an act, it claimed, that would constitute tacit recognition of Israel. Not sharing a common border with the Jewish state, Iraq could afford to shun all contact: Baghdad ordered its forces to return home without so much as opening negotiations. The Jordanian army, now the sole Arab force responsible for the defense of the West Bank, was left in the lurch. Israel, quick to exploit the advantage, massed troops on the border; Tel Aviv refused to sign an armistice with Amman unless it relinquished yet more land. King Abdallah had no choice but to comply.

On the face of it, this sad finale to a disastrous war marked the complete failure of Egyptian policy. Indeed, the defeat of the Egyptian army and the occupation of most of Palestine by the Jews was a disaster in political terms as well. Cairo would certainly experience its deleterious effects for years to come. Nevertheless, the Egyptian government did manage to attain at least one of the major goals that it had originally set for itself: It had prevented the establishment of a Tel Aviv–Amman axis. The war brought political, economic, and demographic changes to Jordan that made King Abdallah more subservient to the Arab League than ever before. The population of Jordan tripled overnight, and the country was now composed primarily of Palestinians, many of whom owed little or no loyalty to the monarchy. Jordan received a greater number of refugees than the other Arab countries combined; these uprooted and angry people formed a ready constituency for the anti-Hashimite propaganda of the Triangle Alliance.

The politics of Jordan now approximated the Iraqi model: Powerful domestic groups regarded the pro-British regime as a den of quislings. Prior to 1948, King Abdallah had displayed an ability, within limits, to defy the other Arab states. Now things would be different. The Palestinian nationalists living under Jordanian rule would function as a fifth column for the Triangle Alliance. The usefulness to Cairo of Palestinian nationalism dramatically demonstrated itself in 1950, when a hostile Egyptian propaganda campaign, combined with the threat to expel Jordan from the Arab League, forced King Abdallah to abandon negotiations for a separate peace with Israel. Jordanian politics had entered a new, ideological era; the masters of the age resided in Cairo.

This crisis of legitimacy in Amman, not to mention the economic consequences of the war, put an end to the Greater Syria Project of King Abdallah, creating the defensive, survival-oriented Jordan we know today. Thus, although the Jordanian threat to the Triangle Alliance still manifested itself as late as 1949, by 1950 it had largely evaporated. The end of the Greater Syria Project did not, however, spell the end of the Syrian question. The war brought to a head the long and deep crisis of legitimacy in Damascus, which suffered three coups d'état in 1949. This turmoil created a power vacuum that invited outside interference; for the next seven years, Iraq would replace Jordan as the major external threat to Syrian republican institutions. The efforts of Egypt and Saudi Arabia to prevent such a merger constituted a major theme of inter-Arab politics leading up to the Suez Crisis.

The continuation of the Syrian question forced Cairo to keep the Arab League at the center of its foreign policy. Undoubtedly the defeat of the Egyptian army strengthened isolationist voices in Cairo. Nonetheless, in the autumn of 1949 Cairo once again opted against isolationism by pressing the other Arab states to create an Arab League Collective Security Pact—a kind of Arab equivalent of NATO (with Egypt playing the role of the United States). The crisis in Syria constituted the immediate background to the proposal to establish a collective security organization, which the Egyptians designed as an ideological weapon for use against the claims of the Syrian supporters of union with Iraq. The scheme of the latter to abolish borders in the Fertile Crescent had the merits of appealing to pan-Arab sentiment and plausibly increasing Syrian security vis-à-vis Israel. The Egyptian government, by calling for the establishment of a formal military alliance under the aegis of the Arab League, provided its Syrian allies with a pan-Arab alternative to Fertile Crescent integration. Thus, the Arab League Collective Security Pact provided its Syrian champions with a means of displaying their pan-Arabism—an unimpeachable value in Syrian politics—while still rejecting the necessity of unity with Iraq.

The scheme laid the foundations for the creation of the Arab military bloc that King Faruq had first sketched for the British in February 1948. That original proposal, it will be recalled, arose against the background, on the one hand, of the Anglo-Jordanian agreement over the future of Arab Palestine, and, on the other, of the struggle between the Turco-Hashimite Entente and the Triangle Alliance. The context in which the concept of Arab collective security resurfaced demonstrates that, even after the Palestine war, a strong commitment to the Arab League was the favored strategy of Cairo for projecting its power into the politics of the Fertile Crescent. As long as the Egyptian government still opposed the expansion of the Hashimites, it had no choice but to rely heavily on the Arab League.

The Collective Security Pact, the brainchild of the Egyptian palace, arose in response to the Iraqi threat, but Cairo also intended it to be a tool for gaining complete independence from Britain. The pact drew sustenance from the popular notion that Arabs should rely only on Arabs for their defense. It posed, therefore, a direct threat to the existing, British security system. The Egyptian government—under Abd al-Nasser, as under the old regime—would in fact present the Arab Collective Security Pact as the most desirable alternative to the various Western proposals that arose in the late 1940s and early 1950s for a new Middle Eastern defense system (Middle East Command, Middle East Defense Organization, etc.). Cairo would argue that, in place of the British security system, the West should base the defense of the Middle East on an independent Arab bloc—a bloc dominated, of course, by Egypt.

Behind the idea of the Arab League Collective Security Pact, therefore, stood a vision of a new regional order. Cairo imagined an Arab world completely independent of Great Britain, presenting a common face to the outside world, and led by Egypt. The very act of supplanting the existing British security system would drastically shift the inter-Arab balance of power against the Hashimite states and in favor of the Triangle Alliance. The Arab League Collective Security Pact, therefore, planted the seeds for nothing less than a revolutionary transformation of the international system in the Middle East. These seeds would sprout only in the mid-1950s, but they were planted years before Abd al-Nasser toppled the Pashas.

When, precisely, did the vision of an independent Arab bloc dominated by Egypt and the Triangle Alliance begin to guide the foreign policy of Cairo? In the absence of official Egyptian documents it is impossible to answer this question with certainty. Nonetheless, several observations will allow us to narrow the range of possibility. When al-Nuqrashi Pasha appealed to the Security Council with a request to terminate the Anglo-Egyptian Treaty of 1936, he implicitly called for an end to the British security system and, therefore, for the creation of a new order. The prime minister would not appear to have outlined—publicly at least—the new order that he wished to see arise. His request to the United States for massive military aid, so that Egypt could take its "rightful place" among the nations suggests, but does not prove conclusively, that he in fact dreamed of something along the lines of the Arab bloc under Egyptian domination.

The position of strategists in Cairo who might have thought along these lines in mid-1947 undoubtedly received a severe blow when the Americans failed to endorse the Egyptian bid for complete independence. Perhaps as a result of Washington's policy, al-Nuqrashi Pasha hesitated to endorse the vision of a bold new order. Certainly the manner in which King Faruq, in February 1948, unveiled the Arab bloc plan suggests that it was the initiative of the palace rather than of the government as a whole. The collapse of Arab resistance in Palestine in April 1948 forced al-Nuqrashi Pasha to make a difficult choice: Should Egypt refrain from fighting and thus allow the Hashimite powers to play the most significant role in Arab politics? Or should Egypt enter the fray so as to play the leading role, on the Arab side, in establishing the post-Mandate order in Palestine? By 11 May, he had decided against leaving the settlement of the Palestine question to the Hashimite armies—he had decided, that is, to fight in order for Egypt to remain the dominant power in the Arab world. This struggle, as we have seen, committed Cairo ideologically to anti-Zionism and strategically to an anti-Hashimite orientation.

The Arab bloc vision of regional order, therefore, definitely served as the policy behind the policy in May 1948. In addition, however, it clearly had strong roots that extended back to March 1947 when al-Nuqrashi first resolved to pull Egypt out of the British orbit. Perhaps one day the official Egyptian documents will shed a clearer light on the debate behind the scenes in Cairo from March 1947 to May 1948.

Despite its enormous costs, which included the defeat of the Egyptian army at the hands of the Israelis, the Arab bloc orientation continued to inform policy after 1948. The depth of the commitment to this strategy resulted from the value to Egypt, especially in the Anglo-Egyptian arena, of being the keystone in the arch—a status that ensured Cairo considerable influence in international affairs. So the advent of the Arab League Collective Security Pact marked a new phase of an old policy. Ostensibly designed to strengthen the Arabs in the face of the Israeli threat, the collective defense scheme actually served Cairo by helping to prevent a Syrian–Iraqi union and by weakening the legitimacy of the British security system in the Middle East. A strong public commitment to Arab solidarity, to anti-imperialism, and to anti-Zionism greatly aided Cairo in its effort to weaken the Hashimites and the British alike.

Thus, the lines of policy that in 1956 catapulted Abd al-Nasser to the forefront of world politics had already been set by the old regime in 1948. Such a policy would remain in place until the 1967 defeat by Israel, which forced Cairo to begin to reconsider the practical value of a pan-Arab orientation.

Notes

Abbreviations

DFPI: *Documents on the Foreign Policy of Israel*
FO: Foreign Office
FORD: Foreign Office Research Department
FRUS: *Foreign Relations of the United States*
HMSO: His Majesty's Stationery Office
NA: National Archives
PP: *Parliamentary Papers*
PRO: Public Record Office
S/S: Secretary of State
WPIS: Weekly Political Intelligence Summary

Chapter 1

1. For the texts of the Notes, see *The Times* (London), 31 January 1946, p. 4.

2. See P. J. Vatikiotis, *The History of Modern Egypt* (London: Weidenfeld and Nicolson, 1991): pp. 288–320; and Royal Institute of International Affairs, *Great Britain and Egypt 1914–1951* (London: RIIA, 1952), pp. 28–31.

3. See, for instance, William Roger Louis, *The British Empire in the Middle East 1945–1951* (Oxford: Oxford University Press, 1984), p. 248.

4. NA, 883.00/7-545, Political Review for June 1945, Tuck to S/S, 5 July 1945.

5. Vatikiotis, *Modern Egypt*, pp. 349–352.

6. Vatikiotis, *Modern Egypt*, pp. 353–356.

7. Vatikiotis, *Modern Egypt*, pp. 354–355.

8. The Chamber of Deputies was constituted as follows: Sa'dists, 125; Liberals, 74; Independent Wafdist Bloc, 29; Nationalists, 7; and Independents, 29; giving a total of 264 deputies. For a report on the election see NA, 883.002/1-1645, Tuck to S/S.

9. For information regarding the committee, see: NA, 883.00/4-245, Tuck to S/S, 24 April 1945. On the palace support for the effort to prosecute al-Nahhas, see NA, 883.00/2-945, Tuck to S/S, 9 February 1945.

10. On Ubayd as a destabilizing factor in the cabinet see: NA, 883.00/4-245, Tuck to S/S, 24 April 1945.

11. For British attempts to discourage the anti–al-Nahhas campaign, see: NA, 883.00/2-945, Tuck to S/S, 9 February 1945; and NA, 883.002/3-745, Winant to S/S, 7 March 1945.

12. As soon as press censorship ended, al-Nahhas published a long petition that he had sent to the chief of the Royal Cabinet demanding the dissolution of the Chamber of Deputies and the holding of new elections; he also published a letter along similar

lines addressed to the British ambassador. This remained thereafter the Wafdist position regarding the Chamber of Deputies. See: NA, 883.00/6-1845, Tuck to S/S, 18 June 1945.

13. See the analysis by the American ambassador: NA, 883.00/9-2445, Tuck to S/S, 24 September 1945.

14. On the relationship between the assassination and the declaration of war and the contemplated seat at the San Francisco Conference, see: NA, 883.002/2-2445, Tuck to S/S, 24 February 1945; and NA, 883.002/2-2545, Tuck to S/S, 25 February 1945.

15. On the San Francisco conference and the hope for a seat on the Security Council, see: NA, 883.00/7-545, "Political Review for June 1945," Tuck to S/S, 5 July 1945. For further evidence that Egyptian opinion in general considered the Charter to have nullified the Anglo-Egyptian Treaty, see the letter to the Secretary of the United Nations from the Workers Committee of National Liberation: NA, 883.00/12-345; and the statement by Ismail Sidqi: NA, 883.00/3-1346, Tuck to S/S, 13 March 1946. This claim would later (in August 1947) form the basis of the appeal made by the Egyptian government to the United Nations, a development which will be examined in chapter 2.

16. On the initial Wafdist dismissal of the Security Council as a tool of the British, see: NA, 883.00/7-545, Political Review for June 1945, Tuck to S/S, 5 July 1945.

17. On the accusations, see: NA, 883.00/9-2445, Tuck to S/S, 24 September 1945.

18. See the comments of Sir Walter Smart to the American Charge d'Affaires: NA, 883.00/11-145, Lyon to S/S, 1 November 1945.

19. See NA, 883.002/12-645, Tuck to S/S, 6 December, 1945

20. On Nuqrashi's poor attempts to shore up his position, see NA, 883.00/9-2445, Tuck to S/S, 24 September 1945; and 883.00/11-145, Lyon to S/S, 1 November 1945.

21. Details of the incident were published at the end of November. It is difficult to explain why these did not come out immediately upon the end of press censorship; perhaps the palace found them embarrassing. For a translation of articles appearing in the press, see: NA, 883.00/11-2445, Tuck to S/S, 24 November 1945

22. NA, 883.00/9-2445, Tuck to S/S, 24 September 1945.

23. NA, 883.00/11-145, Lyon to S/S, 1 November 1945. Lyon refers to "dissident elements" but does not specifically mention Ubayd; on the basis of subsequent developments, however, it is safe to assume that in fact the pressure came from him.

24. NA, 883.00/11-145, Lyon to S/S, 1 November 1945.

25. *The Times* (London), 24 September 1945, 4.

26. NA, 883.00/11-145, Lyon to S/S, 1 November 1945.

27. NA, 883.00/11-145, Lyon to S/S, 1 November 1945.

28. NA, 883.00/9-2445, Tuck to S/S, 24 September 1945.

29. On the attitude of the Muslim Brothers about the British and the Egyptian political system, see Richard P. Mitchell, *The Society of the Muslim Brothers* (Oxford: Oxford University Press, 1969), pp. 217–231; of the Young Egypt Party, see James Jankowski, *Egypt's Young Rebels: "Young Egypt": 1933–1952* (Stanford, Calif.: Hoover Institute, 1975); of the Communists, see Joel Beinin and Zachary Lockman, *Workers on the Nile* (Princeton, N.J.: Princeton University Press, 1987), pp. 310–362.

30. NA, 883.002/12-645, Tuck to S/S, 6 December 1945.

31. On the resignation, see NA, 883.002/11-2745, 27 November 1945; and for a political profile of Ramadan Pasha, see NA, 883.002/12-445.

32. On the crisis, see NA, 883.002/12-245, Lyon to S/S, 2 December 1945; and NA, 883.002/12-645, Tuck to S/S, 6 December 1945.

33. In commenting on the terms of the Note, *Akhbar al-Yawm* urged "that in the event

of failure of the negotiation, Egypt should make herself a test case of the UNO Security Council 'to show whether the principles enunciated at San Francisco are genuine or only the word of the Big Powers.' " See NA, 883.00/12-1745, Tuck to S/S, 17 January 1946.

34. As reported by the American ambassador in NA, 883.00/2-546, Tuck to S/S, 5 February 1946.

35. See the report in NA, 883.00/2-546, Tuck to S/S, 5 February 1946.

36. NA, 883.00/2-546, Tuck to S/S, 5 February 1946.

37. Ibid.

38. On these events, see Mitchell, *Society*, p. 44; and NA, 883.00/2-1346, Tuck to S/S, 13 February 1946.

39. On Ubayd's actions, see NA, 883.00/2-1446, Tuck to S/S, 14 February 1946.

40. For a discussion of Faruq's actions that suggests he wished to mollify the student protesters, see Mitchell, *Society*, pp. 44–45. On the final day of the al-Nuqrashi Cabinet, see NA, 883.00/2-1546, Tuck to S/S, 15 February 1946.

41. For a discussion of the character of the new cabinet, see NA, 883.002/2-1746, Tuck to S/S, 17 February 1946.

42. On the vote in the Chamber of Deputies, see NA, 883.002/2-2046, Tuck to S/S, 20 February 1946.

43. The American ambassador attests to the role of the Wafd: NA, 883.00/2-2246, 22 February 1946; for the role of the Muslim Brothers and their relations with the Wafd see Mitchell, *Society*, pp. 45–46. The British apparently perceived Russian influence in the events, although the Americans remained skeptical: NA, 883.00/2-n2246, Tuck to S/S, 23 February 1946. While the Russian role might be questioned, local Communists no doubt participated: For a suggestion of cooperation between the Wafd and the Communists, see Mitchell, *Society*, p. 45. The American ambassador reported that Faruq summoned the Soviet minister on 21 February.

44. This account is a plausible reconstruction of events based on conflicting accounts. The official British and Egyptian explanations differed over the question of who was responsible for the violence: The Egyptians claimed that a peaceful demonstration had been disrupted by the trucks that stormed the demonstration and ran people down; the British claimed that the protest had turned violent before the arrival of the vehicles. The official accounts are located at NA, 883.00/2-2848, Tuck to S/S, 28 February 1946.

45. NA, 883.00/2-2146, Tuck to S/S, 21 February 1946.

46. NA, 883.00/2-2346, Tuck to S/S, 23 February 1946.

47. See his account at NA, 883.00/2-2848, Tuck to S/S, 28 February 1946.

48. NA, 883.00/2-2346, Tuck to S/S 23 February 1946.

49. Ibid.

50. See NA, 883.00/2-2848, Tuck to S/S, 28 February 1946; and NA, 883.00/2-2346, Tuck to S/S, 23 February 1946.

51. NA, 883.00/2-2246, Tuck to S/S, 22 February 1946.

52. For a full exposition, see Anthony Adamthwaite, "Britain and the World, 1945–1949: The View from the Foreign Office," *International Affairs*, 61 (1985): 223–235.

53. Adamthwaite, in "Britain and the World," quotes Sir Orme Sargent, an undersecretary at the FO: "There are sound reasons for hoping that financial difficulties will be a temporary phenomenon, for this country possesses all the skill and resources required to recover a dominating place in the economic world."

54. On hunkering down, see John Kent, *British Imperial Strategy and the Origins of the Cold War 1944–1949* (London: Leicester University Press, 1993), pp. 55–56, 61–63, 66–67.

55. This forms a major theme of Kent, *British Imperial Strategy*, pp. 33–34, 49–53, 63–65, and, especially, 98–100. See also Louis, *British Empire*, p. 31.

56. On British fears of becoming a client of the Soviet Union, see Kent, *British Imperial Strategy*, p. 99.

57. Raymond J. Sontag and James Stuart Beddie, eds., *Nazi–Soviet Relations 1939–1941* (Washington, D.C.: U.S. Department of State: 1948), pp. 258–259; 244–245, 270.

58. These policies and the Anglo-American response to them are treated in great detail by Bruce R. Kuniholm, *The Origins of the Cold War in the Near East* (Princeton, N.J.: Princeton University Press, 1980).

59. For details on the October agreement, see Kuniholm, *Origins*, p. 109–125.

60. On indirect Soviet support for the Greek Communists, see Kent, *British Imperial Strategy*, p. 54.

61. On the Soviet use of the Greek issue with regard to Romania, see Kent, *British Imperial Strategy*, p. 83; with regard to Iran, see H. T. Montague Bell, ed., *The Annual Register, 1946* (London: Rivingtons, 1947), p. 178.

62. Kent, *British Imperial Strategy*, p. 79–82.

63. See Kent, *British Imperial Strategy*, pp. 80–81 (Libya); 82, 88, 93 (the Dodecanese); and 102–103, 105–106, 108, 113 (Trieste). With regard to Tangier, see *FRUS (Potsdam) 1945*, vol. 2, pp. 1415–1416, 1441, 1460, 1496, 1556. For Syria and Lebanon, see the fuller treatment later in this chapter.

64. In mid-1946 the Soviets backed away from many of their demands on Mediterranean issues. See Kent, *British Imperial Strategy*, p. 101.

65. For the treatment of these issues see *The Official Records of the Security Council*, First Year, First Series, no. 1, pp. 31–71 (Iran); 71–133, 165–173 (Greece); 173–263 (Indonesia); 271–368 (Syria and Lebanon).

66. *FRUS (Potsdam) 1945*, vol. 2, p. 246: "Molotov said that what they had in mind was that the Government of Syria had approached the Soviet Government."

67. For details, see Aviel Roshwald, *Estranged Bedfellows* (Oxford: Oxford University Press, 1990), p. 219. Roshwald interprets the behavior of the Levant states primarily as an attempt to play the United States off the Europeans. While this is no doubt the case, the earlier appeal by Damascus to Moscow suggests that it is only part of the story.

68. Roshwald, *Estranged Bedfellows*, p. 218, explains that the Americans had, in December 1945, applied secret pressure on the British government; Washington "remained hostile to the imperial pretensions of the European powers" and also feared that the retention of forces in the Levant would give the Soviets a pretext for "maintaining their presence in northern Iran."

69. *FRUS (Potsdam) 1945*, vol. 2, pp. 372–373.

70. Avoiding direct intervention in Anglo-Egyptian affairs would appear to have been a constant of Soviet policy during the period 1945–1947. For instance, in March 1947, at the Moscow meeting of the Council of Foreign Ministers, Bevin brought up the matter of Anglo-Egyptian relations to Stalin, who reportedly displayed moderation. According to Bevin, Stalin said "that the Soviet Union had no intention of interfering in the carrying out of British policy in Egypt." See PRO, FO 371/62968/J1431, Moscow to FO, 25 March 1947. When a British spokesman later paraphrased this conversation, the Tass news agency issued a denial but, nonetheless, affirmed that "the U.S.S.R. . . . did not intend to interfere in this matter." See George Kirk, *The Middle East 1945–1950* (Oxford: Oxford University Press, 1954), p. 131.

71. For instance, see: Moscow to FO, 8 August 1946, PRO, FO 371/52551/E7720.

72. When analyzing the failure of his negotiations with the British, Ismail Sidqi writes in his memoirs:

the efforts of one of the greatest Communist states were directed, with all of its power and all of its means, toward thwarting every attempt toward arriving at a rapprochement between Egypt and England. This state succeeded, in particular, in convincing many among us that the Egyptian problem had no solution other than at the hands of the Security Council and the United Nations Organization. . . .

In the Security Council, Sidqi added, Cairo would see to it that Egypt achieved her nationalist goals without Britain being able to isolate her. Ismail Sidqi, *Mudhakkirati*, ed. Sami Abu al-Nur (Cairo: Maktabat madbuli, 1991), p. 253. "Many among us" is, no doubt, a reference to the Wafd and, perhaps, to the Communists as well.

73. Though expressed a year after the events under discussion, the following instructions from Foreign Minister Bevin, weighing the benefit of asking the Americans to press Cairo on the British behalf, may also be taken as indicative of the British attitude throughout 1945–1946: "I strongly advise against United States intervention in Egypt in view of Stalin's declaration of noninterference. . . . I do not want to give the Russians an excuse that the United States are taking a hand in this Anglo-Egyptian business" (Moscow to FO, 31 March 1947, PRO, FO 371/62968/J1511).

74. The British themselves made reference to the Monroe Doctrine; see Kent, *British Imperial Strategy*, p. 90; and Louis, *British Empire*, p. 231.

75. Paul Noble, "The Arab System: Opportunities, Constraints, and Pressures," *The Foreign Policies of Arab States*, ed. Bahgat Korany and Ali E. Hillal Dessouki (Boulder, Colo.: Westview, 1984): pp. 41–77.

76. *The Times* (London), 31 January 1946, p. 4.

77. On the concessions by Bevin, see Louis, *British Empire*, pp. 238–241.

78. NA, 883.00/7-546, Lyon to S/S, 5 July 1946.

79. See, for instance, Cairo to FO, Weekly Appreciation, 9 August 1946, PRO/FO 371/53332.

80. Cairo to FO, Weekly Appreciation, 28 June 1946, PRO/FO 371/53332.

81. Cairo to FO, Campbell, 29 June 1946, PRO/FO 371/53332/J2895.

82. Cairo to FO, Weekly Appreciation, 16 August 1946, PRO/FO 371/53332.

83. See, for instance: NA, 883.00/8-3146, Patterson to S/S, 31 August 1946, and the accompanying memoranda by Ireland.

84. Cairo to FO, Weekly Appreciation, 24 August 1946, PRO/FO 371/53332.

85. On the anti-Communist campaign, see: Cairo to FO, Weekly Appreciation, 12, 19, 28 July, PRO/FO 371/53332. See also: NA, 883.00/7-1246 and 1–1446, Lyon to S/S, 12 and 14 July 1946.

86. See Mitchell, *Society*, pp. 42–43, on the "courtesies" that Sidqi Pasha extended to the Brothers, including the provision of newsprint at a radically reduced price. Note also (pp. 45–47) the theme, developed in the Wafdist press, of an alliance between Sidqi and the Brotherhood.

87. Mitchell, *Society*, p. 48; Cairo to FO, Weekly Appreciation, 13 July 1946, PRO/FO 371/53332.

88. For Sidqi Pasha's comments to the British ambassador regarding the Muslim Brothers' paramilitary forces, see: Cairo to FO, Weekly Appreciation, 22 June 1946, PRO/FO 371/53332. For complaints by the Wafd regarding the velvet-glove treatment by the authorities of the paramilitary organization, see, in the same file, the Weekly Appreciation for 13 July 1946.

89. Mitchell, *Society*, p. 42.

90. For a report on the congress and a translation of the manifesto, see: NA, 883.00/9-546, Tuck to S/S, 5 September 1946.

91. Mitchell, *Society*, pp. 48–50.

92. On the deterioration in the relations between Sidqi Pasha and the other members of the delegation, and on the leaks to the press, see: NA, 883.00/10-246, Tuck to S/S, 2 October 1946, including enclosures.

93. WPIS, No. 358, 4 September 1946.

94. Cairo to FO, Weekly Appreciation, 14 September 1946, PRO/FO 371/53332.

95. Cairo to FO, Weekly Appreciation, 5 October 1946, PRO/FO 371/53332.

96. Ibid.

97. Cairo to FO, Weekly Appreciation, 11 October 1946, PRO/FO 371/53332.

98. For a translation of the manifesto and a discussion of it, see NA, 883.00/10-446, Tuck to S/S, 4 October 1946.

99. On these events, see: Louis, *British Empire*, pp. 248–253.

100. Cairo to FO, Weekly Appreciation, 8 and 16 November 1946, PRO/FO 371/53332.

101. Cairo to FO, Weekly Appreciation, 30 November 1946, PRO/FO 371/53332.

Chapter 2

1. *The Times* (London), 4 March 1947, p. 3.

2. *Official Records of the Security Council*, Second Year, no. 59, pp. 1343–1344.

3. *Official Records of the Security Council*, Second Year, no. 70, p. 1756.

4. Cairo to FO, Campbell, 12 March 1947, PRO/FO 371/62967/J1178.

5. See, for instance, Orme-Sargent to Bevin, FO to Moscow, 28 March 1947, PRO/FO 371/62943/J1409.

6. Cairo to FO, Campbell, 20 March 1947, PRO/FO 371/62968/J1405.

7. *FRUS*, vol. 5 (1947), p. 773.

8. WPIS, no. 384, 12 March 1947; Cairo to FO, Campbell, Weekly Appreciations for 1 and 22 February, and 10 March 1947, PRO/FO 371/63020/J514, J884, and J1147.

9. See for instance, Cairo to FO, Campbell, Weekly Appreciation, 19 January 1947, PRO/FO 371/63020/J303.

10. Cairo to FO, Campbell, 12 March 1947, PRO/FO 371/62967/J1178.

11. Minute by Howe, 18 March 1947, on Cairo to FO, Campbell, 12 March 1947, PRO/FO 371/62967/J1178.

12. Minute by Garran, 1 April 1947, on Cairo to FO, Campbell, 20 March 1947, PRO/FO 371/62968/J1405.

13. Major A.W. Sansom, *I Spied Spies* (London: George G. Harrap, 1965), p. 207.

14. One challenge that the crisis presented to British foreign policy in general, see: Alan Bullock, *Ernest Bevin: Foreign Secretary* (Norton: New York and London, 1983), pp. 361–363.

15. These events certainly raised American fears of a total British collapse: the most compelling account is still Joseph M. Jones, *The Fifteen Weeks* (New York: Viking, 1955), pp. 39–47.

16. Minute by Howe, 18 March 1947, on Cairo to FO, Campbell, 12 March 1947, PRO/FO 371/62967/J1178.

17. From the Address of the president delivered before a joint session of the Senate and the House of Representatives, 12 March 1947; reproduced in Bruce Kuniholm, *The Origins of the Cold War in the Near East* (Princeton, N.J.: Princeton University Press, 1980), pp. 434–439.

18. For a detailed analysis of the place of Palestine in Egyptian foreign policy, see chapter 4.

19. Ahmad Farraj Tayi‘, *Hadith diblumasi*, (Cairo: al-mitba‘a al-fanniyya al-haditha, 1968), p. 12.

20. For the near contemporary perception by a British diplomat that the Egyptians took the Greek and Turkish relationships with the Americans as models, see Kirkbride to Bevin, 26 April 1948, PRO/FO 371/68386/E5468. For an Egyptian statement in this regard (though admittedly made two years later) see: Egypt, Ministry of Foreign Affairs, *Records of Conversations, Notes and Papers Exchanged between the Royal Egyptian Government and the United Kingdom Government* (Cairo: 1950), p. 32. The Egyptian foreign minister stated to the British that his government "cannot help wondering [what is going on] when we see arms flowing from America into the Atlantic countries, Turkey, Greece, and Iran, while Egypt is treated differently."

21. On the role of lend-lease aid in American calculations, see Aaron David Miller, *Search for Security* (Chapel Hill: University of North Carolina Press, 1980), pp. 67–71.

22. Gordon Merriam quoted in Miller, *Search*, p. 66, who cites: "Forecast of Emerging Problems with Reference to the Foreign Petroleum Policy of the Untied States . . . ," 14 January 1943, Folder: "Study Group—Petroleum Policy, Box 19, Petroleum Division [of the State Department] records.

23. This is a major theme of Miller, *Search*, pp. 62–121.

24. Ibid., pp. 110–113.

25. See, for instance, ibid., pp. 72–77.

26. Ibid., pp. 140–149.

27. Ibid., pp. 152–156.

28. See, for instance, the United States–Saudi correspondence regarding King Abdallah's plans to establish a Hashimite Greater Syria: *FRUS*, vol. 5 (1947), pp. 738–759.

29. For some recent works on Palestine, see Ritchie Ovendale, *Britain, the United States, and the End of the Palestine Mandate 1942–1948* (Suffolk: Boydell for the Royal Historical Society, 1989); Martin Jones, *Failure in Palestine* (London: Mansell, 1986); Louis, *British Empire*. Despite not having the benefit of archives, J. C. Hurewitz, *The Struggle for Palestine* (New York: Norton, 1950) still stands up well.

30. *Official Records of the Security Council*, Second Year, no. 70, p. 1749.

31. On the Egyptian appreciation of the legal weakness of the case, see the remarks by the U.S. ambassador in Cairo: *FRUS*, vol. 5 (1947), p. 773. For an American expression of fear regarding the Soviet position, see the telegram from the secretary of state to the embassy in Egypt: *FRUS*, vol. 5 (1947), p. 770. For an expression of American concern regarding the effect on the Arab world of a U.S. rejection of the Egyptian claims, see the telegram from the secretary of state to the Embassy in Egypt: *FRUS*, vol. 5 (1947), p. 775. Although these are intra-American communications, the concerns of Washington would have been apparent to any intelligent reader of newspapers let alone the representatives of the Egyptian state, who conducted daily discussions with U.S. officials in Cairo, Washington, and elsewhere.

32. Note 1 in *FRUS*, vol. 5 (1947), p. 767. No doubt the choice of Moscow as the point from which to relay this information reflected an Egyptian desire to underscore subtly for the Americans the stakes in the matter.

33. *FRUS*, vol. 5 (1947), p. 785.

34. Memorandum of Conversation, ibid., p. 805.

35. These conversations are recorded or summarized in ibid., pp. 785–786; 805–806. See also the report from Cairo upon al-Nuqrashi's return, pp. 811–812.

36. Ibid., p. 785.

37. Ibid., p. 786.

38. For a brief summary of each session, see WPIS, nos. 404–407, 13, 20, and 27 August and 3 September 1947.

39. For British statements on this subject, see the *Official Records of the Security Council*, Second Year, no. 70, p. 1768.

40. *FRUS*, vol. 5 (1947), p. 802.

41. See Kirk, *Middle East*, p. 130; and the British Aide-Memoir in *FRUS*, vol. 5 (1947), 776–777.

42. This explanation was provided by Dean Acheson, the Acting Secretary of State, to the British diplomat who delivered a protest over the trip: see the Memorandum of Conversation in *FRUS*, vol. 5 (1947), pp. 768–769.

43. Ibid., p. 806, note 2.

44. Cairo to FO, Weekly Appreciation, 19 April 1947, PRO/FO 371/63020/J1809.

45. For a very clear discussion of the Anglo-Egyptian financial agreement and its failure, see: NA, 883.5151/10-747, Ireland to S/S, 7 October 1947.

46. *FRUS*, v (1947): pp. 811–812.

47. Ibid., p. 812.

48. Ibid.

Chapter 3

1. Quoted in Daniel Silverfarb, *The Twilight of British Ascendancy in the Middle East* (New York: St. Martin's, 1994), p. 150. For other treatments of this episode and the politics surrounding it, see Majid Khadduri, *Independent Iraq, 1932–1958* (London: Oxford University Press, 1960), pp. 267–270; Hanna Batatu, *The Old Social Classes and the Revolutionary Movements of Iraq* (Princeton, N.J.: Princeton University Press, 1978), pp. 545–566; Louis, *British Empire*, pp. 307–344.

2. Great Britain. *Parliamentary Debates (Hansard) House of Commons*, vol. 446 (London: HMSO, 1948), col. 400.

3. For statements suggesting that British policy toward Iraq took American opinion into account, see Silverfarb, *Twilight*, pp. 127–128.

4. On British concessions to Iraqi nationalism, see ibid., pp. 137–140.

5. Cairo to FO, 10 February 1948, PRO/FO 371/68384/E2054.

6. For the discussions with Azzam Pasha and Hafiz Wahba, see the two letters from Chapman-Andrews to Burrows, 7 February 1948, both in PRO/FO 371/68384/E2054.

7. The character of the Triangle Alliance is analyzed here in chapter 1. For confirmation of its existence from an Egyptian diplomat, who served as the Consul in Jerusalem in 1948, see Ahmad Farraj Tayi', *Safahat matwiyya 'an filastin* (n.d., n.p.), p. 113, who writes:

> It was well known that until 1948—or, for that matter, until the Egyptian Revolution of 23 July 1952—the Arab League was composed of two opposing blocs and a neutral bloc. One of the two opposing blocs contained Egypt, the Kingdom of Saudi Arabia, and Syria; the other contained Jordan and Iraq. The neutral bloc contained the rest of the Arab states [Lebanon and Yemen].

8. See the minute by Garran, 1 April 1947, on Cairo to FO, 20 March 1947, FO 371/62968/J1405

> It has been affirmed by the highest authority . . . that the maintenance of our position of influence in the Middle East is of vital importance to Great Britain and the British Empire. Our position in Egypt is the keystone to our position in the whole area, . . .

9. On Egyptian support for the Alexandria Protocol, see, for instance, "League of Arab States," 24 March 1950, PRO/FO 371/81933/E1071/98.

10. See note 20 in chapter 2.

11. Sidqi, in *Mudhakkirati*, p. 176, states that the agreement bound Egypt to aid Britain in the defense of neighboring countries. This statement receives further elaboration in the diaries of Pierson Dixon, who served on the British negotiating team. See Piers Dixon, *Double Diploma* (London: Hutchinson, 1968): p. 232, where Dixon claims that "aid" means automatic reoccupation of the bases by Britain.

12. Sidqi, *Mudhakkirati*, p. 176–177.

13. Ismail Sidqi takes great pains in his memoirs to prove that the Joint Defense Committee would insure the sovereignty of Egypt. See, for instance, his remarks regarding the benefit for the Canadians of the Canadian–United States Joint Defense Committee, which formed the model for the proposed Anglo-Egyptian Committee, and on which the Canadians were the weaker party: ibid., 192.

14. See, for instance, the Wafd manifesto published in *al-Misri*, 2 October 1946, and translated in Tuck to S/S, 4 October 1946, NA 883.00/10-446. Among other things, the manifesto states that "the proposed alliance may force us to adopt a hostile policy toward a member of the Arab League," and gives Britain "a privileged position in the neighboring or adjoining countries." The Egyptian negotiators, according to the Wafd, "should not conclude treaties with foreign countries which will put heavy responsibilities on the shoulders of the Arabs."

15. See the study by the Foreign Office Research Department [FORD], "The Activities of the Arab League from its Formation in March, 1945 to 15 May, 1948": PRO/FO 371/68352/E13328.

16. Ibid.

17. For the attempt to influence the Saudis and the subsequent expressions of disappointment, see: Cairo to FO, 22 March 1947, PRO/FO 371/62968/J1352; Jedda to FO, 13 March 1947, PRO/FO 371/62943/J1201; and Cairo to Jedda, 22 March 1947, PRO/FO 371/62968/J1380. For the Iraqis, see: PRO/FO 371/61523/E2618.

18. Cairo to FO, 24 March 1947, PRO/FO 371/62968/J1381.

19. FO Minute, Mr. Garran, 19 June 1947, PRO/FO 371/61526/E5890. The claim that the Arab League Covenant forbids separate negotiations on defense reflects more the popular, pan-Arab interpretation of the document than the letter of the text itself.

20. For further evidence of the Iraqi sense of embarrassment with regard to the Anglo-Iraqi connection, and of the sensitivity of Iraq to developments in Anglo-Egyptian relations, see the words by Foreign Office officials Howe and Baxter quoted in Louis, *British Empire*, pp. 323, 326.

21. This, combined with the hostility of the Triangle Alliance to the granting of Jordanian independence, led to an attempt by Jordan to secede from the League in early 1946. See Jones, *Failure in Palestine*, pp. 89–90.

22. For details on this and other activities, see PRO/FO 371/61523.

23. Quoted in M. Colombe, "La Turquie et les Problèmes du Moyen-Orient (1923–1947)," *Cahiers de l'Orient Contemporain*, 11 (12) (1947): 140.

24. Taha al-Hashimi, *Mudhakkirat Taha al-Hashimi*, vol. 2 (Beirut: Dar al-Tali'a, 1978), pp. 160–164.

25. Discussion of undoubtedly the same speech is found in Bruce Maddy-Weitzman, *The Crystallization of the Arab State System 1945–1954* (Syracuse, N.Y.: Syracuse University Press, 1993), p. 27. On p. 191, note 9, al-Pachachi is quoted as remarking on Azzam's speech: "if he had our frontiers, he would talk differently."

26. Al-Hashimi, *Mudhakkirat*, vol. 2, 161.

27. Kirkbride to Bevin, 18 March 1947, PRO/FO 371/61523/E2750.

28. Baghdad to FO, 25 March 1947, PRO/FO 371/61523/E2618.

29. Baghdad to FO, 3 March 1947, PRO/FO 371/61523/E2687.

30. Baghdad to FO, 10 April 1947, PRO/FO 371/61523/E3039. The Iraqis, according to the British ambassador:

> now claim that the Egyptian minister here is on their side and that during his forthcoming visit to Cairo he will tell Nokrashi that in the general interest Azzam should go. . . . I fear, however, that Iraqi efforts will remain clandestine and that there is little or no hope of their coming into the open.

31. Cairo to FO, 2 April 1947, PRO/FO 371/61523/E2883.

32. Amman to FO, 31 March 1947, PRO/FO 371/62968/J1529.

33. See Archie Roosevelt, Jr., "The Kurdish Republic of Mahabad," *The Middle East Journal*, 1 (3) (1947): 247–269.

34. See Colombe, "La Turquie," pp. 131–144.

35. The treaty was negotiated by Nuri al-Said, while he was out of office, and foisted on the government of Tawfiq al-Suwaydi, who demanded that a new article be added stipulating that the treaty did not contravene Iraq's obligations to the Arab League. Opposition in parliament claimed, among other things, that the treaty had been "imposed" on Iraq, that it contravened the Covenant of the Arab League, and that it recognized the borders of Turkey, thereby recognizing the annexation of Alexandretta. See Khadduri, *Independent Iraq*, pp. 346–347. See also Kirk, *Middle East*, pp. 151–152. These attacks by the opposition were staples of the propaganda of the Triangle Alliance, which claimed that the Turks and the Hashimites, as agents for British imperialism, sought to undermine the principles of Arabism.

36. Quoted in *Cahiers de L'Orient Contemporain*, 7 (8) (1946): 505.

37. See Colombe, "La Turquie," pp. 139–140.

38. For the text of the treaty, see *The Middle East Journal*, 1 (2) (1947): 212–213. References to the reaction of the Arab League are found in PRO/FO 371/61523. At the Arab League meeting in March 1947, the Syrians protested the warming of relations between Ankara and Amman; see: Kirkbride to Baxter, 28 March 1947, PRO/FO 371/61523/E3025.

39. *The New York Times*, 22 September 1946.

40. For the text of the treaty, see *The Middle East Journal*, 1 (4) (1947): 449–451.

41. Khadduri, *Independent Iraq*, pp. 343–345.

42. For details of the attitude of the Syrian government, see the study by the Foreign Office Research Department [FORD], dated 10 January 1948, "The Greater Syria Movement," PRO/FO 371/61497/E9137, 11–14.

43. The extent of the legitimacy crisis in Syria, and the vulnerability of the regime to the Greater Syria movement, are analyzed in great depth by Joshua Landis, "Nationalism and the Politics of Za'ama: The Collapse of Republican Syria, 1945–1949" (Ph.D. diss., Princeton University, 1997).

44. *Keesing's Contemporary Archives*, 11–18 January 1947, p. 8375.

45. For proof of the depth of Saudi fears, see: *FRUS*, vol. 5 (1947), pp. 738–759.

46. For examples of protests made to the British, see: PRO/FO 371/61492, 61493, 61494, and 61495.

47. The Saudis had claimed Aqaba and Ma'an from the moment they expelled King Husayn from the Hijaz; they raised the issue whenever they sought to pressure the British to restrain Amman. The question emerged again at the beginning of 1946 when the British granted Jordan independence. See Jones, *Failure in Palestine*, p. 89.

48. Quoted in Kirk, *Middle East*, p. 152, note 2; on the Egyptian fear of a revitalization of the Saadabad Pact, see Colombe, "La Turquie," pp. 138–141.

49. Moscow to FO, 24 January 1947, FO 371/61492/E996. See also the first reference in note 48.

50. See the first reference in note 49.

51. See D. Cameron Watt, "The Saadabad Pact of 8 July 1937," in *The Great Powers in the Middle East 1919–1939*, ed. Uriel Dann (New York: Holmes and Meier, 1988) p. 333–352.

52. Royal Institute of International Affairs, *British Security: A Report by a Chatham House Study Group* (London: RIIA, 1946): 123. Quoted by C. Ernest Dawn in "The Project of Greater Syria" (unpublished Ph.D. diss., Princeton University, 1948), p. 106.

53. With regard to Nuri al-Said's views, see: Stonehewer-Bird to Eyres, 4 February 1947, PRO/FO 371/61492/E1555. Stonehewer-Bird writes that the "fundamental difficulty" in improving Iraqi–Syrian relations:

> will remain and will, I am afraid, be aggravated if Nuri Pasha's plans for creating a 'Northern Bloc' mature. . . . As you know, at the time of the formation of the Arab League, Nuri's plan was originally for a union of the Fertile Crescent, leaving Egypt and Saudi Arabia out of it. He was persuaded, for the sake of unity, to bring Egypt and the Saudi Arabians and later the Yemen in, but he realizes that the League as present constituted is very far from being a unity, and that the Egyptian–Saudi bloc generally with the adherence of Syria use the League to oppose Hashimite plans. His mind is now turning more and more towards his original plan. First of all he intends to further close relations between Iraq and Transjordan. He then hopes to bring Syria into the orbit because, as he told me the other day, he is convinced that the majority of Syrians were opposed to the present Republican regime though they were not necessarily in favor of King Abdullah. . . . Naturally I do all in my power to counsel moderation and the maintenance of unity, peace, and concord. It is Nuri rather than the Regent who is pushing this.

The warm relations between Azzam and members of the Iraqi elite make it inconceivable that a strong whiff of this did not reach Cairo.

54. On the role of the oriental counsellor in general, and on Smart in particular, see Louis, *British Empire*, p. 228, especially note 5.

55. Minute by Smart, 21 January 1947, attached to Campbell to Howe, 25 January 1947, PRO/FO 371/62197/E1219.

56. Cairo to FO, 12 March 1947, PRO/FO 371/62967/J1178.

57. Louis, *British Empire*, p. 326, notes the sense of urgency among the British but does not attribute it to the change in Egyptian policy or the vote in the Arab League.

58. This effort may be followed, from the American point of view, in *FRUS*, vol. 5 (1948), pp. 209–237. The Americans never wholeheartedly supported the British plan, which they feared might also function as a wedge between Riyadh and Washington. See the suggestive comments in Louis, *British Empire*, p. 329.

59. Herein lies the explanation for statements by King Abdullah's enemies regarding the connection between the Greater Syria Project and Zionism. For instance, on 29 August 1947, Jamil Mardam stated in Damascus that the project "was Zionist and imperialist and aims at the partition of Palestine and the establishment therein of a Jewish state." Quoted in FORD, "The Greater Syria Movement," p. 14.

60. *Suriya al-kubra: al-kitab al-urdunni al-abyad* (Amman: Al-mitba'a al-wataniyya, 1947).

61. *Suriya al-Kubra*, p. 38. Also quoted in Dawn, "The Project of Greater Syria," p. 40. Dawn, writing in 1948, notes the British unwillingness to slam the door shut on Greater Syria Project and suggests (p. 106) that the British would eventually use the project in order to solve their dilemma of regional security.

62. Interview with the editor of the Lebanese weekly, *Kull Shay*, 28 March 1947. Since the original source is unavailable to me, this passage is taken from the hasty translation found in Beirut to FO, 29 March 1947, PRO/FO 371/61492/E2760. I added the words in brackets in order to turn the passage into idiomatic English. The only substantive alteration I made was to change "special"—which does not make sense in context—to "particular-istic," on the assumption that the Arabic original was "*khassa*." To cool tempers, the Jordanian government issued a denial of this authentic interview. See: FORD, "The Greater Syria Movement," pp. 9–10; PRO/FO 371/61497/E 9137.

63. The party line of the Triangle Alliance against the Greater Syria Project—that it would extend the range of imperialist influence in the Middle East—is expressed by Khalid al-Azm, *Mudhakkirat Khalid al-'Azm*, vol. 1 (Beirut: Al-dar al-muttahida li'l-nashr, 1972) p. 258. By contrast, the Ba'th party, which placed primary emphasis on unity, supported the project. See FORD, "The Greater Syria Movement," p. 11. The favorable attitude of the Ba'th demonstrates that the "Abdullah-as-stooge" propaganda line cannot be consid-ered to have dealt the project a knockout blow in the arena of ideology, to say nothing of power politics.

64. Kirkbride to Baxter, 21 April 1947, PRO/FO 371/61493/E3600.

65. Cairo to FO, 8 April 1947, PRO/FO 371/61492/E3005.

66. For the assertion by Azzam in late 1947 that Iraq stood behind the Greater Syria Project, see al-Hashimi, *Mudhakkirat*, p. 160.

67. Khadduri, *Independent Iraq*, pp. 343–345.

68. See the discussion of this issue in the Smart memorandum, 21 January 1947, PRO/FO 371/62197/E1219.

Chapter 4

1. This discussion of the trial of Lord Moyne's assassins is based on the thirty-six page report written by the State Department observer Gordon Mattison, which is appended to Tuck to S/S, 19 January 1945, NA 883.00/1-1945. See also the reports in *The Times* (Lon-don), 11, 12, 15, 16, and 19 January 1945.

2. Pinkerton to S/S, 2 February 1945, NA/883.00/2-245.

3. On the arguments of the lawyers, see the report of Mattison, pp. 27–30.

4. The court was composed of five members: three were senior Egyptian judges, and the other two were high-ranking Egyptian army officers. Tuck to S/S, 7 January 1945, NA/883.00/1-745.

5. See: "The Political Consequences . . . ," a Foreign Office Minute by Mr. Garran, 6 January 1947; PRO/FO 371/61874/E2932.

6. On the Muslim Brotherhood and Palestine, see Thomas Mayer's article, "The Mil-itary Force of Islam: the Society of the Muslim Brethren and the Palestine Question, 1945–1948," in *Zionism and Arabism in Palestine and Israel*, ed. E. Kedourie and S. Haim (Lon-don: Frank Cass, 1981), pp. 100–117; reworked in Hebrew as "Agudat ha-Ahim ha-Muslimim ve-She'elat Erez Yisra'el, ba-Shanim 1945–1948," in *Hayinu ke-Holmim*, ed. Yehuda Wallach (Givatayim: Masada, 1985), pp. 353–366. See also Richard Mitchell, *The Society of the Muslim Brothers* (London: Oxford University Press, 1960), pp. 55–57, 63–64, 227–230. On the increasing importance of Islam in politics, see Nadav Safran, *Egypt in Search of Political Community* (Cambridge, Mass.: Harvard University Press, 1961).

7. Gamal Abd al-Nasser, *Falsafat al-thawra* (Cairo, Wizarat al-irshad al-qawmi: n.d.), pp. 11–14. Author's translation.

8. Ibid., p. 17.

9. The Sasson initiative is treated well by Neil Caplan, *Futile Diplomacy*, vol. 2 (London: Frank Cass, 1986), pp. 142–145; and by Avraham Sela, "She'elat Erez Yisra'el ba-Ma'arekhet ha-beyn 'Aravit mi-Hakamat ha-Liga ha-Aravit 'ad Plishat Zva'ot 'Arav le-Erez Yisra'el, 1945–1948" (Ph.D. diss., Hebrew University, 1986) pp. 302–317. Sela's exhaustive (more than 600 pages) work has not received the attention it deserves, even among Israeli scholars. Its influence on this chapter is considerable.

10. On the palace receiving a report, see: Clayton to Smart, 19 August 1946, PRO/FO 141/1090/101/9/46G. Sela, "She'elat Erez Yisra'el," demonstrated to me the value of the files from the Cairo embassy (FO 141).

11. Eliyahu Sasson, *Ba-Derekh el ha-Shalom* (Tel Aviv: Am Oved, 1978), pp. 364–365.

12. Ibid.

13. Ibid. See also: Clayton to Smart, 30 August 1946, PRO/FO 141/1090/101/11/46G; in the same file at—/12/46G, see: Cairo to FO, Campbell, 2 September 1946.

14. Sasson, *Ba-Derekh*, 365.

15. See the report from Bevin on the approach by Nahum Goldmann: Paris to FO, 19 August 1946, PRO/FO 371/52641/E8260.

16. The police informant told Brigadier Clayton, with whom he maintained regular contact, that neither the Jews nor Sidqi knew that he had come to the British. Clayton, with good reason, did not believe him: see "Comments" on Clayton to Smart, 30 August 1946, PRO/FO 141/1090/101/11/46G.

17. This characterization of the independent Arab state envisioned by the policy of the Arab League is based on the plan presented by the League at the London Conference. See: G.B. *PP*, 1946–1947, Cmd. 7044, pp. 9–11. Arab representatives and political commentators traditionally argued that, given the desire of the Zionists to create a state, allowing them any political rights as a community would simply insert into Palestine the thin end of a Jewish wedge.

18. See the section on "The Two Strategies" in chapter 3.

19. The British Ambassador summed up the Egyptian attitude much like Sasson:

There is a tendency among Egyptians to exercise [a] moderating influence on the Arabs, partly because of being really out of the Arab world they do not feel so strongly as the Arabs about Palestine, and partly because they would like to conciliate us over Palestine in the hope that we will respond by being conciliatory about [the] Anglo-Egyptian treaty negotiations. . . . Azzam particularly has shown unexpected moderation recently. . . . (Cairo to FO, 31 August 1946, Campbell, PRO/FO 371/52555/E8732).

20. Chapter 2 analyzes the manner in which these concessions to Britain threw the Sidqi government into crisis.

21. The British ambassador informed Bevin, who suggested sounding out Sidqi, that "if your desire is mainly to secure from Sidky Pasha information as to exactly what he said to Sassoon it is unlikely he will tell the truth unless he thinks we are prepared to enter into a deal" (Cairo to FO, 8 September 1946, Campbell, PRO/FO 371/52556/E8990).

22. After a visit by the anonymous policeman, Clayton wrote to Smart:

The police source has just been to see me. . . . He tells me that he saw Sidky again who has discussed the possibility of exercising pressure on the Arab League over Palestine (in return I suppose for some concession on our part) with Lutfi

Said [the foreign minister] and Kamal Abdurrahim [an undersecretary at the Foreign Ministry]. Sidky is still anxious to know if the proposition is of any interest to us and does not want to take the initiative. (Nor, obviously, do we) (Clayton to Smart, 19 August 1946, PRO/FO 141/1090/101/9/46G).

23. See document by Clayton, entitled "Note," 13 August 1946, PRO/FO 141/1090/101/200/46G.

24. The 1937 Peel Commission report had recommended the partition of Palestine between Jordan and a Jewish state. The Colonial Office traditionally favored this solution.

25. Shortly before Sidqi arrived in Cairo, Abd al-Rahman Azzam, in a conversation with a British diplomat, "was most anxious to avoid an upheaval in the Middle East over Palestine, and thought the only means of doing so was to preserve the status quo. . . . The only real solution was for Great Britain to hold the country as it was without further immigration, and to allow a few years to pass. . . ." Because Azzam expressed support for the continued rule by Britain in Palestine, this sounds like a position that is not hostile to Britain. In the power-political context, however, it translates into a demand that Britain stay mired in the swamp. See: Clayton to Smart, 13 May 1946, PRO/FO 141/1090/101/200/46G.

26. From Kirkbride to Baxter, 28 March 1947, PRO/FO 371/61523/E3025, in which the British Minister in Amman relays an account of the meeting, which he received from the Jordanian foreign minister, Samir al-Rifai. Rifai's account is corroborated by the actual minutes of the meeting as they are described in Sela, "She'elat Erez Yisra'el," pp. 317–321.

27. A translation of the resolution, forwarded by the U.S. State Department to the Foreign Office, can be found at PRO/FO 371/61874/E2615.

28. Al-Hashimi, *Mudhakkirat*, vol. 2 p. 141.

29. Nuri al-Said told the British Ambassador that if the League did not begin to take views of Baghdad into account then Iraq:

> must "suspend her membership" or even withdraw altogether. Iraq could not continue to be dragged along at the heels of Azzam and Egypt—in their use of the League merely as an instrument for furthering their aspiration rather than genuine Arab interests—and still retain her self-respect as an independent sovereign state (Baghdad to FO, 25 March 1947, Stonehewer-Bird, PRO/FO 371/61874/2616).

For a different interpretation of this episode, see Michael Eppel, *The Palestine Conflict in the History of Modern Iraq: The Dynamics of Involvement, 1928–1948* (London: Frank Cass, 1994), pp. 156–157, which cites additional documents. Nuri al-Said was about to step down from office; Eppel suggests that he made the speech in order to force the Jabir government to stay the course. There may be something to this.

30. The diplomacy of Egypt behind the scenes betrays a desire to stall the Palestine issue. Whereas Cairo publicly praised the decision to refer the Mandate to the United Nations, and whereas it supported the decision in the League, it worked to frustrate an initiative that would have made the September session productive. Cairo balked when the British moved to have the secretary-general of the United Nations appoint a preparatory committee (not UNSCOP, which was appointed later by the emergency session) to study the problem before the regular September session. "We are anxious," the Foreign Office explained, "that the United Nations should start work on the Palestine problem before September. If they do not, there is a strong risk that the 1947 Assembly will appoint a committee to examine the problem and to report back in 1948." See: FO to Baghdad, 5 March 1947, PRO/FO 371/61874/E1818. For Egyptian opposition to the committee, see: Amman to FO, Kirkbride, 17 March 1947, PRO/FO 371/61874/E2438.

31. Hurewitz, *The Struggle for Palestine*, pp. 284–285.

32. Great Britain, *Parliamentary Debates (Hansard)*, House of Commons, vol. 433, col. 2007.

33. Minute by Beeley on Campbell to FO, 2 April 1947, PRO/FO 371/61523/E2883.

34. See the FORD, "The Activities of the Arab League," 30 September 1948, p. 4. PRO/FO 371/68352/E13328.

35. This was according to Samir al-Rifai the Jordanian representative to the meeting; see: Kirkbride to Baxter, 28 March 1947, PRO/FO 371/61523/E3025.

36. Sasson, *Ba-Derekh*, p. 368.

37. Al-Hashimi, *Mudhakkirat*, vol. 2, pp. 141–142.

38. On the tension between Syria and Jordan and on the Jordanian proclamation, see Yosef Nevo, *'Abdallah ve 'Araviyei Erez Yisra'el* (Tel Aviv: Makhon Shiloah, 1975), pp. 50–51, which is based on a study of the Arabic press. Rumors abounded, strengthened by the absence of the Jordanian and Iraqi representatives from the opening ceremonies of the League meeting, to the effect that Baghdad and Amman stood perched to break with the League.

39. On this episode, see "The Greater Syria Project Moves to Center Stage," in Chapter 3.

40. Upon reading the telegram, from the British ambassador in Baghdad, that reported on the speech by Nuri al-Said, an official in London wrote: "this is an extraordinary manoeuvre, though it is entirely in line with the report in Sir A. Kirkbride's letter." Unfortunately, the letter of Kirkbride, who was the representative in Amman, has not yet been declassified. This comment, however, proves that people in Jordan knew of Nuri al-Said's intentions before he ever made his speech. See: Baghdad to FO, 25 March 1947, Stonehewer-Bird, PRO/FO 371/61874/E2616. The sealed letter from Kirkbride is located in the same file, at:—/E2452.

41. Al-Hashimi, *Mudhakkirat*, Vol. 2, 142.

42. Kirkbride to Baxter, 28 March 1947, PRO/FO 371/61523/E3025.

43. King Abdallah arrived in London in February 1946 and, within a month, negotiated the independence of his country without serious incident. The treaty that the king signed accorded Britain significant rights over his government: It was, in fact, modeled on the treaty by which Britain originally gave Iraq its independence—in 1930. Thus, although Jordan, in its relations with the Empire, lagged behind the other Arab states by more than a decade, no politically significant groups kicked up a fuss in Amman. See Ron Pundik, *The Struggle for Sovereignty* (Oxford: Blackwell, 1994), p. 45—especially note 47.

44. Kirkbride to Bevin, 26 April 1948, PRO/FO 371/68386/E5468.

45. For an extended discussion of this issue, see Landis, "Nationalism and the Politics of Za'ama," chapter 4.

46. Al-Azm, *Mudhakkirat*, vol. 2, pp. 194–195. Although this coup took place in 1949, the Jordanian threat to Syria was just as grave in the period 1947–1948. I am grateful to Joshua Landis for bringing this passage to my attention, and for sharing his knowledge of Syria with me.

47. For a Hebrew translation of the report, which was prepared by Ismail Safwat, see S. Segev, ed. and trans., *Me'ahorei ha-Paragod* (Tel Aviv: Ma'arakhot, 1954), pp. 66–70.

48. "Al-Jalsa al-sirriyya li-majlis al-shuyukh al-mun'aqad fi 11 mayu 1948 'an masala filistin," *Al-Tali'a* (March 1975): 135. In this account, given by the Egyptian prime minister to the Senate, al-Nuqrashi does not admit that he intended to buy the Arab Legion. He tells the Senate, simply, that he promised to give it aid.

49. Al-Hashimi, *Mudhakkirat*, vol. 2, p. 166. See also Sela, "She'elat Erez Yisra'el," 359–360.

50. Al-Hashimi, *Mudhakkirat* vol. 2, p. 161.

51. See: FORD, "The Greater Syria Movement," p. 10. Pressure on King Abdallah to quit his agitation in favor of Greater Syria came not just from the Triangle Alliance: The Jabir government in Baghdad also requested that Amman remain silent on the subject.

52. Ibid.

53. On the American move toward supporting a United Nations Trusteeship Plan instead of partition, see, for instance, Michael J. Cohen, *Palestine and the Great Powers, 1945–1948* (Princeton, N.J.: Princeton University Press, 1982), pp. 354–368; and Jones, *Failure in Palestine*, pp. 297–301, 332–337.

54. For a contemporary report, see Broadmead (Damascus) to Bevin, 19 February 1948, PRO/FO 371/68368/E2914. The best general treatment of the Army of Liberation is Sela, "She'elat Erez Yisra'el," pp. 456–487.

55. Sela, "She'elat Erez Yisra'el," develops in detail the theme of the Syrian character of the Army of Liberation.

56. Even if leaders in Iraq did harbor plans of dominating the military effort, then the *Wathba*—under whose shadow the Army of Liberation operated—insured that Baghdad would remain mindful of the Triangle Alliance on matters Palestinian.

57. The diary of Taha al-Hashimi demonstrates, at every turn, the good relations he enjoyed with Shukri al-Quwatli and with Abd al-Rahman Azzam.

58. See: Amman to FO, Kirkbride, 13 February 1948, PRO/FO 371/68367/E2185.

59. Fawzi al-Qawuqji, *Filastin fi mudhakkirat Fawzi al-Qawuqji*. ed. Khayriya Qasimiya, vol. 2 (Beirut?: Munazzamat al-tahrir al-filastiniyya, 1975), pp. 135–136.

60. King Abdallah had very close ties to both Nablus and Jenin. See Nevo, *'Abdallah*, pp. 50–51.

61. Given the uncertainty of military commitment of Egypt and Saudi Arabia, this was a strategy born of necessity. Ismail Safwat, for one, expended enormous energy trying to raise money and arms by submitting reports to the Council of the Arab League on the strength of the Jewish forces. For translations into Hebrew of some of these reports, see Segev, *Me'ahorei ha-Paragod*, pp. 66–103. Al-Hashimi, *Mudhakkirat*, vol. 2, pp. 188–190, records a meeting with Shukri al-Quwatli on 5 January 1948; the passage displays the profound sense of isolation felt by the Syrian leadership when faced with, on the one hand, the vacuum in Palestine and the power of Abdallah, and, on the other hand, the uncertainty of the military (and financial) commitment of Saudi Arabia and Egypt.

62. Avi Shlaim, *Collusion across the Jordan* (Oxford: Oxford University Press, 1988), p. 157, bases this judgment on material from the Israeli archives. Shlaim pins his analysis of al-Qawuqji's actions on the nature of the commander's character rather than on the uncertain political context.

63. Sela, "She'elat Erez Yisra'el," pp. 445–456, analyzes this relationship in depth; see the report on the threat to the life of Abd al-Qadir al-Husayni and Hassan Salama posed by the Army of Liberation: Amman to FO, 9 February 1948, Kirkbride, PRO/FO 371/68366/E1889.

64. See the report by Kirkbride on his conversation with al-Alami: Amman to FO, 12 February 1948, PRO/FO 371/68367/E2137.

65. For contemporary assessment that the Syrians created the Army of Liberation to, among other things, forestall action by Hashimite armies, see: Damascus to FO, Broadmead, 5 March 1948, PRO/FO 371/68368/E3113.

66. See the report by Glubb on the competition in the Arab areas between the Mufti's men, the Arab Legion, and al-Qawuqji's army: Packard to Hayter, 5 March 1948, PRO/FO 371/68369/E3371. See the description of poor relations between common Palestinians

and the Army of Liberation in Ahmad Farraj Tayi', *Safahat matwiyya 'an filastin* (n.d., n.p.), pp. 161–164.

67. Sir John Bagot Glubb, *A Soldier with the Arabs* (London: Hodder and Stoughton, 1957), p. 63. This response is not mentioned in the official record, but it is certainly in keeping with the tenor of Foreign Office opinion. For another, detailed discussion of this meeting, see Shlaim, *Collusion*, pp. 132–140.

68. Bevin to Kirkbride, 9 February 1948, PRO/FO 371/68366/E1916.

69. The foreign minister approached the British at least twice, perhaps with variant proposals. See: Cairo to FO, Campbell, 12 February 1948, PRO/FO 371/68367/E2120; and Baghdad to FO, 2 March 1948, Mack, PRO/FO 371/68368/E2947; see also the long minute on the subject by Balfour, 22 March 1948, appended to Jedda to FO, Trott, 11 March 1948, PRO/FO 371/68369/E3366.

70. See the report by Kirkbride on the desirability of Iraqi–Jordanian cooperation, and on the effect it would have on al-Qawuqji, whose army might be co-opted by the Hashimites. Note the remarks by Beeley on 16 February 1948: "The attraction, from King Abdallah's point of view, of bringing the Iraqis in is presumably that this would help to keep the Syrians out. On the other hand the Iraqis would insist on disregarding the UN frontier." Amman to FO, Kirkbride, 13 February 1948, PRO/FO 371/68367/ E2163.

71. The British were also mindful of the effect on Saudi Arabia. See: FO to Baghdad, 27 February 1948, PRO/FO 371/68368/E2564.

72. At issue, ultimately, was not the law itself, but the need to avoid complications with the United States.

73. In Amman to FO, 4 March 1948, PRO/FO 371/68368/E3074, Kirkbride writes: "When he visits Bagdad I hope the prime minister of Transjordan will be able to correct the ideas of the Iraqi ministers as to what action will be possible in Palestine after the end of the mandate."

74. On the search for a security guarantee, see chapter 3, notes 46 and 68; on the supply of arms and money to the Mufti's militia, see the telegrams from Jedda to FO, Trott, 31 January and 2 February 1948, PRO/FO 371/68366/E1494 and—/E1522.

75. See Jedda to FO, Trott, 31 January, 3 February, and 3 February PRO/FO 371/ 68366/E1494,—/E1644, and—/E1657; Amman to FO, Kirkbride, 5 February 1948, PRO/ FO 371/68366/E1750.

76. Evidence suggests that the Saudi action was coordinated with Qawuqji's army. See, for instance, King Abdallah's bitter complaints to Safwat: Amman to FO, Kirkbride, 9 February 1948, PRO/FO 371/68366/E1894. Simultaneously with the Saudi threat, the Army of Liberation, against the will of the Jordanian government, was transporting irregulars to Palestine across Jordanian territory, no doubt in order to avoid complications between Damascus and London. See: Damascus to FO, Broadmead, 30 January 1948, PRO/FO 371/ 68366/1474. King Abdallah's staunchest support inside Syria came from the Attrash family on the Jabal Druze, which had suffered a very bad harvest the year before. By blocking the supply of food to the Jabal, Damascus forced the Attrash to provide soldiers and support for the Army of Liberation, thereby ensuring that the allies of Abdallah involved themselves in the Syrian-dominated war effort: "Although the Attrash family are unwilling to encourage their followers to join this party, poverty and lack of food . . . are likely to force Soltan Pasha's hand." Damascus to FO, Broadmead, 8 March 1948, PRO/FO 371/ 68368/E3130. Like the Syrian state, Jordan faced enemies on all sides.

77. Amman to FO, Kirkbride, 13 February 1948, PRO/FO 371/68367/E2185.

78. Minute by Walker, 14 February 1948:

If the Arab Legion is fully deployed in Palestine restoring order, the security forces in Transjordan after May 15th may be pretty thin. There seems to be a pretty good case for having the RAF units at Amman and Mafraq at the highest possible level by then. In view, also, of the possible attempts by Ibn Saud to march into Maan and Aqaba when the Arab Legion goes into Palestine, it seems a pity that His Majesty's Government have decided that they cannot consider moving the RAF . . . to those places (Kirkbride to Orme Sargent, 11 February 1948. PRO/FO 371/68367/ E2095).

79. See the minute by Buss, 13 February 1948, who endorses the suggestion of the ambassador in Jedda that "the only possible basis of a settlement between the two countries . . . would be some bargain in which the Saudi Kingdom gets, say, Akaba and Maan in exchange for Transjordan expansion in Palestine." Buss comments, with my emphasis added: "In conclusion I suggest that this proposal be regarded as a serious contribution to ideas on a possible settlement of the *Palestine* question" (PRO/FO 371/68368/E2299). See also the numerous minutes on Saudi–Jordanian reconciliation in the same file at—/ E2696. The Foreign Office regarded American participation as crucial.

80. Cairo to FO, Campbell, 7 February 1948, PRO/FO 371/68366/E1832.

81. See chapter 3, note 58.

82. *FRUS*, vol. 5 (1948), p. 223. See also, Louis, *British Empire*, p. 201.

83. See the section on "The Egyptian Response" in chapter 3.

84. Nevo, *Abdallah*, pp. 63–64; the Zionists, according to Nevo, also believed that an unwritten agreement had been struck in London. See the discussion, by the ambassador in Cairo, of related articles in the Egyptian press: Cairo to FO, Campbell, 7 February 1948, PRO/FO 371/68366/E1832.

85. The United Nations partition plan awarded the Western Galilee to the Arab state of Palestine. The Foreign Office, and apparently the Jordanian leadership, did not believe that the Arab Legion had the power to absorb all of Arab Palestine, even with the aid of the Iraqis. This assessment was made at a moment when the reigning assumption held that Jerusalem—where, as it turned out, the Arab Legion actually fought the hardest— would be internationalized. Given the inability of Jordan to absorb all Arab areas, and given the Syrian presence in Palestine, it is reasonable to assume that the Western Galilee would end up in Syrian hands. See: Amman to FO, Kirkbride, 13 February 1948, PRO/ FO 371/68367/E2163—especially the attached minutes. See also Glubb, *A Soldier*, p. 63.

86. Chapman-Andrews to Burrows, 7 February 1948, PRO/FO 371/68384/E2054.

87. Baghdad to FO, Busk, 5 February 1948, PRO/FO 371/68366/E1668.

88. Cairo to FO, Campbell, 12 February 1948, PRO/FO 371/68367/E2120.

89. Cairo to FO, Weekly Appreciation, 16 February 1948, PRO/FO 371/69190/J1151.

Chapter 5

1. "Al-Jalsa al-sirriyya," p. 136.

2. Ibid., p. 145.

3. Cairo to FO, "Weekly Appreciation," 13 May 1948, PRO/FO 371/69190/J3290.

4. "Al-Jalsa al-sirriyya," p. 138.

5. Ibid., p. 139.

6. The reference to the files is intriguing. Sidqi Pasha makes specific reference to files pertaining to the last two years of World War II.

7. "Al-Jalsa al-sirriyya," p. 139.

8. Ibid., p. 137.

9. Ibid., p. 139.

10. Cairo to FO, "Weekly Appreciation," 19 April 1948, PRO/FO 371/69190/J2795.

11. Cairo to FO, "Weekly Appreciation," 6, 14, 19, 27 April, and 4 May 1948, PRO/FO 371/69190/J 2400,—/J2620,—/2795,—/J2898, —/J3224.

12. For the press and political parties, see Cairo to FO, "Weekly Appreciation," 4 May 1948, PRO/FO 371/69190/J3224; for the Muslim Brothers, see Thomas Mayer, "The Military Force of Islam," pp. 100–117.

13. See, for instance, Thomas Mayer, "Egypt's 1948 Invasion of Palestine," *Middle Eastern Studies* 22 (1) (1986): 20–36.

14. Amman to FO, Kirkbride, 25 April 1948, PRO/FO 371/68370/E 5159.

15. Al-Hashimi, *Mudhakkirat*, vol. 2, pp. 213–214.

16. Amman to FO, Kirkbride, 16 April 1948, FO 816/117/S/1014/48.

17. Amman to FO, Kirkbride, 19 April 1948, FO 816/117/S/1014/48.

18. Al-Hashimi, *Mudhakkirat*, vol. 2, p. 214.

19. Ibid., pp. 219–220.

20. Ibid., pp. 220–221.

21. Muhammad 'Ali 'Allubah, *Filastin wa'l-damir al-insani* (Cairo: Dar al-hilal, 1964), p. 142.

22. Cairo to FO, "Weekly Appreciation," 19 April 1948, PRO/FO 371/69190/J2795; al-Hashimi, *Mudhakkirat*, vol. 2, p. 213; Tayi', *Safahat*, p. 112; and, for a related report, see: Cairo to FO, Campbell, 29 April 1948, PRO/FO 371/68371/E5510.

23. 'Alluba, *Filastin*, p. 142.

24. See the two telegrams: Amman to FO, 17 and 21 April 1948, Kirkbride, PRO/FO 816/117/S/1014/48.

25. Al-Hashimi, *Mudhakkirat*, vol. 2, p. 217.

26. Ibid., p. 218.

27. Ibid., p. 219.

28. See Shlaim, *Collusion*, pp. 196–205, for an account of the conflict over the plan that emphasizes the political motives of King Abdallah; see Sela, "She'elat Erez Yisra'el," pp. 558–563, for an account that shows a greater awareness of the political motives of King Abdallah's enemies.

29. Al-Hashimi, *Mudhakkirat*, vol. 2, 220.

30. See ibid. on Abdallah's "desire to tow the Iraqi troops behind him."

31. Sir Alec Kirkbride, *From the Wings: Amman Memoirs 1947–1951* (Frank Cass: London, 1976), p. 24.

32. Al-Hashimi, *Mudhakkirat*, vol. 2, p. 217.

33. Ibid., p. 216.

34. Ibid., p. 217–218.

35. Muhammad Husayn Haykal, *Mudhakkirat fi'l-siyasa al-misriyya*, vol. 3 (Cairo: 1978), pp. 41–44. See Mayer, "Egypt's 1948 Invasion," p. 20.

36. Thomas Mayer follows a similar line of reasoning to argue the same thesis. See his "Arab Unity of Action and the Palestine Question, 1945–1948," *Middle Eastern Studies*, 22 (3) (1986): 331–349.

37. On the threat to the Hashimite House, see Eppel, *The Palestine Conflict*, pp. 179–181.

38. On the meeting, see: Eppel, *The Palestine Conflict*, pp. 184–187; and Mayer, "Egypt's 1948 Invasion," pp. 31–32. Both authors suggest that the regent convinced King Faruq to intervene. Taha al-Hashimi's diary, however, indicates that the Egyptian palace had already decided in favor of action before the regent arrived in Cairo.

39. Amman to FO, Kirkbride, 25 April 1948, PRO/FO 371/68370/E5159.

40. See the comments of Shaykh Hafiz Wahba, quoted in Chapman-Andrews to Burrows, 7 February 1948, PRO/FO 371/68384/E2112.

41. Amman to FO, Kirkbride, 25 April 1948, PRO/FO 371/68370/E5159.

42. On 11 February, Kirkbride reported that "there is no doubt that feeling here on the subject of Palestine is now so intense as to affect the efficiency and loyalty with which such orders are carried out by local officials." Amman to FO, Kirkbride, 11 February 1948, PRO/FO 371/68367/E2046.

43. See the comments by Tawfiq Abu'l-Huda: FO Minute, Pirie-Gordon to Burrows, PRO/FO 371/68366/E1730. Shaykh Hafiz Wahba told the British that a Jordanian minister, Fawzi al-Mulqi, had indirectly informed him about King Abdallah's intention to annex Arab Palestine; see: Cairo to FO, Campbell, 7 February 1948, PRO/FO 371/68366/E1832.

44. "Statement by the Royal Hashimite Diwan," 17 April 1948, PRO/FO 816/117.

45. On the agreement, see Shlaim, *Collusion*, pp. 110–117.

46. On the refusal to acknowledge the agreement, see ibid., pp. 160–179. Shlaim argues that the agreement continued to shape the actions of the two sides and that the attitudes of the Jewish Agency toward King Abdallah played a role in his decision to distance himself. The Shlaim thesis has provoked a controversy. For a critique of the Shlaim thesis and discussion of the debate around it, see Avraham Sela, "Transjordan, Israel, and the 1948 War: Myth, Historiography, and Reality," *Middle Eastern Studies*, 28 (4) (1992): 623–688. Shlaim responded to his critics in "The Debate About 1948," *The International Journal of Middle East Studies*, 27 (1995): 287–304.

47. Amman to FO, Kirkbride, 23 April 1948, PRO/FO 816/117.

48. Amman to FO, Kirkbride, 24 April 1948, PRO/FO 816/117.

49. Al-Qawuqji, vol. 2, p. 135.

50. Tayi', *Safahat*, p. 114.

51. Tayi', *Safahat*, pp. 102–103; see also pp. 105–120.

52. Tayi', *Safahat*, p. 122.

53. Cairo to FO, "Weekly Appreciation," 19 April 1948, PRO/FO 371/69190/J2795.

54. Kirkbride, *From the Wings*, p. 22–23.

55. On the trusteeship, see: Cohen, *Palestine and the Great Powers*, pp. 354–368; and Jones, *Failure in Palestine*, pp. 297–301, 332–337.

56. "Al-Jalsa al-Sirriyya," p. 140.

57. Ibid., p. 141.

58. See the comments on this in A. Eban to C. Weizmann, 10 July 1948, *DFPI*, vol. 1, pp. 312–316.

59. Segev, *Me'ahorei ha-Paragod*, p. 67.

60. Al-Hashimi, *Mudhakkirat*, vol. 2, p. 219.

61. Ibid.

62. "Al-Jalsa al-Sirriyya," p. 141.

63. Ibid., p. 142.

64. The head of the British military mission in Iraq predicted in early March that only one Iraqi battalion would be sent to Palestine, because of low police morale and insufficient means of transport. See: Baghdad to FO, Mack, 8 March 1948, PRO/FO/371/68368/E3302.

65. Tayi', *Safahat*, pp. 127–129.

66. "Al-Jalsa al-Sirriyya," p. 141.

67. Al-Hashimi, *Mudhakkirat*, vol. 2, p. 220; my emphasis added.

68. Ibid.

69. Ibid., p. 219.

Chapter 6

1. Glubb, *A Soldier*, pp. 145–153; Kirkbride, *From the Wings*, pp. 40–44; King Abdallah of Jordan, *My Memoirs Completed*, trans. Harold Glidden (London: Longman, 1978), pp. 20–24; Tayi', *Safahat*, pp. 114–116 ; *FRUS*, vol. 5 (1948), 1197.

2. Glubb, *A Soldier*, p. 150.

3. Ibid., p. 149; Kirkbride, *From the Wings*, p. 40.

4. Ibid., p. 151.

5. Ibid., pp. 151–152.

6. Ibid., p. 145.

7. Ibid., p. 150. For Abu'l-Huda's view, which are identical, see Kirkbride, *From the Wings*, pp. 40–41.

8. Folke Bernadotte, *To Jerusalem*, trans. Joan Bulman (London: Hodder and Stoughton, 1951), pp. 163–164.

9. Unexpurgated version of *To Jerusalem*, published in Sune Persson, *Mediation and Assassination: Count Bernadotte's Mission to Palestine* (London: Ithaca Press, 1979), pp. 141–144; see also Kati Marton, *A Death in Jerusalem* (New York: Arcade, 1994), pp. 166–169.

10. King Abdallah, *My Memoirs Completed*, 8.

11. FORD, "Weekly Summaries on Palestine" (WSP), 14–20 June 1948, PRO/FO 371/68665.

12. Ibid.

13. Al-Hashimi, *Mudhakkirat*, vol. 2 pp. 223–225; Kirkbride, *From the Wings*, p. 41.

14. The Egyptian consul-general in Jerusalem sent a dispatch to Cairo claiming that the Arab Legion had the power to take the new city within a few days, but that the British officers had ordered restraint. See: Tayi', *Safahat*, p. 117.

15. Al-Hashimi, *Mudhakkirat*, p. 224. See a similar comment about the Army of Liberation in King Abdallah, *My Memoirs Completed*, p. 10.

16. Tayi', *Safahat*, p. 116; Kirkbride, *From the Wings*, p. 41; King Abdallah, *My Memoirs Completed*, pp. 22–23.

17. Kirkbride, *From the Wings*, p. 24–25; see also King Abdallah, *My Memoirs Completed*, p. 22; Glubb, *A Soldier*, p. 92.

18. Kirkbride, *From the Wings*, p. 24; Glubb, *A Soldier*, p. 85; and Tayi', *Safahat*, p. 107.

19. Kirkbride, *From the Wings*, p. 34; FORD, WSP, 26 July–1 August 1948, p. 1, PRO/FO 371/68665.

20. FORD, WSP, 24–30 May 1948, p. 5, PRO/FO 371/68665.

21. Kirkbride, *From the Wings*, pp. 34–36.

22. FORD, WSP, 15–23 May 1948, p. 2, PRO/FO 371/68665. Kamil al-Sharif, *Al-ikhwan al-muslimun fi harb filastin* (Cairo: dar al-tawzi' wa'l-nashr al-islamiya, 1984), pp. 130–133; King Abdallah, in *My Memoirs Completed*, pp. 21–22, attributes the arrival of the Egyptian forces on the West Bank to Azzam Pasha.

23. FORD, WSP, 24–30 May 1948, p. 3, PRO/FO 371/68665.

24. Gamal Abd al-Nasser, "Nasser's Memoirs of the First Palestine War," trans. Walid Khalidi, *Journal of Palestine Studies*, 2 (2) (1973): 10.

25. Ibid., p. 13.

26. Al-Sharif, *Al-ikhwan*, pp. 130–133.

27. FORD, WSP, 7–13 June 1948, p. 4, PRO/FO 371/68665. Kirkbride, *From the Wings*, p. 40; al-Sharif, *Al-ikhwan*, pp. 130–133.

28. King Abdallah, *My Memoirs Completed*, pp. 21–22; Kirkbride, *From the Wings*, p. 41.

29. For the actual text of the proposals, see Bernadotte, *To Jerusalem*, pp. 126–131

30. Opinion in Egypt generally considered the proposals to have been made in Britain. See: Cairo to FO, Campbell, Weekly Appreciation, 16 July 1948, PRO/FO 371/69191.

31. Quoted in Marton, *A Death in Jerusalem*, p. 155.

32. For the official Israeli response, see Bernadotte, *To Jerusalem*, pp. 149–152.

33. Cairo to FO, "Weekly Appreciation," 9 July 1948, PRO/FO 371/69191/J4740.

34. Report by the Central Intelligence Agency, 27 July 1948, *FRUS*, vol. 5 (1948), pp. 1244–1245.

35. *FRUS*, vol. 5 (1948), p. 1159. I translated the document from State Departmentese, a language devoid of definite articles, etc.

36. The sources cited in note 1 confirm this conclusion.

37. For instance, a British summary of military activity in Palestine covering the period 24–30 May 1948 stated that: "Major military action has been confined during the last week to two places—Jerusalem itself, and the area of the Jerusalem–Tel Aviv road." In other words, the Jordanian front. FORD, WSP, p. 1, PRO/FO 371/68665.

38. FORD, WSP, 31 May–6 June, p. 1, PRO/FO 371/68665.

39. Ilan Pappé, *Britain and the Arab–Israeli Conflict, 1948–1951* (London: Macmillan, 1988), p. 50, especially note 6.

40. Kirkbride, *From the Wings*, p. 47.

41. Glubb, *A Soldier*, pp. 164–166.

42. Ibid., p. 179.

43. Tayi', *Safahat*, 119–120.

44. See, for instance, ibid., pp. 117–118.

45. Ibid., pp. 131–132.

46. Ibid., pp. 132–133.

47. Cairo to FO, "Weekly Appreciation," 27 August 1948, PRO/FO 371/69191.

48. Cairo to FO, "Weekly Appreciation," 3 September 1948, PRO/FO 371/69191.

49. Tayi', *Safahat*, p. 132.

50. Four days before Riyad al-Sulh arrived in Amman, King Abdallah sent a letter to him answering some of the criticisms that had been leveled against Jordan. Among other things, he wrote as follows:

> When I saw the Arab armies in Egypt to the west and in Syria and Lebanon to the north preparing and proceeding to carry out [the Arab League plan to save Palestine] and then failing to send in even a brigade, showing neither sympathy nor regard for the uprooted people of Palestine but continuing their useless incitement of them and expecting one state [Jordan] to carry out the conquest of Palestine, I kept my place in the vanguard as I had always determined to do.
>
> Winter is approaching and the refugees are without shelter. The responsibility for them and for failing to settle the affair rests on those Arab states which instead of putting forth a military effort looked idly on. The deeds and the steadfastness of my army are sufficient to disprove the slanders that have been fabricated against it (reproduced in King Abdallah, *My Memoirs Completed*, 12).

51. Bernadotte, *To Jerusalem*, p. 201.

52. Ibid., pp. 201–202. My emphasis added.

53. We now have many accounts of the All-Palestine government, almost all of which stress its anti-Jordanian character. See, for instance: Shlaim, *Collusion*, pp. 296–301; Zvi Elpeleg, *The Grand Mufti* (London: Frank Cass, 1993), pp. 99–118; and Tayi', *Safahat*, pp. 147–161.

54. FORD, WSP, 4–10 October 1948, p. 3, PRO/FO 371/68687.

55. The Mufti was persona non-grata in Iraq because of his involvement in the Rashid Ali coup; he was despised by the British, because of his collaboration with the Nazis; and the Americans also, remembered his association with Hitler. The Iraqi animus undoubtedly provides the key for understanding the Egyptian attitude toward Hajj Amin the man. The Mufti's arrival in Gaza coincided with efforts, ultimately successful, to secure the recognition by Baghdad of the All-Palestine Government. Iraq made its recognition conditional on the nonparticipation of Hajj Amin in the government. See FORD, WSP, 11–17 October 1948, p. 3, PRO/FO 371/68687. On the hostility of Iraqi officials to Abdallah, and their leaning in favor of the All-Palestine Government, see: FORD, WSP, 27 September–3 October 1948, p. 3, PRO/FO 371/68687. On Jamal al-Husayni's trip to Baghdad to canvass support, see ibid., p. 4.

56. For the second report of Count Bernadotte, see: FRUS, vol. 5 (1948), pp. 1398–1406.

57. Ibid., p. 1404.

58. Kirkbride, *From the Wings*, p. 59. See also Glubb, *A Soldier*, p. 192; and Shlaim, *Collusion*, pp. 296–301.

59. FORD, WSP, 27 September–3 October 1948, p. 3, PRO/FO 371/68687.

60. FORD, WSP, 20–26 September 1948, p. 5; 27 September–3 October 1948, pp. 2–3, PRO/FO 371/68687.

61. Kirkbride, *From the Wings*, p. 48–49. The Jordanian prime minister later accused the Quwatli regime of attempting to assassinate King Abdallah; see: Kirkbride to Bevin, 21 April 1949, PRO/FO 371/75332/E5395.

62. FRUS, vol. 5 (1948), p. 1419. It is curious that Saudi Arabia is missing from this list of enemies.

63. Riyad's name has been deleted from the published documents in Hebrew, on which my account is based. This mission is treated from different points of view in two other works: Shlaim, *Collusion*, pp. 316–321; and Itamar Rabinovitch, *The Road Not Taken* (Oxford: Oxford University Press, 1991), pp. 172–174.. Shlaim and Rabinovitch, who have seen the original documents, call him "Kamal" and "Kamel," respectively. I gambled on "Kamil."

64. DFPI, vol. 1, p. 632.

65. Ibid., vol. 1, p. 632.

66. Saudi Arabia, Riyad said, had mediated between the two blocs. One wonders why.

67. DFPI, vol. 1, p. 633.

68. Ibid., vol. 2, p. 26.

69. Ibid., vol. 2, pp. 26–27.

70. Ibid., vol. 2, p. 27.

71. On the simultaneous negotiations between Abdallah and the Israelis, of which Cairo may have gotten wind, see Shlaim, *Collusion*, chap. 10.

72. FRUS, vol. 5 (1948), p. 1423.

73. Ibid., p. 1424.

74. Glubb to Goldie, 16 October 1948, Papers of Col. Desmond Goldie; reproduced in Shlaim, *Collusion*, p. 329.

75. FORD, WSP, 6–12 December 1948, PRO/FO 371/68687.

76. FORD, WSP, 6–12 and 13–19 December 1948, PRO/FO 371/68687.

77. Cairo to FO, Campbell, 11 December 1948, PRO/FO 371/68644/E15732.

78. The following account is based on Moshe Sharret's presentation of the Egyptian proposal to the Israeli Cabinet; it appears in David Ben-Gurion, *Medinat Yisrael ha-Mehudeshet*, vol. 1 (Tel Aviv: Am Oved, 1969), pp. 311–316. See also Rabinovitch, *The Road Not Taken*, pp. 173–175.

79. Paris to FO, UN Delegation, 25 November 1948, FO 371/68599/E 15169.
80. Ibid.
81. *FRUS*, vol. 5 (1948), p. 1626.
82. Ibid.
83. Ibid.
84. Cairo to FO, Campbell, 16 December 1948, PRO/FO 371/68644/E16035.
85. Cairo to FO, Campbell, 27 December 1948, PRO/FO 371/68644/E16260.

Bibliography

Archives

Public Record Office, London.
National Archives, Washington, D.C.

Published Documents

Egypt. Ministry of Foreign Affairs. *Records of Conversations, Notes, and Papers Exchanged Between the Royal Government and the United Kingdom Government, March 1950–November 1951.* (Cairo, 1951)

Egypt. Majlis al-Shuyukh. "Al-jalsa al-sirriyya li-majlis al-shuyukh al-mun'aqid fi 11 mayu 1948 'an masalat filistin." *Al-Tali'a*, 11 (3) (1975): 134–146.

Great Britain. *Parliamentary Debates (Hansard), House of Commons* (London: HMSO).

Great Britain. Foreign Office. *Weekly Political Intelligence Summaries* (Millwood, N.Y.: Kraus International Publications, 1983).

Iraq. *Me'ahorei ha-Paragod: Va'ada Parlimentarit 'Iraqit 'al ha-Milhama be-Yisrael.* Trans. Shmuel Segev. (Tel Aviv: Ma'arakhot, 1954).

Israel. *Documents on the Foreign Policy of Israel.* Vol. 1: *14 May–30 September 1948.* Ed. Yehoshua Freundlich (Jerusalem: Government Printer, 1981).

———. *Documents on the Foreign Policy of Israel.* Vol. 2: *October 1948–May 1949.* Ed. Yehoshua Freundlich (Jerusalem: Government Printer, 1984).

———. *Documents on the Foreign Policy of Israel.* Vol. 3: *Armistice Negotiations with the Arab States, December 1948–July 1949.* Ed. Yemima Rosenthal (Jerusalem: Government Printer, 1983).

Jordan. *Suriya al-kubra: al-kitab al-urdunni al-abyad* (Amman: Al-mitba'a al-wataniyya, 1947).

Khalil, Muhammad, ed. *The Arab States and the Arab League.* 2 vols. (Beirut: Khayats, 1962).

United Nations. *Official Records of the Security Council.* First Year, First Series, No. 1.

———. *Official Records of the Security Council.* Second Year, Nos. 59 and 70.

United States. Department of State. *Nazi–Soviet Relations 1939–1941.* Ed. Raymond J. Sontag and James Stuart Beddie (Washington, D.C.: Department of State, 1948).

United States. *Foreign Relations of the United States The Conference of Berlin (The Potsdam Conference) 1945.* Vol. 2 (Washington, D.C.: GPO, 1960).

United States. *Foreign Relations of the United States.* Vol. 8: 1945 (Washington, D.C.: GPO, 1969).

United States. *Foreign Relations of the United States.* Vol. 7: 1946 (Washington, D.C.: GPO, 1969).

United States. *Foreign Relations of the United States.* Vol. 5: 1947 (Washington, D.C.: GPO, 1971).

United States. *Foreign Relations of the United States.* Vol. 5: 1948 (Washington, D.C.: GPO, 1976).

Memoirs and Diaries

Abdallah, King of Jordan. *My Memoirs Completed.* Trans. Harold Glidden (London: Longman, 1978).

Abd al-Nasser, Gamal. *Falsafat al-thawra.* (Cairo: Wizarat al-'irshad al-qawmi: n.d.).

———. "Nasser's Memoirs of the First Palestine War." Trans. Walid Khalidi *Journal of Palestine Studies* 2 (2) (1973): 3–32.

al-Azm, Khalid. *Mudhakkirat Khalid al-Azm* Vols. 1 and 2 (Beirut: Dar al-muttahida li'l-nashr, 1972, 1973).

Ben-Gurion, David. *Medinat Yisrael ha-Mehudeshet.* Vol. 1 (Tel Aviv: 'Am 'Oved, 1969).

Bernadotte, Folke. *To Jerusalem.* Trans. Joan Bulman (London: Hodder and Stoughton, 1951).

Dixon, Piers. *Double Diploma* (London: Hutchinson, 1968).

Glubb, Sir John Bagot. *A Soldier with the Arabs* (London: Hodder and Stoughton, 1957).

al-Hashimi, Taha. *Mudhakkirat Taha al-Hashimi.* Vol. 2 (Beirut: Dar al-tali'a, 1978).

Haykal, Muhammad Husayn. *Mudhakkirat fi'l-siyasa al-misriyya.* Vol. 2 (Cairo: Matba'at misr sharika musahima misriyya, 1953).

al-Jamali, Muhammad Fadil, *Dhikrayat wa-'ibar* (Beirut: Dar al-katib al-jadid, 1964).

Jawdat, 'Ali. *Dhikrayat, 1900–1958* (Beirut: Mitba'at al-wafa', 1967).

Kirkbride, Sir Alec. *From the Wings: Amman Memoirs 1947–1951* (London: Frank Cass, 1976).

al-Qawuqji, Fawzi. *Filastin fi mudhakkirat Fawzi al-Qawuqji.* Vol. 2. Ed. Khayriya Qasimiya (Beirut?: Munazzamat al-tahrir al-filastiniyya, 1975).

———. "Memoirs, 1948, Part I." *Journal of Palestine Studies,* 1 (4) (1972): 27–58.

el-Sadat, Anwar. *In Search of Identity* (New York: Harper and Row, 1977).

Sansom, Major A. W. *I Spied Spies* (London: George G. Harrap, 1965).

al-Suwaydi, Tawfiq. *Mudhakkirati* (Beirut: Dar al-katib al-'arabi, 1969).

Sidqi, Ismail. *Mudhakkirati.* Ed. Sami Abu al-Nur (Cairo: Maktabat madbuli, 1991).

al-Tal, Abdallah. *Karithat filastin* (Cairo: Dar al-qalam, 1959).

Tayi', Ahmad Farraj. *Hadith diblumasi* (Cairo: al-mitba'a al-fanniyya al-haditha, 1968).

———. *Safahat matwiyya 'an filastin* (n.d., n.p.).

Wahba, Hafiz. *Khamsun 'aman* (Cairo?: Mustafa al-Babi?, 1960).

Secondary Sources

Abd al-Mun'im, Muhammad Faysal. *Asrar: 1948* (Cairo: Maktabat al-qahira al-haditha, 1968).

Abidi, A. Haydar Hassan. *Jordan—A Political Study, 1948–1957* (London: Asia, 1965).

Adamthwaite, Anthony. "Britain and the World, 1945–1949: The View from the Foreign Office." *International Affairs,* 61 (1985): 223–235.

Alami, Musa. "The Lesson of Palestine." *Middle East Journal,* 3 (4) (1949): 373–405.

Allubah, Muhammad Ali. *Filastin wa'l-damir al-insani* (Cairo: Dar al-hilal, 1964).

Bar-Josef, Uri. *The Best of Enemies; Israel and Transjordan in the War of 1948* (London: Frank Cass, 1987).

Batatu, Hanna. *The Old Social Classes and the Revolutionary Movements of Iraq* (Princeton, N.J.: Princeton University Press, 1978).

Be'eri, Israel. *Army Officers in Arab Politics and Society* (Jerusalem: Israel University Press, 1969).

Beinin, Joel, and Zachary Lockman. *Workers on the Nile* (Princeton, N.J.: Princeton University Press, 1987).

Bullock, Alan. *Ernest Bevin, Foreign Secretary, 1945–1951* (London: Heinemann, 1983).

Caplan, Neil. *Futile Diplomacy*. Vol. 2 (London: Frank Cass, 1986).

Cohen, Gabriel. "Mediniyut Britanya 'Erev Milhemet Ha'atzma'ut." In *Hayinu Keholmim*, ed. Yehuda Wallach, pp. 13–177 (Ramat Gan, Israel: Massada, 1985).

Colombe, M. "La Turquie et les Problèmes du Moyen-Orient (1923–1947)." *Cahiers de L'Orient Contemporain* 11 (12) (1947): 140.

Coury, Ralph M. "Who 'Invented' Egyptian Arab Nationalism?" *International Journal of Middle East Studies* 14 (3–4) (1982): 249–81, 419–34.

al-Dali, Wahid. *Asrar al-jami'at al-'arabiyya wa-'Abd al-Rahman 'Azzam* (Cairo: Matabi' ruz al-yusuf, 1982).

Dawn, C. Ernest. "The Formation of Pan-Arab Ideology in the Inter-War Years." *International Journal of Middle East Studies*, 20 (1) (1988): 67–91.

———. "The Project of Greater Syria." Ph.D. diss.: Princeton University, 1948.

Elpeleg, Zvi. *The Grand Mufti* (London: Frank Cass, 1993).

Eppel, Michael. "The Iraqi Domestic Scene and Its Bearing on the Question of Palestine, 1947." *Asian and African Studies*, 24 (1) (1990): 51–73.

———. *The Palestine Conflict in the History of Modern Iraq: The Dynamics of Involvement, 1928–1948* (London: Frank Cass, 1994).

Fabunmi, L. A. *The Sudan in Anglo-Egyptian Relations* (London: Longmans, Green, 1960).

Gelber, Yoav. "The Negotiations Between the Jewish Agency and Transjordan, 1946–1948." *Studies in Zionism*, 6 (1) (1985): 53–83.

Gershoni, Israel. "The Arab League as an Arab Enterprise." *Jerusalem Quarterly*, 40 (1986): 88–101.

———. *The Emergence of Pan-Arabism in Egypt* (Tel Aviv: Shiloah Institute, 1981).

———. "Ha-Le'om ha-'Aravi, Beyt Hashim, ve-Suriya ha-Gedola bi-khtavav shel 'Abdallah." *Ha-Mizrah ha-Hadash* 25 (1–2) (1975): 1–26, 161–83.

Gershoni, Israel, and James Jankowski. *Egypt, Islam and the Arabs* (New York: Oxford University Press, 1987).

Goren, Asher. *Ha-liga ha-'Aravit* (Tel Aviv: 'Eynot, 1954).

Hahn, Peter L. *The United States, Great Britain, and Egypt, 1945–1956* (Chapel Hill and London: University of North Carolina Press, 1991).

Hurewitz, J. C. *The Struggle for Palestine* (New York: Norton, 1950).

Issawi, Charles. *Egypt at Mid-Century* (London: Oxford University Press, 1954).

Jankowski, James. "The Egyptian Wafd and Arab Nationalism, 1918–1944." In *Nationalism and International Politics in the Middle East: Essays in Honour of Elie Kedourie*, ed Edward Ingram, pp. 164–186 (London: Frank Cass, 1988).

———. *Egypt's Young Rebels: "Young Egypt": 1933–1952.* (Stanford, Calif.: Hoover Institute, 1975).

———. "Zionism and the Jews in Egyptian National Opinion, 1900–1939." In *Egypt and Palestine*, ed. Amnon Cohen and Gabriel Baer, pp. 314–331. (Jerusalem: Ben-Zvi Institute, 1984).

Jones, Joseph M. *The Fifteen Weeks* (New York: Viking, 1955).

Jones, Martin. *Failure in Palestine* (London: Mansell, 1986).

Kent, John. *British Imperial Strategy and the Origins of the Cold War 1944–1949.* (London: Leicester University Press, 1993).

———. "The Egyptian Base and the Defence of the Middle East, 1954–1954." *Journal of Imperial and Commonwealth History* 21 (3) (1993): 45–65.

Khadduri, Majid. *Independent Iraq, 1932–1958* (London: Oxford University Press, 1960).

———. "The Scheme of Fertile Crescent Unity." In *The Near East and the Great Powers,* ed. Richard N. Frye, pp. 137–77 (Cambridge, Mass.: Harvard University Press, 1951).

Khalidi, Walid. "The Arab Perspective." In *The End of the Palestine Mandate,* ed. William Roger Louis and Robert W. Stookey, pp. 104–36 (Austin: University of Texas Press, 1986).

Kimche, Jon, and David Kimche. *Both Sides of the Hill* (London: Secker and Warburg, 1960).

Kirk, George. *The Middle East in the War* (London: Oxford University Press, 1953).

———. *The Middle East 1945–1950.* (London: Oxford University Press, 1954).

Kuniholm, Bruce R. *The Origins of the Cold War in the Near East* (Princeton, N.J.: Princeton University Press, 1980).

Landis, Joshua. "Nationalism and the Politics of Za'ama: The Collapse of Republican Syria, 1945–1949." Ph.D. diss., Princeton University, 1997.

Little, Douglas. "Cold War and Covert Action: The United States and Syria 1945–1958." *Middle East Journal* 44 (1) (1990): 51–75.

Louis, William Roger. *The British Empire in the Middle East 1945–1951* (Oxford: Oxford University Press, 1984).

———. "Jordan and Iraq: Efforts at Intra-Hashimite Unity." *Middle Eastern Studies* 26 (1) (1990): 65–75.

Maddy-Weitzman, Bruce. *The Crystallization of the Arab State System 1945–1954* (Syracuse: Syracuse Universiy Press, 1993).

Marr, Phoebe. *The Modern History of Iraq* (Boulder, Colo.: Westview, 1985).

Marton, Kati. *A Death in Jerusalem* (New York: Arcade, 1994).

Mayer, Thomas. *Egypt and the Palestine Question, 1936–1945* (Berlin: Klaus Schwarz, 1983).

———. "Egypt's 1948 Invasion of Palestine." *Middle Eastern Studies* 22 (1) (1986): 20–36.

———. "The Military Force of Islam: the Society of the Muslim Brethren and the Palestine Question, 1945–1948." In *Zionism and Arabism in Palestine and Israel,* ed. E. Kedourie and S. Haim, pp. 100–117. (London: Frank Cass, 1981).

Miller, Aaron David. *Search for Security* (Chapel Hill: University of North Carolina Press, 1980).

Mitchell, Richard P. *The Society of the Muslim Brothers* (Oxford: Oxford University Press, 1969).

Montague Bell, H. T., ed. *The Annual Register, 1946* (London: Longmans, Green and Co., 1947).

Morris, Benny. *The Birth of the Palestinian Refugee Problem, 1947–1949* (Cambridge: Cambridge University Press, 1987).

———. "The Crystallization of Israeli Policy against a Return of the Arab Refugees: April–December 1948." *Studies in Zionism,* 6 (1) (l985): 85–118.

Muwafi, Abd al-Hamid Muhammad. *Misr fi jami'at al-duwwal al-'arabiyya* (Cairo: Al-hay'a al-misriyya al-'amma li'l-kuttab, 1983).

Nakash, Yitzhak. *The Shi'is of Iraq* (Princeton, N.J.: Princeton University Press, 1994).

Nevo, Yosef. *'Abdallah ve 'Araviyei Erez Yisra'el* (Tel Aviv: Makhon Shiloah, 1975).

———. "The Arabs of Palestine 1947–1948: Military and Political Activity." *Middle Eastern Studies,* 23 (1) (1987): 3–38.

Nevo, Yosef, and Ilan Pappé, eds. *Jordan in the Middle East* (Ilford, Essex: Frank Cass, 1994).

Noble, Paul. "The Arab System: Opportunities, Constraints, and Pressures." In *The Foreign Policies of Arab States*, ed. Bahgat Korany and Ali E. Hillal Dessouki, pp. 41–77 (Boulder, Colo.: Westview, 1984).

Ovendale, Ritchie. *Britain, the United States, and the End of the Palestine Mandate 1942–1948* (Suffolk: Boydell for the Royal Historical Society, 1989).

Pappé, Ilan. *Britain and the Arab–Israeli Conflict, 1948–1951.* (London: Macmillan, 1988).

———. *The Making of the Arab-Israeli Conflict, 1947–1951.* (London: Tauris, 1992).

Persson, Sune O. *Mediation and Assassination: Count Bernadotte's Mission to Palestine in 1948.* (London: Ithaca Press, 1979).

Pipes, Daniel. *Greater Syria* (New York: Oxford University Press, 1990).

———. "Radical Politics and the Syrian Social Nationalist Party." *International Journal of Middle East Studies*, 20(3) (1988): 303–324.

Plascov, Avi. *The Palestinian Refugees in Jordan, 1948–1957* (London: Frank Cass, 1981).

Porath, Yehoshua. "Abdallah's Greater Syria Programme." *Middle Eastern Studies*, 20 (2) (1984): 172–189.

———. *In Search of Arab Unity, 1930–1945* (London: Frank Cass, 1986).

———. "Nuri al-Saʿid's Arab Unity Programme." *Middle Eastern Studies*, 20 (4) (1984): 76–98.

Pundik, Ron. *The Struggle for Sovereignty* (Oxford: Blackwell, 1994).

Rabinovitch, Itamar. *The Road Not Taken* (New York: Oxford University Press, 1991).

Roosevelt, Archie. "The Kurdish Republic of Mahabad." *The Middle East Journal* 1 (3) (1947): 247–269.

Roshwald, Aviel. *Estranged Bedfellows* (Oxford: Oxford University Press, 1990).

———. *Great Britain and Egypt 1914–1951* (London: RIIA, 1952).

Royal Institute of International Affairs. *British Security: A Report by a Chatham House Study Group* (London: RIIA, 1946).

Rubin, Barry. *The Arab States and the Palestine Conflict* (Syracuse, N.Y.: Syracuse University Press, 1981).

Safran, Nadav. *Egypt in Search of Political Community* (Cambridge, Mass.: Harvard University Press, 1961).

Sasson, Eliyahu. *Ba-Derekh el ha-Shalom* (Tel Aviv, ʿAm ʿOved: 1978).

Schueftan, Dan. *Optzia Yardenit* (Tel Aviv: Ha-Kibbutz ha-Meuhad, 1986).

Seale, Patrick. *The Struggle for Syria* (London: Oxford University Press, 1965).

Sela, Avraham. "Israel, Transjordan, and the 1948 War: Myth, Historiography, and Reality." *Middle Eastern Studies* 28 (4) (1992): 623–688.

———. *Mi-Magaʿim le-masa 'Umatan* (Tel Aviv: Dayan Center, Tel Aviv University, 1985).

———. "She'elat Erez Yisrael ba-Maʿarekhet ha-beyn-ʿAravit me-Hakamat ha-Liga ha-ʿAravit ʿad Plishat Zvaʾot ʿArav le-Erez Yisrael, 1945–1948." Ph.D. diss., Hebrew University, 1986.

al-Sharif, Kamil. *Al-ikhwan al-muslimun fi harb filastin* (Cairo: dar al-tawziʿ waʾl-nashr al-islamiya, 1984).

Shimoni, Yaacov. "Ha-ʿAravim Likrat Milhemet Yisrael-ʿArav, 1945–1948." *Ha-Mizrah ha-Hadash* 12 (3) (1962): 189–211.

Shlaim, Avi. *Collusion across the Jordan* (Oxford: Oxford University Press, 1987).

———. "The Debate About 1948." *The International Journal of Middle East Studies* 27 (1995): 287–304.

Silverfarb, Daniel. *The Twilight of British Ascendancy in the Middle East* (New York: St. Martin's, 1994).

Simon, Reeva S. "The Hashemite 'Conspiracy': Hashemite Unity Attempts, 1921–1958." *International Journal of Middle East Studies* 5 (1974): 314–327.

Susser, Asher and Aryeh Shmuelevitz, eds. *The Hashemites in the Modern Arab World* (London: Frank Cass, 1995).

Tignor, Robert L. *The State, Private Enterprise and Economic Change in Egypt, 1918–1952* (Princeton, N.J.: Princeton University Press, 1984).

Vatikiotis, P. J. *The History of Modern Egypt* (London: Weidenfeld and Nicholson, 1991).

Watt, D. Cameron. "The Saadabad Pact of 8 July 1937." In *The Great Powers in the Middle East 1919–1939*, ed. Uriel Dann, pp. 333–352. (New York: Holmes and Meier, 1988).

Wilson, Mary C. *King Abdullah, Britain, and the Making of Jordan* (Cambridge: Cambridge University Press, 1987).

Index

Abd al-Ilah, 66, 81, 104, 108, 135, 161
  and King Faruq, 142
Abdallah, King (Jordan)
  and Arab League, 78–80, 143–144, 193–194
  Arab states' fear of, 82–84, 86, 112–127, 133–138, 191–192
  Greater Syria Project of, 87–91, 107–110
  wartime policies of, 158–159, 170–172
Abd al-Nasser, Gamal, 4, 5, 79, 149, 183
  and Palestine question, 96–98, 164–165
  inherits grand strategy, 195–196
Abu'l-Huda, Tawfiq, 135, 156–157, 172
  meeting with Ernest Bevin of, 121–126
Afghanistan, 84
al-Alami, Musa, 120
Alexandretta, 82
Alexandria Protocol, 71
All-Palestine Government, 174–179, 182, 186
Anglo-American Committee of Inquiry, 57
Anglo-Egyptian Agreement (1954), 12
Anglo-Egyptian Treaty (1936), 9–17, 72–73
Arab League
  and Army of Liberation, 117–121
  and problem of Jordanian power, 115–116, 121–122, 126–127
  as regional defense organization, 68–75, 194–196
  as tool of Triangle Alliance, 76–80, 85–87, 92–93, 100–107
Arab Legion
  and Britain, 111–112, 148–149
  Egyptian attitudes toward, 113–116, 151–152
  and Jordanian plans for expansion, 121–122
  and Palestine war, 160, 161, 169–173, 174, 178
Ardahan, 25–26
Army of Liberation, *See* Arab League;
  al-Qawuqji, Fawzi
Atlantic Charter, 15
Attlee, Clement, 11, 49
Azerbaijan, 25–26
al-Azm, Khalid, 112
Azzam, Abd al-Rahman, *See also* Arab League
  as Egyptian agent, 48, 74, 150, 152, 154, 159
  relations with Britain, 68, 85, 106–107, 145–147

relations with Iraq and Jordan, 77–80, 110, 113–116, 126–127, 133–136, 138–140, 162, 172
relations with Jewish Agency, 99–100

Baghdad Pact, 70, 85, 114
Bank of England, 63
Balfour Declaration, 95, 101
al-Banna, Hasan, 40
al-Barzani, Mustafa, 26
Beeley, Harold, 106–107
Belgium, 52
Ben Gurion, David, 166–181
Ben-Zuri, Eliyahu, 94–95, 98
Bernadotte, Count Folke
  on Egyptian policy, 175–176
  first proposals of, 160, 161, 166–169
  on Jordanian policy, 158–159
  second proposals of, 177–178, 179, 183, 187
Bevin, Ernest, 35–36, 98. *See also* Bevin-Sidqi
  Agreement
  meeting with Tawfiq Abu'l-Huda, 121–126
Bevin-Sidqi Agreement, 9–12, 41–46, 72–73, 77
Britain
  economic problems of, 49–51, 62–63
  geopolitical strategy of, 23–33, 84–87
  and Palestine war, 121–123, 144–147, 187–188, 191–192
  relations with Arab League, 77–80, 125–127
  relations with Egypt, 9–12, 22–23, 33–36, 41–49, 67–69, 91–93, 95–98, 102–103, 105–107, 144–147, 187–188
  relations with Iraq, 66–67, 76–77
  relations with Jordan, 88–91, 111–112, 148–149
Burma, 50, 75

Campbell, Ronald, 86–87, 93, 191–192
Central Intelligence Agency, 51, 167, 174
Churchill, Winston, 29–30, 35
Colombia, 60
Communist Party, 17–19, 30, 39, 40, 59
Conciliation Commission, 186–189. *See also*
  United Nations
Cyprus, 32
Czechoslovakia, 129